Just Me and My Films

Around My World in 80 Films

By Dave Small

For my Gran and my brother Mark,

no longer with me,

but always in my heart.

Contents

Part Four – A Degree in the Classics

Intermission

Part Four - Continued

Introduction

Hello.

Makes you notice doesn't it. A little bit of darkness. Refines the senses. Focuses the mind.

It's time to enjoy the big screen experience, with no distractions, no sudden ring tones, no glaring screens, no talking.

So sit back, relax, switch off your phone and switch off from the outside world.

Not my words, but if you've been to a certain chain of cinemas in the last few years then you may recognise these lines.

My own cinematic journey began way before such announcements were needed. There were no sudden ringtones, as mobile phones had not even been invented yet. You knew the film was about to start as the very bored refreshments seller, usually a grumpy and slightly scary old woman, exited the auditorium with her selection of Strawberry Splits, Orange Maids, Choc Ices and bags of Butterkist Butterkist Ra-Ra-Ra, before the lights didn't dim, but were just turned abruptly off.

The film wasn't being screened in super ultra-high definition widescreen with panoramic Dolby super woofer surround sound for your enhanced visual and aural pleasure. The chairs you were sitting on weren't VIP leather ones, contoured to one's posterior, with perfectly sized drinks holders in the arms. Sometimes they had springs sticking through the worn out, always hideously patterned fabric, or they squeaked loudly and embarrassingly whenever you shifted position. But then again, neither did it cost an arm and a leg just to buy a soft drink, but you did get warned rather ominously about making juvenile slurping noises with your straws from some evil Tannoy announcement, probably by the grumpy, slightly scary old woman who had just sold you the drink in the first place.

Back then, going to the cinema was not the rather soulless experience it can be today. Every auditorium, unless it's one of the many wonderful independent cinemas we still have, looks exactly the same as the next one. Mainstream chain cinemas no longer have the same, if any, personality, and we all know that personality goes a long way.

I honestly can't say that my enjoyment of a film nowadays is any more enhanced by these so called improvements. The film, if it's good enough, will make all those other things pale into insignificance, as the cinema, however luxurious or insalubrious, has the ability to transport us to another world, another time, even another dimension. It can make us weep with joy and sadness, sometimes both at the same time; it can scare the living daylights out of us; it can fill us with hope and optimism for a better world, or it can teach us harsh truths.

Whatever it does, it can allow us to escape reality for a couple of hours. Not just the film itself, but the act of being in a darkened room, sharing the same experience with others, coming out into the bright daylight, or into the gloomy drizzle, to remind us that where we have just been has a certain magic about it.

That's why we love the cinema so much, and why we will continue to go there, even when there are now so many other ways of consuming films. Only the cinema can create this sense of magic and catharsis.

This book is not a list of my favourite films, nor is it a rather pompous and frankly dull critique of the films. I am certainly not a film reviewer, and would never just give my opinions on a list of films. What follows is the films that have played a significant role in my life, and have helped to shape me into the man I am now, some forty-three years since going to the cinema for the first time. Not all, but most, have been watched in a cinema, and all have given me indelible memories. I haven't watched them all again to remind me of their qualities or otherwise, I have just delved into the memories that each film has left me with, and how they have become part of my life, and maybe some of your lives too.

Some of the films many people will have seen several, if not countless times. Some films only a few may have seen, if at all. The ones you have seen, I hope they will bring flooding back your own memories of them. Those you haven't seen, it may pique your interest to check them out and create your own individual memories of them. It's up to you.

All I ask is that you sit back, relax, switch off your phone (if you want), and switch off from the outside world.

Part One

Childish Delight

King Kong (1976)   Dir: John Guillermin

Ironically, I'm starting with possibly the only film I did not see all the way through, as I had to leave the cinema after about half an hour. I've sat through some awful films in my life, some just bad, some mind-numbingly boring, others bewilderingly bemusing, but I persevered with them, in the vain hope that they may improve. However, this first film on my journey had nothing to do with how bad, boring or bemusing the film was.

The truth is, I was absolutely petrified and had to be taken out of the cinema by my dad, as my parents were genuinely concerned for the potentially huge and damaging effects on my four-year old mental health. They thought I would be scared, and indeed scarred for life if I continued to watch a 50-foot ape cause carnage, whilst all the while caring for the most beautiful damsel in distress I'd ever seen, not that I'd seen many of those in the four years and three months I'd been alive. My mum was neither a damsel, nor was she in much distress as far as I could see, apart from when my older brother wouldn't go to bed, or my dad had broken wind in her vicinity.

The first time I was ever taken to the cinema by my parents must have been some time in the summer of 1977. This film had been released the previous Christmas, but back then the cinemas were not slaves to the studios as they seem to be now, and could show films again when they wished. It must have been in the summer of 1977 as my family went on a week's holiday to Whitby and I distinctly remember getting lost on the beach on a lovely hot day, something you don't get many of in Whitby, and especially at Christmas.

I remember wandering off, making sure I knew where my mum, dad and brother were all sitting, before promptly forgetting where they were and starting to panic. So as any four year old would do in a time of crisis, I sat down and cried. Eventually I could see my dad's legs coming towards me and he scooped me up and took me gratefully and rather pathetically back to the safety of our windbreak.

I also remember getting myself locked in a toilet somewhere, and once again resorting to crying loudly until my dad had to come and rescue me. Those two days, and the memory of this film, are the only ones I have of that holiday. I'm sure I had a lovely week, and have spent many happy days in Whitby since then. I haven't even got lost once (yet), although my wife would probably have preferred it if I had, just to give her some peace and quiet. I also can work out how to unlock toilet doors now. Just about.

So, one evening, my mum and dad took me and my brother for a treat to see this monster of a film. It turned out to be not such a treat for me. It was rated as the equivalent of a PG back then, so my parents must have had faith in my abilities to withstand such horrors that were about to unfold on the cinema screen, despite having proved to them that I was a bit of a cry-baby.

The film's director had just made "The Towering Inferno", that most cliched of disaster movies, and the trailer to "King Kong" was one of those typical bombastic, disaster fuelled trailers in the same ilk as his previous film, and other disastrous epics such as "Earthquake" and "Airport" (either of the 1970, 1975 or 1977 versions) all brilliantly lampooned in "Airplane", a few years later, and we were all very excited by the prospect of watching such awesome wonders on the big screen.

The line "And introducing Jessica Lange" was enough for me though, as my four year old heart had fallen in love with this goddess. To me, she was absolutely gorgeous, and it was probably the scene when Kong takes a gentle hold of his beautiful sacrifice and holds her up to his mouth, with everyone, certainly me anyway, expecting her to be eaten in one gulp, that proved too much for me. I must have started to cry at that point, and had to be taken out of the cinema by my dad, as I don't remember anything else from the film after then.

Instead of seeing the rest of the film, my dad and I walked along the beach and we collected some interesting looking shells which I gave to my mum after she brought my brother out, who delighted and revelled in the fact that I hadn't seen the whole film because I was such a wuss. They emerged into the warm Whitby evening from their trip to an uncharted island populated by rather savage beasts, and even more savage humans. My mum kept those shells and put them in a jar on the side of our bath, so that every time I washed my hair with Matey shampoo (ironically marketed as a shampoo which wouldn't cause tears!), they reminded me of the embarrassment of that evening in which tears certainly had flowed.

And so, I missed Kong not devouring the beauty after all, but giving his tiny human piece of perfection the tender care she so obviously needed; I missed the brave but rather stupid men who were attempting to rescue her get thrown off a large log over a ravine by Kong giving it a little twist; and most importantly of all I missed the finale where Kong climbs to the top of not the Empire State Building, but the top of the World Trade Centre, before (spoiler alert!) crashing to his death after being attacked not by biplanes as in the original 1933 version, or Peter Jackson's remake in 2005, but rather sinister looking helicopters, which peppered the mighty beast until it could take no more.

I've obviously seen the film since my traumatic experience as a four year old, and have even managed to get right through until the end without even being near to tears. Well almost, as Kong's death does bring a tear to my eye. I've also seen the two other versions, the first one with Fay Wray as the damsel in distress, and the third version with the lovely Naomi Watts in that role. Both are excellent films in their own right, and my own son was only five when I took him to see the 2005 version. He must have been so much braver than me as he wasn't a sissy at all and thoroughly enjoyed the experience, although I was quite proud of him when he almost cried at Kong's death too.

Looking at the 1976 version now, the sight of the Twin Towers of the World Trade Centre in this post 9/11 world seems quite eerie. The producer of the film decided to use this landmark as a way of showing off New York's updated skyline, as the World Trade Centre had only been opened a few years earlier, just as the Empire State building had only been completed a couple of years before Fay Wray was taken protectively to the top of it.

As we all know, it wouldn't be helicopters that would bring those towers down. This is probably one of the reasons why the film is hardly ever shown on TV these days, and is probably the least loved of all three versions, but for me, I have real soft spot for it. It makes me feel like a proper grown up whenever I watch it, now that I no longer need to be provided with tissues before a viewing.

And of course, there is the rather ethereal and divine Jessica Lange to hold my attention. As a teenager, I may have needed tissues for another reason during one of her later films, after watching Jack Nicholson and her on a kitchen table in the 1981 remake of "The Postman Always Rings Twice" But that's another story.

Star Wars (1977)   **Dir: George Lucas**

It might seem a bit of a cliché to have this as my first full film, but for any boy who was born in 1973, as I was, this film is probably the first for many other thousands of four or five year old younglings. That may seem rather sexist, as I'm sure that many girls went to see the film too. But back in 1977, or January 1978 when it was released across the UK, the film was seen as predominantly a boys' film, and one which me and all my other male reception school friends went to see during our very first year at school.

Not that girls can't enjoy the film. Indeed, I have a female colleague who is the nerdiest, the geekiest, the most knowledgeable fan of the whole franchise I have ever met. She knows things about each film that life is too short to fill your head with. And she would take that as a compliment by the way.

For me, and thousands of others across the country, the film remains indelibly etched in our memories, not only because it was our first experience of the big screen, but because of the many timeless vignettes it seared into our minds, instantly creating the almost mythological status it has now acquired for everybody else. When the first thing you ever see on a cinema screen (the first half hour of King Kong excluded) is the now synonymous line "A long time ago in a galaxy far, far away…" you know you are going to be transported to not only another world, but also another galaxy and another time. Throw in the mind blowing blast of John Williams' score, and I was instantly hooked.

It didn't matter that the scrolling text which followed was going up the screen so fast that my mum gave up trying to whisper it to me. Even though I was a fairly good reader by then, I still couldn't keep up with it, and wouldn't have understood it even if I had. But it didn't matter, as then the camera pans down to a lone planet in the distance, before what seems like a huge spaceship hurtles towards it, with lasers blasting out of its rear end. That in itself was awesome, but then only a second or two later, the spaceship we all thought was huge is then swamped, engulfed and overwhelmed by a mind-bogglingly massive Imperial Star Destroyer. The whole screen is literally taken up with the vastness of the pursuing ship, making the first one look almost Lilliputian in its feebleness.

When you're four, and the screen itself is fifty times higher than you and 100 times wider (my maths could be slightly wrong there), and the spaceship that has just taken over this whole screen, you are in no doubt that this is going to be a story about the plucky little guys fighting against a huge evil super power. I was transfixed, even though I didn't really have a clue what was going on, where it was happening, who the characters were, or indeed why it was happening. I certainly couldn't have cared less how it was happening; it just was, and for the next two hours, I was overwhelmed too.

This almost mythological opening was completely intended by George Lucas to bring a fairy tale quality to the film. For a four year old boy, who wasn't interested in stupid princesses falling in love, and living happily ever after with their heroic rescuer, this was my kind of fairy tale, although much the same happens in Star Wars too. This super powered, light sabring fairy tale from another galaxy did have a handsome, humble hero, falling in love with a most beautiful princess, and like many thousands of others, I fell in love with Princess Leia too, despite her weird hairdo. Who knows, if she had unfurled her strange headphone hair, she may have looked like Rapunzel too.

14

As far as the actual storyline went, the intricacies of the plot went way over my head, but for a four year old, it was simply a goodies v baddies story, with the baddies ultimately defeated and the goodies being rewarded. The characters' names passed me by too, apart from Luke Skywalker, as that was the only one which seemed vaguely normal. My school friends weren't sure of the names either. We just referred to CP-3O as "the golden man", R2-D2 as "the bleeping bin", and Chewbacca as "Gorilla Man", but we all knew Luke's name, because secretly we all wanted to be him.

Luke was the one who got the nicest smile from the princess at the end when the medals were handed out; he was the one who rescued the princess, although Leia was pretty kick-ass herself, especially when she takes control of the so-called rescue by Luke and Han and blasts a hole in the wall, only to put them all in another kind of mortal danger in the garbage vault with the creepy monster swimming around in it; and he was the one who fought with the coolest weapon ever, a blue light sabre.

The vignettes that I remember the most vividly more often than not included Luke. Apart from the opening shot, the entrance of Vader, and the death of OB1, everything else that is seared into my mind involves Luke: his home in a hole in the desert , which I got to visit on a family holiday to Tunisia a few years later; his daring X-Wing fighter manoeuvres as he sped along the Death Star just before he blows it up; and most vividly of all, him swinging across the chasm in the belly of the Death Star to escape from the approaching Stormtroopers with Leia clutching onto his neck after kissing him on the cheek and wishing him good luck.

He didn't really need that much luck as it happened, as the Stormtroopers couldn't seem to hit anything with their blaster guns. Had they not had any training on how to aim at all? That swing from his tiny rope which he got from his belt to me was the ultimate in fairy tale hero stuff, and because of that, he was the one we all wanted to be. And a few months later, I actually got to be him. Sort of.

Every summer my home town of Carnforth had a summer carnival, where there would be themed decorated floats parading through the town's streets, before all ending up on the school playing fields where there would be a funfair. The summer of 1978 was when my street would decide to go for a Star Wars themed float. So a local building suppliers' lorry was decorated appropriately with stars made out of tin foil, and we all got dressed up to join in. I have no recollection of who my mum and dad dressed as, if indeed they dressed as anyone, but me and my brother were Luke Skywalker, with dressing gowns tied at the waist with leather belts, and wellies as our costumes, with a painted cardboard roll as our light sabres.

We passed for Luke Skywalker at least, but one of the older lads on our street out did everyone, and made himself the most awesome and frankly scary Darth Vader outfit. When I saw him I was instantly transported back to the cinema, and hid behind my mum's legs hoping that he didn't pick me off the floor by my neck with one hand. Our float may well have won some sort of award, probably "Highly Commended" which basically means it was good, but not as good as at least three others in the parade.

I got some of the action figures for my birthday that year, including Chewbacca, whose name I now knew, and obviously Luke Skywalker himself, and an X-Wing fighter to zoom around my bedroom with. The Millennium Falcon was the one everyone wanted, but they were so expensive, and only the rich, spoilt kids got those where I lived. But I really wasn't bothered as I had the hero's fighter ship to play with, and not some sidekick whose ship was a bit of an old rust bucket. So what if it was the ship that made the Kessel Run in less than twelve parsecs? Han Solo was only in it for the money, whereas Luke was in it for love.

A theme seems to be developing here, and that is a damsel in distress. Both films I have mentioned so far have included a brave, strong male rescuing a fair maiden from seemingly inescapable peril (although in King Kong whether it was Jeff Bridges or Kong as the hero is debateable, Bridges was almost as hairy as Kong after all). Maybe this is the ultimate reason why I loved Star Wars so much. Maybe I just wanted to save my very own damsel in distress.

This theme would continue later on in my life too, when at the age of twenty-three I met a single mum who had recently left her husband after realising what a prick he was, asking her to marry me and becoming a dad to her two year old daughter. Although she wasn't in that much distress when I met her, she was finding life tough as a single mum, emotionally and financially, and so I suppose I did help her in some way. She was certainly a damsel though, the most beautiful damsel I'd ever seen since falling in love with Princess Leia nineteen years previously.

Our first date was a trip to the cinema, and although she really wanted to go and see the very romantic, moving and ever so grown up "The English Patient", "Star Wars" had just been re-released in HD. I hadn't seen it on the big screen since I was four and so somehow I persuaded her that this would be the one to watch. She relented, but never fails to remind me of her sacrifice for me that night. She didn't seem to mind it too much, apart from when I started quoting OB1 Kenobi's line of "The sand people are easily startled, but they'll soon be back, and in greater numbers". And yet she still wasn't put off by me.

She put up with my desire to be a child again and my faux nerdiness. She even bought me a life sized cardboard cut-out of Princess Leia (the frankly much sexier version wearing her bronze bra from "The Return of the Jedi" rather than the weird hairdo white hooded long dress affair) and carried it from Soho all the way back to our flat on buses and Tubes, much to the annoyance of the London commuters.

We've been married for twenty-two years now.

The force must be with me after all.

Herbie Goes Bananas (1980)   Dir: Vincent McEveety

One of the people this book is dedicated to is my Gran. She was a wonderful, generous and kind lady who I have nothing but the fondest and happiest memories of. This chapter will go a long way to explaining why. She is possibly the main reason why I fell in love with not just films, but the actual act of going to the cinema, the whole experience of it, from the anticipation before, to the cathartic re-emergence into the sunlight of reality afterwards.

When I was a young boy, she lived with her own mother, my Great Granny, or Nan as I used to call her, as her own husband had died in a car crash literally three weeks after my own mum had been born. She already had a son, who would have been my uncle Barry, but he had been born with a heart defect, and had died at the age of just eleven. So, this woman, after just surviving the war and having my mum, was left on her own with a baby girl, a very ill son, grieving for her husband, and a sick son, who eight years later, she would be grieving for too.

I cannot imagine how she coped with such loss, and so with no husband to support her with two children, one of whom was severely ill, her best option was to move back in with her own mother, where they both helped to raise my mum, and her brother, until his much too early death.

My Gran did a fantastic job, despite her awful situation, and was able to get my mum into Lancaster Girls' Grammar School, and nurtured her into the all-round wonderful person my mum is, and always has been.

I only ever remember her giggling and being happy, and my brother and I would spend a lot of time at my Gran and Nan's house, after school some evenings and particularly in the school holidays. My Gran loved to find us lots of fun things to do, as much as the activities of the late 1970s could be described as fun. It's surprising how entertaining a game of Pick-Up Sticks can be, where you have to extract pointed sticks from a pile with your own pointed stick, or baking biscuits with her, or playing hide and seek. She never seemed to mind me and my brother's need for attention and our constant need to be fed. She was only too pleased to do it.

Another thing she was only too pleased to do was to take us out for a trip to the pictures, as she called them, and every school holiday for what must have been about four years, I was taken to the cinema either in Lancaster or Morecambe. This is when I truly fell in love with the cinema, and consequently fell more in love with my Gran. Maybe she just enjoyed getting out from under her own mother's feet, and to feel as if she was being a mother to two boys, seeing as she had lost her only son at such a young age. I certainly loved being with her, and she provided me with so many of the happiest memories of my childhood between those glorious, innocent ages of four to nine years old.

Back then she had a little yellow Mini, and whenever it was a trip to the cinema to see whatever was on, we would pile into her tiny little yellow car and be taken out for a treat, with sweets always provided, a lolly at the cinema, and always laughter and giggles on the way there and back.

Despite my Gran living in Lancaster, for some reason (probably a trip to the outdoor market was needed for some groceries) we would mostly go to the cinema in Morecambe, which was situated right next door to The Winter Gardens on the Promenade. This fine late Victorian building had only just shut down when I started going to the cinema, but in its heyday had seen over 2000 people at a time watching the very best the music hall and variety scene could offer. Laurel and Hardy, George Formby, and even the great Laurence Oliver had all performed there, Olivier making the film "The Entertainer" there in 1960, all about the life of the once great music hall performer Archie Rice.

By 1977 it had fallen into disrepair and neglect, as most of Morecambe's once wonderful attractions had done. If they hadn't yet, then they were well on their way to becoming faded glories of a once proud English seaside resort. Little did I know of the great performers that had been only a few yards from where I would sit in the cinema. But I didn't care, I was watching the stars of today, and the stars of tomorrow in front of the big screen with my big orange lolly in my hand which made my lips go orange it was that juicy.

I remember that the screen at Morecambe was nothing special before the film started, it was always covered with curtains before they would magically open to show us all the usual mix of local adverts for a carpet shop, or a bathroom suppliers, or Lyon's Maid ice creams.

The cinema in Lancaster was a different affair though, and the trips there were even more special. This was the same cinema that my Gran had been to watch "Gone With the Wind" in, back in 1939 when she was just sweet sixteen. It seems a completely bygone time now, another era, where she and her friends would get themselves dressed up for a night out at the pictures watching Clark Gable and Vivien Leigh. They would queue down the street and round the corner to get into the cinema, and then get a bag of chips and the bus home afterwards.

Watching that film, being transported to the cotton plantations of America's deep south, all in glorious Technicolour, must have seemed like the most thrilling experience ever. I've only ever watched "Gone With the Wind" once, and I'm sure it did not give me the same thrill that my own Gran must have got from that first bright and radiant screening she enjoyed all those years ago.

This cinema was also special to me for another couple of reasons. Firstly, there was a winding set of stairs leading up to the box office and the entrances to the two screens, and when there was a queue for a certain film coming all the way down to the street, you slowly shuffled up the steps, looking at all the posters for the upcoming films, putting them on your cinematic wish list, and marvelling at the life size cut-outs of the stars perched on each landing where the steps turned in direction slightly. All the while you had a nagging concern about whether you would actually get in to see the film. There were no ticketing arrangements, or pre-booked seats then. It was simply a first come first served basis, and if you had not got there early enough, the further up the stairs you got, the higher the anxiety rose as this meant the fuller the auditorium was.

Many times you would have queued up for at least half an hour, reaching the final landing with the box office in sight, only to be told by one of the rather threatening looking ushers that only the next ten people would be able to get in. It was obvious that there were at least twenty people in front of you, and so you'd walk back down the stairs grumbling, wishing you'd got there earlier, vowing to do so next time, if indeed there would be a next time for that particular film. And of course, back then, films did not become available to stream or go to DVD release or even VHS release for years afterwards. If you didn't time your arrival properly, that could easily be your chance to see that film gone, the one that everyone else had seen, and the one you would now have to wait months, if not years to watch.

My Gran used to take me and my brother usually in the afternoons so we would rarely experience this feeling back then, and let's face it, the films we went to see were hardly huge box office smashes, certainly nothing like "Gone With the Wind", and there was rarely a queue at all.

Once we successfully got into the auditorium, the next wonder would be there for me to enjoy. Instead of a curtain covering the screen, as at the Morecambe cinema, the screen in the Lancaster cinema would already be uncovered, and it would be filled with the most hypnotic patterns floating across the screen.

I'm not sure how it was done, probably something to do with different coloured dyes and bubbles, but the whole screen was taken up with all these different coloured bubbles, some big, some small, some passing behind each other, some bouncing off each other. Some even merged into one bigger bubble and created yet more beautiful colours in this kaleidoscopic visual trip. I used to hope we could get into the cinema as early as possible so that I could eat my sweets and suck my lolly, all the while being mesmerised by the beautiful and entrancing shapes floating around for me. I was almost disappointed when the adverts and trailers came on before the actual film started.

Watching those patterns for two hours would have been more fun than some of the films actually, because back then, in the late 1970s and early 1980s, there was a lot of dross being churned out for the kids on their school holidays. My Gran took me and my brother to loads of these films, and we lapped them all up gleefully, even if they were instantly forgettable. I'm struggling to remember anything about most of them anyway.

Disney seemed to have the monopoly back then for any film that was suitable for kids, and they churned them out at a rate of knots. When I used to teach Media Studies at A Level, I used to do a series of lessons on the impact of Disney on popular culture and how CGI films started challenging their supremacy in the animated films market. So here is a brief insight into one of my lessons.

Everyone knows Disney for their animation but unfortunately these films took so long to make. After "Snow White and the Seven Dwarfs", the corporation's first full length animated feature film was released in 1937, it took them another three years for their next one. And like London buses, two came along at once, in "Pinocchio" and "Fantasia", both being released in 1940. "Dumbo" flew onto our screens in 1941, before millions of kids' childhood innocence was destroyed when Bambi's dad got killed in 1942.

After recovering from the Second World War, "Cinderella was released in 1950, along with "Alice in Wonderland" the following year, and "Peter Pan" a couple of years after that. Next was "Lady and the Tramp" in 1955, and then another four years until "Sleeping Beauty" would be awoken by a kiss from her handsome prince. During the 1960s, there would only be three more animated films, "101 Dalmatians" in 1961, "The Sword in the Stone" in 1963, and then the last ever film Walt Disney himself would be responsible for, the much loved "The Jungle Book" in 1967.

The 1970s would start with "The Aristocats" in 1970, "Robin Hood", just after I was born in 1973, and probably the first two Disney animated films my Gran took me to see, as I was just about old enough then, which were "Winnie the Pooh" and "The Rescuers", both of 1977.

Disney knew they had to produce more than just three or four films a decade to survive, and that is just what they did. By 1950 they realised that it was quicker, easier, and definitely cheaper to roll out many live action films, starting with "Treasure Island" in the summer of 1950. In the 1950s alone there were eighteen live action films produced by the Disney Corporation, including such memorable "classics" as "Johnny Tremain", "The Littlest Outlaw", and "Third Man on the Mountain", and if anyone out there says they vividly remember these films, then fair play to you.

These live action films were being released literally a few months apart, with as many as six films being released in one single calendar year. Between the release of "101 Dalmatians" and "The Sword in the Stone", only two years apart, sixteen live action films were put out onto our cinemas by Disney. There would be another sixteen before "The Jungle Book" was released, one of these being "Mary Poppins" so they weren't all just forgettable fodder, although again I doubt if anyone remembers some of the others from this period, "The Monkey's Uncle" and "Follow Me, Boys", being two rather dubiously named examples. And some people say that Media Studies is just a Mickey Mouse subject!

***

Looking at the list of Disney films in the 1970s, "Winnie the Pooh" was most probably the first ever film that my Gran took me to watch, but I saw many of the films which followed. I definitely remember "The Rescuers", as Gran bought me a little jigsaw puzzle with a scene from the film on it, which I completed over and over again. I also remember "Herbie Goes to Monte Carlo", and "Pete's Dragon", both of 1977. I distinctly remember sobbing at the moment Elliot the dragon has to say goodbye to Pete at the very end, something I would experience very keenly again five years later when another Elliot had to say goodbye to his friend.

I also remember vaguely going to watch "The Cat from Outer Space", strangely enough about a talking cat from another planet, and "The Black Hole", both of which were fairly dire. Disney kept re-releasing their animated films too, and I remember seeing many of these older classics, including "Bedknobs and Broomsticks" and was particularly fascinated with the football match that is played by the weirdest football teams ever. At that point, I was starting to develop a love for my other great passion, falling in love with football too, and the rules of that match between animated animals confused me, as they didn't seem to correspond with the rules of proper football that I was beginning to learn. The offside law was confusing enough for a six year old without a load of cartoon characters blatantly flouting these rules!

By the 1980s, I was a much more grown up seven year old, and was taken to watch "Popeye", with Robin Williams in his first ever big screen appearance, and the rather bizarre "Condorman" in 1981 with Michael Crawford, known only to me for doing brilliant Frank Spencer impersonations, much better than Lenny Henry anyway, in a spoof superhero caper. My eight year old mind loved it though. I think I liked it so much that I nearly wet myself laughing and almost did a whoopsie on the carpet!

The only other film I remember was the film in the title of this chapter "Herbie Goes Bananas". Actually I remember very little about the film itself, apart from some manic car chases and all round crazy antics from a sentient car which could understand and also communicate with its human owners. What a riot it was.

I pick this because even though my Gran had her yellow Mini, I used to imagine that because it was yellow, the same colour as a banana, then there was some sort of similarity between the two cars. My Gran's driving was very often just as crazy and manic as Herbie's, and so getting to and from the cinema was a real life movie scene at times. Her parking was certainly rather haphazard if I remember rightly. I'd ask if we could go out for a drive in Herbie, just for a bit of entertainment when a trip to the cinema wasn't on the agenda that day. Gran's driving certainly provided enough entertainment of sorts for that day.

She even took us to see a re-release of "Born Free" one day, and it was only after about twenty minutes into the film that she realised she'd taken us into the wrong auditorium. I can't remember what we had been watching, but it certainly wasn't Joy Adamson with Elsa the lioness. For all I knew it may have been something highly inappropriate that we'd been mistakenly taken to, although I'm guessing I would have remembered it if Leatherface had started carving up his victims with his chainsaw. It was probably something like the film version of "Battlestar Galactica" which was probably improved by me missing out the first twenty minutes actually.

Sadly, by the age of eight, my brother was too cool to spend time with his Gran and younger brother any more as he was now eleven, and would be off to secondary school, and I would no longer go for days out to the cinema with my Gran, but those four years or so started me off properly on my cinematic journey. I'd seen some great films, and also some awful ones, but at least I'd been driven there in my very own version of Herbie, even if my Gran's driving was rather bananas at times, but I wouldn't change it for the world.

Superman (1978)   Dir: Richard Donner

I've always been rather dubious about Superman. Not the film, which I quite enjoyed, but the actual character of Superman himself. Can he even be classed as a real super hero? I would suggest not. Like the other iconic DC "super" hero, Batman, who does not actually have any superpowers at all, simply being a very rich guy with lots of fancy gadgets, so Superman's claims to being super in the human sense are rather exaggerated.

He is almost too super to be believed. He can do almost anything, even being able to fly, his only weakness seemingly being, rather randomly, an inability to see through lead. This film proved that he can even make the planet spin back round and thus reversing time. Rather far-fetched to me. And he's not even from our planet. In fact he's more of an alien in human form who can do just about anything, rather than a run-of-the-mill ordinary guy who just so happens to have acquired abnormal, and thus super, abilities. Superman didn't gain these powers, he was born with them, which is cheating if you ask me.

If you want a true super hero, then look no further than the amazing, the ultimate, the spectacular, the insert your own hyperbole, the one and only Spiderman. Now he is what I call a superhero, but alas his first cinematic outing was very far from super. It was truly awful frankly, and is an embarrassing stain on Peter Parker's legacy, to use another hyperbole.

Ever since I can remember, I have loved Spiderman. From the earliest of ages I was reading comics in which I learnt the back story to our friendly neighbourhood Spidey, and thought he was the coolest thing ever. I would draw pictures of him, and send them into Tony Hart's TV programme, in the vain hope that they might get featured on the segment called The Gallery, where kids' artwork was featured. My pictures never were, because they were crap, really, truly bad, mainly because I couldn't draw at all. My pictures of Spiderman climbing up a wall made him look frankly deformed, rather than the most awesome superhero out there. I even wrote in to "Jim'll Fix It", asking if I could meet my hero. Thank God my dream did not come true as I might have had to sit on Jimmy Saville's knee. Not even Spiderman, or even Superman, could have fixed that situation.

So, when my parents told me that a new film version of Spiderman, a pilot film to whet my appetite for a subsequent TV series was being made, I was, quite understandably, climbing the walls to go and see it. However, the film and TV series, released in America in 1977 when I was four, would not be released in good old Blighty until 1981, and so I would have to wait another four years before being able to see my hero on the big screen, rather than in a comic, or in one of my crap drawings. This just built up my anticipation even more.

In the meantime I would just have to make do with the release of the first ever film of the far inferior hero, the one and only Superman, starring Marlon Brando of all people, despite me not knowing who the hell he was, which films he'd starred in, or indeed anything of the huge legacy he had created in the history of cinema.

So, in the absence of Spiderman, and my parents' ability to take me, my Gran made me an offer I couldn't refuse, and we went to watch a man who for some reason couldn't seem to dress himself properly, and would prefer to put his underpants on outside his trousers. And he had a kiss curl. And he wore glasses. And he wore a cape ("No capes" – Edna Mode in "The Incredibles"). But for a few months he would briefly displace my affections for the real superhero that is Spiderman, a man who knew where his underwear should be.

"Superman: The Movie", to give it its precise title, just so we all knew it was a film and not a really long TV show, was released just before Christmas in 1978, and presumably, I, along with thousands of other five- year olds, was taken to see it over the Christmas holidays of that year. I didn't really understand what was going on in the first part of the film, the bit that Marlon Brando got paid vast amounts of money for, and the bit I enjoyed the most was Clark Kent's childhood. I vividly remember him lifting the truck up in front of his soon to be adoptive parents, and I loved the bit when, as a teenager, he runs alongside the train and jumps in front of it, to the amazement of all, before arriving at his destination going before all his peers who rather meanly wouldn't let him in their car.

It was only once Clark Kent grew up and became Christopher Reeve that I didn't particularly like it anymore. Kent was just too bumbling, too nerdy, and too much of an idiot to actually care about. But at least he could get changed quickly in a phone box, before catching falling helicopters with one hand whilst saving his own damsel in distress.

The poster tag line for the film is "You'll believe a man can fly", and I did, sort of. Without the use of CGI, the director did an admirable job of making our outer underweared hero seem as though he was actually flying. No wires could be seen or anything to give the game away, which did impress me. I was mostly impressed when he bridged the gap in the railway track to prevent a huge crash, but as I said earlier, the bit where he flies so quickly around the world that he actually reverses time was just going too far.

Another thing which I wasn't too keen on was just how rubbish the villain was. Lex Luthor, played brilliantly by another great, Gene Hackman, who again I had no idea of his legacy, was just not villainous enough. From my comic book experience, supervillains were not only scary and despotic, but they also looked quite cool too. Think of The Green Goblin, Mysterio, The Vulture, The Lizard and particularly Doctor Octopus from Spiderman. All these were proper villains, not just some bald headed idiot with a fancy pool and a bimbo for a girlfriend. I just didn't care that much whether the evil Lex would actually defeat the Man of Steel, but the film passed the time of day and made my craving for the Spiderman film less urgent.

I even got my Gran to make me a cape out of some red material, put a hairclip in my fringe to try and give me a kiss curl, and definitely wore my red Y-fronts outside my trousers for a day or two. Then I realised I just looked stupid and came to my senses. Maybe my Spidey sense kicked in to remind me that I was being a traitor.

The wait for my real super hero would have to continue, and I would even get the chance to watch not just one, but two Superman films before the Spiderman one would come out. "Superman 2", directed this time by Richard Lester, arrived at Easter 1981, a couple of weeks before my eighth birthday, and this time at least the villains were better. The trio led by Terence Stamp's General Zod gave Superman a run for his money this time, as did Lois Lane, even persuading him to reveal his identity so they could go for a romantic trip to Niagara Falls, in one of the tackiest hotels you could ever wish to stay in. But he still did not match up to Peter Parker and his alter ego, the web-slinging, web-headed, wallcrawling one and only Spiderman.

And so, in September 1981, the first full length live action motion picture of Spiderman swung onto our screens, and my wait was finally over. To say I was underwhelmed would be a super understatement. The film was so bad, almost laughable, and was nothing like the comic book world I had been living in.

For a start, instead of Spidey swinging between the skyscrapers of a dark and foreboding New York City, he inhabited the sunshine of Los Angeles, surrounded by Californian absurdities. He couldn't even swing properly, he just sort of crawled along the floor with the camera tilted to one side to make it look, very unconvincingly, that he could climb up walls. The super villains were just a load of rather stereotypical, to the point of being almost racist, Japanese baddies, and the whole thing was just quite pitiful. At least I had sort of believed that Superman could fly, but I definitely did not believe that Spiderman could swing, and I don't mean in the wife swapping sense. My hero was played by Nicholas Hammond, who had played the part of Friedrich, one of the annoying Von Trapp children in "The Sound of Music". He should have stuck to playing with lonely goat herds quite frankly.

I would have to wait another twenty-one years before my dream was finally realised, once CGI had been invented, for a proper Spiderman film to come out. This version, directed by Sam Raimi, he of "The Evil Dead", with Tobey Maguire making his first outing as my hero, was much more of what I had been hoping for, but now that I was almost at the end of my twenties, a father of two kids by now, it didn't have quite the same appeal. I still got the thrill I was hoping for, especially when Spidey swung from the skyscrapers, but frankly there wasn't enough shots like that. The villain, Willem Dafoe's Green Goblin was also a bit of a disappointment, his rigid and not that scary mask taking away from his evil persona which I remembered from the comics of my boyhood, but he was still miles better than Lex Luthor.

It wouldn't be until the release of "Spiderman 2", a couple of years later, that my craving for the ultimate in not just Spiderman films, but any superhero film would be satisfied. I would argue that this is the greatest superhero film ever. Alfred Molina's Doctor Octopus was exactly how I wanted him to be, and loads more panoramic shots of Spidey swinging around New York were included. It was heaven for me as a thirty-one year old kid, and put anything that Superman or Batman could offer to shame. It was just a pity that I had to be in my thirties for me to feel like I was eight years old again.

The Spy Who Loved Me (1977)   Dir: Lewis Gilbert

My favourite episode of "I'm Alan Partridge" is the one titled, "Never Say Alan Again", mostly due to the fact that Alan, unable to have his Bondathon Bank Holiday weekend due to his assistant Lynne spilling an oversized jug of Sunny D over all his VHS tapes, proceeds to hilariously narrate the opening sequence of this film, my first ever Bond film, and still my all-time favourite.

The title song "Nobody Does it Better", by Carly Simon evokes so many memories for me, as that was one of the only decent songs my mum and dad had in their vinyl collection, along with the obligatory copy of Don McLean's "American Pie", and rather randomly a 7" single of "Chanson D'Amour" by The Manhattan

Transfer. Alan Partridge certainly proved that indeed nobody could do it better than his hilarious narration.

I think I could have had a good go at matching him, as I've seen the film so many times, but I still wouldn't have known that the man on the submarine who first uses the periscope used to be in "The Onedin Line", but I did know that the "Russian shits in black jumpsuits", did not in fact have "lemon piping" down their arms and legs, but a rather rusty, orangey piping instead, although Bond was wearing a very fetching shade of lemon ski suit.

I loved that film when I first saw it at the cinema, probably a couple of years after it had been first released, and whenever it is on TV, even now, I will gladly sit and watch it, usually narrating along for the benefit, or more rather, to the chagrin, of my long suffering wife. It is definitely one of my guilty pleasures, but I'm not sure I even feel guilty about liking it.

Although it is very much of its time, with some two dimensional characters played awfully by the most wooden of actors (and that's just Bond himself!), it also includes some questionable views towards women, bordering on the misogynistic, and some of the cheesiest lines of dialogue ever. But I don't care; it's brilliant fun. And of course it's got another damsel in distress, the smoulderingly beautiful Barbara Bach, Ringo Starr's wife, who plays a not so kick-ass Russian agent called Major Anya Amasova, with a code name of Triple XXX, who Bond obviously gets into bed by the end.

Ringo Starr was definitely batting above his average there, and Mrs Merton's question to Debbie McGee springs to mind when I think of how a rather odd looking scouser married the most beautiful woman in the world, or so I thought at that point, pushing Jessica Lange into second place; "So what was it Barbara that first attracted you to the multi-millionaire Ringo Starr?"

The film basically starts and ends with Bond in bed with a beautiful woman. In between these romantic interludes we get the ultimate in Bond megalomaniac villains, who has a terrifying henchman with metal teeth, and the only accessory any self-respecting megalomaniac needs - a huge tank full of man-eating and very hungry sharks. There are also some very cool helicopters, the usual selection of gunmen, who, Stormtrooperesque, never seemed to be able to hit their target, and a wide range of exotic locations, from the tombs and pyramids of Egypt, to Alpine mountains, and cliff top roads overlooking the clear blue Mediterranean Sea. We are also treated to a Union Jack parachute, some awesome gadgets provided by Q, the best of these being of course a Lotus Esprit that fires rockets and can turn itself into a submarine. What's not to like?

Mum and dad got me a replica toy of that most cool of cars, with various buttons to press, which would release its sub-aqua manoeuvrable fins, and also fire rockets about ten inches into the air from its boot. I'm guessing it wouldn't have been the most practical of cars to do the weekly big shop in, unless of course you lived on an island and the only supermarket meant a trip to the mainland by boat. It would have its benefits then I suppose.

I would sit in the bath, next to the jar of shells I had collected from the beach after my failed and fateful trip to see "King Kong", and run the white car over our very 70s avocado bathroom tiles, before it would leap into the air, transforming mid-air into a submersible. I also had a toy shark which would try and attack it, but of course Bond's gadgets would always come up trumps.

Jaws the toy shark (as I unimaginatively named it) would also be no match for the other Jaws, the metal-toothed machine of a man who, like a vampire with deadly braces, bit people on the neck to kill them. He seemed indestructible, and even when Bond cunningly used a giant magnet to throw him into the aforementioned tank of man-eating sharks, he became a shark-eating man and easily survived.

I cowered behind the seats in the cinema whenever he was on the screen, although I did manage to stay in the auditorium at least. He terrified me, and his relentless ability to survive whatever situation he was put in, made his ability to survive almost as remarkable as Bond's. Maybe the producers cannily thought he could be used in the next film, which he duly was, in 1979's "Moonraker", in which he not only survives an exploding space station, but finds love, despite his magnetic gnashers, and becomes a loveable goodie by the end.

By this film, Roger Moore had become the ultimate Bond for me. Most people would vote Sean Connery, with his panther-like walk, as their favourite James Bond, but it very much depends on everyone's individual era. Kids these days will no doubt have Daniel Craig at the top of their list, if they have even seen the older films and the previous incarnations of Bond. And that's how it was for me.

"Goldfinger", "Dr. No" and "You Only Live Twice", to name just three of Connery's outings as Bond, are all great Bond films, all with many seminal and genre defining moments in them. But to me they just seemed a bit outdated by the time Roger Moore brought his suave sophistication, his roaming eyebrows and his great collection of sports casual wear onto the screen. But then again, looking back on these films now, they seem just as outdated as Connery's efforts, not least because in "Moonraker", we get yet another gorgeous Bond Girl, Lois Chiles, playing a character called Holly Goodhead.

Dr. Goodhead (at least she wasn't just a bimbo, she was a doctor after all) became my new most beautiful woman in the world, usurping the place of Mrs Ringo Starr, even though I had no idea of the rather rude connotations her name brought to older viewers. I was such a sweet and innocent little boy and had no idea that less sweet and innocent men were smiling knowingly at her character's name, as they had been used to such suggestive names already by then. Let's have a quick look at some of the more ridiculously named Bond girls.

We start of course with "Honey Ryder" from "Dr. No", played by the sweetest and almost divine Ursula Andress, with Eunice Gayson playing the rather obscenely named "Sylvia Trench" in the same film and also "From Russia with Love". We also get in that film the rather titillatingly named "Tatiana Romanova", played by Daniela Bianchi, and then the ultimate in suggestive Bond names, the frankly pornstaresque "Pussy Galore" from "Goldfinger", iconically played by Honor Blackman. "Domino Derval", played by Claudine Auger, was another pushover in Bond's merry game of females in "Thunderball", before Connery's era was finished off with the almost male pornstaresque named "Plenty O'Toole", played by Lana Wood in "Diamonds are Forever".

Roger Moore's era begins with Jane Seymour, playing "Solitaire", in "Live and Let Die", a name which Bond seemed to take as a challenge, doing his utmost to make sure she would not be alone, and certainly not in bed, and then in "The Man with the Golden Gun" we get "Mary Goodnight", played by Britt Ekland. I'm sure many men dreamed of having a good night with her.

And so we come to Barbara Bach's Russian Agent "Triple XXX", and onto the delectable "Dr. Goodhead". There is a certain tongue-in-cheek, almost seaside postcard, Carry-On Film charm to these character names, but all I was thinking was that she didn't just have a good head, she had the most perfect everything, and her apparently admirable abilities in the fellatio department never crossed my mind. I told you, I was sweet and innocent.

Now that I'm not quite so sweet and innocent, I'm not going to write a worthy piece about the degrading and misogynistic nature of Bond films. There have been plenty of books on the subject, which are well worth a read. All I knew back then was that I was in love with Dr. Holly Goodhead, and when completing my "Moonraker" sticker album, I would keep a spare sticker of her in my wallet that I kept my 50p a week pocket money in, and another would be stuck on my bedside cabinet, so that the last image I would have in my head, a head that was no longer as good as it used to be, before drifting off to sleep would be the lovely Lois Chiles in her not particularly flattering yellow spacesuit. I would then drift off into space with her, Barabarella style, dreaming that she too would need to remove her spacesuit.

Moore's next two Bond films, 1981's "For Your Eyes Only" and two years later, "Octopussy" (even the title sounds rude now), continued in the same vein, and along with the two already mentioned, I loved all four. In a Top 10 list of Greatest Ever Bond films, maybe only "The Spy Who Loved Me" would get onto that list, but I don't care. To me those four films, between 1977 and 1983, were the seminal films of my Bond childhood, and will quite happily watch them whenever they are on TV, narrating along Alan Partridge style to my heart's content, whilst telling my wife to "Stop getting Bond wrong!" But alas, she has usually left the room by that point to go and do something much more interesting than watch a secret agent outwit and outsmart evil and deadly megalomaniacs with a penchant for man-eating sharks.

The Empire Strikes Back (1980)   Dir: Irvin Kershner

In between the two Superman films, I had to reacquaint myself with the force, as did millions of others around the world. I was now seven years old and was now in the upper infants class, so my Jedi training was going quite well. I now knew all the characters' names, and even kind of understood where OB1 Kenobi's body had disappeared to after Vader had struck him down in the first film. I awaited the release of the second Star Wars film with eager anticipation.

Many of my school friends had been to see it before me, and they came back to school with whisperings of the plot and did not care less about anything such as a spoiler alert. Before I got to eventually see the film, I knew to expect to see the back of Vader's head without his helmet on, and that Luke would meet a little green man in a swamp, as well as having his hand chopped off by his father. I still didn't fully realise the significance of the last crucial piece of information, but the film was in no way spoiled despite these rather significant plot points being leaked to me prior to my viewing.

This time the anticipation was even greater than for the original film. I was only four back then and did not know what to expect. It was just a day out in another galaxy far, far away as far as I was concerned back then, but this time it was starting to become the almost mythical pilgrimage it has become for many others.

The vignettes I remember vividly this time are of course the battle on the snow planet with the mighty AT-AT walkers making their doom filled procession towards the rebel base, with Luke bringing one down with a piece of wire, a bit of a flaw in the Empire's basic design of these fearsome machines.

I was also appalled by Han having to put Luke inside a dead two legged camel type thing, and could almost smell the stench when Han muttered the line "And I thought they smelt bad…on the outside", which was hilariously parodied in Seth Macfarlane's "Family Guy" version of the film many years later.

I found the bit with the little green guy in the swamp a bit boring to be honest, as I didn't really understand what he was talking about. Power of The Force understand not I did. But I very much remember Han Solo being lowered into the carbon-freezing machine, and Luke's hand getting chopped off before falling down what looked like an awesome slide to what surely would be his demise.

I also remember becoming more transfixed with Princess Leia, now that she had sorted her hair out, but for some reason I left the cinema not with the same exhilaration as I did the first. Maybe it was because the film does not have a distinct ending, with a big medal ceremony and prizes being awarded to the victors. I suppose the title of the film itself should have given me an inkling that it might not be quite so triumphal as the first film. But I was not unhappy about the film, as I knew that all good fairy tales would end happily ever after. I would just have to wait another couple of years, with another couple of years of studying The Force to really appreciate the second film.

I now, like most other Star Wars fans, consider this second film to be the best of all the films. Not because of the set pieces, which may not be quite so dramatic as in other films, but because of the plot and story development, which are much more mature than the almost comic book simplicity of the first film. But it would not be until the final part of the trilogy that my tutelage would be complete.

Before that though, I had to watch Han Solo go and look for ancient artefacts with his trusty whip, and I would need to go on my own adventure to the almost mythological and certainly historic site (judging by the average age of its residents) of Eastbourne.

Raiders of the Lost Ark (1981)   Dir: Steven Spielberg

As a boy, I lived in the small town of Carnforth, in North Lancashire, and let me make it clear that my parents did not go on a 650 mile round trip just to take me and my brother to watch this perfect slice of adventure and escapism. We were on a week's holiday in sunny St. Leonards on Sea, and apart from a trip to the site of the Battle of Hastings, as I was a bit obsessed with it after studying it at school the previous month, standing on what may well have been, but let's face it, probably wasn't the exact spot where King Harold got an arrow stuck in his eye, the only other highlight of the week was an evening out in Eastbourne (a round trip of a much more sensible 35 miles) to watch a film I'd never heard of.

I wasn't even aware that "Raiders of the Lost Ark" had been released, had no idea that Harrison Ford, or Han Solo, as I referred to him at that point, was the star, or even what it was about. I certainly had no clue as to who directed it. Little did I know that this would be the start of a deep love affair with Steven Spielberg, one that would be nurtured and nourished over the rest of my life, but particularly in the next few highly formative years of my cinematic journey.

However, this wasn't the first Spielberg film I'd been to see at the cinema, my Gran having taken us to see "Close Encounters of the Third Kind", over the Easter holidays in 1978, whilst I was still only four years old. It was far too grown up for me, and I was still comparing it to "Star Wars" and frankly I found it boring in comparison. There were no princesses to be rescued, or light sabre fights, or even men that looked like big gorillas, or clad in gold metal. All I remember about Spielberg's classic first science-fiction film was Richard Dreyfuss making a mountain out of mashed potato, the five note melody played, and the huge UFO landing to reveal the weird looking alien. But this balmy summer's evening trip to Eastbourne would leave me thoroughly entertained, definitely entranced, and hugely enthralled.

"Raiders of the Lost Ark", despite being a huge box office popcorn film, is still one of the greatest films ever made, and in my mind, the best film ever made in the adventure genre. It had everything, and that was just the opening sequence, which left me almost breathless with excitement and anticipation for the rest of the film.

That iconic opening sequence is a microcosm of what the rest of the film will provide. It has genuine, almost heart-stopping tension, as Indy attempts to pull himself up and through the rapidly closing door; it has real horror, when Indy's non too trustworthy guide, played by Doctor Octopus himself, Alfred Molina comes to a very spiky end; it has humour, when Indy is just about to pick the golden head from its plinth, as we cut back to his guide copying the movements of Indy's nervous fingers; and of course it has a spectacular finale in which the huge boulder rolls menacingly towards our hero, smashing everything to smithereens in its doom-laden way, before Indy finally escapes with darts flying all around him from the local tribespeople, being ordered to do so by a greedy and selfish baddie.

Even the very final scene in the sequence provides a combination of terror and humour as Indy finds himself sharing a seat in the plane with a snake, before literally flying off into the sunset.

The rest of the film just amplifies each of these emotions, and even adds a little romance into the mix too. The humour comes from one of Dr Jones' students distracting him from his teaching with her eye lids that have a personal message for her eminent teacher on them. The sight of the Nazi agent Toht trying to cool his hand down, which has been badly burned by the headpiece he so desperately wanted to hold of made us all giggle, as did the scene when the same villainous Nazi scares Marion by getting out what looks like an instrument of extreme and eye watering torture, only to use it to hang his coat up with. Even in scenes of apparent tension there is humour; the sword wielding henchmen who challenges Indy to a duel is then abruptly shot by our hero, which again caused much mirth.

Romance is provided with the scene on the boat where Marion kisses all the parts of Indy's body that don't hurt, those parts being his elbow and his lips, but even here, humour preceded this tenderness, when Marion flips over the mirror and smacks Indy in the chin.

Tension is provided when Indy thinks he has lost Marion and desperately searches for her in the laundry baskets, only to think she has been killed, and of course the literally writhingly horrible scene where he and Marion are trapped in the snake filled tomb.

Horror is definitely there at the very end of the film once the Ark is finally opened, and the Nazi faces horrifically melt, and Toht and Belloc's faces turn into skulls which are literally blown away by the holy, or rather unholy forces emanating from the golden bed linen box. And we even get a black humoured sense of cynicism at the very end when we see how the "top men" are looking after the Ark by nailing it shut and placing it in a vast warehouse full of other identical packing cases.

The whole film is perfect. It is the most brilliant combination of all that is good about cinematic storytelling, creating, not to put too fine a point on it, a work of art. I know it is not a deep thinking masterpiece, worthy of several viewings just to fathom out the film's true ultimate meaning, but nevertheless it is a masterpiece, and even though I don't need to watch it multiple times to work out its meaning, I have watched it countless times simply because I know that it will entertain me and make me feel eight years old again. That, as far as I'm concerned, is the mark of a masterpiece, not because you learn something new about it on each viewing, but because you know exactly what to expect, knowing the script almost word for word, knowing that it will still make you as thrilled and excited as you did the first time you saw it.

It had such an effect on our whole family, and the ride back to Eastbourne was one of the happiest journeys we have ever had together, all of us quoting our favourite bits. That's another mark of a masterpiece, the ability to bring different generations together and unify them. It was one of the best nights that I had ever spent with my family, certainly the best night I had ever spent with them in Eastbourne. But of course it was, and will forever be, our only ever night out in Eastbourne. But what a night it was.

I was so affected by the film that once we got back to school, with me starting Year 4 by now, my new teacher asked us all to write about our favourite memory of the school holiday, and I quickly penned my first ever film review. Not that I've done much film reviewing actually, but I distinctly remember writing about Indiana Jones being not a famous "archaeologist", but a famous "architect", which my teacher duly corrected for me in the margin. My rather sweet mistake didn't spoil her enjoyment of my efforts, although I wonder what the film would have been like if Indy had been an architect. I probably wouldn't have been writing this sentence now if it had. Good job Mr. Spielberg didn't make the same mistake.

Jaws (1975)   Dir: Steven Spielberg

Along with "Jaws" I also include its sequel "Jaws 2". I am loathed to put these two films in the same bracket, one being another masterful work of cinematic art, and the other very much less so. I bet you can't work out which is which. I only put them together because the first time I saw them was as a double bill put on at the cinema in Lancaster, and no it wasn't my Gran getting the auditoria mixed up again when I should have been watching another crap Disney live action film. It was in fact my dad who took both me and my brother to watch these films. I distinctly remember it as it was possibly the only ever time my dad took us to the pictures without my mum being there too.

I'm not sure of the circumstances, but for some reason dad just told us both that we were going to the cinema to watch a couple of films. And it was even on a school night, with the first instalment starting around 7pm, and after a brief interval, the sequel would be shown at 9pm. We didn't get back until well after 11pm, which, on a school night, for an eight year old, was unheard of. Even when I went with him to watch our football team play, we would always be back just after 10pm. I felt like Cinderella being allowed to go to the ball.

When dad said that we were going to watch "Jaws", my brother was over the moon. He was three years older than me, and had heard so much about the film that he was the most excited I think I'd ever seen him. This was a proper grown up film, and I'm not quite sure how we got in to see it, seeing as neither me and my brother were way below the appropriate age limit to watch them. But let's face it, the cinema staff at our local cinema on a Monday evening were not about to turn us away. They were probably just glad of the custom. I don't think the censorship guidelines were adhered to much back then, and I'm so glad they weren't because we had a brilliant evening, us boys together watching people getting torn to shreds by two ridiculously massive and seemingly never sated sharks.

Since that evening, I must have watched the original and hugely superior film at least fifty times, whereas I think I've only ever seen the sequel once more. I was not aware back then just how inferior any of the other "Jaws" films are, with me still not realising this fact until I went to see the third instalment, a few years later, with some school friends this time, with us all sitting with cardboard glasses with one red lens and one blue.

"Jaws 3D" was one of a few films to be released using this novelty technology around the mid-eighties, and instead of severed limbs floating to the sea bed, they would always mysteriously float towards the camera, making us lean back in our seats as the mangled leg seemed to float out of the screen towards us.

I was probably still only ten years of age when I saw this one, but by now I realised just how naff the other films were, and just how flawless the original was, and still is. Even now, whenever it is on the TV, I always end up watching it, quoting the lines word perfectly, although at least I don't soil myself any more when the severed head reveals itself in the wreckage of the boat whilst Richard Dreyfuss is having a look around for clues. He certainly found one that evening.

I'll deal with the second film first, and the only things I remember was that Roy Scheider must have thought himself to be the unluckiest Police Chief in the world, but probably one of the luckiest actors ever. I wonder what he got paid to make this pile of dross, but as I said, my eight year old mind was not as discerning as it is now. I still loved watching small children and cocky teenagers being threatened by a large fin, various innocent people getting eaten alive, and the ending, where the shark bites an electrical cable and is fried to death. All these are still rooted in my memory. But that's about all I can remember about that one.

As for the original, well where should I start? The beginning might be the best idea, and what an opening it is. I was terrified, but also ever so slightly titillated knowing that the shark's first victim was completely naked as she skinny dipped in the sea. The iconic music did everything else for me, hooking me in completely, and making me hungry for more. A bit like the shark really.

I was obviously quite disturbed by the sight of a young lad, probably around the same age as me, floating around on a lilo, as I had done many times before, being chewed up in a fountain of gushing blood, before his rather pathetic piece of rubber mattress floats onto the shore, surrounded by his own blood. That could have been me, but then again, killer Great White sharks tend not to roam the English Channel, or the North Sea just off the coast of Whitby, at least not in my fledgling experience.

I always remember how the boy's mum slaps the Police Chief, blaming him for her son's death, rather than the greedy Mayor of Amity Island. I also remember just how old she looked. She looked more like his grandmother than his mum, but I suppose all that sunbathing has a certain effect on the skin. I was actually more upset about the guy whose dog goes missing. It's all very well losing a son to a blood thirsty scavenger, but imagine your dog getting eaten alive. How awful.

Yes I did almost wet myself when the head emerges suddenly from the boat wreckage, freaking Richard Dreyfuss out, and obviously the death of the old sea dog Quint, where he gets severed in two, his bottom half inside the shark's mouth before it bites down, sending blood spewing out of his mouth before being taken out to sea to be enjoyed properly as a main course.

The superlative ending, with Roy Scheider sinking ever further into the ocean, before finally hitting the gas canister, making the shark explode into thousands of gruesome bits, showering the sea with flesh and bits of chewed up Quint also, quite understandably, made a rather large impression on me. So much so, that the next day, I got my new set of Berol felt tip pens out and drew pictures of the shark's demise from both films.

I was very proud of these pictures; my drawing skills had come on a bit since those early pictures of a deformed Spiderman, and they were stuck lovingly above my bed, so that I would constantly be reminded of how one of God's beautiful, if rather vicious, creatures was blown to bits or electrocuted into oblivion. These ones were too good to be sent to Tony Hart. These were just for my own personal viewing.

As an adult or a child, we all remember these parts of the film, but as I have got older, I prefer the less gruesome aspects of

Spielberg's storytelling. I love in particular the domesticity of the film, the way the Police Chief has a normal, fairly humdrum existence, just trying to bring up his kids, along with his wife, who I had a little bit of a crush on. When she looks at the picture of a shark attacking a boat in a book and then shrieks out to her son in panic to get out of her boat and "Listen to your father" makes me realise, that as a father myself, we can at times be right, and know more than our wives, although admittedly only on very few and precious occasions.

I also love the scene where Brody is exhausted and is rubbing his face at the dinner table, with his son imitating his exact movements, before he realises what his son is doing and pulls a face at him. These little details show us that he is just a man, and certainly is no superhero, and has to deal with normal life as well as the huge problem of a massive shark killing the people he is employed to protect. And to top it off, he has a fear of going in a boat, just to exacerbate his woes.

The scene in the boat where Brody, Quint and Hooper are getting drunk and singing is also a favourite of mine. Whenever I've been tired, and quite often when I'm driving with the kids in the back of the car, we would all sing "Show me the way to go home, I'm tired and I want to go to bed" to keep me alert. I also love the humour brought into the scene with Hooper and Brody comparing their scars, before Quint spoils the hilarity when he recounts his ordeal as he floated in the shark infested waters after the USS Indianapolis had been torpedoed.

I eventually got around to looking this gruesome episode of the Second world war up on the internet to find out just how much of an ordeal it was. Let me tell you, Quint wasn't making it up or exaggerating it. In fact, if anything he downplayed the torture those men went through as the swarms of sharks helped themselves to a floating bit of buffet.

That's why the film works so well. Not only is it a piece of escapist nonsense, but it is also rooted in reality and domesticity, showing how real people would react in such circumstances. And that's why millions of people around the world, whether they were on a lilo off the coast of England, or in a pedalo on the Mediterranean, or diving amongst the coral reefs of Australia, were wary forever more of whether a huge man eating shark might be out looking for a bite to eat, even though statistically, this would not happen. I'd probably be a bit more wary in Australia though, rather than Whitby.

E.T. the Extra-Terrestrial (1982)   Dir: Steven Spielberg

If you've ever seen the clip of Henry Thomas auditioning for the role of Elliot in this film, you'll understand why he got the part. He captured everything that was needed, which is why this film affected me so much. He wasn't acting, he was feeling the role, using truly remarkable empathy to convey an utter sense of vulnerability, confusion, protectiveness and bewilderment at the prospect of his new friend being taken away from him. And of course his new friend wasn't even human, but a frankly almost pre-historic dwarf with impressively long fingers, an extendable neck, and a head shaped a bit like an oversized rugby ball. And yet Elliott was devoted to him so much that millions of us, me certainly included, sobbed with he was finally parted from his extra-terrestrial friend.

This to me is probably my favourite of all Spielberg's films. Not because I have seen it more than any of the others. In fact I have watched it nowhere near the amount of times I have watched the other two Spielberg films already mentioned, namely "Raiders of the Lost Ark", and "Jaws". That's probably because it's a tough watch at times, and I have to emotionally prepare myself for it, unlike the thrills of Indiana Jones searching for treasure, or a shark causing mayhem.

Those films were perfect in so many ways, but it was only once I saw "E.T." that I realised just how powerfully emotional a film could be. Maybe it had something to do with me being around the same age as Elliott, and always being a bit of a loner, with only a bigger brother for company a lot of the time, and he wasn't that keen on spending too much time with a little pipsqueak like me. Elliott even played with Star Wars figures, as I had done many times, although I never owned Lando Calrissian or Boba Fett as Elliott did.

"E.T." had a profound effect on me, and I will always cherish the memories the film brings back to me. It was released in December 1982 when I was nine years old, and presumably went to see it sometime soon after its release. I distinctly recall that mum and dad took me to see it on a Saturday afternoon, and I distinctly remember the excitement and anticipation as I slowly got to the top of the stairwell at Lancaster cinema.

The auditorium was packed, and the whole afternoon had a magical feel to it, not just because of the film itself, but because of the feeling of safety and protection I got from sitting in between my mum and dad, watching a film that is really not a film just for kids. Anyone of any age can enjoy this film, and I was packed into the cinema with a huge range of ages and different types of people. This was when I realised just how unifying a film can be, all sharing in the emotions of Elliott and his little alien friend.

As we were all filing out of the cinema, in an almost eerie quietness, punctuated with the occasional sniffle as most people were attempting to either disguise their tears, or just allowing them, like me, to trickle down their cheeks. The two women in front of me, probably both in their twenties with no children with them, were both sobbing too, and one said to the other, "That was the saddest, happiest film I've ever seen". That summed it up for me. Spielberg, like a modern day cinematic version of Dickens, knew exactly how to emotionally manipulate his audience in order to elicit the most profound sense of catharsis most of us had ever experienced. He again showed us all what a master craftsman he was, in whatever genre he chose to explore.

The film touched me on so many different levels. Obviously the developing friendship between Elliott and E.T. was deeply moving, but again, as in "Jaws" the simple and honest domesticity of the film connected with me. This time, the family dynamic was of a single mum trying to bring her three kids up the best she could, despite their father never being present in the film, having moved to Mexico with his new girlfriend.

And yet it was she who was feeding them and providing a safe environment for them to grow up, despite the usual trials and tribulations siblings can bring to each other, in particular the excellent use of the insult "Penis breath" which Elliot shouts in his brother's face, causing his mum to be angry and laugh at his verbal ingenuity at the same time. It made me intensely grateful that I indeed did have both my parents sitting next to me, and never had had to deal with such complicated emotions.

I felt everything that Elliott felt, not simply because he was my age, but it probably had something to do with the director shooting the film from the eye-level of a child to further connect us with both E.T. and Elliot. I palpably felt the confusion of

Elliott, knowing deep down that E.T. had to "phone home" and yet desperately wanting him to stay with him.

I felt the magic, and almost believed in the magic, as Elliott's BMX starts to fly with E.T. sitting in the basket on the front, silhouetted by the huge moon, which became the iconic image we were left with after the film ended.

I sobbed in anguish when E.T.'s heart light finally fades and then is extinguished when he is being treated by the medics and scientists, my mum squeezing my hand to make sure I was ok. And I also sobbed with a mixture of relief, joy, disbelief and pure delight when the heart light flickered back to life, and Elliott's face lit up with the same emotions I've just mentioned.

I was thrilled with the final chase, where Elliot and his brother are in the ambulance, and Elliott finally manages to pull the connector from the long tube that is attached to the back, allowing them to meet up with their mates on their BMXs. When the boys see E.T. for the first time as he emerges from the back of the ambulance, Elliott delivers one of the greatest lines of dialogue ever. He tells them that "he is a man from outer space and we're taking him back to his spaceship."

One of the boys replies, with a tongue in cheek nod from Spielberg towards that other most famous of Science Fiction franchises, "Star Trek", "Can't he just beam up or something?" which leaves Elliott totally exasperated.

Elliot comes out with the actually quite profound line of "This is reality!" blurring the lines between fantasy and reality for us cinema goers. It certainly felt like reality to me at that point.

The boys, with E.T. in Elliot's basket, once again are seemingly in the clear, only to have to use more evasive manoeuvres on their BMXs, swooping up and down the hills, actually jumping over the police car waiting for them, before inevitably being trapped, with a gun pointing at them from the end of the street.

The thrills and tension turned into that sense of pure magic again when E.T. makes the whole gang of boys fly above the trees on their bikes to finally evade capture, allowing the most heartbreakingly beautiful and evocative farewell scene ever to happen. I'm actually welling up now as I write this, as all those emotions I had then are coming flooding back to me.

The finale is just heart wrenching. We are pleased that E.T. is going back home, but heartbroken that he will no longer be there for Elliott. The farewells each of the three children give to E.T. are more emotional than the next, and my tears had already started with Drew Barrymore's character Gertie, as she gives E.T. the geranium plant, and he tells her to "Be good". A few sobs came out not just from me, but around the whole cinema when Michael, Elliott's brother receives a heartfelt thank you from E.T.

Then there were wailing sounds heard (and that was just from my dad) when Elliott says his final farewell to E.T., with the most tender of hugs between the two sending me over the edge, and I joined in with the wailing, especially when Spielberg cuts to a shot of Elliott's mum crying too. E.T.'s finger lights up, touches Elliot on the forehead, and tells him that "I'll be right here", to let us all know that he will never forget him, and that he will always be in Elliot's head, and certainly in his heart.

Spielberg then creates that final image for us of the spaceship's door closing in a circular manner, allowing the last image of E.T. to be the heart light glowing brightly with gratitude, hope, and love, before the ship flies off into space leaving a rainbow in the sky, and John Williams' sweeping and soaring score lifting us all off our seats too. It is pure cinematic magic.

Again, it might not be the most important of films in terms of gravity of subject matter, but it is a work of art; a work of art of almost divine proportions, as of course there is also the Christian allegory side to the story, in which, just like Jesus, E.T. is sent down from above, dies, but then rises again, before ascending back to where he came from, bringing hope, redemption and especially love to those he meets. The last words Elliott says to his friend just before E.T.'s heart light bursts back into life are "I love you", allowing the miracle to take place

Indeed, Richard Attenborough, who picked up eight Oscars for "Gandhi" in the same year, including Best Picture and Best Director, always maintained, with typical humility for such a great man, that "E.T." is a far greater film, as it does what only the cinema can do – create magic. Attenborough's biopic was brilliant, and the worthiest of winners. It told a hugely important story, one that truly deserved to be told, but it didn't create pure magic as "E.T." does.

I know which film I'd have voted for.

The African Queen (1951)   Dir: John Huston

You may be wondering why this rather incongruous film appears at this point. I was still only eight or nine years old, but there were a few grown up films I saw at this time in my life too. The previously mentioned "Gandhi" was one of them. My parents had really wanted to see it, but with no access to childcare, they decided to take me and my brother along for the ride one evening to watch a film which was over three hours long and definitely had no light sabres, aliens, or sharks at all. To be honest I remember very little about the film.

Maybe this was because my mum and dad didn't think I'd be able to take the film in, and suggested I take something to colour in whilst I was sitting in the dark with them if I got bored. My colouring in skills were severely put to the test that day. I wish I hadn't bothered as I'm sure I would have been able to take some enjoyment and knowledge from the film.

The most vivid memory of this epic was the massacre at Amritsar, where hundreds of Sikhs were gunned down by British soldiers, and the lasting image I have is of the well in the middle of the square, which was stained with blood, as people tried desperately to escape the bullets. I remember this came just before the interval, another first for me, as I'd never been to a film where I could top up my lolly count at half time.

I've obviously watched the film since and am pleased to say that I am able to remember lots more about it now, but at the age of eight, I was still quite proud of being taken to a proper grown up film which had a profoundly serious message and an essential lesson for us all to be learned from it, which is of course why it beat "E.T." to the Best Picture Oscar, and Dickie Attenborough beat Spielberg to the Best Director prize. Spielberg certainly didn't hold it against him, giving him one of the main roles in another of his films, "Jurassic Park", eleven years later.

Another of Dickie's films, this time as an actor, also left a huge impression on me around this time. It must have been around Christmas 1980 or 1981 that I first sat and watched "The Great Escape", with my family, probably on Boxing Day after getting momentarily bored of my new train set or Scalextric track. This momentary ennui with making my JPS Formula One car zoom round the track turned into at least a three hour hiatus, as the moment I started watching this great film, I was instantly hooked.

The all-star cast, most of whom I'd never heard of, apart from James Garner because of my parents' enjoyment of "The Rockford Files" and Gordon Jackson, because of my brother's obsession with the TV series "The Professionals", and my mum's fondness for "Upstairs, Downstairs", made a huge impression on me despite not knowing who most of them were. I didn't have a clue who Dickie Attenborough, Charles Bronson, James Coburn, Donald Pleasance, David McCallum or even the great Steve McQueen were, but after this film I certainly did.

Instead of James Garner being Jim Rockford, he would forever be the guy who tried to escape with the blind Donald Pleasance, ultimately failing, being recaptured in his attempts to save his blind friend

Gordon Jackson was no longer Bodie and Doyle's boss, but the man who is tricked by a Gestapo officer, who addresses him in English, with Jackson stupidly replying in English too, giving his and Dickie Attenborough's masquerade as Frenchmen away, leading to them being executed by a machine gun in an open field.

I was captivated by Bronson's ultra-macho character Danny, "The Tunnel King", especially when his machismo is shattered, and he breaks down, admitting to being claustrophobic. And as for Steve McQueen as Hilts, anyone who has seen the film remembers him bouncing his baseball in the cooler. And speaking of cool, McQueen was the coolest thing I'd ever seen on a motorbike (apart from my toy Evil Knievel) as he jumped over barbed wire blockades, ultimately being recaptured, and thrown back in the cooler, with the final image of the film being the German guard pausing to hear the familiar sounds of Hilts' baseball yet again. It was a much better way to spend Boxing Day than watching cars go round in a figure of eight to the point of near hypnosis. I'd rather be hypnotised by a brilliant story, the fact that it was based on real events making it even more brilliant.

But the one grown up film I also vividly recall from this time, was one that I had never heard of, didn't even know what it was called, let alone knew who the stars were, and didn't find the answers to these questions out until many years later.

You must remember that back then in the early 1980s, we did not have the multitude of choices on TV that we have today. We had the total sum of three channels: BBC1, BBC2 and ITV. And that was it. Three channels. It's hard to imagine now. So you ended up watching whatever was on, and couldn't just flick to one of the hundreds of channels available now, or stream something on catchup. Back then I watched so many old films simply because there was nothing else on. I grew up watching old Laurel and Hardy films, and old westerns, as these were better than watching another episode of "Crossroads".

It was one such evening in which I had the front room to myself when I first encountered "The African Queen", John Huston's classic, starring two of the biggest stars that cinema has ever produced, in this age, or any other age for that matter: Katharine Hepburn and Humphrey Bogart. But I had no idea who they were.

I'd only ever heard Bogart's name when impressionists on TV, most probably Mike Yarwood, had done Bogey's voice as part of his act. Obviously the key to the humour here is knowing who the impression is of, and I didn't know who Humphrey Bogart was, had no idea what he looked like, and definitely was in the dark about what he sounded like. And yet here I was, watching him on TV fall in love with another great, possibly the greatest ever (the most Oscars for Best Actress, with four to her name), the one and only Katherine Hepburn. It would be much later in my life that these two's legacies would be fully explored and appreciated by me.

So, with the living room all to myself one evening after tea, I was flicking between channels, looking for something to mildly entertain me. The only choices I probably had were the News or Regional News on BBC1 and ITV, and an eight year old's thirst for current affairs was naturally not so urgent as it is now, so BBC2 would have to do.

My only choice, apart from updates on the state of the nation, which let's be honest, wasn't that great in the early 1980s, was whatever was showing on the channel that another Attenborough, David this time, had helped to create. I couldn't thank him enough that evening as I flicked onto the channel and became seduced by a film all about a rum and gin-swilling captain of the eponymously named boat, and the tensions between him and his only other passenger, Hepburn's straight-laced missionary, Rose Sayer.

I didn't even see the beginning of the film, and so had no clue as to why these two opposites were stuck on this boat together in the middle of deepest darkest Africa. But there was something about their characters, and Bogart and Hepburn's masterful portrayals of them that hooked me in, just as Bogart's Charlie Allnut was being hooked in by Rose's charms.

I loved their bickering and squabbling, and was overjoyed at the end when they realised they actually loved each other and got married, even though they were facing being hanged. But of course it all ends well, and I went up to bed that evening with a warm glow, even though I still did not know which film I had just watched or who these people I had spent the last couple of hours with were.

I only found this information out probably about eleven or twelve years later when reading a book all about classic films, or the 100 Films You Must See Before You Die type of book, that I realised that I could already tick this one off my list. At that point, the plot of the film I had seen many years previously now all made sense, and so I watched it again as soon as I could, making sure I watched the first crucial half hour this time, to relive that evening in front of my TV when I was eight years old. And I've loved it ever since.

But that's enough of delving into the past, it's time to get back to my next new release at the cinema, which ironically caused me to have to go much further back in time.

I had to once again travel to a long time ago, in a galaxy far, far away.

The Return of the Jedi (1983) Dir: Richard Marquand

My tutelage in the ways of The Force was near to completion by now. I had reached the milestone of double figures in terms of age, and was keen to finish my Jedi journey, as was just about every other ten year old in the world.

Even though this film is generally considered to be the weakest of the original trilogy, this is the one I remember the most and still prefer it to any of the other six films which have subsequently been released, although it's not hard to like any film, Star Wars related or not, more than "The Phantom Menace". By now I understood fully the previous two film's plots and had even digested the rather startling piece of hereditary information Vader had given to Luke at the end of the previous instalment.

The opening of this film was memorable for two things. Firstly, the disgusting sight of Jabba the Hutt, (the first time anyone had ever seen him) reclining like a huge slug on his throne, whilst having his every need met by his weird array of servant creatures brought repulsion to my eyes. This repulsion was beautifully balanced though with the most attractive sight I'd ever seen in not just a Star Wars film, but any film for that matter.

Princess Leia in her slave outfit, bronze bikini and all, was a magnet for my eyes, and all I wanted at that point was a big life sized cardboard cut-out of her to put in my bedroom. That would have to wait though. From the headphone hair of the first film, to the gilet wearing kick ass commander of the second film, she was now more like a futuristic version of Salome, and it wouldn't be long before she would get her prize too, although she wouldn't have to dance at least to earn it. She'd be required to put a bit more effort in than that, having to use the chain she was tied to Jabba with to strangle the big fat slug until his eyes popped out, and his loathsome tongue fell lifelessly out of his disgusting slit of a mouth.

But before that Luke would have to kill a huge monster in a deadly pit, with Jabba's entourage looking on excitedly, in a hugely unfair gladiatorial battle. Jabba was not entertained, it's safe to say, so Luke, Leia, and the recently defrosted Han are taken to another pit, this time with teeth, in the desert to be formally executed. But of course Jabba did not realise how strong the force was with this young Jedi Master, and how strong Leia must have been to actually choke the fat bastard to death, allowing all our gang of goodies, Chewie, C3-P0 and R2-D2 included, to speed off into the desert leaving the hungry hole in the ground to have to make do with a few of Jabba's mates as a light hors d'oeuvre.

Sad was I when Yoda died, but at least Luke now knew what he had to do in terms of having a bit of a chat with his dad, and fighting off those rather incestuous urges he had been having for Leia, who he now discovered to be his twin sister.

All that was left was for the whole Evil Empire, an organisation so powerful that it could literally blow up planets with the press of a button, to be defeated by a bunch of cute little teddy bears. And some better-late-than-never fatherly help for his son, with Vader chucking the Emperor down a big hole, and yet another rather basic flaw in the second Death Star's structural design allowing it to be destroyed, but this time not by Luke, but by Lando, who was now one of the Goodies, and I don't mean one of Bill Oddie's mates.

The whole finale on the forest moon of Endor was hugely entertaining, with breathless speeder chases through the trees, C3-PO being hailed as a God by the furry foes who turn into furry friends, with Luke, Han and Chewie all being spit-roasted, and two-legged versions of AT-ATs being destroyed with the simple use of logs was great fun, although the final scene was a slightly underwhelming, with hazy visions of OB1 and his new best mate Anakin all joining in with the teddy bears' picnic in the tree tops.

And so my time as a Padawan was complete. I could now progress to becoming a Jedi apprentice, so that I could teach my own younglings the ways of The Force once I became a father seventeen years later. And yes, on the census form in 2011, me and my son's religion is now formally that of Jedi.

Taught him well I have.

Indiana Jones and the   **Dir: Steven Spielberg**

Temple of Doom (1984)

Now that I'd served my time at Jedi school, putting in the
required amount of extra-curricular hours in, it was also time for
me to move on in terms of normal curricular education. The final
part of my childhood obsession with Spielberg came just as I was
in between primary and secondary schools, in the summer of
1984. This was probably the last film I saw at the cinema before I
made the big step up to big school, and for many people it did not
live up to the brilliance of "Raiders of the Lost Ark", but I
disagreed.

Maybe I agree with them now, but at the time, I certainly thought
it was just as good. I definitely enjoyed it just as much, but this
might have had something to do with the opening scene being
filled with pretty dancing girls, led by Spielberg's future wife
Kate Capshaw, singing a multi-lingual rendition of "Anything
Goes". It was his tribute to old Busby Berkley routines, and even
though it was nothing like the opening scene from "Raiders", it
still gave me enormous satisfaction, especially as the song turns
into a Shanghai surprise, with a frenetic and frantic gun battle
breaking out in Club Obi Wan, a nice touch by Spielberg to his
friend and Executive Producer, George Lucas.

The opening scene was definitely different, presumably Spielberg
didn't want to just make a replica of the first film, opting to make
the whole film have a different, more fantastic feel to it. There
were no Nazis this time, no searching around for Christian
artefacts, and definitely no melting faces. What he did give us
instead was a different, yet also very similar film.

The setting may be different, the characters, with the introduction
of a more stereotypically feminine female lead than Karen

Black's rather ballsy Marion, and a new character, played by the then twelve year old Ke Huy Quan, as Indy's new sidekick, Short Round, were different too, but the general tone, the humour, the breath taking set pieces, and the gimmicks we all loved from the first film all remained the same. I loved it because of the different similarities, or similar differences it contained, whichever way you want to put it.

The set pieces, starting with the opening night club scene, are up there with the best that Spielberg has ever done. I loved the hair raising sledge ride down the Himalayan mountain side after Indy's pilots decide to jump out, leaving our heroes with only a rubber dinghy to use as both parachute and sledge.

I loved the banquet scene at Pankot Palace, especially the monkey brains and the other dishes of truly gruesome cuisine. I loved the insect infested spiked chamber which almost turns Indy into a human pin cushion, only to be saved once the rather masculinely named Willie puts her hand into the creepiest and crawliest hole ever, despite breaking one of her nails, and pushes the stone in to stop the roof's deadly descent.

I especially loved watching the ritualistic sacrifice, where our baddie, Mola Ram, shows quite a heartless lack of care and attention to his victim, ripping the poor man's heart out with his fingers, showing it still beating to his now definitely heartless victim, before he is put out of his misery and lowered into a fiery pit of hellish lava.

I loved the roller-coaster ride in the mine carts through the tunnels, putting anything Alton Towers has to offer to shame, and I also loved the iconic rope bridge scene, with Indy trapped between two sets of Thuggee reinforcements, with his only option being to chop the bridge in two, allowing the hungry crocodiles to feast on anyone who inevitably fell into the river below. It really was raining men for those delighted crocodiles that day.

The final scene is a bit cheesy though, with Indy becoming a much cooler version of the Pied Piper, as he leads all the enslaved children back to their families, before returning to normal life, whatever normal life was for Indiana Jones, as constantly being involved in death defying situations, usually with only a whip for comfort seemed to be normal for him

Looking back on it now, "Temple of Doom" is not as good as "Raiders of the Lost Ark". It was never going to be as good as that perfect film. In fact there are very few films, and certainly not in the adventure genre that are as good, but it is still up there as one of my favourite childhood films.

I saw it just before my parents took me and my brother for a week in Cornwall that year, to St. Ives in fact, and as I was going to St. Ives, I read a new book which my mum had bought me from cover to cover, all about the making of the film. I knew everything there was to know about the film once we got there and probably read it at least three times more that week. I learned what each of the dishes was actually made of in the banquet scene, and how the special effects were created, and became very jealous of the boy playing Short Round as he got to do all that cool stuff with Harrison Ford at only a year older than I was at that point. Lucky git.

I also got some insight into Spielberg's last two films, the aforementioned "Raiders of the Lost Ark" and "E.T.", learning how animatronic models were used for the Extra Terrestrial, as well as little people dressed up as him, one of them being another twelve year old boy who had been born without legs and so had become an expert at walking on his hands. Not so lucky git. As far as I was concerned, it was the book that kept on giving, and further fuelled my obsession with all things Spielberg related.

Once we got back home from Cornwall, I may have even persuaded my mum to come with me again to the cinema so that I could watch the whole film once more, this time armed with the knowledge and the facts I had learned from my book, facts and knowledge that my poor mum had to listen to constantly, on the way to the cinema, on the way back, and probably during the film too. She didn't seem to mind though. After all, she had bought me the book in the first place. At least she knew that I'd read it.

And so off on my journey to big school it was, with all its new technology, like computers and stuff, and into my life would enter another new piece of technology, one that would give me much more opportunity to continue and expand my own cinematic journey. A video recorder. And not a Betamax one either. A real VHS player, although it still may well have been a top loader, and it definitely made a rather deafening, and frankly menacing sound when it was rewinding. I didn't mind though. I could now watch films whenever I wanted, or at least when my brother rented them out from the local video shop, which was very frequently indeed.

Part Two

Adolescent Growing Pains

Rocky 2 (1982)   Dir: Sylvester Stallone

It had taken months of nagging from my older brother to finally convince my parents, especially my dad, that a video recorder was indeed an essential part of any respectable household. It was the "respectable" aspect that my dad was scared about, fearing that mine and my brother's young corruptible minds would be filled with sin and evil, especially as our local video shop, indeed the only video shop in the town, contained such infamous titles as "Driller Killer", "I Spit on Your Grave", and "The Texas Chainsaw Massacre".

The titles of these films alone caused my dad to panic. I've only ever seen one of these films, and thoroughly enjoyed, if that is the right word, watching Leatherface and his completely messed up family do despicable things to a group of innocent teenagers. I hasten to add that I was well into my thirties when I saw it though and was not corrupted at all by its gore. I had already been corrupted long before then, and not by video nasties.

My brother instead worked on my mum, advising her of the many benefits of a video recorder, being able to tape programmes she loved whilst she was out, and being able to keep them forever if she so wished. If mum agreed, then so inevitably would dad.

My brother's main aim though was so he could watch "Rocky 3", which he had become obsessed with after the release of the iconic theme track "Eye of the Tiger", by Survivor, which seemed to spend ages at No.1 in the charts.

Sylvester Stallone had originally asked Queen if he could use "Another One Bites the Dust" for the opening montage but was refused permission, and so this awesome track with its hypnotic opening riff was used instead. I can't imagine now what the film would have been like without it. Still awesome actually, in the cheesiest of ways.

Mum eventually relented, and so my brother, and consequently me, were introduced to Rocky Balboa, a character who has become iconic for millions of teenage boys, and a few girls, who grew up in the 1980s. I still watch any of these first four Rocky films again whenever they are on TV now, despite having them all on DVD, and knowing them almost word perfectly, particularly "Rocky 2".

You might note that the order I watched them in was out of synch, watching them in the following order: 3, 2, 1, 4, with the original film being my least favourite, despite it having won the Best Picture Oscar, and its director, John Avildsen (who?) won Best Director, along with the award for Best Editing. The film remained off my radar for a few months due to the fact that my brother never got around to renting it out until he had watched the third and second films so many times that he thought it was time to see where the whole saga began.

Although it is a more grown up film, and in terms of plot and character development, is far superior to the others, probably because it wasn't directed by its star, it didn't have the same appeal as the other instalments in the series, mainly due to the fact that there wasn't actually that much action in the boxing ring itself, and that of course was what a ten and thirteen year old boy craved at that point. It did contain the brilliant line, "You're gonna eat lightnin' and you're gonna crap thunder!" though from Rocky's trainer Mickey, played by Burgess Meredith, who I'd only ever come across as The Penguin in the "Batman" TV series with Adam West. "Rocky" didn't have enough Pow!, Crack! and Ummph! for us two boys, and it certainly didn't contain the most spellbindingly gorgeous Catwoman in it either.

What "Rocky" lacked was certainly made up for in the third film, with its instantly gratifying opening montage in which Rocky literally punches opponents off the floor and out of the ring, and it also had the baddest of badass baddies, the ferocious Clubber Lang, played by Mr. T, who would then go onto developing an irrational hatred of getting onto planes in "The A Team". He was savage in the ring, as was the bizarre matchup between Rocky and Thunderlips the wrestler, played by Hulk Hogan, which of course Rocky gains a respectable draw in, despite almost having his back broken and a horde of swimsuit clad beauties climbing onto his back to protect their master from Rocky's relentless fists.

It was the second film which I have the most affection for though, simply because it had been shown on TV so I could actually tape it on one of my new Scotch videotapes ("Re-record, not fade away"). As "Rocky 3" had only been rented out for one day, and granted, my brother and I probably watched it at least three times that particular day, with "Rocky 2", I could now watch it to my heart's content whenever I wanted.

I loved the recap at the beginning from the end of the first film, the only bit of "Rocky" we actually enjoyed, and I loved Rocky's ineptitude at asking Adrian to marry him, and his even greater ineptitude when it came to spending his newly gained money wisely.

When the rather drippy Adrian has to take the job in the pet shop whilst heavily pregnant, not wanting Rocky to fight again due to the possibility of him becoming blind, eventually collapsing and falling into a coma, I was there every single second with Rocky by his new bride's bedside, and when she woke up and tells Rocky to go and win, having obviously had some sort of epiphany whilst in her coma, or more likely not wanting to lug bags of pet food around anymore, I was jumping for joy, especially when Mickey the trainer shouts out "What are we waiting for?" to cue the best montage ever, ending with Rocky's iconic run through the streets of Philadelphia, becoming another Pied Piper of sorts, before ending up on the steps of the Philadelphia Museum of Art, surrounded by his adoring throng of fans. If I could, I would have sprinted alongside him too at that point.

His eventual victory to take the title from Apollo Creed almost made me cry, especially with his final manic shout out to his wife at home, "Yo Adrian, I did it!", but of course I was at big school now, and I didn't cry at films any more. Well, not as much any way.

By the time "Rocky 4" came out in 1985, I was old enough to go with my big brother to watch it at the cinema, and by now was starting to realise how unrealistic and somewhat comic book the films were, and even I found the fact that Rocky, who had retired by now after all, got back in the ring to pummel another mean baddie, this time in the guise of Ivan Drago, played by He-Man himself, Dolph Lundgren, to be just a bit too far-fetched.

The usual montage was there, but instead of chasing chickens around as in the second and third films, he went to Siberia and lifted logs and pulled sleds around, so that he could not only beat his man mountain machine of an opponent, but also bring about world peace and end the Cold War all at the same time. "If I can change, then you can change. We can all change!" If only Rocky had been the chief negotiator in peace talks between the USA and the USSR.

When the film was released on video a year or so later, I reserved it for a day in my school holidays, so that I could repeat what me and my brother did with the third film, and watch it as many times as possible in twenty four hours. I was rather disappointed that whoever had rented it the day before had not brought it back by 11 am when the video shop opened, only returning it at the much more convenient time for him of around 7pm. This would impact the amount of times I would be able to watch it that evening, and had to watch it the following day at least twice to make up for it. And yes, the robot which Rocky gives to Paulie for his birthday got on my nerves every single time.

Even now, when I'm lying in bed flicking through the channels on TV, waiting for my wife to finish her ablutions and join me, she always groans when she finds that I have found any of the "Rocky" films being shown, as she knows that she may as well read or go on her phone for the rest of the evening, and try and ignore my narration and speaking the lines aloud whilst I relive my youth again.

Whenever I get into my gym gear to go and be energetic for a short period of time, her usual response to me is, "Are you going to go and chase chickens again?" She knows all too well that I haven't fully grasped what the eye of the tiger actually is, and that I'll be spending most of my time sitting in either the steam room, the sauna or the jacuzzi. But at least I'll play that song on my drive down to the gym to get me in the mood for a blood pumping jacuzzi session.

An American Werewolf in London (1981)   Dir: John Landis

Another benefit of our video recorder was that it did allow me to watch films that I wasn't allowed to see, or ones that hadn't actually been in the cinema. One such film was "The Karate Kid", which everyone I knew seemed to have seen on video, apart from me. Still to this day I've never met anyone who actually saw it at the cinema, if it ever had a theatrical release in the first place. Once I saw it, probably at the age of eleven, I instantly realised why everyone had been raving about it so much. It was ace.

Mr. Miyagi's fiendish training regime, which masqueraded as a way of getting Daniel Son to do a variety of households chores for him, with his iconic line "Wax on, wax off," is recognisable to anyone from my generation, as is the film's finale, with Daniel Son waiting patiently, arms raised, a manic look in his eyes, before delivering what is apparently called a Crane kick straight to the face of his cocky blond bastard of an opponent. He is then hugged by a very young Elizabeth Shue before going onto make the inevitable sequel, and causing everyone I knew to try and recreate that kick in the school playground, causing a few injuries, and not just to those who were being kicked, but the ones attempting it in the first place as well.

We would all go and watch the second film at the cinema, and I even took my first proper girlfriend to watch it, with Peter Cetera's song "The Glory of Love", becoming, in the words of Simon Bates on Radio 1, "our tune". The film itself was not a patch on the original, but at least I got to slow dance with my girlfriend Tracy to our song at the school disco.

The other benefit of the VHS player was that if I wasn't allowed to watch a certain film, then at least one of my mates would be, and would probably have taped it too. This is how I came to watch still one of my all-time favourite films, all about a couple of young American lads who decide to go to a pub called "The Slaughtered Lamb", and probably wish they hadn't bothered, despite Rik Mayall being in there having a game of chess.

"An American Werewolf in London", had become famous for its special effects, with the transformation from man to lycanthrope gaining almost mythical status amongst us eleven and twelve year olds. The film was released in 1981 at the cinema, and with it being an X certificate back then, there was no way that me, or even my older brother, still only thirteen when it was released on VHS, was going to be able to pass ourselves off as eighteen to enable us to rent the video.

So, when it was first shown on TV in what must have been late 1984, one Sunday evening if I remember rightly, my brother and I were just a tad excited. My dad himself was quite keen to see what all the fuss was about too, and so us boys, just as we had for the "Jaws" double bill two or three years earlier, settled down for what should have been a feast of gore and horror, laced with some of the funniest black humour you could ever wish to see in a film, with a spattering of naked nurse on offer too, with Jenny Agutter showing that she indeed had grown up since the last time I had seen her in "The Railway Children".

But we only managed to watch the first five minutes, as my dad abruptly turned it off and told us it wasn't appropriate. This was nothing to do with the many gory killings, or the ridiculously scary dream sequences, which still make me jump now when Nurse Alex goes to open the curtains before being savagely stabbed by one of the demon Nazis that David has just dreamt have massacred his family whilst being forced to watch, before having his throat slit. Why my dad turned it off had nothing to do with the blood thirsty murders carried out by a half man half wolf who seemed to be able to negotiate Tottenham Court Road Tube station with ease.

My dad's sudden halting of proceedings was due to the bad language used at the start of the film, when David and his soon to be not quite dead, but very definitely killed companion Jack are discussing the merits of a girl they both know, with some rather prevalent use of the F word included as they stroll across the North Yorkshire moors. My dad, a Christian man with a deep and living faith, despite having worked on building sites or workshops where such "industrial" language was commonplace, did not want that kind of language to be brought into his home, especially on a Sunday, and so off the TV went.

To be honest, even if there hadn't have been much swearing at all, I'm not sure he would have let me watch the scary bits, and if dad may well have enjoyed the nude shower scene, my mum would definitely have turned it off at that point, before I'd seen any glimpse of Jenny Agutter's nipples, or indeed a glimpse of the werewolf at all. Both my parents would most certainly not have put up with the scene in the porn theatre, where a now very decomposed Jack allows David to meet all his victims in person, with fairly lurid sex noises going on in the background.

Mum and dad have always been rather censorious when it comes to anything like sex or swearing. They took us to see "Ghostbusters" one night during the Christmas holidays of 1984, and the atmosphere was very tense throughout the film, with me thinking at one point that we were going to be embarrassingly dragged out of the cinema by my disapproving parents after they had heard a few naughty words. The mood become even tenser in the car on our journey home, due to the amount of swearing in the film we had just endured, something that I don't recall the film being especially laden with, but it had obviously offended my parents' rather saintly ears. I've hated "Ghostbusters" ever since, not because of the language, but because it's just not very good.

And as for any sex scenes, I remember sitting down one evening with my mum to watch "Yanks", with Richard Gere as its rather dreamy hero, who I'm sure mum had a bit of a crush on, making girls' hearts flutter in the North of England, after being posted

74

there during the second World War. We were having a lovely evening, with mum looking dreamily at the screen until Gere got a little too affectionate with one girl, and mum suddenly awoke from her trance, switched over to another channel, with the words "I don't think we need to see any more of this part thank you very much," before turning back once the deed had been done, once Gere had reached completion so to speak. So instead of watching a tender love scene which impacted the story, making the tearful farewell at the end of the film even more poignant, I had to probably watch five minutes of "Terry and June", or something similarly banal.

As for "An American Werewolf in London" though, my brother and I were not to be thwarted. It must have been the school holidays, as the next day after it had been shown on TV, word got round that one of our mutual mates, one with rather less officious parents, had the house to himself, and had taped the film from the previous night.

So, we managed to watch the remaining 1 hour 32 minutes, surrounded by about twenty very curious lads crammed into a front room, creating our very own little cinema where X certificates no longer mattered, although the twenty inch screen was not quite as big as the one our local cinema had to offer.

All of us slavered slightly when David and Alex washed each other very thoroughly in the shower, and we were all awe struck and quite disbelieving of what we were actually witnessing when David finally transformed into the werewolf, with "Blue Moon" serenading us in the background. It blew us all away, and I have loved the film ever since, and always will do. It is the perfect blend of horror and humour, and one that never gets old with repeated viewings, which I have certainly given it, to the point of knowing it almost word perfectly again.

If ever I'm out walking on the fells of The Lake District, or more often the Yorkshire Dales, I never forget to say "oops" to myself if I stray from the path. I just make sure I avoid pubs with evil looking symbols inscribed on their walls for my post hike pint.

Beat Street (1984)   Dir: Stan Lathan

Three absolute classics now to reminisce about. Well, one of them is a classic of sorts in its rather niche genre, whilst the other two are just really bad films, despite one of them starring none other than Nicole Kidman, in what would be only her second appearance in a full length film. Little did I know back then as a ten year old boy that about twenty years later I would be gobsmacked by her performance as Satine in "Moulin Rouge", and fall under her diamond spell. I wasn't exactly under her spell whilst watching "BMX Bandits" though, after I had accompanied my brother Mark to the cinema, as he was frankly obsessed with anything BMX related.

It had all started the year before really, with "E.T." accelerating his already new found fondness for Bicycle Motocross. The sight of BMXs in a huge Hollywood movie made everyone want to get in on the craze that my brother had already gone crazy for. After that film, he asked our Nan, who was a mean knitter, to knit him a balaclava just like the one Elliott's mate wears in the final chase scene. Her first effort didn't quite go as planned, with the hole in the front being far too big, so that the whole of my brother's face was on show, making him look more like Russ Abbot's character Basildon Bond rather than a cool Californian teenager.

Her second effort was more like it, and Mark, now satisfied that he looked cool enough, would practise his bunny hops, wheelies, and bar spins on our street, to the amazement of quite a few of the other kids, especially the younger kids like me who watched on in awe.

So, when he heard that a new film would be coming out at the cinema, without the need for a stupid alien dwarf to get in the way of his BMX enthusiasm, he bunny hopped at the chance. I think this may well have been another one my poor Gran had to endure, as quite honestly it was a very bad film, with not much of a plot, and the BMX stunts weren't even that good. My brother could have got into that film as one of the stars, and only a year or so later he was given a starring role, when the Boys' Brigade company my dad had started up in my home town of Carnforth was invited to perform at the Blackpool Tower Circus, with my brother being the main star, sort of.

The sketch would involve my brother coming out into the ring, the one in which Peter Kay filmed one of his first ever DVD performances, and showing off some of his stunts, whilst me and a group of other younger kids tried to copy him, unsuccessfully I might add. But then my brother crashes, and despite his protective gear, looks to be injured. Us smaller kids then zoomed off to get help, telling some of the older boys, who were playing medical staff, to come and help. Dutifully the "paramedics" rush on, but instead of paying close medical attention to my brother, all they did was make sure his bike was taken care of, whilst he lay groaning at the side of the stage. A stretcher was even brought on to carefully take the BMX to intensive care, with the medics hoping to God that they will be able to save the Shimano brakes, or the Mitsubishi Competition 3 tyres.

Although all very amateurish, which was kind of its charm, it went down a storm, getting us many laughs, before another company came on and performed a skit of their own, or wowed us all with their ability to march and perform drill instructions with perfect timing, and even did them at double pace for their finale. A great day was had by all, and certainly a better day than the day me and my brother went to watch Nicole Kidman and some other Aussie kids do some fairly rubbish stunts on their bikes whilst trying to thwart a bank robbery.

After my brother got bored of his BMX phase, he moved onto the next craze which was sweeping across America and consequently Britain, especially the tough graffiti laced streets of Carnforth, North Lancs, which my brother would like to think was his own version of a Bronx ghetto.

Never was there a more inappropriately named piece of kit than my brother's medium sized tape player. It was definitely no "ghetto blaster". It certainly didn't blast, not getting anywhere near all the way to eleven, and we absolutely didn't live in a ghetto, just a fairly pleasant and quiet cul de sac opposite my old primary school. Our hood had a complete lack of racial or ethnic diversity. It was hardly an urban melting pot where crews would battle it out with their moves and their spray cans to win supremacy.

My brother and his rather motley crew of mates would get their bit of lino and show off in the school playground. He was a big year 10 by then, with me only just having started secondary school. I got lots of street cred because of him, partly because he could do not just your bog standard back spins, knee spins, crabs, and swipes, but he had also almost mastered windmills and even had a decent go at head spins. He also managed to get some very attractive year 10 girls to come round to our house, girls who I had fancied for ages, and here they were, coming round to my house, but only to watch Mark make their head spin with his head spin.

Call me a cynic, but it was as though film studios were just trying to cash in on these rather short-lived and fleeting teenage crazes. First there had been a film all about BMXs, and then came along a film all about breakdancing, imaginatively called "Breakdance", although any similarity to the real world of Hip Hop and B-Boys this new film had was purely by coincidence rather than by design. In fact it had very little resemblance at all, and was actually quite laughable. It wasn't even called "Breakdance" in America, being released under the far slicker and much catchier "Breakin'" with the missin' "g" and the apostrophe instantly giving it more hop, although it was still not too hip.

The story involved some posh white dancer girl who wanted to try out some new more urban moves, and so befriends a couple of hip young B-Boys to teach her. Even their names, Ozone and Turbo were an affront to hip hop culture, with Kelly the white girl being inadvertently turned into a breakfast cereal with her new "street" name of "Special K".

The dancing was hardly that cool either. The moves were not particularly new or difficult and the outfits were just bad eighties bagginess, with even leg warmers still being worn. It was just a watered down white version of something dynamic and ground breaking, something which black culture could truly call its own, a bit like Pat Boone covering early Rock n Roll classics by Little Richard.

The producers tried desperately to give the film some sort of credibility by paying Ice-T probably a vast sum of money to appear in it, but ended up seeming more like iced tea rather than the badass hip hop legend he was back then.

It was all a bit naff really, and only partly satisfied my brother's quest for urban street culture. It did at least have a good song in it, with Chaka Khan's "Ain't Nobody", appearing on the soundtrack, making the top ten, and then her version of Prince's "I Feel For You" getting to No.1 in the charts, even though Ozone and Turbo appeared in the lurid, and definitely not street, video accompanying the song, the one we all watched on "Top of the Pops".

To get his much more realistic slice of New York street culture, my brother would have to rent out the video of "Beat Street", which he would watch again and again. At least this film was actually set in the Bronx, and was actually filmed there along with parts of Brooklyn and Queens, and featured real stars of the Breakdancing scene, as well as some real graffiti on real subway trains. It also featured some proper pioneers of hip hop music including Grandmaster Melle Mel and the Furious Five, Doug E. Fresh, and the legend that is Afrika Bambaataa.

The film impressed my brother very much and the bit he watched repeatedly was the battle in the club between The New York City Breakers and The Rock Steady Crew, featuring some quite incredible and unbelievable dance moves, which were more gymnastics than dance actually. He was most impressed with a head spin which seemed to carry on for ages, and not just windmills, but baby windmills, in which the legs are crossed, making it harder to gain and keep momentum.

My brother Mark made it his mission to add baby windmills to his repertoire, and after enough practice, he mastered them to ensure even more fit girls wanted to come round to our house. This breakdancing malarkey had some benefits after all, although it didn't seem to do much for my brother's back, as he suffered from chronic back pain later on in life. I'm sure his desire to impress girls whilst spinning round on his back had something to do with his rather fragile discs in his spine.

"Beat Street" was by far a much cooler, a much hipper, and a much grittier film about hip hop culture, and put "Breakin'" to shame, with or without the apostrophe. But that didn't stop me and my brother going to see the inevitable sequel to "Breakdance", imaginatively entitled "Breakdance 2" but this time with the added "Electric Boogaloo" in its title, which just about summed up how bad this effort was.

As I said earlier, it was as though film studios were trying to just fleece young teenagers out of their pocket money by churning out dross for them to lap up. But at least Ice-T kept it real by appearing yet again, for probably another vast amount of money. He was hardly an OG, or Original Gangsta anymore.

More like OMG actually.

First Blood (1981)   Dir: Ted Kotcheff

During this period of mine and my brother's lives, apart from spinning round on his head, he was also watching Sylvester Stallone's transition from using his fists, to using guns. In fact not just guns, but also knives, bows and arrows, rocket launchers, pointy sticks, his bare hands, anything that could be used to hurt or kill other people actually.

I was first introduced to John Rambo in "First Blood" on video, and have had an uneasy relationship with him ever since. I maintain to this day, much to my wife's annoyance every time that the film is shown on TV, which is quite frequently, that this film is not just your bog standard guns and mayhem comic book caper that the other films in the series have become. Stallone's first outing as John Rambo, the Vietnam veteran struggling to

81

cope with civilian life, does have a serious point to make about the treatment veterans of that war received, albeit in a none too subtle way.

Stallone never really did subtle very well, especially in the follow up of 1985, but at least he tried to develop the character in "First Blood" into a fully formed three dimensional one, with a back story and valid reasons as to why he then decided to maim, kill and generally blow everyone up.

The scene where our "hero" is stuck in the mine, talking to his former Colonel from Vietnam, although rather "over the top" to reference another of Stallone's films from the mid-eighties which I saw at the cinema, does at least try to convey some heartfelt emotion, showing the mentally ravaged effects on men like John Rambo, who had been given no help to reintegrate, no support for the horrors they had witnessed, and certainly no thanks for their efforts in what was an ultimately pointless and failed war.

Of course there have been much better films to have tackled the subject, namely Oliver Stone's "Born on the Fourth of July", but in that later film you don't get the sight of a man stitching his own arm back together, setting primal and savage traps for police officers to get impaled upon, or blowing up petrol stations with rocket launchers. And when I was twelve, I wasn't really that bothered about the personal anguish the war had caused. I was more bothered about watching a man smash through roadblocks in an army truck after having wasted lots of innocent police officers, led by Brian Dennehy's stubborn and rather bloody minded Chief of Police. It wasn't just his mind that was bloody by the end of the film.

Whenever I watch the film now, it takes me right back to being a twelve year old, and although I now realise how obvious and rather clumsy the deeper message is in the film, I still watch it with fondness, something that cannot be said for the follow up film, a film which I rarely watch again, only ever dipping into it for a few laughs.

"Rambo: First Blood Part II" destroys quite literally any sympathy or respect I had for John Rambo, and consequently Sylvester Stallone, due to its bombastic combination of gratuitous machismo, ridiculously comic book violence, and a certain amount of racial stereotyping in its portrayal of the Vietnamese, and the evil Soviet baddie, played by Steven Berkoff. Whatever good Rocky did by putting an end to the Cold War ,was then obliterated by Rambo. But it made Stallone an awful lot of money, which in the true spirit of American capitalism, is all that mattered.

My brother was fifteen at the time the film was released at the cinema, and if I remember rightly, was given an 18 certificate. The cinema staff were much more officious when it came to letting fifteen year olds in than our local video shop owner, but my brother tried anyway, and to his eternal disbelief but huge relief, he actually got into see this carnage fest.

I remember him coming into my room that evening, and in hushed whispered tones, after closing the door very quietly, told me of his adventure of that afternoon, knowing full well that my parents would never have allowed him to have seen such sinful nonsense.

He told me of the torture scenes in which Rambo was gleefully electrocuted, after he had been pulled out of a leech infested pit of mud. He told me of a range of ever increasingly ridiculous killings, usually caused by Rambo's new weapon of choice, a bow with exploding arrows, and a new means of deadly transport, something which he didn't get to use in "First Blood", a helicopter with massive guns and rockets which were liberally fired at anything and anyone that moved.

He also told me of the beautiful Vietnamese girl who Rambo tries to save, the only redeeming feature of the film as far as I am concerned, but here again, this rather forced love interest is brutally killed. Even a moment of tenderness is obliterated in this film. At least in the first film there wasn't any sort of love interest, unless of course you count Rambo's love for his country as a love interest.

If ever there was a film which used a sledgehammer to crack an egg, then "Rambo" is it. Stallone even tries to give the film the same heartfelt message at the very end. After two hours of utter mayhem and managing to reverse any sympathy we had for his views on the treatment of Vietnam veterans, Rambo insists to Colonel Trautman that he "only wants his country to love its soldiers as much as its soldiers love it". Profound words there from a man who has just annihilated with extreme prejudice masses of gooks, so that he can bring his comrades back home.

The whole film has a nasty side to its comic book façade. It makes a mockery of some genuine issues, and then has the audacity to attempt to make a serious point to try and justify its gratuitous violence and racial hypocrisy.

By this time though, my brother Mark had another action figure to play with, and I don't mean Action Man, although our next film was a real life embodiment of Action Man, with the camouflage and scars to match. Instead of Rocky's fists and Rambo's knives, we would now become obsessed with Arnie's guns, both literal and metaphorical ones.

The Terminator (1984)   Dir: James Cameron

One of the best things about having an older brother, combined with a rather lax and unscrupulous video shop owner, was that I got to watch some really cool films which I shouldn't have been watching for another six or seven years yet. I was now around twelve years old, and my brother was fifteen, and so my brother, with a little help from our friendly neighbourhood video shop owner, was able to rent 18 certificate films, and I could watch them too, if my brother was feeling brotherly towards me.

He had a TV and video in his bedroom by now, and mum and dad seemed very pleased that we were spending so much time together, allowing our sibling rivalries to be put to one side and developing new found bonds. What they didn't realise was that we were watching very violent, but super cool films involving lots of guns, lots of swearing, and lots of carnage. It was a great way to bond actually.

There were now two video shops in my home town, and at least one of them would be prepared to conveniently bend the rules, knowing full well that Mark was not eighteen yet, but they didn't seem to mind. We certainly didn't. It was great.

One of the first 18 certificate films he rented, such was the aura around this film, was "The Terminator", which to this day is still a fantastic film, and Arnold Schwarzenegger's finest to date. This is mainly due to the fact that he plays a robot, which does not require the widest of emotional ranges in terms of acting.

Arnie (I can't be bothered to keep typing his surname) had started his own cinematic journey by being the star of a documentary "Pumping Iron", about body building, competing against The Hulk, or at least the actor who played him, Lou Ferrigno. He then went to get bit parts in a few smaller films, before landing the leading role in "Conan the Barbarian", and its sequel "Conan the Destroyer".

His muscles and brawn were perfectly suited to this role as a fearless, invincible fighter, seeking revenge on Darth Vader, whilst rescuing The Exorcist's daughter. And no, I haven't just mixed up three very different films, as the man he seeks revenge on in "Conan the Barbarian" was played by the actor who voiced Darth Vader, James Earl Jones, whilst the father of the princess he was rescuing was played by Max Von Sydow, who had only a few years before struggled to rid Regan of her demon whilst shouting "The power of Christ compels you!" repeatedly at her.

But it wasn't until James Cameron, the King of the World himself after he directed "Titanic" some thirteen years later, offered him the role of a menacing and seemingly unstoppable cyborg, that Arnie would really hit the big time. And me and my brother were very thankful that he did.

Let's face it, Arnie was never going to win any awards for his acting abilities, but he would become one of the most iconic action heroes, or in this case, action villains in cinema history, and me and my brother were there in my brother's room to witness his rise to gun-toting, mayhem-causing, cheesy one-line delivering greatness.

One of his greatest lines in "The Terminator" was one of the first times I had heard the F word used so blatantly. I think the first time I'd heard it was in John Carpenter's "Escape From New York", when Kurt Russell's Snake Plissken utters the word, shocking me with his verbal diarrhoea, another film incidentally in which Donald Pleasance needed help to escape from somewhere. But when Arnie delivers the line "Fuck you asshole" to one of his prying neighbours, I was no longer shocked; I was impressed. He then proceeds to cut open his arm to reveal the mechanics of his metal skeleton, and removes his eye with the same knife, plopping it into the sink for us all to behold.

I was now in a forbidden world, one in which such forbidden-in-our-house words were used with gay abandon, and I don't mean Arnie was being a bit camp. He was the ultimate in masculinity, despite being not actually human. His nemesis, Kyle Reese, was also pretty cool, and definitely prettier than Arnie, saving his damsel in distress, the rather feeble Sarah Connor from being blown away by the cyborg.

The whole film was transfixing, from the opening scenes where Arnie randomly shoots other Sarah Connors until he eventually finds the one he is after in a nightclub, only for Kyle to blast him out of the window with his pump action shotgun, pumping iron into Arnie repeatedly. The police station scene where Arnie delivers his other great one-liner of the film "I'll be back", was also pretty damn cool, with Arnie being shot at from all angles, whilst still destroying the whole police force with Sarah hiding under a desk.

There is even time for Kyle and Sarah to do some of their own pumping, creating the mindfuck that is Sarah's baby John Connor, who would actually send Kyle to save his own mum from the future. Work that one out if you can.

We didn't care about the time travelling logistics or quandaries this union would create, as of course we then get the final chase, with Arnie marauding along the road in his tanker, only for it to be blown up, revealing the true horror of The Terminator, and signifying the end for Arnie, but certainly not the end for the cyborg.

The finale in the factory is relentless, a bit like the cyborg himself, or rather I should say "itself" by now, seeing as all traces of humanity had now been eradicated, something that Arnie did a great job of doing anyway. The machine just keeps on coming for Sarah in his quest to kill her, and even when it is in pieces, with no bottom half, it still manages to crawl menacingly at her, only being finally terminated by a now much less feeble Sarah. Sarah would of course go onto become the opposite of feeble, in time for the sequel, which wouldn't be for another seven years, plenty of time for her to get muscles and go a bit bonkers after giving birth to the man who saved her life in the first place.

Me and my brother devoured this film, and is again another film which I will watch at whatever point it is up to if I'm flicking around the channels on TV. It is a classic of its genre, and as I said, Arnie's greatest film. He was now considered a hot ticket, and his quite startling rise to the cinematic stratosphere took on a very steep trajectory from this point on, but from now on he would be playing good guys, if you could call a guy good who basically kills and maims people with great aplomb.

His next film would be "Red Sonja", in which he would team up with Ivan Drago's wife Brigitte Nielsen. Arnie and Sly Stallone would become massive stars, and massive rivals, with Sly winning the battle for Nielsen's hand in marriage and also starring with his new wife in "Cobra", another one of mine and Mark's favourites, mainly due to the brutal mayhem caused by the psychotic villain who had a really evil looking knife.

Arnie's next film was "Commando", another one of his "great" films, if these films could ever be called great. There was certainly a great deal of carnage, but not much else. Barry Norman definitely thought this. My brother had stayed up late one evening just so he could watch Norman's review of "Commando", and get to see some clips of the film.

In the morning he told me how the BBC film critic had absolutely panned the film, and held similar views as mine on "Rambo", and was as scathing about it as he possibly could be, with good reason I might add. But this made Mark more determined to see this slice of mayhem, about a marine saving his daughter from a gang of evil baddies, with the help of a huge amount of huge guns. To thirteen and sixteen year old boys though, it was perfect viewing. At least this film didn't try and dress its violence up as anything else other than cartoonesque fun, unlike Stallone's rather pompous ending to "Rambo: First Blood Part II".

Next came "Raw Deal", "Predator" and "The Running Man", all perfect vehicles to show off Arnie's rather limited skills, all of which we watched enthusiastically, until my brother found a new obsession in the second summer of love of 1988, deciding to leave me to watch Arnie alone whilst he went off raving to acid-house music. But he did at least give me a few more cinematic gems to remember him by, one of which would involve another cyborg.

"I'd buy that for a dollar!"

Robocop (1987)   Dir: Paul Verhoeven

I first saw a poster for this film whilst on a school skiing trip in the middle of year 10, thinking that it looked good, even if it did look a bit formulaic; yet another action hero type film, a poor man's "Terminator" probably. My cinematic tastes had matured to an extent by now, even realising what a silly film "Commando" was, but secretly still loving it.

When the film eventually was available to rent, I was in the middle of my revision for my GCSE exams. I arrived home from school and saw that my brother had rented "Robocop" out, and I thought I'd just pop it on to see what it was like, thinking that I'd probably turn it off after ten minutes or so if the same formula as the Arnie films was used yet again.

I not only didn't turn it off, but was instantly hooked. I'd never heard of its director Paul Verhoeven, who incidentally would go onto use Arnie in his next film, and had no idea how violent and at times gory it would be, how cool the special effects would be, how funny it could be, or just how pulsating the narrative was, making me not only watch it that night, but try and fit another viewing in straight after school the following day, disrupting my carefully planned out revision timetable, before it would have to be returned to the video shop.

Revision would just have to wait for Robocop. In fact most things would not get in the way of Robocop, seeing as he was a huge metal killing machine with a nifty way of spinning his gun after filling his deserving of such a death victims with many bullets. After all, this killing machine was a good guy, and not the bad guy Terminator type of killing machine. This machine at least had a conscience buried deep somewhere behind his hard shiny exterior.

Verhoeven's use of satirical adverts and tongue in cheek news reports was probably the thing that hooked me in the most, making me realise that this wasn't just another Arnie gun-fest. There was an extremely violent film with a bit more intelligence to it than those films. Not much more, but still enough to make me realise it was worth watching.

Once it had hooked me, it reeled me in with probably the most graphic scene I had ever seen in my life at that point, when our hero, Officer Murphy, goes to investigate a crime and ends up meeting the archest and cruellest of villains, Clarence Bodicker. I couldn't help thinking what a pathetic sounding name that was for one of the most sadistic, evil bastards I'd ever come across, certainly in a film.

His name reminded me of my first ever pet, Clarence the cat, who was almost as evil as the man who had just been responsible for blowing a man's limbs away with shotguns, as my feline, so-called friend had abandoned me to go and live with a little old lady who lived further down my street. Ever since then, I've had an irrational aversion to cats, thinking of them in much the same way as I viewed the gun-toting, cocaine-fuelled Clarence from "Robocop". I much prefer the loyalty and devotion of dogs, at least they don't sod off and live with a stranger just because there was better and more food available. And neither do they blow you to bits with massive guns.

Clarence's sadism is riotously revealed when he disarms Murphy, before blowing the poor cop's hand clean off, and then allowing his gang of misfits and weirdos to use Murphy as target practice, shooting his body to bits, literally blasting it away until not that much of him actually remains, but crucially just enough for what's left of him to be turned into Robocop.

The scene in which the other alternative in law enforcement, the ED-209, is being given its trial run, going horribly wrong and leaving one of the executives filled with bullets from the arms of the very scary, but very naughty machine, was also quite startling in its brutality. I could not quite believe just how unashamedly graphic the film was. Verhoeven certainly did not pull any punches with his violence. It was over the top, over the mark at times, but for most fourteen year old lads, me included, it sent us over the moon.

The sequence where Robocop is finally revealed, shot from the perspective of the cyborg himself, is lovingly referenced in Simon Pegg's opening to one of the episodes of "Spaced", still to this day my favourite ever sitcom, mainly due to the homages to many of the films mentioned in this book. It builds up our anticipation for what Robocop will actually look like, and then when his covering is finally removed, after getting a drunken yet very sexy kiss from one of his inventors, we are not disappointed. Well I certainly wasn't.

He had cheesy yet cool catchphrases to go with his cool metallic armour, like "Stay out of trouble", and "Dead or alive, you're coming with me", and when he shoots a would be rapist between the legs of his would be victim, leaving her completely unhurt, but him in a pool of blood, writhing in agony, he couldn't get much cooler. It took balls for him to do that, something that the would be rapist would never have again.

By now I didn't care less about the intelligence or otherwise of this film any more, I just wanted more gore and violence, as any self-respecting fourteen year old lad would do, and actually got a bit bored when Robocop discovered who he used to be, and the almost touching way he tries to reconnect with his wife and children, accepting who, or rather what, he has been turned into now This scene did at least make sure he got his revenge.

The finale at the old abandoned steel mill, another similarity to "The Terminator", certainly delivers gore and violence, with one of Clarence's gang, the annoying ginger one, having his skin melted off by a vat of toxic waste, before being run over by

Clarence himself, causing his head to memorably fly up into the air like a rugby ball that's been skied.

The actual death of Clarence is a little underwhelming, just getting stabbed in the neck with Robocop's metal spike which he used to extract data from machines. This time it would extract blood, lots of it as it gushed from Clarence's jugular. No melted face or flying head for him, but that of course is not the end of the film, as the real baddie has to be dealt with too. Robocop blasts Dick Jones into oblivion, falling to his death, screaming as the camera looks down on him, and the world can live in peace again, in the knowledge that any crimes will be dealt with by Robocop very severely, very ruthlessly, and most importantly of all, very entertainingly. "I'd buy that for a dollar!"

Another film me and my brother loved in which the baddie falls screaming to his death, and possibly the first 18 certificate film I dared to rent out for myself, was "Die Hard", in which Bruce Willis threw off his image as a smartass private detective solving crimes with Cybil Shepherd, to being a smartass cop kicking some terrorist butt, but this time with the help of a fat little cop call Al.

No robots or even cyborgs this time, but still some great deaths, some great set pieces, and some great lines to remember as our bare footed hero blows the gang of uber villains away, leaving Alan Rickman to fall out of the window of the Nakatomi Plaza, giving us all a great present on Christmas Eve. We all gleefully shouted, "Yippee Kay Yay Motherfucker", as Hans Gruber met his rather vertical end, something Father Christmas would certainly not be too pleased about.

But who needed Father Christmas as a fifteen year-old when you had John McClane instead? "Ho ho ho!"

Escape to Victory (1981)   **Dir: John Huston**

I'm conscious of the fact that most of the films in this section have involved lots of violence, either legal violence in a boxing ring, or definitely illegal violence with either guns, rocket launchers or werewolves. I just want to reassure you that my early teenage years were not just filled with blood, guts and gore. There were many other films I watched back then in which there were hardly any deaths at all, if indeed any, and certainly not intentional ones.

Another film my brother, and consequently I became obsessed with was another film Mark loved due to Sylvester Stallone being in it. But I became obsessed with it not because of any film stars that were in it. I was more bothered about someone who had graced a football field, rather than the silver screen. I'm talking about probably the greatest footballer of all time, and no I don't mean John Wark, Russell Osman, Ossie Ardiles, Mike Summerbee, or even England's World Cup winning captain, Bobby Moore. I mean of course, Pele.

This film combined my two favourite things at that time in my life, films and football, although I'm not sure which order they would come in. My love for "The Great Escape" probably had something to do with my fondness for the film, as well as Michael Caine and Max Von Sydow being its two proper actors. I still didn't class Sly Stallone as a proper actor, being of only slightly better acting ability than his rival Arnie. Thankfully, Arnie was not in this film, although he would have made a terrifying Nazi soldier, or a pretty big goalkeeper to have to try and score against. In fact, it would have been great to have the final match played with Stallone in one goal and Schwarzenegger in the other. Like the famous coffee shop scene in "Heat" with two greats opposite one another. Sort of.

I loved the film partly due to the storyline, and the daring escape Stallone's character Hatch makes to gain contact with the French resistance and make the necessary plans for them to dig a massive tunnel to break through into the bath of the football team's changing room during the film's finale.

I also remembered how Michael Caine had to snap the poor goalkeeper's arm, by kicking it and making a rather excruciatingly horrible cracking sound, so as to allow Hatch to become the team's goalkeeper, even though he was truly awful. He was only slightly worse than the Scotland keeper, Alan Rough, back then. Sorry to all my Scottish readers, but I think that by the end of the film I'd rather have had Sylvester Stallone in goal for the team I supported than Alan Rough, especially after his heroic penalty save at the very end of the match to make the score between the allied inmates and the German team a respectable, if improbable 4-4.

This of course caused a proper old school pitch invasion, something you rarely see at football matches now, with the crowd bursting through the gates, allowing the prisoners of war to escape anyway, making the efforts of the French resistance tunnellers a huge waste of time. And they couldn't even have a bath to clean themselves up afterwards seeing as though they had just wrecked it.

But it was the football which I loved the most. I finally saw the great Polish footballer Deyna on a football pitch. I had only ever come across him in a pack of top trumps before, in which if you used his number of appearances for his country as the figure to beat, you knew that no other card in the pack could beat it. I'd never actually seen this Polish legend though, and yet there he was on the same pitch as some British stars, an Argentinian star, and a Brazilian legend, all being coached by one of the biggest

Hollywood legends ever. It put the charity matches of today such as Soccer Aid to shame quite frankly.

And it was Pele's overhead kick which is embedded in my memory as a thing of absolute perfection and glorious beauty, especially as it was shown at full pace, slow motion, and from every possible angle. It was the ultimate bicycle kick, and never let anyone say they've seen a better one, even you Peter Crouch.

The amount of times I attempted to replicate that strike from Pele just caused me to get a badly bruised back, rather than the glory he received. I wonder how many goes Pele needed before he got it just right. Not as many as me I bet, and I never even got it just right at all.

The Naked Gun (1988)   Dir: David Zucker

I started my last chapter being conscious of there being a lack of non-violent films in this section, and I am now conscious that there have been no comedies mentioned yet. Yes, many of the films I have written about so far have comic elements to them, but there is no specific one which can be categorised as an out and out comedy. This needs to be rectified, but before that I must give an honourable mention to another perfect film, one which again, though not classed as a comedy, has many comic elements included. I am also conscious that this section of the book has not contained any films I actually went to see at the cinema. Something else to put right.

"Back to the Future" was released in late 1985 when I was twelve, and I so desperately wanted to see it. My brother and I were now at that awkward age where we didn't really want to be accompanied by our parents, certainly in my brother's case, as he was fifteen by now, and had already got into see "Rambo" if you remember. So, out of the kindness of his heart, he offered to take me to the cinema to see the film, despite this slice of perfect story telling having very few guns, only one murder which turns out to be not actually a muder, and very little violence in it at all, unless of course you count being covered in horse manure as violence. It did have a very fast car in it though.

That DeLorean disguised as a time machine has become iconic for any cinema goer in the eighties, and the whole film gave me, and my brother, who secretly loved it too, so much fun that evening. The film is perfect in so many different ways. It has a great story, great characters, with great dialogue, great humour, great set piece sequences, particularly the very tense and brilliantly executed final scene where Marty and Doc are battling to time their 88mph dash to coincide with the lightning bolt, and some great songs too.

As you can probably tell, I thought it was great, and I don't mean that in any sort of flippant way. It truly is a cinematic great, a real gem, which I could happily watch again and again. I loved how Robert Zemeckis captured the atmosphere of the 1950s. I've always loved the music of the fifties, and it has been known in our household for me to serenade my dog with The Penguins' "Earth Angel" when she's lying on the sofa next to me.

The prom scene which features that Doo-Wop classic, in which Marty has to make sure his dad gets together with his mum, is brilliant on so many different levels. When the chorus of the song crescendos in time perfectly with Marty's parents' kiss, after Marty has collapsed on stage before springing back up, allowing the fading figures in the photograph to come back to life, so to speak, is one of cinema's greatest scenes, not just of the eighties, or even the fifties, but any era.

The combination of romance, music, tension, catharsis, and ultimately triumph is something I will never get bored of, and if you've watched it, you know exactly which bit I'm talking about. If you haven't watched it, what are you waiting for? Go and do it now. This instant. A pity we can't all travel back in time to watch it at the cinema again for the first time, just as I did when I was twelve.

I was still not old enough really to go to the cinema on my own, or even with friends of mine, all of the same age. This would have meant a perilous bus or train journey, and then a doom laden walk through the crime ridden streets of Lancaster, or so my parents thought back then. Not really, but they didn't want me doing such a thing without the protection of my big brother. Not until I was thirteen anyway, and became a much more mature teenager, rather than a little kid of twelve.

Being a teenager meant that I could now do what my brother had done with "Rambo", that is to get into a film which was deemed to be unsuitable and inappropriate for me. However, whereas he did it first with an 18 certificate film when he was only fifteen, I thought I'd go for the safer option of trying to get into a 15 certificate film at the tender age of thirteen. And the film I would choose to pop my cherry with in this regard would not have too much violence really, hardly any guns at all, but it did have a huge knife. And a fit girl. So I thought it would be very appropriate for me actually.

"Crocodile Dundee", Paul Hogan's first outing on the big screen, was released almost a year to the day after "Back to the Future", so I was now big and hard enough to go without my brother. However, I would need someone bigger than me to stand next to in the queue. The week before, one of my mates had tried to get in to see it, but had been refused entry due to his very cute and unfortunately very boyish looking face. And he had just turned fourteen a few days before. He got mercilessly ripped by us all at school that week, and so I had to make sure that he could not do the same to me.

My plan was to go with my tallest mate available, the one who is now 6 foot 6 inches tall, and even then, when we were both thirteen, was probably 6 feet tall already. He looked fifteen just by his height, so if he got himself a ticket and got mine at the same time, without me having to put on a very deep voice and memorise my new birth date, then that would be the best plan.

Thankfully the plan worked a treat, and me, my tall mate, and a few others packed into the cinema full of other thirteen year olds and settled down to watch an Australian guy attempt to work out why the hell he was in New York. I remember very little about the film actually, only the bit where he gets out his huge bush knife which he used to kill any of the multitude of animals that want to kill you in Australia, scaring some would-be muggers away, with the line "Call that a knife? Now that's a knife!"

I was so relieved to have actually got into see the film that I didn't really watch it at all. Either that, or it was just a bit rubbish, and not worth the bother in the first place. I suspect the latter.

I had to tell my mum and dad that I had gone to watch Eddie Murphy's "The Golden Child" once I got home, as they would not have approved of me breaking the law, especially to see such a bad film. To this day I have still never seen the Eddie Murphy film, and don't recall ever having watched "Crocodile Dundee" all the way through again either.

Both films had elements of comedy in them I believe, but now that I had proved to my parents that I could survive the urban jungle of Lancaster, it was now a free for all, and I would go to the cinema with my mates most weekends from then on, either on a Saturday afternoon, or, more excitingly, on a Friday evening, not getting home until about eleven o'clock.

"Crocodile Dundee" had not satisfied my comedic thirst. I needed to see a proper comedy. My brother had taped "Stir Crazy", starring Richard Pryor and Gene Wilder, and we watched that over and over, almost wetting ourselves at times, with the duo's attempts to fit in with the other inmates causing much hilarity, but this was still only at home on the TV screen. I wanted a proper comedy on a proper big screen.

My first opportunity was the Steve Martin and John Candy vehicle, (or vehicles more like) "Planes, Trains and Automobiles", and this was one of me and my mates' rare Friday night adventures, making the whole experience even more grown up. We got there early enough to bag seats on the back row, and were even accompanied by some girls, although we were too cool to want to go out with any of them. Or maybe they just didn't fancy us.

Either way, we laughed wildly at this actually very sweet and charming film, which also happened to include some very funny scenes. The scen when the two stars are careering out of control between two huge lorries, and Martin looks over at Candy to find him dressed as The Devil, laughing manically, had us all in stitches, as did Candy's attempts to sell his Casio watch, as that was what most of us were only able to afford as a piece of digital horological wrist wear at the age of thirteen.

For some reason though, only me and the lad who was sitting next to me found funny the part when Martin attempts to get the others on the bus to sing along with him, starting up a rendition of "Three Coins in the Fountain", in which nobody else joins in, only to be raucously outdone by Candy's version of "Meet the Flintstones".

In fact we didn't just find it funny, we found it absolutely hilarious for some reason. Whereas there was a mild titter amongst the audience, from us came huge belly laughs of hysteria, causing a few tuts and shushes from not just our mates, but from others in the auditorium. Maybe we were just trying to show off in front of the girls, attempting to impress them with our wacky humour. It's safe to say that it didn't work.

So, with my cinematic comedy cherry now popped too, I wanted more. Other films came and went, including "Biloxi Blues" with Matthew Broderick, which would lead me to discover "Ferris Bueller's Day Off", in which Broderick would trick his school's Principal into thinking he was his girlfriend's father who had come to pick up the lovely Mia Sara from school, before giving her a very inappropriate "fatherly" kiss to welcome her into his car. "Do you have a kiss for Daddy?"

But it wasn't until the UK release of "The Naked Gun" in early 1989 that my need for comedy gold would be met. Granted, although not the most subtle of comedies, remember I was still only fifteen at this point, and clever, subtle comedy was not what fifteen year old lads either want nor actually get, it certainly filled the comedic hole in my life.

The comedy me and my mates wanted had to be quite childish to the point of being just plain silly, with the humour usually being derived from bodily functions. Oh, and if there was a sexy female in there too, that would be good also. Tick, tick, in terms of those criteria then.

The jokes were simplistic, puerile, and went nowhere near over our heads, instead smacking us straight in the faces with their combination of daft sight or sound gags and a certain amount of unsubtle smuttiness. Exactly what we wanted. Leslie Nielsen was hilarious as the bandy legged detective, harking back to the old school hilarity Peter Sellers used to create for my dad and brother in "The Pink Panther" films. I was a little bit young to remember them too well, and so Nielsen was the next best thing.

The scene where he still has his microphone attached whilst in the toilet, leading to the finest array of bodily function sounds I'd only ever heard before in "Blazing Saddles" caused almost as much noise to come out of me and my mates, with only a little bit of wee being emitted, unlike Nielsen's seemingly never ending "comfort break".

I loved the cheesy one liner visual puns, when he orders a Black Russian drink for example, and when he is searching through some drawers to apparently find what he has been looking for, dramatically saying the word "Bingo!" before pulling out an actual bingo card. I suppose you have to be watching it really to get the humour. Describing comedy never really works, although the line "Nice beaver!" which he says with a completely deadpan face to Priscilla Presley as he watches her climb into her attic whilst she wears a skirt, only for her to produce an actual stuffed beaver on a plinth, needs no more explanation for it to be both smutty and hilarious at the same time. For a group of fifteen year old lads this was comedy genius.

The film would be quoted endlessly in the school yard for weeks afterwards, and even now I still use lines from this film in certain situations, although I never get to use the beaver line very often at all unsurprisingly. The TV series the film was based on "Police Squad" was then shown on TV, and we would all become addicted to that too. It also caused me to have an irresistible compulsion to finally watch the original Zucker, Abrahams and

Zucker comedy, another one with Leslie Nielsen in it, and still one of the funniest films ever made in my rather childish opinion. Ladies and gentlemen, I give you the one and only, the hilarious, the stupidly silly "Airplane!"

I'd seen bits of this classic before, but never the whole film. It had been talked about so often by others, especially the bit where a naked woman with a fantastic pair of breasts randomly appears on screen whilst the rest of the passengers are panicking, that I just had to see it. "The Naked Gun" had whet my appetite, but "Airplane!" would provide the main course, and what a bellyful, or rather belly laugh, it proved to be.

There are so many memorable lines and scenes from that film that there's no point in listing them all. We all have our favourites, but I'm just going to share with you the first three that come into my head.

In no particular order:

1. The disco dancing scene where Striker throws Elaine so high she goes out of shot, only for Striker to catch her again a few seconds later from the side.
2. The pilot, Captain Oveur, with the little lad on his knee, where he asks the wide eyed young visitor to the cock pit if he likes films about Gladiators.
3. Kramer's entrance to the airport terminal in which he beats up many different groups of people, who all offer him some sort of leaflet, including a bunch of Hare Krishnas.

As I said, it needs to be watched for the humour to be conveyed properly. There are so many more moments of comedy gold that I could on for ages, something none of us want. If you don't get the jokes then you need to watch it. Those of you who do get the jokes, you're probably laughing right now, remembering the bits I've just described, possibly thinking of your own favourite bits, and most definitely getting the urge to watch it again as soon as possible.

That's what I'm going to do later tonight, but first I have to come up with an appropriately cheesy and rather childish way of ending this chapter.

Surely there must be a decent line I can think of you ask. No, sorry, I can't think of one at all actually, so I'll just have to end it here.

And don't call me Shirley.

Part Three

Grown Up Films and Girls

Indiana Jones and   Dir: Steven Spielberg

the Last Crusade (1989)

The title film of this chapter may well be misleading, as this film surely cannot be counted as a proper grown up film, seeing as the other two films in the trilogy (I refuse to count "The Kingdom of the Crystal Skull" as part of the series) were dealt with in the first part of this book, and were a massive part of my childhood. And I thought I told you not to call me Shirley! Who said I was childish? Well, by now I was a very much more mature sixteen year old young academic, who had just finished his GCSEs, and was determined to study four A Levels and then gain a degree. But that did not mean that I didn't want to go and see the next Indiana Jones film. I was still enough of a kid to do that.

Just because I had now completed five years at big school, sprouted hairs and even spoke with a much less squeaky voice since my last adventure with Indy, I figured that these films could be enjoyed by anyone of any age, and so off to the cinema I trotted to catch up again with my old friend.

This time, however, I did not go with my parents, my brother, or even any of my mates. This time I would take a girl, one of a few who would be treated to a trip to the cinema with me over the next couple of years. And no, I didn't know about the trick from "Diner" with the popcorn box. Not yet anyway.

I'd been seeing this particular girl for a couple of months by the time Indy took out his whip again, and as she was a year younger than me, I thought I'd play it safe. You can't go wrong with an Indiana Jones film, and so we had a lovely evening holding hands, watching our hero get back to what he was most loved for.

After the relative negative response to the second film, which went off in a different direction from the first film, much like the line on the map which shows Indy's journey as it stops at different points. With the third instalment, Spielberg thought he'd go back to the original formula, not that I hadn't enjoyed the second film. In fact I think I preferred it to this last film, as this one seemed to have run out of ideas slightly, going back to Indy trying to find a most holy of Christian relics before the evil Nazis get their hands on it.

Not that it isn't still a great film, especially the opening sequence with River Phoenix playing a young Indy, as we find out how he became so adept with a whip, and why he had such a phobia of snakes, although that doesn't explain why I have a massive fear of snakes too. Maybe the scene with the asps and the cobra in "Raiders of the Lost Ark" gave me my particular hatred of the slithering horrors.

We got to see not just Indy as a boy, but also Indy's dad, in the guise of Sean Connery as the bespectacled, rambunctious and rather obstreperous Professor Henry Jones, who insists on still calling his son Junior. The love interest this time, for both men as it turns out, is the foxy but ultimately deceiving Elsa, played by Alison Doody. This Elsa wanted to find the Holy Grail so much that she couldn't let it go, ultimately betraying our hero, before Indy finds the Grail, saves the day and his dad, and gains eternal life. Not bad for a day's work.

As far as eternal life goes, and I don't want to sound grandiose, but these three films have become eternal in some way, and will live on for many generations to come. They certainly get shown on TV enough times for us all never to forget them, and quite rightly so. All three films and the character of Indiana Jones have certainly become part of my life, and millions of others' lives around the world, which is why I was actually quite disappointed that Spielberg decided to resurrect the character almost twenty years later for a much inferior fourth film. He didn't need resurrecting, he was still very much alive in our memories and our hearts, becoming entrenched in my childhood, as well as many adult lives too.

Indy didn't get the girl in this film, and neither did I, as my girlfriend and I split up soon after this film. At least my girl didn't fall to her death into a lava filled crevasse. Well it was her loss, as she missed out on me taking her to see "Back to the Future Part 2" a few months later, and she may well have even got to see the third and final film in this near perfect trilogy too, despite the second part being a bit of a let-down, after the perfection of the first film.

If only she'd given me the chance, I could have taken her forward in time, then back in time, then forward and back yet again, before finally ending up not in the 1980s, but the 1880s.

As I said, her loss.

Dead Poets' Society (1989)   Dir: Peter Weir

I'd started my A Levels now, moving from my local secondary school to the Boys' Grammar school in Lancaster, and it was all a bit of a shock to me when I first moved. My teachers would now refer to me by my surname and the whole place seemed very traditional, very stuffy, and very different to what I had been used to for the first five years of big school.

One teacher that stood out for me, and one of the main reasons why I became a teacher myself, particularly an English teacher, was my own A Level English Literature teacher. Not only did he call his students by their first names, but he was prepared to do things his way and make his lessons not only fun and entertaining, but also academically challenging. I looked forward to his lessons more than any others with his combination of humour, anecdotes and surprise, as well as a real love and passion for his subject. I hope I have been able to do the same in my own lessons. So when this film came out, it made a huge impact on me.

I'd only been at the school for a few weeks when it was released, and I identified so much with the whole film, especially Ethan Hawke's character of Todd Anderson, the new boy starting a new school, coming to terms with his new environment and new expectations. To him, Robin Williams' English teacher John Keating, was the shining light of hope in this brave new world of academia, strict rules, and tradition. My own English teacher became a somewhat similar figure to me.

My own teacher never wanted to be compared with Mr. Keating, and actually disagreed with his methods in many ways, but I couldn't help comparing the two. Although we never ripped pages out of textbooks, or were taken out into the yard to find our own silly walk, or even heard the word "excrement" come out of his mouth, he made me realise the beauty of Literature and poetry, and the enjoyment it could bring.

The line in the film when Keating talks about poetry being a reason as to why we live, compared to the necessary but more functional subjects like maths and science: "Medicine, law, business, engineering, these are all noble pursuits, and necessary to sustain life. But poetry, beauty, romance, love, these are what we stay alive for", is the one which made a huge impact on me. I certainly felt like seizing the day too because of my English teacher.

Another character in the film, Knox Overstreet, seizes the day by eventually plucking up the courage to ask a girl he has fallen head over heels in love with on a date, and I identified with him too. After my previous girlfriend had fizzled away, I had become enchanted by another girl. She was gorgeous, and actually reminded me of the girl Overstreet had become enthralled by. I too had finally plucked up the courage to ask my fair maiden out on a date, and this was the film I took her to see.

The film connected with me not just on the academic, intellectual level provided by Mr. Keating, but also on a romantic level. I, just like Overstreet, was sitting next to a goddess, and also like that nervous young man in the film, I couldn't quite believe that she had agreed to spend an evening with me.

I didn't know what to do. I was so in awe of her sitting next to me that I didn't try anything with her, and spent most of the film working up to holding her hand. She made me feel like a stupid kid again, with our hands embarrassingly within touching distance of each other, yet remaining firmly an inch away from each other. But when Overstreet bolstered himself with the motto "Carpe Diem" and finally took hold of his girl's hand, then so did I with mine.

Incredibly, she didn't seem to mind my hand nestling hers. We didn't look at each other, and I spent the rest of the film in a state of disbelief that she hadn't pulled her hand away. It was a moment of both bliss and anguish, as I had no idea what to do next. It was as if she was a butterfly that might fly away if I tried anything else, and I didn't even attempt to kiss her as I dropped her back at her house before getting the bus back home.

Maybe my nerves got the better of me and I missed my chance, and although we saw each other again, she told me that she wasn't ready for a boyfriend and wanted to concentrate on her studies. She will always be the one that got away for me. Maybe I should have seized the day a bit more looking back on it now.

Seven years later, after I had not only finished my A Levels, but also completed my degree in English Literature, trained as a teacher, and successfully managed to navigate my way through my first year as a teacher, I came home in the summer holidays for a week or so to catch up with my parents. The same girl I had taken to see "Dead Poets' Society" was also back home, and with us both not being in a relationship, I thought I would seize the day once more.

This time we went to see "The Truth About Cats and Dogs", a film I love and have real affection for, and another film with a deeply romantic heart, a bit like me. But yet again, my nerves got the better of me, and although I never even tried holding her hand this time, I walked her back to her house, just as I had done all those years ago as a nervous sixteen year old, and again didn't attempt to even kiss her. As I said, she was the one that got away.

"Dead Poets' Society" is a film that is very special to me indeed. Apart from the rather embarrassing romantic element, it has profoundly influenced me as a teacher. I have always tried to convey my passion for certain books and characters, and have attempted to make my students connect with them, at times in somewhat unconventional ways.

Thankfully none of my students have ever killed themselves (at least I hope not) after having a new found passion for something which was forbidden by their parents brutally quashed, just like Robert Sean Leonard's character Neil Perry does in the film, after his father, played by none other than Kurtwood Smith, the same actor who played the sadistic psycho Clarence Bodicker in

"Robocop", refuses to allow his son to indulge in his new found love for acting.

I've also never had my students standing on their desks to show their allegiance and devotion to me, a scene in the film which never fails to make me shed a tear even now. However, I have stood on a desk for my own students.

In an attempt to convey the ridiculousness of Malvolio's yellow stockings in "Twelfth Night", I always used to put on a pair of very long and hideously yellow football socks whilst reading that particular scene from Shakespeare's beautifully romantic play. As Malvolio reveals his garish outfit to Olivia, I would then jump on my desk and reveal my own yellow legs, having pulled my socks up, as far as my suit trousers would allow, causing much mirth amongst the class. I didn't go so far as cross gartering though.

Whatever it did, it made my students realise just what an idiot Malvolio must have looked. On many occasions when I have met former students after they have gone out into the big bad world of normal life, they always remind me of my standing on desk antics and my bright yellow, but very shapely legs. Hopefully, they have also seen "Dead Poets' Society" by now too, and have seized their own day.

After this film, and yet another girl slipped by, I went back determinedly to see whether the girl I went to see "Indiana Jones and the Last Crusade" with was still up for any sort of romantic involvement, and so, as that was the only thing I knew or felt comfortable with, I invited her to the cinema again. The only film showing that week, apart from a kids' film which neither of us wanted to see, was James Cameron's "The Abyss", and all I remember about it was the first sighting of the amazing special effects Cameron would use with amazing results in the follow up to the only other film I had seen of his, in "Terminator 2: Judgement Day", a couple of years later.

Maybe I should have just not bothered, as she once again showed very little, if any interest in me as a potential suitor, and she went back to a previous boyfriend, leaving me in my own romantic abyss.

Another girl came along, and this time I thought that a viewing of that most wonderfully romantic, and extremely funny film "When Harry Met Sally", should do the trick. Surely I couldn't go wrong with this film, despite the not particularly romantic but definitely hilarious fake orgasm scene, causing me and my date to feel a little awkward. But once again, I was left dissatisfied and frustrated, although not quite in the same way as Meg Ryan, when nothing would come from this date either. I was starting to think that I was just wasting my money by paying for two cinema tickets instead of just mine

It was nearly the end of the eighties by now, and so I decided to give up on girls and concentrate on not only my A Level studies, but also my study of films. It was time to see as many films as possible, and not just mainstream ones released in mainstream cinemas. In fact the films I would throw myself into would not even have to be in the English language.

It was now time to discover the joys and delights of Arthouse cinema, subtitles and all. Carpe Diem!

Mississippi Burning (1989)   Dir: Alan Parker

During my two years studying some of the classic works of English Literature at A Level, I also made it a mission of mine to study, or at least watch, some of the greatest classics in the medium of film. This is where my local independent theatre and cinema came in very handy.

The Dukes Theatre in Lancaster was where I was taken as a boy to watch pantomimes at Christmas and ever since have had a severe aversion to this particular form of "entertainment". This was due to a huge hairy spider being lowered down onto my head when I was probably four years old in a scene which involved Little Miss Muffet. I was busy watching the action on stage when unbeknownst to me, this massive insect with an evil grin on its face was stealthily lowered into the audience by some evil git working some sort of wire, scaring, or in my case petrifying whoever it landed on. Oblivious to its almost deadly descent, it was gently placed on top of my head and I shrieked loudly, very nearly soiled myself, and started to cry. Again. I have hated pantomimes ever since.

Apart from terrifying pantomimes, the theatre put on some brilliant theatre, and when there was no performance, they would use the theatre to put films on, with a screen being unveiled from behind the curtain. Mainstream films never made it there, but the type of films which would never have been seen if it wasn't for little gems of cinemas like this. It certainly allowed me to expand my cinematic knowledge and maturity.

This arty, intellectual, and sometimes rather pretentious ("Pretentious? Moi?") journey started just before my GCSE exams, when me and a friend decided that we wanted to see what a cinema that didn't show trailers for overblown, bombastic thrillers, or even have adverts for the local carpet shop was like, and picked the first film we thought would suitably develop our love of film and our so-called intellectual voracity. We plumped, rather randomly, on "The Accidental Tourist", starring William Hurt, Kathleen Turner and Geena Davis, who I had only ever

114

seen before having sex with a fly in David Cronenberg's brilliant remake of the 1958 original, "The Fly".

We did not know much about the film, and were pleasantly surprised by the civility of the whole experience. There were no annoying kids, the sort only a year or so ago I had been, making their juvenile slurping noises with their slush puppies, or laughing far too loudly at bits that weren't even that funny.

The film too was a pleasant surprise and we enjoyed it immensely, having a very serious conversation about its merits on our way home. Now, suitably intellectually charged, we vowed to keep going to The Dukes and watching as many of this type of film that we could. It wasn't any more expensive than our local Odeon, and you didn't have to sit through trailers or adverts. All you had to do was quietly watch the film, preferably with a very concentrated, very earnest, and almost haughty look on your face. We definitely could manage that.

This film was one of the nominees for that year's Best Picture Oscar, and as we had already seen "Rain Man" in the main cinema, in which Dustin Hoffman gave his second Best Actor performance, and "Working Girl", in which Melanie Griffith and Sigourney Weaver fought not only against the sexism found in the business world, but also for the affections of the surprisingly, almost revelatory comedic Harrison Ford, who I had never seen without a blaster gun or a whip up to that point, me and my mate decided that seeing as though we had already seen three out of the five Best Picture nominees, we might as well do the full set.

Next on our list was "Dangerous Liaisons", which would mean another trip to The Dukes, but it was so worth it. We both fell head over heels in love with not only Uma Thurman, but the stunning Michelle Pfeiffer.

115

I'd seen her already in "The Witches of Eastwick", "Married to the Mob" and "Tequila Sunrise" before, so was well aware of her charms, but it wasn't until I saw her in full eighteenth century French regalia that I realised just how beautiful she was.

She was utterly stunning back then, and I remember watching Barry Norman interview her around that time, and even he went all boyish and adolescently clumsy with her, stumbling over some of his questions such was her magnetism. From that point on she became my new objet d'amour, my obsession becoming ever more intense after I saw her cavorting on a piano wearing the most sumptuous of red dresses in "The Fabulous Baker Boys", and then was sent into another realm once she donned her PVC outfit as Catwoman, in "Batman Returns", about the only reason I could think of to betray my love for Spiderman and go and watch his not-even-super super rival.

The last film on our list would be the most significant for me, not just because of the subject matter, the fact that it was based on real events, or Gene Hackman's stunning performance, which was better in my opinion than Hoffman's portrayal of an autistic savant, and should have won him the Oscar instead. It would also be memorable for where I saw the film and who I was with. It was a night at the cinema I'll never forget.

Just after we'd all finished our GCSE exams, me and five mates decided we wanted to have a bit of an adventure of our own. So, we packed our rucksacks, got our bikes and went to Lancaster train station. This in itself was an eight mile ride from my home town, and with a heavy rucksack, with various bits of camping equipment haphazardly stuffed in, it made my ability to actually ride the bike quite haphazard too.

Once we rather wobblingly arrived at Lancaster, we all piled on a train for Windermere, where we then cycled through to Ambleside, with our final destination being Great Langdale Campsite deep in the glorious Langdale Valley, still one of my favourite places not just in the Lake District, but anywhere in the world.

We finally reached the campsite and pitched our tents, again in a fairly haphazard way. The plan was to spend a few days there, do a bit of walking in the fells, swim in some of the lakes and rivers, and get a few beers in and generally forget about anything school related. We'd left school now, for good, or at least until our A Levels started, but that would only be by choice rather than legality, and we had a great time, with no parents or teachers to keep us in check.

We did all the activities mentioned above, swimming and bathing in the River Brathay, climbing up to Stickle Tarn before swimming in that too, and having the aforementioned beers most evenings, even though we were still only sixteen. We fancied doing something different one evening, and as the local cinema in Ambleside was showing "Mississippi Burning", then that was the obvious choice. We just hoped the cinema staff would be as lenient as the local off-licence proprietor had been when it came to getting in to see the film, as it was an 18 certificate.

In order to watch the film, we would have to cycle back into Ambleside, but this time without the rucksacks to make us look like unsteady tightrope walkers swaying around, where we would grab something to eat before watching what was to be a seminal film in my life up to that point, and still is in many ways over thirty years later.

Everything went smoothly, and the cycle ride into Ambleside was glorious in the early evening sunlight. Despite not having my very tall mate with me that evening, the one who had helped me to get into see "Crocodile Dundee" three years previously, the cinema staff were only too pleased to allow six young lads to come in and pay them money.

The film itself left a massive impression on me, right from the opening scene in which the civil rights workers' car is followed through the dark by the ominous headlamps of some less than friendly, and downright murderous racists, which included the Deputy Chief of Police, played by Brad Dourif, the stuttering Billy Bibbit from "One Flew Over the Cuckoo's Nest", and one of the scariest and most despicable characters I'd ever come across, in Michael Rooker's sadistic racist, Frank Bailey. He even made Clarence from "Robocop" seem quite mild such was the ferocity of his loathing, made even more frightening as he was not some fictional character from a comic book film, but a real person, with real hatred.

The intensity and threat created by the music, something I'd only ever witnessed in "Jaws" before, made the scene horrifically hypnotic, and we were all gripped, much like Frank Bailey's balls were by Gene Hackman later in the film.

The whole film was a powerhouse, with brilliant performances from all the leads, including Willem Dafoe, and Frances McDormand as the long suffering and abused wife of the Deputy, who finally finds the courage to break her alibi for her weasel of a husband, allowing Hackman's Mr. Anderson to unleash his own brand of justice after the more usual and definitely more legal form of justice from his superior had failed to make a breakthrough.

This then leads to R. Lee Ermey as the town's Mayor being memorably "interrogated" by the scariest black guy ever. We watched in delight as he pissed himself after being threatened to have his balls cut off, just as a black kid had had done to him.

The film left a huge impression on me not just that evening, but for the rest of my life, as I'm sure it did for my mates too. We all came out of the cinema with a mixture of sobriety, anger and a strange exhilaration. We also somehow felt older. I certainly felt as though I had matured within the last two hours, and had grown in stature. I had just seen a very important film, one from which I had learnt immensely, and one which had opened my eyes.

My fairly callow, innocent eyes had become more experienced, even though I was too young to have seen the film in the first place apparently. I had experienced it with some great mates, in a fantastic venue, in a wonderful part of the world, all combining to make it a truly memorable, even life changing and life affirming evening for me, despite the horror of the film's subject matter.

All we needed to do now was to cycle back to our tents We thought we would fortify ourselves with a couple of beers before we made the very dark, very quiet and very meandering journey back to the campsite. If the lack of a rucksack had made the journey to the cinema much easier, then the beers which we consumed afterwards had the opposite effect, and we all wobbled our way precariously back to the campsite, with only the moonlight to help us see.

But at least we didn't have three or four cars with their beaming headlamps ominously following us, just as those murdered civil rights workers had in Mississippi back in 1964.

Cyrano de Bergerac (1990)   **Dir: Jean-Paul Rappeneau**

Now that me and my best mate had ticked off the five "isms" of
the 1989 Best Picture nominees, namely autism, sexism, racism,
voyeurism and tourism, we were not content with just films in the
English Language. We wanted the full set which included the
bonus film of the Best Foreign Language Film, and the
opportunity to use our most earnest and intellectual faces yet.

"Pelle the Conqueror", a Danish film starring Max Von Sydow,
also nominated for Best Actor, who I had only seen before in
"Escape to Victory" was also being shown at The Dukes Theatre
in Lancaster, and so we ticked that off our list too. This film
would be the real start of our cinematic expansion into genuine
Arthouse films, as a film such as this would never have been
shown anywhere but an independent Arthouse cinema. It
certainly didn't make it to the Lancaster Odeon. Over the next
two years we would go and see so many films at The Dukes that I
may well have missed a few from the following list.

One of the earliest films I saw, after my initial introduction via
"The Accidental Tourist" was the very funny but very black teen
comedy "Heathers" with Christian Slater teaching Winona Ryder
how to get rid of her not so friendly friends.

Then came a spell of David Lynch films, which the theatre put on
to tie in with the release of his newest film "Wild at Heart", with
Nicolas Cage and Laura Dern attempting to avoid some very
strange hired killers, including Willem Dafoe in a much less
sympathetic role than the last one I saw him in. They also
screened "Blue Velvet", "The Elephant Man" and his first full
length film, the bizarre yet strangely fascinating "Eraserhead", all
of which we watched with a mixture of horror, sympathy and a
certain amount of bewilderment.

Another film which would certainly cause bemusement, but also a huge fascination for us, partly because it featured Helen Mirren wearing black stockings, and having sex in a toilet, was Peter Greenaway's "The Cook, the Thief, his Wife and her Lover." The use of colour by Greenaway, the use of music by Michael Nyman, and the fact that one of the title characters ends up having to eat another of the title characters were enough to make this film certainly memorable for us, and not just because of Helen Mirren's stockings.

We would also see Michael Rooker, the most racist of the many racist bastards from "Mississippi Burning" in "Henry: Portrait of a Serial Killer", and witnessed an even more evil and horrific characterisation from this very fine actor.

Another film including a Henry was also watched, although Fred Ward's depiction of the rather sex crazed Henry Miller, author of the erotic and, at the time, banned "Tropic of Cancer", along with its sequel, "Tropic of Capricorn", was definitely not as disturbing as Rooker's portrayal of the eponymous serial killer. Me and my mate only went to watch this because it promised us more opportunities to view Uma Thurman in various states of undress and sexual situations, which would also include Anais Nin, played by Maria de Madeiros, who would also go onto ride away on a chopper, not a motor cycle, with Bruce Willis in "Pulp Fiction" a few years later.

This was the first of a few erotic films we went to see, with the flimsy excuse that they were Arthouse films justifying the fact that we wanted to see rude things on screen. "Sex, Lies and Videotape", with just the first word of the title being enough to intrigue and lure our curious young minds to see it was also watched. But the ultimate erotic film we would see was the

Japanese film, "Ai no Korida", or "In the Realm of the Senses" to give it its anglicised title.

The story of a former prostitute who begins a passionate and torrid love affair with her employer was certainly diverting, particularly as the sex scenes were apparently unsimulated. But let's face it, we were only waiting for the bit where the torridness became a little too painful, causing her to accidentally strangle her lover to death, and then cut his cock off to keep as a rather gruesome memento of their relationship. It certainly made us cross our legs anyway.

We would uncross them again for one of the sexiest films we saw during that period, a little known gem of a film, directed by Dennis Hopper, starring the 1980s heart throb Don Johnson from "Miami Vice", who was married to Melanie Griffith by this point. He starred alongside two gorgeous women, who almost acted like the angel and the Devil on Johnson's shoulders, Virginia Madsen, the blonde, tempting him with her sultriest of charms, whilst Jennifer Connelly, the brunette, was his angel, but of course he was still tempted by her equally gorgeous charms. It was Hopper's best film since "Easy Rider" as a director, and he may even at this point have stopped taking hallucinogenic drugs by then. More on that later.

After all this soft porn, we needed a bit of gritty urban hard hitting drama. Spike Lee's "Do the Right Thing" followed by "Jungle Fever" would fill that particular void, allowing us to see another star of "Pulp Fiction" and someone who would become coolness personified, Samuel L. Jackson.

We also discovered "Last Exit to Brooklyn", with Jennifer Jason Leigh, and Alexis Arquette as a transgender who was suffering horrible abuse, something which would lead to her own gender realignment surgery in 2006, before presenting herself again as a man in 2013. Her role in this film seemed an ominous foreshadowing of her own troubled relationship with her gender.

Another troubled soul, at least in his role in this film, was Jonny Depp in John Waters' "Cry Baby" which also starred Traci Lords and Ricki Lake, who incidentally had also appeared in "Last Exit to Brooklyn", in her pre chat show fame, after she had made her debut in another of John Waters' off beat musicals, "Hairspray", which I would go onto love once I saw it on stage almost thirty years later. "Cry Baby" was great fun. Very camp, very melodramatic and very funny. Just like John Waters himself.

We also introduced ourselves to someone else who would become a major part of my cinematic life. In fact it wouldn't just be some one but two people whose films I would love, the Coen brothers, Joel and Ethan.

The first of their films we watched was "Miller's Crossing" with Gabriel Byrne and Albert Finney, who I'd loved as a kid when he played Scrooge, still to this day one of my dad's favourite films, especially the song "Thank you very much", which I have sung and danced to many a time in the classroom as an accompaniment to my students' study of "A Christmas Carol". We would also meet again from Spike Lee's films one of the Coen brothers' favourite actors, John Turturro, an actor I have always admired.

"The Grifters", Stephen Frears' modern day Film Noir, starring Anjelica Huston, John Cusack and the gorgeous Annette Bening, was definitely worth a watch, as was "Rosencrantz and Guildenstern are Dead", Tom Stoppard's adaptation of his own play, which starred Gary Oldman and Tim Roth as the title characters from Shakespeare's "Hamlet".

We would watch films by Jim Sheridan, such as "My Left Foot", in which Daniel Day-Lewis gave his first Oscar winning performance, and also the follow up, "The Field" starring Richard Harris, and the Elephant Man himself, John Hurt, who I had first seen with an alien exploding out of his belly. We would also watch a film which managed to be brilliantly funny and terrifying at the same time, the almost mainstream B-Movie homage, "Tremors", with Fred Ward this time tackling giant man eating worms rather than man eating women as in "Henry and June".

When the sequel to Roman Polanski's "Chinatown" came out, we went to watch a double bill with a very late ending after fitting in both the original film and "The Two Jakes" in one evening. I fell a little bit more in love with Faye Dunaway, who I had first fallen in love with after watching "Bonnie and Clyde" at the age of fourteen or so, and consequently did not like Polanski's sequel to "Chinatown" very much, basically due to Dunaway's absence from this film.

Our foreign affair would also continue, with two of the Spanish director Pedro Almodóvar's films, namely "Women on the Verge of a Nervous Breakdown" and "Tie Me Up, Tie Me Down, which again were only watched, particularly the latter film, because of the slightly suggestive and titillating title.

From Spanish to German next, with Wim Wenders' "Wings of Desire", where two angels come down to earth. Me and my mate came down to earth too with this one, it being slightly over our not-intellectual-enough heads, and I remember very little about it other than the brilliant use of both colour, and black and white shots to show the different perspectives of angels and humans. It starred Bruno Ganz, who would go onto shout furiously at everyone he possibly could before he and his new bride would take a cyanide capsule and shoot each other in "Downfall", the brilliant account of Hitler's final hours in his Berlin bunker.

After a Danish film, a Japanese, two Spanish and a German one, we thought it was about time we indulged in a bit of French cinema, and the first great French film we would see would be the title film of this chapter, "Cyrano de Bergerac" starring Gerard Depardieu as the soldier with a talent for composing poetry mid sword fight, with a rapier sharp wit, who also happens to have an enormous nose.

I sort of knew the story after seeing the film "Roxanne", starring Steve Martin and Darryl Hannah, but was eager to see the proper story in all its French glory. We went to see it at The Dukes in Lancaster, and the next day I impressed my English teacher by telling him I'd been to see it, something he hadn't yet done, as he too was a huge film fan. By the time he could get to the cinema, it had finished its run in Lancaster and was only being shown twenty-five miles away at The Brewery Arts Centre in Kendal. He went the following day and told me how when he arrived there was literally no one else waiting to see the film. The staff told him this and asked if he could see it another night so they could finish early.

Seeing as he'd travelled quite a long way and postponed marking my class's essays that night, something he couldn't put off any longer, he politely told them that he would still like to see the film, even if he was the only one in there. So, he got to see Gerard Depardieu woo his beloved Roxanne in a cinema all to himself, something I have yet to experience for any film I have watched.

We wanted to see the film again as well, and so, as I had now passed my driving test and my dad had allowed me to borrow his

125

car, we made our own journey up to Kendal to watch the film all over again. Alas, there were at least four other people there with us that night, but we enjoyed it even more the second time, not having to take as much care over the subtitles this time as we already knew the story.

This foray into French folie, inspired by the brilliant Depardieu, caused me to search out one of his earlier films, "Jean de Florette" and its sequel "Manon des Sources". These lovely films were luckily being screened on TV over consecutive nights one Bank Holiday weekend. By now, like my brother, I had a TV and video in my own room too, and recorded both films so I could watch them as and when I liked.

It turned out that I would only watch the first film, the one with Depardieu in once, maybe twice, but its sequel, the one without Depardieu would be viewed on many, many occasions. This was not due to its beautifully crafted script, its subtle and touching performances from its actors, nor for the gorgeous countryside of Provence being on display, all of which the film had in abundance. It was down to Michelle Pfeiffer being knocked off her perch by another, someone who I was even more in love with than Catwoman, either Julie Newmar or Pfeiffer herself. To make my new love even more sophisticated, she just happened to be French. Her name was Emmanuelle Beart, and she was the most wondrous female I had ever encountered, in a long list of wondrous females I had now fallen in love with on screen.

Forget the actual film "Emmanuelle" or even the joke of a film "Carry On Emmanuelle", this Emmanuelle was the ultimate in loveliness, being of the Brigitte Bardot school of beauty. Along with A Level English Literature, I was studying French too, and now Miss Beart gave me the necessary impetus to study French in much more detail, although I doubted whether the outline of

Emmanuelle Beart's lips and the shapeliness of her figure would actually come up as questions on my A Level French exam. But at least I could try and understand what she was saying without reading the subtitles, something I hardly did anyway when she was on screen, as my eyes were always transfixed on her face.

But that's enough French romance for now. I need to get back to some good old-fashioned American schmaltz, with a bit of film-noir thrown in too.

Dead Men Don't Wear Plaid (1982)   Dir: Carl Reiner

Wednesday afternoons at my new school always meant one thing: sport. I have always loved sport, but have never been very good at either rugby or cricket, being a very definite football man myself. If you have read my first book, "Just Me and My Football", you'll hopefully remember that anyone at Lancaster Royal Grammar School who wasn't involved with the rugby or cricket teams were not exactly catered for in the same way. Being thrown a football and being told to get on with it, with the only other lads available to play being completely useless at anything sport related, but unbelievably brilliant at anything Physics or Chemistry related.

I tried a bit of cross country running, but that was far too much of an effort and really boring actually. I also tried to revive my table tennis playing days at one point, but the same problem occurred. All the best opponents, who would have made my sport afternoons worthwhile and enjoyable, were all trying to hurt each other whilst chasing an egg on the rugby pitch. I came up with a plan as to a far better way of using my Wednesday afternoons.

I'd always enjoyed going out on my bike, and so I approached my form tutor and asked whether it would be ok if I left school at lunchtime, and went home, so that I could then go out for a bike

127

ride every Wednesday afternoon. He thought this sounded like a decent idea, and me being the trustworthy type, and him being the gullible type, he signed my idea off, meaning I basically had the afternoon all to myself.

Occasionally I would browse in the bookshops in Lancaster, or go home and catch up with homework, and sometimes I even went out on my bike for an actual bike ride. However, the most frequent of activities would be to go to the cinema and watch those mainstream films which I had been missing whilst going to The Dukes Theatre for my fill of Arthouse cinema.

I saw load of films whilst bunking off on those Wednesday afternoons, some good, some bad, and some very forgettable. Films such as "Bird on a Wire", "Gremlins 2", "Dick Tracy", "Black Rain", "Memphis Belle", "Days of Thunder" were all fairly forgettable, with some of these falling into the bad category too.

Some of the better ones I saw were the excellent thriller "Presumed Innocent", "The War of the Roses", "Die Hard 2", "The Hunt for Red October", "City Slickers" and "Hotshots" which surely wasn't as good as Zucker and Abrahams' previous films. And what did I say about calling me Shirley?

I also saw some romantic films which would have been better if I'd had a girl with me, but seeing as though I'd given up on that front, I was very happy to go alone. I saw both "Ghost" and "Pretty Woman", two of the biggest romcoms of all time whilst sat by myself in the cinema in Lancaster.

Some people have told me that it's a bit weird to go to the cinema on my own, but I've never minded sitting there in the dark all by myself. It's not as if I'm going to be chatting away to anyone, and it was certainly cheaper than paying for another girl to accompany me, only for them to not bother seeing me again.

One of the better films which I saw during this period, in fact one of the best films of not just 1990, but any year actually, was "Sea of Love" with Al Pacino and Ellen Barkin. This was a brilliantly taut thriller which kept me guessing, much like "Presumed Innocent" had done. Both of these films were classy, intelligent, and smart thrillers which made me realise what fun mainstream films could be, even if they didn't have subtitles.

So I got my Arthouse fix usually at the weekend, whereas my mainstream diet would be sated on Wednesday afternoons, in the dark, on often warm and sunny afternoons. But it was still better than chasing an egg around, or getting hit in the bollocks with a cricket ball.

Another set of films I remember seeing at this point all starred Steve Martin, who, after the success of the previously mentioned "Roxanne", and "Planes, Trains and Automobiles", seemed to release a film every few months from then on. After those two films came "Dirty Rotten Scoundrels" with Michael Caine having hung up his football coaching boots, and then "Parenthood", which was one of the first of those Wednesday afternoon cinema trips I would enjoy.

This ensemble piece, although schmaltzy and at times a little too desperate to be liked, was a lovely film, and one which even as a sixteen year old, who had no experience of being a parent, and at that time in my life, definitely had no immediate plans to become one either, has stayed with me and will gladly watch again whenever it is on TV. Now that I am a parent, three times over, the film has taken on so many different layers of significance for me, and I can not only enjoy it, but empathise with its characters on a much deeper level now.

Next came the much more forgettable "My Blue Heaven", "LA Story", and "Father of the Bride", but it was another of Steve Martin's much earlier films which stuck with me most from this period, and I definitely didn't see it on a Wednesday afternoon at the cinema.

During this period I'd discovered Martin's back catalogue, and loved his hilarious cameo as the sadistic dentist in "Little Shop of Horrors" in which he had first teamed up with his co-star of "My Blue Heaven", Rick Moranis. His rendition of the song "Be a Dentist" is one of the best, certainly one of the funniest cinematic musical numbers ever. I also loved "The Man With Two Brains" where he played the genius and slightly bonkers Dr. Hfuhruhurr. Those two adjectives could also be used just for his name itself, and the film was one of his best early efforts, developing his acting style as well as his comedic style from the madcap physicality of films like "The Jerk" four years earlier.

But it was one of the films in between these two which is still my all-time favourite Steve Martin movie, mainly because he was by no means the main star. In fact in comparison to some of the film's stars, his name should have been way down the list in terms of cinema greats.

In "Dead Men Don't Wear Plaid", Martin's co-star was the sumptuous Rachel Ward, she of "The Thorn Birds" the TV mini-series my mum had swooned over due to Richard Chamberlain's sexy heart throb of a priest. Well this time it was my turn to swoon, with Rachel Ward possibly overtaking my affections for Emmanuelle Beart, if only briefly.

However, Miss Ward was not the main co-star. For that title you could take your pick from any of the following: Alan Ladd, Barbara Stanwyck, Ray Milland, Ava Gardner, Burt Lancaster, Humphrey Bogart, Cary Grant, Ingrid Bergman, Veronica Lake, Edward Arnold, Kirk Douglas, Fred MacMurray, James Cagney, Joan Crawford, Lana Turner, or Bette Davis.

It's up to you to choose your favourite from that highly impressive list, but if you don't know who all of them are, or any of them for that matter, then you are in the same boat as me when I first saw it, and yet my lack of knowledge of the legacies of these true movie greats did not cause my enjoyment of the film to be detrimentally affected in any way. It maybe even caused my enjoyment to be heightened due to my ignorance.

I came across this little gem when my English teacher gave his class a rather unconventional homework in the last week before Christmas. He asked us all to look through the Christmas TV guides and come back with a list of five films we would recommend for the other members of the class. I obviously took this very seriously.

Most of the class came back with the usual fare of either traditional Christmas films or typical dross that most teenage boys like. I can't remember what my first four were, but I saw that "Dead Men Don't Wear Plaid" was being shown one evening, tucked away in the schedule probably about 11pm on Channel 4 I think. Anyway, I was intrigued to find out what it was as I had recently seen "The Man With Two Brains" and wanted to know more about the Steve Martin's earlier work. It looked like a fun film, and one that was certainly worth a recommendation, so onto my list it went, knowing that none of the other members of my class would have anything so obscure on theirs.

The next lesson we all read our lists out, and my teacher was impressed, if a little annoyed with my fifth and final choice, as he himself had picked the same film, and wanted to take all the glory for this recommendation, and show off his far superior knowledge of films. I stole his fire though. My other class mates probably thought I was just trying to show off, which of course I was to an extent, but my teacher's opinion of me was begrudgingly heightened due to my own knowledge and good taste in films.

Over the Christmas break I watched many of the films that had been recommended by the class, the ones I hadn't already seen that is, and looked forward to seeing what "Dead Men Don't Wear Plaid" was actually like, and whether my hunch was justified. I was not disappointed.

Steve Martin plays a 1940s private detective, Rigby Reardon, who gets a visit from Rachel Ward as the femme fatale Juliet Forrest, who asks Reardon to investigate her father's death. We soon learn of Reardon's aversion to the use of the words "cleaning woman", although you'll need to have seen it to get the joke. Still to this day I can't help but snigger whenever I hear those words, and can't help but imitate Martin's voice as he struggles to say the doom laden phrase, although I don't have the same violent reaction as he does.

On his quest to help Miss Forrest, the film is intercut with scenes from a range of classic Film Noir thrillers from the 1930s and 40s, including "Sorry, Wrong Number", "The Killers", The Big Sleep", "In a Lonely Place", "Suspicion", "Notorious", the original "The Postman Always Rings Twice", the one with Lana Turner, and definitely not the one I was so taken with in my younger adolescent days starring Jessica Lange, "Humoresque", and my own personal favourite, which will be dealt with later, Billy Wilder's great "Double Indemnity".

"Dead Men Don't Wear Plaid" ingeniously uses the footage from the old films, interspersing actual dialogue with that of Steve Martin himself to make it seamlessly look as though Rigby Reardon inhabits the same dark, gloomy world as the true cinema greats of these classic films.

It is not just ingenious, but is very, very funny, and again has become one of my all-time favourite films, especially after I discovered all the classic films which had been used once I got to university a couple of years later. Once I'd watched many of the films, "Dead Men Don't Wear Plaid" became a so much richer source of fun and enjoyment, paying lovingly affectionate homage to the Film Noir genre.

Its director Carl Reiner, who had made both "The Man With Two Brains" and "The Jerk" with Martin, is also the father of Rob Reiner, who of course directed "When Harry Met Sally", and was married to the woman who delivered the timeless line "I'll have what she's having!" in the fake orgasm deli scene from that film.

His son Rob had been responsible for a few other brilliant films which I then discovered, including the spoof rockumentary "This is Spinal Tap", from which I'll never be able to look at a picture of Stonehenge in the same way again, "Stand by Me", which I'd already seen of course, having fallen in love with the title song on Top of the Pops when it was No.1 for ages in 1986, "The Princess Bride", and my own personal favourite, "The Sure Thing", with John Cusack desperately trying to get his end away with the rather wonderful Nicolette Sheridan.

My discovery of all these gems was down to my initial discovery of "Dead Men Don't Wear Plaid", and that piece of homework set by my A Level English teacher in the run up to Christmas 1989. It was possibly the most fruitful, and definitely most enjoyable piece of homework I've ever done. Certainly better than doing an essay on "Twelfth Night".

I'd rather shave my tongue than do another essay on Shakespeare.

Apocalypse Now (1979)   Dir: Francis Ford Coppola

One of the other films I went to see on those Wednesday afternoons was another film which had an interval, just as "Gandhi" had done eight years before. "Born on the Fourth of July", would certainly be a different experience for me though, and I definitely didn't need any colouring books with me this time to keep me from being bored.

Oliver Stone's tour de force about the life of Ron Kovic, who struggled to come to terms with his sense of betrayed patriotism, his new inability to walk, and the way his whole life had been turned upside down by the Vietnam War, as with so many other young men, was the second film in what would become his Vietnam trilogy. It was certainly a more mature and insightful attempt to tackle the issue than Sylvester Stallone's "First Blood" a few years earlier, although I have watched Stone's film nowhere near as many times as Stallone's.

This film would be the start of my own Vietnam phase, taking in as many films about the subject as possible. One of these was "Good Morning Vietnam", with Robin Williams in a very different role from that of John Keating, although he basically was playing himself as well as the DJ Adrian Cronauer. I bought the soundtrack to this film and was introduced to some great tracks, as well as some hilarious ad libbing from Williams. On that camping trip me and my mates took after our GCSE exams, one of my mates would let not just us, but the whole campsite, and possibly most of the Lake District know that he was awake by putting his head out of his tent and bellowing at the very top of his voice "Goooooooood Mornin' Vietnaaaaaam!" I'm sure the other campers appreciated this very much indeed.

I also discovered one of my favourite ever songs of all time, Smokey Robinson's "Tracks of my Tears" after watching Oliver Stone's first Vietnam film, "Platoon", which portrayed a much grittier side to the war, as did the underrated "Casualties of War" by Brian de Palma, with Michael J. Fox in a massively different role than the ones we'd got used to seeing him in.

I would also discover Stanley Kubrick for the first time with "Full Metal Jacket", a film about Vietnam that had been shot entirely in England. From the opening scene, in which the new recruits have their heads shaved, before meeting R. Lee Ermey as their drill sergeant blew me away, a little like Private Pyle's head was blown away at the end of the first half of the film, although my mind blowing experience was certainly less messy than his. That film, especially the first half, was one of the most gripping and powerful films I had ever seen, and to this day, me love it long time.

It was now time to watch the ultimate in Vietnam movies, Coppola's almost mythical flawed masterpiece, "Apocalypse Now". I had read Joseph Conrad's novel "Heart of Darkness" around that time, and the documentary about the making of the film, "Hearts of Darkness" was about to be released, and so I thought I'd better get up to speed.

My brother had raved about it when it had been shown on TV for the first time, but I was too young to watch it, or so my dad said, and it had eluded me ever since. I'd heard all sorts of stories about the film, and how brilliant it was, especially as I was now heavily into the music of The Doors, and knew that their classic song "The End", an epic eleven and a half minute track, was partly used in the opening sequence of "Apocalypse Now".

For me, the film had been more a case of Apocalypse When? Well it was now time to rectify that, and it has lived with me ever since.

From the opening shot of the trees exploding into a huge ball of fire, with Jim Morrison's mournful voice haunting the whole screen, to the dancing Playboy bunnies, to Robert Duvall's Colonel Kilgore breathing in the fumes of the napalm before coming out with his timeless line, "Smells like...victory!", to a seventeen-year old Laurence Fishburne, who would go onto become Morpheus in "The Matrix" getting shot in the head after only a day or so before he had been dancing to the Stones' "Satisfaction" and shooting innocent Vietnamese children, to Chef freaking out at the sight of a tiger, I was mesmerised by the film.

The obvious scene to focus on though is the brutal, yet brilliantly enthralling helicopter attack, with Wagner's "Ride of the Valkyries" blaring out to "scare the shit" out of the gooks. This scene seemed to sum up the whole Vietnam War – it was callous, brutal, unfair, annihilative, completely senseless, and yet somehow rivetingly spellbinding. It made the viewer question the War's morality, whilst at the same time feel guilty for being excited by it. This paradox made a much bigger impact on me than any of the other films about the Vietnam War.

The final section of the film, with Dennis Hopper literally off his face on acid whilst filming, with Marlon Brando's megalomaniac Colonel Kurtz finally being slaughtered by Willard, is where the flaw comes in the film. Coppola did not seem to know how to end the film, a point he himself made in the excellent documentary I would go onto watch about the making of the film, "Hearts of Darkness", which is perhaps a better film ironically than the film of its subject matter, and if you have seen "Apocalypse Now" then you need to see this essential companion piece too.

With "Apocalypse Now", it was as though I had almost come of age, and put any sort of childishness into my past. As soon as I could, I bought myself a poster of the film from Affleck's Palace on one of me and my mates' regular trips into Madchester, so that I could almost worship at the film's altar every morning in front of my bed.

But soon enough I would discover another film from the same year as Coppola's flawed masterpiece which would restore my faith in being silly and childish, and would be worshipped by me for all the reasons my mum and dad had refused to watch it in the first place.

Monty Python's Life of Brian (1979)   Dir: Terry Jones

By this point in my life I'd also discovered "Monty Python's Flying Circus", even buying the collected scripts from every episode so that I could learn them, just like the guy in "Sliding Doors" must have done when he quotes the Spanish Inquisition scene on his way to wooing one of the Gwyneth Paltrows in that lovely film.

I'd already seen my comedy godfathers' first film, "Monty Python and the Holy Grail", and found it absolutely hilarious, especially the fight scene in which the knight gets all his limbs chopped off by John Cleese, "Tis but a scratch!", and the killer flying rabbit who ruthlessly decapitates its unsuspecting victims. Another favourite scene is when the guards are watching John Cleese as Launcelot charge towards them but never seeming to get any closer, until suddenly he springs upon them, slicing them up, before causing carnage in the castle.

In a battle between the two films I've mentioned in which the object of the quest is The Holy Grail, I think I prefer the silly version compared to the less silly "Indiana Jones and the Last Crusade". I can't imagine Indiana Jones being sent off to find a shrubbery for the Knights who say "Ni!".

The only reason I hadn't seen "Life of Brian" was because my parents were very much of the Malcolm Muggeridge school of thinking, and believed the film to be a sinful work of blasphemy, even though neither my parents nor Muggeridge had actually seen the film. Their loss as far as I'm concerned. They will never be able to pick up on the many cultural references which have become entrenched in our society because of the film.

Only last week on "Match of the Day" when Gary Lineker, Alan Shearer and Ian Wright were discussing the ten best Premier League managers as there was no actual football to show due to the Coronavirus lockdown, Lineker mentioned all of Sir Alex Ferguson's achievements in the game, ending with the line "But apart from that, what has Ferguson ever done for the game?" echoing John Cleese's line from the film about what the Romans had ever done for us. My dad may well not have picked up on this joke, and he never misses Match of the Day, or indeed church the following morning, apart from when there is a coronavirus lockdown of course.

So, I would not have been allowed to have watched the film in my own house, and only watched it because one of my mates had a free house one Saturday evening and us two, along with my two other oldest and closest friends decided we needed a good bit of lampooning of organised religion, and so rented it out from the video shop and settled down for a comedic feast. It felt like I was being a very naughty boy that evening.

The film is not of course any sort of direct attack on my parents' Christian beliefs, but a satire on the dangers and ludicrous nature of organised religion which can lead to dogma and fanaticism, which I think we can all agree sometimes leads to rather irrational, and very often dangerous behaviour.

Jesus even features in the film, in one of the very first scenes when he is giving his Sermon on the Mount, only for a squabble to break out between Eric Idle and Big Nose Michael Palin. This is in no way offensive to Jesus, but it is merely suggesting that not everyone who wanted to listen to the Messiah's words could actually hear what was being said.

It is a work of comedy genius, and has so many memorable scenes in it. I especially loved Palin's ex-leper, who calls his healer Jesus a "bloody do-gooder" which I accept may be ever so slightly blasphemous. The Judean People's Front and The People's Front of Judea scene has been used on many occasions to ridicule political parties, as well as its more serious targets of divisions within the same religion who all worship the same God. I think the troubles of Northern Ireland proves the legitimacy of that joke.

The scene in which Pontius Pilate scalds his guards for tittering so at his accent, before testing their resolve by mentioning Biggus Dickus, the high wanking officer, is another one that has gone into not just comedy folklore, but the culture of our country. Whenever Woy Hodgson spoke when he was England football manager, I simply cannot help but think of the scene where the crowd attempt to get Woger weleased, or even the wobber and wapist, the weally wevolting Wodewick weleased is nothing

139

short of puerile but brilliant comedy. How is that being blasphemous? It may well be offensive to people with speech impediments, but it certainly is not blasphemous.

One of the mates I was watching it with has quite a bad stutter, and he didn't seem to mind the next scene where Michael Palin, as the over sensitive crucifixion officer is trying to communicate with Eric Idle who has the most debilitating stutter. Instead of being offended, he just laughed, not just laughed, but laughed enormously, or should I say en-n-n-n-n-n-n-n-ormously?

And then of course there is the final crucifixion scene, and yes it makes light of Christ's death, and I can see why my mum and dad may not like this scene, seeing as it belittles the pain and anguish their Lord suffered as he was dying for all our sins.

But the message Eric Idle sings from his cross, about always looking on the bright side of life, seems to me to be a much more useful tenet to adhere to than one which believes in eternal damnation in the fiery pit for all those sinners who have not given their lives to the Lord God almighty, and certainly for those who have watched and maybe even enjoyed possibly the greatest comedy film in the history of cinema.

That'll be the rest of us then.

That thought is enough to make all of us be in the dumps, but let's not be silly chumps, let's just purse our lips and whistle, that's the thing. And always look on the …

Goodfellas (1990)   Dir: Martin Scorsese

I was a now a proper cinema aficionado, or so I thought, and had even started reading Empire Magazine voraciously, usually at least three times from cover to cover every issue, and had now started to tick off the films on the magazine's separate pull-out booklet on the 100 Greatest Films. I took the magazine's opinions as law, and so did not question their choices. I also did not question the opinions of my English teacher, whether it be on literature, or more importantly, films.

After my recommendation of "Dead Men Don't Wear Plaid", which had stolen his fire somewhat, he knew that I was very keen on discovering as many films as possible, and we would often chat after lessons about the films we had either seen, or wanted to see. These chats would often become part of lessons actually, and many of the other boys, or young men, as we now classed ourselves, would join in.

If we weren't feeling completely enthusiastic about discussing the merits or otherwise of the particular book we were studying at the time, whether it was Thomas Hardy's "Far From the Madding Crowd", "Long Day's Journey into Night", Eugene O'Neill's great American domestic tragedy for the stage, or my personal favourite, "The Great Gatsby", which of course he had shown us the film of, starring Robert Redford and Woody Allen's wife at the time, Mia Farrow, before he started to get rather too affectionate for their adopted daughter, we would more often than not be able to divert our teacher onto a discussion about films.

This is also a trait I developed as a teacher, and my classes all know that due to my personal interests of football and films, that they can always waste a bit of the lesson by asking me about either of these subjects, and our attention will always be diverted away from the use of oxymoron in a particular poem we are meant to be studying.

I don't consider it a waste of time though as, in my not quite as professional as it should be opinion, chatting about football and films is certainly not a waste of time. My job as a teacher is to connect with my students as well as teach them English, and if a few minutes chatting about a film I have seen, or what the game of football I went to watch over the weekend was like, then that is all part of the pedagogic process. That's my excuse anyway.

In my A Level classes as a student myself, we would often have discussions about films, and I followed up almost quite devoutly on my teacher's recommendations. After watching "The Great Gatsby" as a complement to our study of the book, which also starred Sam Waterston, I was recommended to watch another of his films, "Capricorn One" a conspiracy theory film about the possibility of a faked moon landing, which also starred Elliot Gould, James Brolin, who ends up having to eat a raw snake in the desert whilst trying to evade his pursuers who are desperately trying to prevent him from becoming a whistle-blower on the deception, and also OJ Simpson, who I had only seen before being constantly injured with hilarious results in "The Naked Gun".

He also recommended the excellent sci-fi film "The Andromeda Strain", which is another as taut as a fiddle string thriller about a global health crisis sweeping the world, and the scientists' efforts to control it, something rather topical right now, as I write this during the Coronavirus lockdown of 2020.

Sam Waterston also featured in another film he recommended, "Crimes and Misdemeanours" also starring Mia Farrow, and would lead me to discover the world of Woody Allen, one which I am eternally grateful for. After seeing the film, my teacher and I discussed our favourite lines, mine being "The last time I was inside a woman was when I visited the Statue of Liberty", whereas he topped that with "A strange man just defecated on my sister."

As a result, I delved into many of the films of Woody Allen, and watched "Hannah and her Sisters", "Annie Hall", "Manhattan", "Radio Days" and my own personal favourite, "The Purple Rose of Cairo", which ironically is the least Allenesque of all these films, with Mia Farrow this time playing a cinema obsessed singleton in the 1930s, who falls madly in love with Jeff Daniels who plays her hero in her favourite film, who then steps out of the screen into her reality, with the beautiful line "I just met a wonderful new man. He's fictional but you can't have everything" being my personal favourite.

My teacher also recommended "Postcards from the Edge," which was written by Carrie Fisher, Princess Leia herself, in a thinly veiled autobiographical account of her drug laden past, living a Hollywood life as the daughter of Debbie Reynolds and Eddie Fisher, with Meryl Streep playing the character based on Fisher, and Shirley MacLaine as her rather bonkers mother.

From this account of a struggle to find sobriety amongst the madness of Hollywood, showing just how ridiculous the world of the cinema can be, I was also recommended the most sublime film about the beauty of the cinema, and one which would go onto win the Best Foreign Language Film at the Oscars. Even though it is in a foreign language, Italian if you were wondering, this beautiful little film showed how cinema can transcend language altogether with the images on screen. The montage of kisses which were forced to be cut from their original screenings is still one of the most romantic, passionate and moving scenes I've ever witnessed, and is almost bringing a tear to my eye just remembering it now.

I also remember one of my A Level English lessons in which very little study of any book was done, although the film in question was based on a science-fiction classic by Philip K. Dick entitled, "We Can Remember it For You Wholesale". Paul Verhoeven wisely changed the title of the book for his film to "Total Recall", with Arnold Schwarzenegger playing a much more intelligent role than some of his earlier stuff, but still delivering great lines after killing people, most notably "Consider that a divorce" after he has shot his apparent wife, played by Sharon Stone, in the head.

We spent a whole lesson discussing the merits or otherwise of the film, and got quite deeply into the many different theories as to who Arnie's character Quaid really was, whether or not he was a goodie, or a baddie, with evidence provided for both cases by a few of the class who had seen it, some of us more than once. To this day, that film still confuses me after that discussion we had thirty years ago.

One film my teacher did not need to recommend though was Martin Scorsese's "Goodfellas". I had read enough about this film for me to know it was a must-see, whether my teacher had recommended it or not.

If you're reading this book in the first place, I assume you are interested in films to some degree, so I'm also assuming you've seen "Goodfellas" too, so there's no need for me to mention the film's opening scene with Robert De Niro, Joe Pesci and Ray Liotta driving late at night in their car, before hearing a noise from their car boot, or trunk of course, leading to a much more heavy handed use of a kitchen knife than Jamie Oliver would be used to, although I'm not too sure about Gordon Ramsay.

There's no need to mention how brilliant the narrative of the film is, with a young Henry Hill becoming part of the mob, or how cool the soundtrack was, with a mixture of romantic 50s Phil Spector stuff, such as The Crystals' "Then He Kissed Me" to absolute stormers like The Stones' "Gimme Shelter", and Muddy Waters' "Mannish Boy".

I certainly don't need to mention Joe Pesci's now over quoted "Funny how?" scene, in which his character personified threat and menace just with a few words and a look in his eyes, and as for the bodies turning up in rubbish skips, or dumpsters as I should call them, and frozen stiff in refrigerated trucks, there's no need to mention those either.

The film is filled with so many classic and memorable scenes that you'll know them anyway, so I'll dispense with listing them here. Oh wait, I've just done it. But one scene I do want to definitely mention is the final section of the film, in which Henry narrates, almost by the second, his manic, coke-fuelled day which leads to his arrest and ultimate decision to become a part of the witness protection program, betraying all his former associates and friends.

The scene is gripping in its intensity, not just because of the pace of it, but also because of the looming sense of threat posed by the overhead helicopter following him around all day. Combined with scenes of domesticity, such as the preparation of that evening's meal, to lines of cocaine being voraciously snorted with his girlfriend, whilst also trying to keep his wife in the dark again, the whole section is a real tour de force, one of Scorsese's best ever, but of course I didn't know that then when I first saw the film, as I'd never seen any of the other truly classic works of art by this brilliant director. I needed to put that right as soon as possible.

So next came "Mean Streets", and "Raging Bull", which I need to watch again actually as I haven't seen either now for years. I want to see just how good the boxing scenes are and how they compare to the more comic book fights in the "Rocky" films. We all know how much weight De Niro had to put on, well maybe not the exact amount of weight, but whatever it was, it was a lot, showing just how far he was prepared to go for such a role, which is of course a testament to Martin Scorsese too.

I also discovered "The King of Comedy" in which De Niro plays a hugely different character from the other films he had done so far with Scorsese, another film I've loved ever since. But there was one film missing from my list, and I know you know which one it is. If you don't, then my only response would have to be "You talkin' to me?"

Taxi Driver (1976)   Dir: Martin Scorsese

Now that I'd passed my driving test, a whole new world of cinematic possibilities opened up for me and my mates: the world of the Multiplex. If there was nothing on in Lancaster, either at The Dukes or the Odeon, or indeed the Brewery Arts Centre in Kendal, there was always one place we could guarantee that at least one film we'd want to watch would be on. In fact it was more likely that there would be at least three or four films that we'd be interested in, and we'd fill our boots with cinematic treats as often as we could. We certainly feasted on the much wider range of snacks than we were used to.

Preston's newly opened UCI multiplex cinema offered us not only sweets, but opened up a whole new world of hot dogs, drinks and varieties of popcorn, but probably didn't offer such treats as an Orange Maid or Strawberry Mivvi, which was possibly the cinema's only downside. The screens were bigger, the sound was better, and the choice of films was huge. We would often take in not just one film in an evening, but make it into a double bill. The whole experience was exciting, and by

146

now we were able to go to the pub before, after, and sometimes in between films.

We watched another De Niro film, "Awakenings" in which he played the antithesis to Travis Bickle or Jimmy Conway. This time he played Leonard Lowe, a catatonic sufferer of encephalitis lethargia, a disease which caused its unfortunate victim to be in a constant state of inertia, either awake or asleep, who is awakened temporarily by Robin Williams' new methods of treatment, only to return to his original state.

We watched whatever film was on, even if we weren't that interested in any which were on offer. I even went to watch the not particularly memorable "Mermaids" on my own, as my mates wanted to go and see something else which I wasn't bothered about seeing. I probably should have just gone with them, as Cher, Christina Ricci, Winona Ryder and Bob Hoskins didn't really do much for me that night. "Thelma and Louise" was a much better film, and one which we all went to see together, although I'm not sure the theme of female empowerment which the film proudly extols was meant for a group of four seventeen and eighteen year old lads.

We were more interested in Geena Davis getting her kit off with Brad Pitt, who we knew even back then would become a huge star. Little did I know then that Pitt the younger and definitely Pitt the sexier would go onto feature in some of the films which will be mentioned later in this book, films which have become very significant for me. His body was certainly significant to most females who watched "Thelma and Louise", as he shows Thelma how he robbed a convenience store with a hairdryer. Well, sort of.

After having watched both "Field of Dreams" and "Bull Durham" at The Dukes Theatre in Lancaster, one film that I did want to watch, and saw it at least twice, despite it being over three hours long, was Kevin Costner's epic Oscar winning "Dances With Wolves". I loved it, and never felt that it was too long. The way I see it is if someone says a film is too long, that must mean they have got bored with it. A film is never too long, just too boring, and this film never seemed too long or too boring at any time.

The film has had its critics and its detractors, but that's mainly due to Kevin Costner being a bit of a dick, but to me "Dances With Wolves" is one of my guilty pleasures. No it's not one of my guilty pleasures at all. It's simply one of my pleasures, and another film I will gladly watch again and again, despite its length, and despite it usually meaning a very late night, or when we watched it first at the cinema, a very late journey home, usually not getting back until after midnight, with school to get up for in the morning.

However, there was one film which meant a return journey home of much later than midnight, seeing as it didn't even start until midnight, but the midnight showing of "Taxi Driver" at the UCI in Preston was so worth it.

I couldn't quite believe that the one film missing from the Scorsese films on my Empire Magazine list did not have to be watched on a TV screen after having been rented out from my trusty old local video shop, but would be shown in all its glorious darkness on the big screen, just as it would have been when it was first released. This was an opportunity not to be missed, and one which I grabbed with both hands

My first ever viewing of this film was another seminal moment in my cinematic journey from boy to man. I was astonished by it, watching Travis Bickle's slow descent into insanity after being rejected by Cybil Shepherd, and becoming fascinated with Jodie Foster as a teenage prostitute working for the very seedy Harvey Keitel.

The final scene blew me away then, and still blows me away now whenever I watch it again, just like Travis blew his victims and consequently his own demons away with his selection of guns and sliding mechanisms he'd attached to his arms. If ever there was a film which gave an insight into the evil aspects of adult life, ironically involving a girl who was at least three years younger than I was at the time I first watched it, living in a world of overwhelming sin and immorality, then "Taxi Driver" is it.

The scene in which Martin Scorsese himself plays a husband of a cheating wife, sitting in the back of Bickle's cab outside the apartment in which his wife is doing the cheating sums the film up. The sordid, graphic and just plain nasty way the character speaks not only to Bickle, but also about his wife, and what he plans to do to her is chilling in its sense of menace, portraying the grim underbelly of New York life in shocking bluntness, even brusqueness. It left a very bitter taste in my mouth, which was of course its intention. It was probably the darkest film I had ever seen up to that point in my life, and remains up there even now. In fact there's not too many films at all which can match it in terms of its mordant cynicism. But as a seventeen-year old, as I then was, who was exploring all aspects of cinema, then it was a hugely significant moment for me.

I was just glad to get home in my own, or rather my dad's car which he allowed me to use that evening, without the need for any sort of taxi being used. I was also relieved that I hadn't invited a girl to see that film with me, as it may not have been the most romantic of dates. It may have been slightly more successful than going to a porn theatre on a date though.

Unlike Travis Bickle, I didn't make that mistake.

One Flew Over the Cuckoo's Nest (1975) Dir: Milos Forman

My actual A Level exams were fast approaching by now, but that did not stop me from watching as many films as I could. I was recording any film I thought worthy of a couple of hours of my life, and watching them as a way of relaxing after doing my exam revision in the early evening. Watching a film was a perfect way to escape from the incessant quotes and potential exam questions I had running though my head. I was determined not only to pass my A Levels, but also to tick off as many from my list of must-see films as I could. I watched anything and everything, some awful films, some good films, and a few great ones too during my revision period and the ensuing summer..

Once my exams were over, and I had a long glorious summer ahead of me, free from any sort of school work, I made it a personal mission of mine to tick off a few classic films I had not yet seen, and quite a few that I had not even heard of. A couple of these were two classic films from the silent era, Sergei Eisenstein's "Battleship Potemkin" from 1925, and "Metropolis", Fritz Lang's science fiction masterpiece, and to my amazement both films were being shown at The Dukes Theatre as part of a silent film season, which I greedily lapped up.

As a complement to the first of these films, Eisenstein's account of the 1905 Russian Revolution, with the finale taking place on the Odessa steps, I also watched Brian De Palma's "The Untouchables", with Kevin Costner's Elliot Ness attempting to bring down Robert De Niro's Al Capone, with a little help from Sean Connery in his only Oscar winning performance. This film would use the Odessa Steps scene as both inspiration and homage, and it was a brilliant watch, as was the first film, despite its age.

"Metropolis" too was a mind blowing film, considering it was made way before special effects had been properly used, let alone such a novelty as talking. Both of these silent films were accompanied by a live score being played in the theatre too, and it was a real privilege to have witnessed these cinematic masterpieces. I was so proud of my little local Arthouse cinema to allow me the opportunity of seeing such rare works of art. As a complement to "Metropolis" I also saw Whit Stillman's "Metropolitan", although the first nine letters of the films' titles were the only thing they had in common, apart from both being excellent.

As previously mentioned, in the chapter about "Apocalypse Now", I was a huge fan of the music of The Doors at this point in my life, and luckily enough for me, the day before my eighteenth birthday, Oliver Stone's biopic about the band was released, with Val Kilmer playing "The Lizard King" Jim Morrison. Needless to say I went to see the film, at least twice actually, and was suitably enthralled. It definitely lit my fire anyway

This late 1960s vibe then led me to watch another film from that drug fuelled era, a film which became an important one for me, as it has been for millions of other. "Easy Rider" was written and directed by the crazy Dennis Hopper, who also featured in "Apocalypse Now", off his face on hallucinogens, as he was for the duration of the filming of "Easy Rider" with Peter Fonda as his co-rider and collaborator, and I added this film to my poster collection, which already included one of the best films of the late 70s, and now as my own tribute to Dennis Hopper's passion for excessive drug taking, one of the best films of the late 60s,

"Apocalypse Now" and "Easy Rider" being released ten years apart from each other.

I decided that these two posters, along with my huge one of Spiderman (not drawn by me thankfully) would be taken to university with me to show anyone who came to my room how cool and hip I was. It is safe to say that they never fooled anyone. I was the least cool and the least hip student ever. And I couldn't even ride a motorbike.

Apart from the cool motorbikes and the trippy mood of the film, it also featured a young Jack Nicholson, giving a memorable, if short appearance. He stole the film in a way and made me very keen to see even more of his films. There were quite a few of his on my list, but they would have to wait until after I got back from my own road trip, or rather my own rail trip.

My month long Inter-Railing trip around Europe with five other mates, began in Paris, after stumbling off the train from Boulogne after very little sleep on the ferry. Instead of going to the glorious sights of the city of love, like the Eiffel Tower, the Arc de Triomphe, or a cruise along the River Seine to see if we could see Quasimodo on the top of Notre Dame, we spent a few hours in a graveyard instead.

Our obsession with The Doors led us to Pere Lachaise Cemetery so we could pay our respects to Jim Morrison. We were so pretentious back then, and once we finally found the grave, it was just surrounded by layabouts tripping their tits off on acid or mushrooms. It was not exactly the spiritual experience I was perhaps hoping for and probably not worth the trip on the Metro to find it, but at least I got to see some other graves, like Georges Bizet, Marcel Proust, and possibly the greatest of them all, Oscar Wilde. He, like Jim Morrison, had a certain hankering for hallucinogens, although absinthe and acid are very different apparently. I wouldn't know of course as I was a good boy. Whatever similarities these two poets had, I bet Oscar didn't look as cool as Jim in a pair of leather trousers, but I could be wrong.

After various stop offs, including Venice, Athens and a couple of Greek Islands, our rail trip took us as far as Istanbul, and even here I was able to tick off another film from my list. After having been to the Blue Mosque, the Grand Bazaar, experienced a rather tortuous Turkish massage, and had the most expensive shoe shine in this great city's history, which is also mentioned in my first book, "Just Me and My Football", we saw that a cinema we'd passed a couple of times was showing "Amadeus" in English, but with Turkish subtitles. We decided to have a night at the pictures in the company of Mozart, another film which I've watched many times since, although without the need for a very confusing language to be at the bottom of the screen. Next time I watch it on DVD I may just have the Turkish subtitles on anyway for old time's sake.

***

Once arriving back home after my European adventure, I threw myself headlong into my list of films. I was conscious of not having seen two of the greatest films ever made, or so my Empire supplement told me, and after having been blown away by "Goodfellas", one of my mates made me an offer I couldn't refuse and suggested that we watch "The Godfather" and its sequel. This was a rites of passage moment for us both. I had read so much about the films, and my brother had always revered them, telling me with glee about the horse's head in the bed scene, that it was time to finally watch them both, which we did over the course of two consecutive nights.

I'm only being honest, but I was slightly underwhelmed by the films on first viewing. If someone had offered me at that point in my life the choice between Scorsese's classic or Coppola's classic, I would without doubt have chosen "Goodfellas". Maybe I was just too young to appreciate the films and just how brilliant they actually were, and of course still are.

Now I am older, possibly wiser, but probably not more mature, I have come to realise just how significant "The Godfather" and its sequel are. Perhaps part of this deeper appreciation is because I am a father myself now, and understand what "The Godfather" is essentially about: family. The scene with Michael and his father in the garden when Vito expresses regret that Michael did not become a senator or governor, allowing him to hold legitimate power, sums the film up. It is beautifully acted, subtly written and directed, and shows just how deep, and indeed how inexorable the family bond is in the film. Family is at the heart and soul of the film, in not just the familial sense, but the idea of respect, loyalty, love and honour too.

I forgot just how outrageously brilliant an actor Marlon Brando was, with Al Pacino being not just his successor in terms of the Corleone family, but also in terms of acting ability. Brando rightfully won the Best Actor Oscar, even though he refused to accept it, due to his protest at the way Native Americans were being treated. Both performances are sheer tours de force, delivered by two masterful artists at the peak of their powers.

Apart from the obvious stand out scenes, such as the opening Wedding sequence, the killing of the Chief of Police in the restaurant, and Sonny's brutal assassination in which he must have had at least a hundred bullets fired into him, the final baptism sequence is stunning. With Michael renouncing sin, becoming Godfather to his nephew, the scene is intercut with the

154

ruthless murders of the heads of his rival families, allowing him to become The Godfather in the other sense of the word, providing an alibi for him at the same time. The journey to become ruthlessness personified is now complete. It is a truly staggering scene, and one which, as I said, was just too subtle for me when I was basically still a kid.

"Goodfellas", a powerhouse of a movie, is not exactly renowned for its subtlety. "The Godfather" is the finest of vintage wines, blended beautifully and satisfyingly, whereas "Goodfellas" is a huge line of cocaine, more exciting and brutal, but not as subtle or as delicate.

The sequel, which many people consider to be even better than the first film, still has family at the heart of it. This time though, whereas family gave Michael strength in the first film, the disintegration of the family is the crux to this film. We watch Michael left alone at the end, with both his brothers now dead, estranged from his wife, ultimately all powerful but completely alone.

Family is seen to be a weakness in this film, yet also can be used as a weapon with Pentangeli's brother being flown over in the investigation hearing just to sit there completely silent and let Pentangeli know that if he testifies against the Corleones then his family will suffer back in Sicily. It is possibly the most important piece of sitting silent there has ever been in a film. Family, as well as providing strength, can also be an Achilles heel, which again shows the power that the theme of family has in this sequel.

I disagree that the film is even better than the first, mainly due to the fact that Marlon Brando's phenomenal acting never appears in it, although of course Vito Corleone does. The flashback scenes, with De Niro playing the young Vito, who witnesses not only his brother's death at his father's funeral, but also the brutal murder of his mother right in front of his nine year old eyes, shows us brilliantly the beginnings of the saga.

The flashback scenes are worthy of anything in the first film, with one of the iconic moments being him being left all alone in quarantine for three months on Ellis Island, before the film cuts back to the present with Michael's son, Vito's grandson Anthony at the same age, surrounded by hundreds of people at his first Communion as a contrast.

Vito's rise to power with his associate Genco, who is played by Frank Sivero, who would also go onto feature with De Niro in "Goodfellas" as Frank Carbone, the one who ends up frozen in the meat van, is beautifully and subtly played. Even Vito's first murder, with Fanucci being shot with a gun enveloped in a towel, which catches fire, is brutal yet also exquisite, whereas Vito's ultimate revenge on Don Ciccio, the man who was responsible for his family's deaths back when he was nine, is just brutal.

The film lacks Brando, but gains another acting great in De Niro, but it is the fact that Vito Corleone, the first and original Godfather still features which makes this film great too. Either way, it is a film which matures from the first film, and one again which you need to be of a certain vintage yourself to truly appreciate.

***

There has been very little mention of the horror genre so far in this book, and the truth is, I've never been a huge fan of it. There would be two films that would change that to an extent. The first was another of Brian De Palma's brilliantly directed films, "Carrie" which gripped me right from the opening scene, in which Sissy Spacek gets tampons thrown at her in the school showers by a bunch of complete bitches, through to her being taken to the prom by the very lovely Tommy Ross, who had such a gleaming smile, despite it being against the wishes of her terrifying religious freak of a mother, played by Piper Laurie.

The tension in the scene as we await the pig's blood to be tipped onto Carrie's unsuspecting head is masterfully created by De Palma, before Carrie unleashes hellfire on everyone in the room, both students and teachers, even the lovely gym teacher who had tried to help her in the first place. Despite John Travolta having danced away from the scene, he still gets dealt with appropriately. Let's just say that Carrie was totally devoted to blowing his car up and watching him die in a huge fireball.

The scene which gripped me the most though was Carrie's mother's crucifixion scene, with Carrie having had just about enough of her freakishness, and so decides to pin her own mother to the wall with loads of flying kitchen knives. And of course the very final scene is definitely "gripping" for Amy Irving, who would go onto become Steven Spielberg's first wife, after Brian De Palma had introduced them. If you haven't seen the film then I won't spoil it for you, but it definitely gripped me. It scared the hell out of me actually.

It certainly sacred the hell out of my wife, although of course she was not my wife back then. I watched "Carrie" again fairly recently, and my wife told me how her own mother, in a rather sick tribute to Piper Laurie, had played the most gruesome trick on her and her younger brother.

At the age of only twelve, my wife to be and her eight year old little brother had nagged their mum into being allowed to stay up and watch the film for what must have been its first showing on TV. She had eventually relented, partly because she wanted to watch it herself, but had ideas of her own for her two wide eyed little children.

Back then her local butcher would give her a bag of pig's innards for the family dog, after she had bought the meat for her human children. This obviously came with a plentiful supply of pig's blood, the same sort of blood Carrie has tipped all over her pretty prom dress, causing the murderous rampage in the first place. My future mother-in-law, after the final scene had already scared the life out of her kids, thought she would put her own supply of pig's blood to good use, or some sort of use anyway, although "good" is probably not the right adjective.

She went into the kitchen to get the dog's food ready for the morning, but thought it would be fun to stick her arm in the bag of pig flesh, covering it to her elbow in blood, and waited behind the door for her unsuspecting, and already shaking with fright daughter, to wander in to get a drink. Just as her daughter came through the door, she stuck her blood covered arm out, causing her own sweet and innocent little girl to scream the highest pitched scream she had ever screamed, and ran back into the living room to join her brother.

Like some sort of real life horror monster, her mother then proceeded to chase her two children around the living room and up the stairs, where they managed to lock themselves in the bathroom, clinging onto each other for dear life, whilst the one person they relied on for their safety, their own mother, stood outside cackling, almost wetting herself with laughter.

I've always loved my wife's dark sense of humour, and this episode went a long way to explain where it came from. She's got nowhere near the same sense of black and bloody comedy that her own mother had though, something which I, and our kids, are grateful for.

Since then I've also watched the rather pointless remake of the film, with Chloe Grace Moretz as the title character. The film is good, but is in no way an improvement on the original. It just made me think why film makers choose to remake films that are already great to start with. Surely if you want to remake something, then choose a film which was not very good to start with, something that thankfully hasn't been done to my next film.

If "Carrie" had gripped me, then "The Shining" would not only grip me but make me view the winner of the 1973, 74, and 77 Grand National in a completely different light. Red Rum, the horse, would not feature in the film, but anyone who has seen the film, which is most film lovers, and certainly all Kubrick and horror lovers, then the name conjures up a very different image than Aintree racecourse.

"Redrum" in "The Shining", conjures up the image of a small boy who talks to his finger, who replies in a very disturbing voice, after having seen the creepiest set of twin girls ever, before being savagely attacked by his own father. Nothing to do with the Grand National at all.

The film is creepy on so many levels, with a brilliantly chilling performance from Jack Nicholson, who also of course kills Hong Kong Phooey in the course of the film. Scatman Crothers, the voice of the casually racist, but oh so innocently named cartoon character, one of my favourite cartoons as a boy actually, had already suffered at the hands of Jack Nicholson in the next film I absolutely had to tick off my list, although in this film at least Nicholson only got him very drunk, rather than brutally murder him with an axe.

159

"One Flew Over the Cuckoo's Nest" was a film I had been so looking forward to, as at the time, it was only the second film ever to have won all five top Oscars, Best Picture, Director, Actor, Actress and Screenplay, with "Frank Capra's "It Happened One Night" being the first in 1934. Since then this achievement has only been done one more time, with "The Silence of the Lambs" winning all five too, although I would argue that Anthony Hopkins' Hannibal Lecter should really have been nominated in the Best Supporting Actor category, as he is not actually on screen that much. But I'm not going to start an argument about it. Especially with Hannibal Lecter.

This was a film which simply needed to be watched, and one that needs to be watched by everyone in the entire world due to its brilliance. I just wish Ken Kesey, the author of the fantastic novel on which the film is based, someone else who spent most of his life off his face on mind bending drugs, had seen it before he died, having staunchly refused to watch the adaptation of his book.

He missed out on a truly great piece of cinematic storytelling, which is not just powerful in its message, but also spine-tinglingly acted and directed. The final image of Chief Bromden running away to his literal and metaphorical freedom, after having been released from his mind's confinement by Randall P. McMurphy, whilst Christopher Lloyd's Taber watches on with a look of manic defiance is one of the truly great final shots in the history of cinema. Even though I have seen the film at least twenty times, my spine tingles every time.

Since I first watched it, the film has taken on new levels of significance for me. I've loved some of the lines delivered by the self-proclaimed "God damn marvel of modern science" McMurphy ever since that first initial viewing, a few of my favourites being his suggestion that instead of being in the hospital, Billy Bibbit should be outside, "bird-dogging chicks and bangin' beaver", his reply of "The next woman who takes me on is gonna light up like a pinball machine and pay off in silver dollars", after returning from his electro-shock so called therapy, and his really quite profound assertion that "I tried, didn't I? Goddamn it! At least I did that", after attempting to lift the seemingly immovable water fountain control panel. And still to this day I can't help but say "Medication time" whenever I have to take some paracetamol.

Many of the scenes in the film have taken on new meanings for me down to the fact that I have now been a teacher for twenty five years, and have had to deal with situations almost as bonkers as McMurphy himself encounters. Some of my classes remind me of the scene in which Harding, or Hardon as McMurphy calls him, is recounting his sexual problems with his wife, before the whole discussion turns into something from a mental hospital, which is of course what it is.

I've had many situations where the students have reacted to something or someone in a similar way, leaving me just standing there bemused by what I am witnessing, a little like McMurphy's face when he first sees what his new set of friends are like. I have been in the same situation as Nurse Ratched, trying to remain calm, but also trying to restore some sort of order.

I've had many McMurphy type characters in my lessons, those who want to disrupt, but not for the same reasons as McMurphy, and many a time I've felt like I was battling against "the mental defective league in formation".

This all sounds rather unprofessional, but most teachers at some point must have felt the same thing, especially if they teach

161

children with additional needs. Some of these kids suffer from a huge lack of self-confidence, believing themselves to be stupid and idiotic, as their own parents have told them that enough times for them to believe it.

Often I just want to use the words of McMurphy and tell them "You're not an idiot, huh? You're not a goddamn looney now!...You're no crazier than the average asshole!" but of course I'd probably get into trouble for saying that. I just hope I have had the same positive effect on some of my students as McMurphy had on his "students".

The look of pride on the patients' faces as they return from their impromptu fishing trip, showing off their catch reminds me of some of the students' faces I have taught when they have finally managed to achieve something they thought was beyond them. It gives me a real sense of pride too knowing that I have had that sort of effect. I just hope I don't get sent for a lobotomy now for saying that, what with the Nurse Ratched type of educational authorities being in charge now.

I have actually used a crucial scene from the film as a way of getting some creative internal monologue writing from my own A Level students when we have been studying the book. At the end of the party with Turkle having passed out, along with most of the patients, McMurphy pauses and is seen to just take a moment and reflect on his "achievements". The camera lingers for at least thirty seconds on his face as he surveys. I have often got my students to use their skills of empathy to write what they think is going through McMurphy's head at that particular moment, with some great responses being written by my students. I'm not sure I'd be allowed to do that now in the current Ratched style education climate either. But who cares, I'll do it again anyway.

Screw the system, which is of course the book and the film's central message.

And so, with another classic film ticked off my list, the end of September arrived, and I prepared to go on another adventure, this time leaving my teachers, my friends and my parents and go off to university. All my mates were going off to different establishments and we all gradually departed one by one. I was the last one to leave and the day before my journey down south to study for a degree in English Literature, largely inspired by my film loving English teacher, who incidentally would also teach my son A Level Literature twenty five years later, I thought I would go to the cinema one last time.

With no one left to go with, I happily went back to the cinema in Lancaster, where it had all started for me as a four year old boy, reminiscing about my journey from boy to man, pondering my future, and watched "Terminator 2: Judgement Day".

Hasta La Vista Baby!

Part Four

A Degree in the Classics

A Clockwork Orange (1971)   Dir: Stanley Kubrick

I arrived at the University of Reading, and immediately put up my posters of Spiderman, "Apocalypse Now" and "Easy Rider" in an attempt to look worldly and interesting. But I needn't have bothered, as without her even seeing my posters yet, in Freshers' Week, I met a lovely girl who was doing the same course as me. We got chatting and discovered that we both loved films, although her knowledge of the history of cinema was way more expansive than mine. Our main degrees were in English Literature, but in our first year, all students had to choose two other courses to do for the first two terms. We had Freshers' Week to not just get drunk, but also choose these two extra courses.

The one I really wanted to do as one of my supplementary courses was one on American Film, but it proved to be very popular and I was left disappointed, leaving me with the rather pointless and definitely not as interesting Sociology and Philosophy courses. Instead of being able to study some truly great works of cinematic art, I had to learn about Descartes. Rather than his famous philosophical tenet of "I think, therefore I am", my own personal tenet at that time was "I watch films, therefore I am". I was left naval gazing rather than film watching.

Thankfully, the girl I had met, and who I was becoming closer to, not just in terms of our taste in films, had got onto the course, and so she became almost my tutor in film for the next couple of years. I certainly enjoyed the one to one tutorial sessions we would have, and not just on film.

However, before our private tutorials, seminars, and sometimes even lectures, when I wasn't concentrating enough, started, I finally got to see a film which I'd heard about, but never been able to watch. This was due to the simple reason that it had been banned, not by any morally zealous censorial committee, but by the director of the film himself.

Stanley Kubrick's adaptation of one of my favourite novels at that point in my life, "A Clockwork Orange", by Anthony Burgess, had been withdrawn by its distributor Warner Brothers at the request of Kubrick himself. This was due to the spate of copycat violence which occurred after the film's initial release in December 1971.

During a manslaughter trial the following March, where a fourteen year old male accused of the manslaughter of a fellow classmate, the film was cited as playing a significant factor in the crime, as well as the senseless murder of an elderly man by a sixteen year old boy who had been told of similar violence in the film, and a rape case in which the attackers sang along to "Singin' in the Rain", just as Alex and his droogs had done in the film, caused Kubrick to realise that maybe Art was having too much of a negative effect on reality. He had received death threats and so asked for the film to be withdrawn, meaning that I had never had the chance to watch it and see what all the fuss was about.

However, during my Freshers' Week, apart from the lovely girl I have already mentioned, I also met a lad who had a pirate copy of Kubrick's banned film. This was an opportunity not to be missed, not just in terms of watching the actual film, but also as a way of maybe getting closer to the aforementioned girl. So I asked if I could borrow it and invited my new girl friend, who I very much hoped would become my actual girlfriend, round to my room to watch it on my trusty old 14 inch TV screen, which was sat on top of a knackered old video recorder I had brought down to Reading with me.

She accepted my invitation and we bonded whilst watching a very violent and quite nasty film all about a dystopian society where ultra-violence is regarded as cool. It wasn't the most romantic of dates, but she appreciated the fact that I had given her the chance to watch this film which had been taboo, and one which she too had never had the chance to tick off her list either.

To be honest, the film is my least favourite of all Kubrick films. Despite it being nominated for Best Picture, I didn't like it then and I still don't like it now, even after it had been re-released after Kubrick's death in 1999, allowing everyone else to see the beatings, the murders, the rapes and the tortures. There is a real malevolence about it, and the violence is gratuitous to the point of being sensational, which is maybe the point of it in the first place.

However, the film crucially omits the rather more redemptive ending that the book originally included. The American publisher of the book, and so the copy which Kubrick read and based his screenplay on, does not include the final chapter of the original book in which Alex learns from his past errors and becomes a better, more morally conscious person. The film does not include this to give it a sense of hope and redemption, which is maybe why it just remains a nasty film.

I'm still glad I watched it though, and was definitely glad that my girl friend did indeed become my girlfriend soon after. So thanks Stanley, some good came out of your film after all.

Psycho (1960)   Dir: Alfred Hitchcock

And so my degree started, not just in terms of classic Literature, but also in terms of my advanced undergraduate education in film, particularly American film, with my own, very private, tutor. Her first module of her American Film course, ironically enough, was on the films of Alfred Hitchcock, a man who was born in Leytonstone, East London. She was required to attend viewings of these films on Thursday evenings on a separate campus, which meant that she obviously would need someone to walk her there and back to keep her safe from the notoriously crime ridden streets of leafy Berkshire. She invited me to be the man to do this, and suggested I may as well sneak in and watch the films with her.

The first of these Thursday night Hitchcock dates was his most famous film of all, but certainly not my favourite, "Psycho". I'd never seen it, although I'd obviously heard all about it, particularly the shower scene. What I wasn't expecting was just how scary the scene is when we finally discover the depths of Norman Bates' depravity, and the unsettling, eerie final chilling image of Bates' face which merges into the rotting skull of his dead mother.

I very much enjoyed the film, and even though my girlfriend wouldn't let me hold her hand during the film as she was too busy writing notes, she certainly allowed me the privilege on the walk back to our Hall of Residence, where we would discuss in minute, and rather pretentious detail, the finer points of the film.

Apparently it is significant that the first drop of rain on Janet Leigh's windscreen as she leaves Phoenix, Arizona is exactly the same shape as the first drop of blood on the shower curtain once she arrives at the Bates Motel and is freshening up, so to speak. I'm not sure how that added to the film's deeper meanings, but I found it utterly enthralling all the same, especially as my girlfriend, who I was besotted with, had taught me it. She was not just the object of my heart's desire; she was also becoming my Svengali in terms of cinema. I was only too willing to be taken in hand by her.

The next week's viewing would be "The Birds", which personally I found much more frightening than "Psycho". Maybe it was because it was in colour, as I was not used to watching black and white films. Not yet anyway. My Svengali had plans on that front too.

Tippi Hedren was brilliant in the role of the constantly avian threatened Melanie Daniels. Her completely stressed and harassed look wasn't surprising really as Hitchcock himself had seemed to have been a source of constant and personal threat to Hedren, Melanie Griffiths' mother, during the shooting of the film, and definitely not the avian type of threat. Hitchcock was so enamoured of her that he cast her as the lead in his next film, "Marnie", alongside Sean Connery, which would also be the next film I would see on a Thursday night, although I certainly did not treat my leading lady in the same way as Hitchcock had done with his.

My girlfriend was able to borrow films from the film department's extensive video library, and so, being able to watch these in my room without the need to be amongst other film students, we got closer and closer whilst watching "Rear Window", which introduced me to the delights of James Stewart and particularly the heavenly delights of Grace Kelly, who I'd only ever heard of when my mum told me about her death whilst we were on holiday when I was just eight years of age. I instantly fell in love with her of course, as did just about any man who had ever met her or laid eyes on her, whether they be a Prince or not, which I most definitely wasn't.

Next came another of the Amazing Grace and Hitchcock's collaborations, "Dial M for Murder", before we ended the module with "Rope" in which the whole film seems to take place over one continuous shot, but in fact is made up of several eight minute takes cut together ingeniously.

Then we watched "Torn Curtain", with Paul Newman and the most incongruously cast Julie Andrews as the female lead. She was obviously trying to get away from the spoonful of sugar image she had created for herself in "The Sound of Music" and "Mary Poppins", one which she would go even further to dispel from our minds with her appearance with Dudley Moore and the ravishing Bo Derek in "10", thirteen years later.

Next came the great "North by Northwest", with my love for Grace Kelly being overtaken briefly by Eva Marie Saint. Grace recaptured the top spot once I'd seen another of Cary Grant's Hitchcock films, "To Catch a Thief", in which her sumptuousness is beyond compare, as well as Grant's suaveness, and "Strangers on a Train", which would come to have much more significance for me after I left university – the title of the film anyway, not the film itself.

The other film I must mention is my own personal favourite of Hitchcock's, which is "Vertigo" with James Stewart pairing up this time with Kim Novak, another blonde who Hitchcock seemed to take his own very personal interest in. I shared his obsession with beautiful blondes, although my obsessions never became scary and threatening, although the way I met my wife, who just so happens to be blonde, could be seen to verge on the stalkerish, which is where the title of "Strangers on a Train" would pick up its rather apt importance. More on that later, although I will, say we have been happily and definitely unsinisterly married now for almost twenty two years, before you all start thinking I'm a weirdo.

The film is possibly my favourite due to James Stewart being in it rather than Kim Novak. Stewart was quickly becoming one of my favourite actors by now, and within the next year or so he would take on huge significance for me not just in terms of my film life, but also my personal life too. Again, more on that later.

Not content with just Hitchcock's American films, my girlfriend would also introduce me to some of his earlier, black and white films, some of which had been made in England, including "The 39 Steps", which was definitely not the Robert Powell version I'd seen as a kid, "The Lady Vanishes", and "Rebecca" the film version of Daphne Du Maurier's novel with Joan Fontaine and Laurence Oliver in the lead roles.

From there we became spellbound by "Suspicion", "Notorious" and "Spellbound" itself, in which the famous dream sequence had been created by Salvador Dali. We also caught up with "Mr. and Mrs Smith", a very different film from the Brad Pitt and Angelina Jolie version many years later. Carole Lombard definitely didn't appear wearing black PVC and stockings in Hitchcock's version. Maybe I would have remembered it more if she had done.

I'm starting to sound rather too much like Hitchcock now, so I think I'll end this chapter before it gets too weird. Hitchcock may have been a great director, one of the all-time greats in fact, but his treatment of women was definitely less than great, and is something I don't want to be associated with. My mother taught me how to respect women, although my love for her will hopefully not manifest itself in the same way as Norman Bates' did.

And we all know what a psycho he was.

Boyz n the Hood (1991)   **Dir: John Singleton**

A few weeks into my degree, I went to stay with my mate, the one who I had gone to see all the arthouse films at The Dukes Theatre in Lancaster with. He was now taking a gap year and working in London, earning some money before he would do some trekking in the Himalayas later in the year.

He was staying with his uncle in London, in Canonbury, a short walk from Highbury and Islington Tube station, and so he invited me to come into the Big Smoke for the weekend, something I was only too pleased to do, seeing as I'd never really been into London before, apart from as a kid with my parents. I was well up for a weekend on the mean streets of the capital, although the streets where he was staying were hardly mean. He would take me somewhere meaner and more daunting later that evening after having arrived at his uncle's house early on the Friday evening.

We wanted to go to the cinema, just as we had done countless times before, but this time the venue would be very different to the ones we had been used to. John Singleton's debut film, the now seminal story of early 90s gang life in the 'hoods of South Central Los Angeles, had been released that very day, so as we were now tough inner city boys (yeah right), we thought we'd see what real urban life was like.

The nearest cinema to us was one in Dalston, an area which had a much bigger black population than we'd ever experienced, and as close to a 'hood as we could get. Us callow little white boys were a little bit nervous about our walk to the cinema, as we would have to walk the streets of this dark and dangerous drug infested part of the sprawling metropolis, or so we naively thought it would be. Surprise, surprise, our fears and our perceptions of Dalston were completely changed as we very safely walked to the cinema, through multiculturalism we'd never come across before, having our wide white eyes opened up.

The film itself was brilliant, with Cuba Gooding Jr and Laurence Fishburne giving outstanding performances. I'd last seen Fishburne getting shot as he headed up stream on his way to help Martin Sheen kill Marlon Brando in "Apocalypse Now", and nobody had ever seen Gooding Jr before as it was his breakthrough film, playing Tre Styles, son to Fishburne's brilliantly named Furious Styles, as he fights to keep his son from becoming entrenched in the gang culture of South Central, the part of Los Angeles which would erupt into riotous violence the following year after the LA Police's arrest and brutal beating of Rodney King.

One line I will always remember from the film, and one which would have much greater significance for me a few years later, was Furious' advice of "Any fool with a dick can make a baby, but only a real man can raise his children." Again, more on why that would become so significant for me later on. At the time I watched the film, I was blown away with just how authentic the film was, pulling no punches in its portrayal of gang culture, something I had never experienced anything like, apart from the fake gang culture my brother had attempted to recreate during his breakdancing days with his membership of a "crew". But that gang culture was very definitely the white, insipid version portrayed in "Breakdance", unlike this much more "Beat Street" version of "Boyz n the Hood".

Ice T had appeared in that earlier calamity of a film, but this film would feature another Ice, Ice Cube, with T attempting to rectify his reputation with an appearance in Mario Van Peebles' "New Jack City", with Wesley Snipes, which I would also see a few weeks later. But it was Singleton's film which had the biggest impact on me, and not just in terms of its cinematic qualities. It would also influence my love for gaming, and in particular my obsession with playing "GTA: San Andreas", many years later.

I played that game for hours, preferring to immerse myself in LA gang culture from the safety of my sofa in a different type of LA, that of the postcode of LA1 in Lancaster, where I would settle down to bring up my own family ten years after having watched the film set in the real LA. The game was heavily influenced by "Boyz n the Hood", with many references to the film within the game, including similar clothes to Cuba Gooding Jr's yellow shirted Tre Styles, and Ice T further regaining his 'hood reputation by providing the voice of Madd Dogg.

After the film had finished, me and my mate, now much more urbanised than a couple of hours before, walked back to Canonbury, again without even the slightest involvement in a drive by, and decided that we would just be white boy tourists for the rest of the weekend, going into central London on the Saturday to experience Chinatown, with no Jack Nicholson or Faye Dunaway in sight anywhere, and we even had a wander around Hampstead Heath on the Sunday as an antidote to the mean streets of Dalston, which turned out to be far from mean actually. It had certainly opened my eyes up, maybe if only to my own innocent and inherent casual racism, something which I am eternally grateful to Tre and Furious Styles for doing.

Big respect to them both.

The Deer Hunter (1978)   Dir: Michael Cimino

A couple of weeks after my foray into the dark underbelly of London and LA, I returned the favour to my mate and invited him to come to my place in Reading for the weekend, which he duly took me up on. Instead of going to the cinema on the Friday evening, we instead decided to partake of the usual student pastime of getting absolutely hammered, which we did very successfully if I remember rightly, although I remember very little of the actual evening itself.

All I know is that we both woke up with huge hangovers and for nothing better to do, we thought we'd pop into town and go to the cinema, as we always used to do. However, the film we would choose to go and see would not be the most effective of hangover cures. Instead of it being a nice soothing remedy in a darkened room, it would end up mashing our heads even more.

"Jacob's Ladder", starred Tim Robbins as a Vietnam veteran struggling with mad, wild and frankly terrifying hallucinations, after he had been part of a government experiment during the war into a new drug called "The Ladder". This narcotic which had been created would cause its users to experience increased aggression, bringing primal urges to the forefront of their minds without the ability for their conscious mind to suppress them. It had first been tested on monkeys and then on a group of enemy soldiers, with truly gruesome results.

If you haven't seen the film, you can only imagine the sorts of horrors these men suffered from both during the war and in its aftermath. All I will say is that the carnage created did not ease the pain of a throbbing headache and a general feeling of regret and nausea which I was definitely feeling that afternoon due to my excessive intake the previous evening.

Along with "Born on the Fourth of July", and of course "First Blood" and "Rambo", this was another film dealing with the after effects of the Vietnam War which I had now added to my cannon, but there were a couple more films which I knew of which deserved to be watched too, and two films that definitely dealt with that war's aftermath in rather more mature and subtle ways than the methods preferred by Sylvester Stallone. My girlfriend, after all the Hitchcock stuff we'd been watching, was only too glad to watch them with me too, and handily, she was able to borrow them for us from the Film Department's library.

"Coming Home", with Jane Fonda falling in love with Jon Voight as an injured veteran whose views on the war have not only changed him, but eventually change Fonda's more traditionalist outlook, is a beautiful piece of cinema. It deals movingly with the literally paralysing physical effects of the war, as well as the emotional and mental turmoil it also brought. Both Fonda and Voight deservedly won the respective Oscars the following year in the Best Actor category, although the film itself would be slightly overshadowed by the next film I would watch, another film in the same year dealing with the same subject. It seemed that America was still dealing with its own hangover from that conflict in South East Asia.

The Oscars for Best Picture and Best Director, along with Christopher Walken's stunning performance in the Best Supporting Actor category would all go to Michael Cimino's epic masterpiece "The Deer Hunter", although its main star Robert De Niro would have to wait another couple of years for his Best Actor Oscar for "Raging Bull".

Bizarrely, I'd heard of "The Deer Hunter" first when I was reading a copy of "Smash Hits", which my brother had bought in 1984 after the release of Bananarama's single "Robert de Niro's Waiting", in which he was talking Italian apparently, even though he'd spoken very little Italian in any of the films he'd featured in so far.

"Smash Hits" provided an article for us pre-teens, explaining who Robert de Niro in fact was, and mentioned that he had starred in the Oscar winning film of 1979, although I was unaware of its content matter as the ten year old I was at the time I read the article, and certainly when I was only five on its actual release date, being still wrapped up in the delights of "Star Wars" and "The Cat from Outer Space" at that point.

By the time I watched "The Deer Hunter", I was well aware of who De Niro was, and was actually a bit ashamed of myself for never having watched his most famous film to date at that point, despite it not having been directed by Martin Scorsese. The scenes set in Pennsylvania, the wedding scene and Michael's return from Vietnam, did not really leave that much of an impression on me, despite the fact that John Cazale, who had played Michael Corleone's rather useless older brother Fredo in both parts of "The Godfather" had filmed these scenes whilst actually dying of cancer. He died just after filming was completed and never saw the finished film.

As for the scenes set in Vietnam itself, I challenge anyone to watch them without having an impression left upon them. And a mind-blowing one at that, almost literally. Just like Christopher Walken's character Nick's brains are blown away in the final Russian Roulette scene, so I was blown away by the sheer brutality, intensity, and unpredictability of the earlier scene in which De Niro and Walken are forced to play the game for the entertainment of their captors. If they didn't play, they would be put in a rat and dead body infested cage in the river, and left to drown in the most horrific of circumstances.

Like the scene I mentioned in "The Godfather", with Pacino and Brando giving tour de force performances from artists at the very peak of their powers, so it was in this scene, although this one lacked the subtlety of the other piece of brilliance. I suppose subtlety is not one of the things a scene in which your life is literally being taken into your own hands, whilst being surrounded by haggling and cackling gooks, who are only keeping you alive for their own entertainment, lends itself to. It was one of the most powerful pieces of cinema I had ever seen, and one which remains so over forty years later.

I had finally completed my own journey into the heart of darkness of Vietnam films and thought I would take a break from them. I'd seen things man, and now it was time for something a little less disturbing. Well, not really actually, but at least this next film would not have any Russian Roulette scenes in it.

But it would contain guns. Lots of them. And they would all be fired to the soundtrack of K-Billy's Super Sounds of the 70s.

Reservoir Dogs (1992)   **Dir: Quentin Tarantino**

I not only watched films with my new girlfriend in my room, but continued going to watch them on the big screen too. However, the nearest big screen for us would not mean a trip into town to the actual cinema, but a trip to our usual lecture theatre in the centre of campus, literally a five minute walk away.

When we weren't all being either bored stiff, or enlightened intellectually during the day whilst listening to one of our tutors drone on, in the evening the main lecture theatre was transformed into a cinema which would show all the arthouse type films I'd become accustomed to watching before I moved down south. The seats weren't as comfy though, but at least if the film was dull we could put our head on the desk and have a nap, which is of course what we all wanted to do during the day's lectures as well.

Many evenings were spent watching an eclectic mix of British, American and European cinema with the films I remember most being, in no particular order: the adaptation of David Mamet's stage play of "Glengarry Glen Ross", with Al Pacino giving yet another barnstorming performance in one of the sweariest films I'd ever seen; Neil Jordan's "The Crying Game", and no I did not see the twist coming; "High Heels", another of Pedro Almodóvar's slightly manic and frantic melodramas; "Barton Fink", the Coen Brothers' excellent follow up to "Miller's Crossing" with the two Johns, Goodman and Turturro impressing me immensely; and David Cronenberg's adaptation of "Naked Lunch", William S. Burroughs' beat novel, which had Robocop himself, Peter Weller, as a bug exterminator who becomes involved in some sort of secret government plot whilst hallucinating wildly on the substance he uses to kill bugs with.

There was a no smoking policy in the lecture theatre, but for some reason that evening's screening was filled with so called students who I had never seen before on campus, especially in the lecture theatre, who made the whole room stink of weed, which kind of added to the bizarre nature of the film.

We then discovered a few more of Cronenberg's earlier, weirder, and crazier creations, with "Shivers", "Rabid" "Scanners", "Videodrome", and my personal favourite "The Dead Zone", with Christopher Walken again being very intense indeed, all being shown as part of a season on BBC2, with Alex Cox introducing each one as part of his brilliant "Moviedrome" series. We lapped them all up, but I would certainly feel more uneasy the next time I took a bath after watching "Shivers". It certainly gave me them.

In complete contrast to David Cronenberg was one of the loveliest and gentlest of films I think I have ever seen. For some reason, despite it having been released a couple of years previously, "Cinema Paradiso" was shown in our lecture theatre, and seeing as it had won the Oscar for Best Foreign Language Film in 1990, I jumped at the chance to watch it, as it had passed me by somehow on its initial release.

This beautiful little film, a love letter to cinema itself, ends with the now grown up little boy Toto returning to his Sicilian home to attend the funeral of Alfredo, the projectionist at the village cinema, Cinema Paradiso, and the man who had instilled into the young boy his love for the cinema. The final sequence where all the censored kisses from a huge array of classic films, clips that Toto never got to see as a boy as they were deemed too suggestive, had been spliced together by Alfredo in his final gift to Toto. The montage of kisses is truly magical and hugely romantic, although it did remind me of my own mum's censoring of "Yanks" a few years before when I was still a young boy, and much too young to watch any "kissing" on screen.

Two of my favourite films we would see would be in the French language, although both were not French. The French film was the highly inventive, original and quite dazzlingly dark "Delicatessen", which I enjoyed enormously although I almost became a vegetarian afterwards, but thankfully soon got over that impulse; the other film, "Man Bites Dog", a Belgian one, was a hugely entertaining, dark and twisted, blackest of black comedies about a serial killer who has agreed to be followed by a group of young documentary makers, as a way of providing insight into our anti-hero's chosen career. We certainly get an insight, as well as a lot of laughs along the way. The funniest bit is when he literally scares an old lady to death, sneaking up on her, before shouting loudly into her ear, and then boasts about how he doesn't always have to use guns and make a mess.

Perhaps the artiest of arthouse films we would watch was not French, or Belgian, or even Spanish or Italian. There was one nation's films I needed to dip into, namely that of Sweden, and I got the opportunity to see the most famous Swedish film of them all: Ingmar Bergman's "The Seventh Seal", where my old friend The Exorcist, Max Von Sydow, famously plays a game of chess with Death.

Maybe I was just not arty and intellectual enough, but the film bored me to Death, whether he played chess or not. I know it may be considered a true cinematic masterpiece, but life is just too short to go back and re-evaluate a Swedish language black and white film about Death.

There are many other films I'd prefer to revisit before I actually meet Death himself, and maybe even get to play a game of chess with him too, one of these being the least intellectual film I think I'd ever seen. Russ Meyer's "Beyond the Valley of the Dolls" was also being screened in our lecture theatre, and seeing as the only other Russ I'd heard of was Russ Abbott, then this film had some comic potential, and certainly sounded more fun than "The Seventh Seal". I was not wrong. We had a great night watching the most gaudy and garish of sexploitation films.

The following week another of Meyer's brassy, brazen, and brilliant films, "Faster Pussycat, Kill, Kill" was screened, which we again eagerly lapped up as the perfect antidote to Ingmar Bergman's brand of sombre solemnity. Even though Bergman's film was on my Empire Magazine list of films I must watch, I was much more pleased to have experienced "Faster Pussycat, Kill, Kill", which most definitely was not on the list. I'm sure it's on some sort of list, and most definitely would be on the list if it had been compiled by the director of my next film, a film I don't need to revisit at all because I know it so well, and yet keep finding myself drawn back to it at regular intervals.

"Reservoir Dogs", was a film I knew very little about when it was first released, let alone its director or even which actors were in it. It was first shown to an audience at the Sundance Film Festival in January 1992, before being shown in Europe at the Cannes Film Festival in May that year. It was gradually released throughout European countries at intervals, but did not officially get its release until January 1993 in the UK. Maybe that is why it had slipped under my radar.

My girlfriend and I prided ourselves on having seen most, if not all of Barry Norman's Top 10 films of the year, which he would announce in the run up to Christmas. His Top 10 of 1992 included "Reservoir Dogs", even though neither of us had had the chance to see it yet. And why not? The answer to Barry's unrhetorical question this time was because us mere mortals were not lucky enough to have had tickets for the glittering Film Festival in Cannes, unlike the immortal Barry Norman.

So, as soon as it was released, and was considered arthouse enough to be screened in our lecture theatre, we were both very keen to complete 1992's list, despite it being 1993 by now. We were not disappointed, and instantly could see why Barry had put it on his list.

Right from the opening scene, with the machine gun delivery of the bristling dialogue, the type of screen dialogue we'd never heard before, with the discussion of the meaning of Madonna's "Like a Virgin", and the argument over whether to tip or not, we knew this was going to be good. Then once the soundtrack kicked in, with the iconic shot of the black suited gangsters walking towards the camera in slow motion, before it abruptly cuts to Tim

182

Roth screaming in agony and covered in blood in the back of Harvey Keitel's car, we were mesmerised, intrigued, and completely hooked by this cocky new director's style.

The unusualness of the narrative structure, the brutality of the violence, the coolness of the songs, the ferocity of the guns, and the uncompromising uniqueness of the script all combined to make this a film it is impossible not to remember. We all know the torture scene with Michael Madsen's Mr. Blonde dancing to the very groovy Stealers Wheel's "Stuck in the Middle". And we can all remember how Mr. Blonde wants to go all Vincent Van Gogh on poor old Marvin Nash. I remember the physical reaction I had during that scene, and whilst turning my face away, I remember seeing everybody else in the lecture theatre having the same reaction too.

The biggest physical reaction I had though was when Nice Guy Eddie, played by Chris Penn, entered the scene to try and calm things down, accusing Mr. Orange of being the rat, before he just shoots dead the barely alive cop, blowing away any sort of hope the film gave me, that maybe somewhere there would be some sort of redemptive moment. But no, he was just killed like a wounded horse, and I physically let out a moan of despair, knowing that there would be no light at the end of the tunnel for any of these men.

It is hugely significant that they all shoot each other in the final scene, and even more significant that the last image we see is of Mr. White being blown away by police gunfire, after he had done the same to at least two cops earlier. The last sound we hear is of gunfire, which is the most apt way to end such a ferocious and fierce film.

None of us knew back then just how big a part of film history and even popular culture Mr. Tarantino would become. I even went to see the film again the following evening, on my own this time, making full sense of the interwoven narrative this time, and the torture scene still had almost as much impact on the second viewing too. It was a film which demanded, almost threatened its audience to sit up and watch.

It most definitely wasn't a little doggie of a film. It had bite, and it certainly bit me.

Basic Instinct (1992)   Dir: Paul Verhoeven

You may be wondering why this film is included, seeing as the title of this section included the word "classics", something which this monstrosity of a film is not. But then again, I never said that all the films in this book would be good. But I suppose this film has become one of those "so bad it's good" kind of classics.

It was certainly not the sort of film which would have been shown in the campus lecture theatre. During the week, my girlfriend and I would have our scholarly and more erudite taste buds whetted either by going to the lecture theatre film screenings, or watching some of the older classics in my room on my trusty old video recorder. However, that didn't mean that I didn't want my more mainstream, and frankly more fun taste buds stimulated too, with the latest releases at the cinema.

Reading had two cinemas, an Odeon and a Regal I think, and we were always sure to be able to find something, usually on a Friday or Saturday evening, which would satisfy our cravings for the proper cinema experience, popcorn and all. We would normally start our evening by treating ourselves to a meal at Pizza Hut, before washing it down with a film. We saw loads of films at the proper cinema, some great ones, some good ones, some bad ones, and some truly awful ones too. Paul Verhoeven's next film, after I had been so impressed with "Robocop" and "Total Recall" would fall into this final category.

"Basic Instinct", really is a bad film, but entertaining all the same, providing us with the kind of junk food experience we all enjoy every once in a while. Michael Douglas, the great Kirk Douglas' son, is the man who had basically been responsible for getting "One Flew Over the Cuckoo's Nest" made, as well as starring in some brilliant films in his earlier career such as "The China Syndrome", with Jane Fonda, a film my girlfriend had recommended that I watch and had been hugely impressed with.

"Fatal Attraction", too was an excellent film, introducing us all to the phrase "Bunny Boiler" in a genuinely classy thriller. Oliver Stone's "Wall Street" too is considered a classic of the 1980s, brilliantly depicting the consumerist obsession of that period, with Douglas brilliantly delivering his famous speech about how greed is good. "Romancing the Stone" and "The Jewel of the Nile" are cracking adventure films, and his reunion with Kathleen Turner in "The War of the Roses" was great fun too.

I wasn't particularly keen on "Black Rain", which was another film I had seen on my Wednesday afternoon bunking off sessions at sixth form, but I was still willing to give Douglas the benefit of the doubt with "Basic Instinct", despite Barry Norman having slated it a few nights previously on Film 92.

Barry's main problem with the film was how Sharon Stone flashed her fanny at us all in a rather gratuitous manner, which was of course the main reason I was so keen to give Michael Douglas the benefit of the doubt in the first place. It wasn't just this now hugely lampooned scene which was gratuitous; every aspect of the film was gratuitous.

The script, the acting, the dialogue, the car chases, the club scenes, the sex, the jumpers Douglas wore, are all far too overblown and garish. It was about as subtle as a brick in the face. Compared to his earlier whodunnit thriller, the aforementioned "Fatal Attraction" or other films in the genre, like the outstanding "Jagged Edge" with Jeff Bridges, or Kevin Costner's "No Way Out", "Basic Instinct" is a just a bit of a joke film, but maybe that's why I still like it, and will happily watch it, if I come across it whilst channel hopping on the TV. It certainly left an impression on me, but maybe not for the right reasons.

Douglas' next film went some way to restoring his reputation, being extremely annoyed at a cheeseburger in "Falling Down", but it would be another of his films we went to see which would go a long way to getting Michael Douglas back in my good books, but it probably had more to do with his co-star, the gorgeous Annette Bening.

"The American President" is a lovely film, in the style of Frank Capra, which is a huge compliment from me as you will discover later, and one which seems at the moment a much needed antidote to the current American President, who is the antithesis of everything Michael Douglas' President Andrew Shepherd was. If only art would imitate life sometimes.

My high regard for Miss Bening started after I had seen her in "The Grifters", in which she wore a head scarf much better than my Gran used to. She also appeared in "Postcards From the Edge", before starring with Harrison Ford in the rather forgettable "Regarding Henry", which was ironically about how forgetful Henry had become, losing his memory completely, something I too seem to have done about this film, apart from Miss Bening's loveliness of course.

But it was her appearance in another film which my girlfriend and I enjoyed one Friday night which would make me really stand to attention. Her appearance with Warren Beatty in the underrated gangster biopic of Ben "Bugsy" Siegel, oddly enough called "Bugsy", really made my eyes wide open. Like the philandering Warren Beatty himself, I could not take my eyes off her. Whatever film she is in, her performances alone are worth watching, and I'm sure a couple of her subsequent films will get a mention later on too.

Now that I've mentioned Harrison Ford, we enjoyed immensely on another Friday evening one of his best films ever. "The Fugitive", is a great film, with great performances from Ford himself and Tommy Lee Jones, the man charged with apprehending Dr. Richard Kimble, after he escapes the most spectacular of train crashes. It is very often shown again on TV, and is another film I will very happily find myself watching to its conclusion, even though I know exactly what is going to happen.

Many people forget what a versatile performer Harrison Ford was. He could so easily have become typecast in action hero roles, such were the popularity of the Star Wars and Indiana Jones films. But he made sure he chose very diverse roles to show off his considerable talents. Yes he may never have won an Oscar for his acting, only ever having been nominated once, for his performance in "Witness", another memorable film of the mid-eighties, but he has been in so many excellent films. "Blade Runner" of course is a sci-fi classic, and his performances in "The Mosquito Coast", "Frantic" and the previously mentioned "Working Girl" are all well worth watching.

Another film I have previously mentioned, "Presumed Innocent" in which he starred alongside John McClane's wife, Bonnie Bedelia, also featured someone who my A Level English teacher had introduced me to, the delectable Greta Scacchi. He had a bit of a school boy crush on her, and waxed lyrical to us boys about her beauty and charms, although her charms were used in a not particularly charming way in the steamy "Heat and Dust" and also in the very mischievous "White Mischief".

Greta Scacchi was to my English teacher what Annette Bening had become to me, and I would see her in "The Player", Robert Altman's inventive and dark satire on Hollywood, with Tim Robbins attempting to keep his head above water in the shark infested waters of Hollywood, as well as avoiding a murder charge.

I remember the film not just because of Greta Scacchi, but also the ridiculously long, technically amazing opening scene, where Altman pays homage to other great one-shot scenes, such as Orson Welles' opening shot in "Touch of Evil". It is also memorable for the ridiculous amount of cameo performances, with many great actors appearing as themselves to give the fictional story more authenticity.

Other films I would enjoy, most of them falling into at least the "good" category, would be "The Godfather Part 3", which frankly let the other two films down, preventing the now three Godfather films from being a truly great trilogy, and "A Few Good Men", with Jack Nicholson getting very angry indeed at Tom Cruise when he demands to know the truth.

I was enthralled by Terry Gilliam's "The Fisher King", with Robin Williams playing a rather eccentric homeless man who brings redemption of sorts to the suicidal Jeff Bridges. One scene in particular enthralled me, which has remained with me almost thirty years on: the dance scene in Grand Central Station. It is one of the most staggeringly beautiful pieces of cinema you could wish to see, and one which I need to watch again as soon as possible.

We very much enjoyed Francis Ford Coppola's next film, "Bram Stoker's Dracula", with Gary Oldman as the fiendish Count. Little did I know then that my own son would attend the same theatre school as Gary Oldman, Rose Bruford College, some twenty eight years later. Oldman, after winning the Oscar for Best Actor for playing Churchill in "Darkest Hour", returned to his old school and gave my son and his peers the chance to talk to him about his career, which was a very generous thing of him to do. My son was certainly thrilled to have met Count Dracula, which is more than can be said of Keanu Reeves.

Continuing the Gothic theme, we also came alive whilst watching "Mary Shelley's Frankenstein", with Kenneth Branagh using the same tactic as Coppola by using the author's name to give his film more gravitas and credibility, and also as a means of getting away from the usual image we have of Frankenstein's monster. Robert De Niro certainly did not have any bolts coming out of his neck, although Helena Bonham-Carter had her heart coming out of her body in a particularly gruesome scene.

Whenever I have taught the novel in my English classes, or the stage adaptation to the younger students, I very much enjoy showing them that particular scene in which Frankenstein's new bride is treated extremely heartlessly by Frankenstein's monster. It certainly stops my classes from falling asleep at least.

Helena Bonham-Carter would be treated much more pleasantly in "A Room with a View" and after seeing that beautiful film, I had gone onto watch Bonham-Carter's co-star, the similarly double-barrelled named Daniel Day-Lewis in "My Left Foot", as mentioned during my sixth form years. My girlfriend and I would also watch three more of his films on those Friday evenings in Reading.

The first would be Michael Mann's "The Last of the Mohicans", in which Day-Lewis was very certain that he would find Madeleine Stowe, repeatedly assuring her of this in front of a lovely cascading waterfall, before teaming up again with Jim Sheridan in "In the Name of the Father", as the wrongly convicted Gerry Conlon, who spent years in prison after being coerced into confessing involvement in an IRA bombing.

The third film we would watch was probably the most memorable, but not because of Daniel Day-Lewis at all. "The Age of Innocence" was Martin Scorsese's latest film, and certainly his least violent film to date. Despite the rather radical departure from his usual type of film, I still enjoyed it, though not because of its leading man or its director, both of whom I admired immensely, but because of the leading lady. Michelle Pfeiffer, as the Countess Olenska, reminded me just how gorgeous she was, and reminded me of why both I and Barry Norman had fallen in love with her a few years previously.

The final film I am mentioning in this chapter fell very definitely into the "awful" category, along with "Basic Instinct", and this film couldn't even claim to be so bad that it was good. It was just very bad. On my nineteenth birthday, my girlfriend "treated" me to a viewing of "Hook", Steven Spielberg's reworking of the Peter Pan story, and frankly I wish she hadn't bothered.

We had a lovely Chinese meal afterwards, but the film itself was a pitiful starter course to our evening. And as for my dessert, well let's just say I enjoyed it more than watching Robin Williams and Dustin Hoffman fly around in tights.

This was the first Spielberg film in which I had not come out of the cinema utterly enthralled. As I came out of Neverland and re-entered the real world after watching "Hook", instead of that feeling which Spielberg had given me as a kid as I watched all those early films of his, all those films which had made me fall in love with the cinema in the first place, the feeling had been replaced with a sense of flatness and genuine ennui. It felt as though my childhood had most definitely ended as I reached my twentieth year; even Spielberg was letting me down now.

With my own age of innocence coming to an end, it was time to rectify that by discovering possibly the most wonderful film of all time. It is a film which still restores my sense of innocence each and every time I watch it, each and every Christmas Eve.

It's a Wonderful Life (1946)   Dir: Frank Capra

I'm slightly embarrassed to admit it now that I'd never heard of this film before my girlfriend suggested that we watch it on our first Christmas Eve together. I'd gone down to meet her family and stay for a few days over Christmas, and as we had taken her dog out for as many walks as she could manage, and been to the pub as many times as I could manage, she noticed that this film was being shown on the TV on Christmas Eve afternoon. She was not only surprised that I'd never heard of it, let alone seen it, but I think she was actually rather mortified with me, and no doubt her affection, and indeed respect for me went down a little. But this would give her another chance to educate me in the way of classic film. And this one certainly falls into that category.

So, with her family all sitting comfortably, with she and I snuggled up on the sofa next to her little brother, I took part in a family tradition of hers, which has now become part of my own family's too, although with a completely different girl as my wife

191

now. She didn't tell me anything about the film, what to expect or how wonderful it would be, and just told me to sit and enjoy it. Like a good boy I sat quietly, and didn't moan about it being old and black and white, and within seconds I was engrossed in the story of a man who would go onto become my role model and a yardstick for my life, which has been almost as wonderful.

I am also slightly embarrassed to admit that on first viewing I was a little disappointed with the film's ending. I rather naively thought that George Bailey's happiness relied on the fact that he was able to finally get enough money together to pay off his debt to Mr. Potter (Peter Kay's inspiration for Brian Potter in "Phoenix Nights"), when I have come to realise in my wiser years how that money is just a symbol of the love and gratitude other people have for him. The money was given happily by those who knew him, and indeed those who had never met him due to the kindness he has shown to others and the huge positive impact he has had on everyone. His happiness does not depend on money, but being able to bring happiness to others. Surely that is what life should be about. It is the simplest of messages, in the simplest of films, which makes it the most wonderful of films.

It is wonderful on so many levels. Firstly, it is as romantic as they come, with George and Mary's courtship being portrayed tenderly and humourously, especially when Mary has to hide in the bush after losing her dressing gown with George wondering how he should deal with this "very interesting situation".

The lasso the moon sequence is truly beautiful, with George's line of "I'll give you the moon...then you can swallow it, and it'll dissolve, and the moonbeams would shoot out of your fingers and your toes and the ends of your hair", and as for the scene when they are both talking into the telephone to Sam Wainwright, their lips getting closer and closer, well that is just a gorgeous scene full of palpable tenderness.

The film is a comic masterpiece too in many ways, from George and Mary falling into the swimming pool but continuing to dance, to Clarence's lines about Mark Twain, causing the bridge master to fall off his chair when George's clothes are drying out, to George realising that he can't hear properly anymore, that his lip is bleeding once again, and finding Zuzu's petals in his pocket to his absolute delight, all of which bring absolute delight to us too. He's even delighted with his impending incarceration "Isn't it wonderful? I'm going to jail!", such is the film's unyielding refusal to give into pessimism.

Many people don't like the film because of its schmaltziness, and its boundless optimism and positivity, but underneath this heart-warming story of one man's life and how he has had such a profound effect on those around him, there are some really profound philosophical and political messages in it too, messages which, now more than ever, the world needs to embrace again, if it ever did in the first place.

The line "Just remember this Mr. Potter: that this rabble you're talking about, they do most of the working and paying and living and dying in this community. Well, is it too much to have them work and pay and live and die in a couple of decent rooms and a bath?" is deeply moving and sums up the heart of the film, and should sum up any Government's approach to welfare. It is a cry of anger and desperation from George, but one which could also be aimed against the Potter like leaders of this world right now, without the need for me to mention any names.

Potter sums up the capitalist greed, the every man for himself attitude which prevents the many from succeeding in life, and

George sums it up again perfectly when talking about how his own father was the antithesis to Potter's selfish brand of commercial gain where people are simply treated like commodities: "People were human beings to him, but to you, a warped frustrated old man, they're cattle. Well, in my book he died a much richer man than you'll ever be."

This is a film which should not just be watched at Christmas. Yes it may be set on Christmas Eve, but it is a film which should be watched whenever we feel that the bad guys are seeming to be winning. Indeed, I watch it whenever I feel like that, be it Christmas, Easter, July, November, whenever I feel my life source just needs a bit of a top up. And that's what the film has the never ending ability to do – it makes your own life and life in general so much better, so much richer, and so much more precious, which is a testament to the power of the film and the power of the cinema.

It should be on the National Curriculum actually. Forget learning what modal verbs are, I'm an English teacher and am still not sure what they are, but what I am sure of is that everyone, particularly children, can learn from this most wonderful of films. Maybe not children in particular, maybe adults need to watch it more often just to remind themselves what real hope and goodness felt like, before life got in the way. It should be compulsory viewing for everybody, whatever walk of life they are in, as its message is truly universal.

Life is indeed a miraculous gift, so make sure you use it wisely and most importantly, kindly. Just make sure that if you were given the gift of seeing life without you ever having been in it, would the world be a better place, or as with the absence of George Bailey's wonderful life, a much worse place?

I told you the message was simple.

Be like George Bailey.

JFK (1991)   Dir: Oliver Stone

From one of the simplest, most beautiful films ever made, to one of the most complicated, and ugly films. Ugly not in the sense of its look, but it certainly shows the ugliness of humanity.

After his massive critical and commercial success with "Dances With Wolves", Kevin Costner was not just the flavour of the month, but the flavour of the early nineties. Whatever he touched seemed to turn to gold, from "Robin Hood: Prince of Thieves" which although enjoyable, was responsible for allowing Bryan Adams' song "Everything I Do" to remain at No.1 for a seemingly interminable eternity during not just the summer of 1991, but way into Autumn too, staying there for sixteen weeks, the longest unbroken run at the top of the charts ever. He even won an Oscar for Best Song for it. How? Why? Questions to this day which will never be answered sufficiently.

The film in which the song came from was an enjoyable romp, with the film being stolen by the Sheriff of Nottingham, played memorably by the now late, great, Alan Rickman, who I'd first seen trying to kill Bruce Willis, but who I'd last seen in "Truly, Madly, Deeply", as the ghost who comes back to provide some solace for his inconsolable wife, extraordinarily played by Juliet Stevenson.

This was another film I'd seen at The Dukes Theatre, and I distinctly remember just how moving and real Stevenson's sobbing scene was. She didn't just cry but she wailed, with tears, mucus, and the most agonising grief pouring out of her in one of the most astonishing pieces of acting I'd ever seen. That film

195

made the far less subtle, and consequently far more commercially successful "Ghost", with Lord Patrick of Swayze playing the ghost, seem like a kids' film in comparison. "Truly, Madly, Deeply" was a grown up film, and possibly one which I wasn't ready for yet at the age of seventeen. I need to revisit it actually now that I'm married and know what it is to truly, madly, and deeply love someone.

Costner's next film would be with Oliver Stone, who was working his way through seminal moments of 1960s American history, with his epic take on the conspiracy behind the assassination of John F. Kennedy in 1963. Costner would play the main character, the lawyer Jim Garrison, who discovers in very minute, painstakingly long winded, and not particularly entertaining detail that perhaps Lee Harvey Oswald was not the man who assassinated JFK.

I was a big fan of Oliver Stone, as he liked his films to be not very subtle, a bit like me, and so I had been looking forward to this film for months before it was released in January 1992. At the time, I was impressed with it, but looking back now, it took far too long to say something which we probably all knew anyway.

Maybe we didn't all know the exact involvement the CIA had in the death of their own President, or the many, many, many other factors which Stone makes sure he covers. He certainly left no stone unturned, but ironically left me turning away from Stone. It was a bit boring frankly, and to understand the minutiae of detail given to us by Stone, with many of the finest actors in the world all having small roles, required a degree in American politics, American history and American paranoia, something which Oliver Stone seemed determined to provide for us all.

It is a very admirable film, and I'm glad the dark underbelly of America was uncovered, but at the end I was none the wiser as to who actually shot JFK. All I now knew was that it probably wasn't Lee Harvey Oswald, and that a multitude of dark forces played their parts in his assassination.

One assassination in which there was no doubt as to who committed it, was that of Lee Harvey Oswald himself. Everyone knew who did it as it was seen live on TV in front of millions, if not billions of people.

Jumping on the bandwagon which Oliver Stone's film had got into motion came another film, providing even more convoluted conspiracy theory details. This time it would be about the man who shot the man who shot (allegedly) JFK, thus not allowing him to stand trial, namely Jack Ruby, in the imaginatively titled film "Ruby". Unfortunately, this Ruby didn't take his love to town, but took his gun to Dallas.

Danny Aiello played Jack Ruby, an actor I'd first seen in Madonna's video for "Papa Don't Preach", with the gorgeous Sherilyn Fenn playing the ultimate blonde bombshell Candy Cane, his headline stripper in his run-down Dallas strip club. Unsurprisingly, I remembered her performance more than Danny Aiello's, although I remember very little about the film at all actually.

Sherilyn Fenn would go onto star in another much more significant film in not just my life but that of most of my English classes, when she had her neck broken by John Malkovich's Lennie Small (no relation) in Gary Sinise's "Of Mice and Men". I know the film almost word for word, as I have seen it probably more than any other film, simply because I have read the novel on which it is based so many times with so many classes over the past twenty five years, always showing them the film to complement the reading, and almost crying at the end every single time still to this day. Fenn played the vulnerable, flirtatious, and ultimately deadly Curley's Wife to perfection, allowing her soft velvety dark hair to be stroked a little too much by Lennie. Even if she'd have been a blonde bombshell, as she was in "Ruby", she still would have been a bit too much for Lennie Small to handle.

If only Lennie had never handled her at all then maybe she wouldn't have died, but then of course neither would Lennie. Sorry for the spoiler, but I'm used to my classes already knowing the end, as every set of books I hand out to them during the lessons have mostly had the most succinct but most unhelpful piece of graffiti scrawled on the first page, simply telling the new recipient of the book that "George shoots Lennie", which kind of gives away the story for the eager new readers.

From "Ruby", a spin off from the JFK craze featuring a blonde bombshell, came another one using JFK's assassination as its premise, and featuring another blonde bombshell, which was probably my main motivation to go and see it, as this time the blonde would be my old flame, Michelle Pfeiffer.

"Love Field" was another film my girlfriend and I went to see in Reading, which had Miss Pfeiffer as a housewife, obsessed with Jackie Kennedy, travelling to Washington to attend the funeral, and learning much more about herself along the way. Again, apart from Miss Pfeiffer's platinum blonde hair, it is a film I remember little of, and maybe I should revisit again, to watch it for something other than a desire to see the delights of Michelle Pfeiffer, but at least it didn't just give me more conspiracy theories. I'd had enough of them by now.

The most enjoyable, and certainly for me, the most memorable film to come out of this obsession in the early 90s for JFK based films, was a film which thankfully only used the assassination of JFK as a much more tenuous plot link. "In the Line of Fire" starring Clint Eastwood, is a brilliant thriller, which keeps its audience on the edge of its seat, despite us knowing that the planned assassination of the head of state is bound to fail, much like Fred Zinnemann's taut and classy "The Day of the Jackal" in which we know that Edward Fox's plan to assassinate Charles de Gaulle will ultimately fail, as of course Charles de Gaulle was not assassinated by anyone, fictional or not.

That's the skill of both these films, to keep us guessing how close the killer, in the case of "In the Line of Fire", John Malkovich, will get to actually carrying out their plan. The enjoyment comes in watching the would-be killer's plan take shape, and watching the man charged with stopping the killer getting closer to foiling the plot, until the climax where the bullet is actually fired, like a time bomb ticking down until the explosive ending.

"In the Line of Fire" would also feature one of the hardest of hard men Clint Eastwood crying on screen, as he remembers his failure to protect JFK when assigned to protect him, hence the link with "JFK" the film. But in this film there would be no attempt to change the world and change everyone's minds, just a genuine attempt to entertain us, something which the director Wolfgang Petersen, Clint Eastwood and Rene Russo manage to do magnificently. Again, like "The Day of the Jackal", it is a film which I always end up watching if I flick onto it on TV, if only to marvel at the ingenuity of the guns the would-be assassins invent for their failed attempts, or to marvel at how fat John Malkovich had to get for the role. Or maybe it's just to see Clint crying.

The obsession with JFK's assassination would continue right up until 2013, with the excellent "Parkland" being released in the UK fifty years to the day after the actual assassination took place. This film does not go into any convoluted conspiracy theories thankfully, simply recounting the chaotic events that occurred at Dallas' Parkland Hospital where Kennedy was taken and desperately worked on in a failed attempt to save his life.

It is really quite gruesome and graphic at times, and no that isn't a comment on Zac Efron's acting, although it may well have been said about "The Greatest Showman", one of Efron's most popular films, which simply did not do it for me at all, and I do love a good musical. Maybe he should have made a musical about the assassination of JFK instead. Now that would be a film worth seeing, as long as Mel Brooks directed it. It would be up there with "Springtime for Hitler" in terms of bad taste, which wouldn't be a bad thing. I'm not sure Oliver Stone would have approved though.

And speaking of bad taste, I'm sure a certain character from this next film has had a few bad tastes in his mouth, although at least he'd be able to wash them away with a nice Chianti.

The Silence of the Lambs (1991)   Dir: Jonathan Demme

This film caused a bit of a stir when it came out, and rightly so actually. The story itself was shocking enough, about a man who liked to imprison his victims down a hole, starve them, and then skin them so that he can wear their flesh. Add into this psychotic mix the help of Hannibal Lecter, who likes to eat his own victims, then it was no wonder that the film caused such a rumpus.

Underneath all the media hype surrounding the film is a brilliant thriller, split mainly into two parts, with Lecter's escape marking the end of part one, and the hunt for Buffalo Bill as the second part. It is part one which everyone remembers most, simply because of Anthony Hopkins' portrayal of such a cold, ruthless but also quite culinary killer. Everyone knows the scene in which Jodie Foster, as Clarice Starling, goes to visit Lecter in his cell for the first time. It has been parodied enough times, particularly by French and Saunders, that is has become a part of cinema history and mainstream popular culture.

The scariest scene for me though, was Lecter's actual escape. I had no idea where he had gone, and then to reveal himself in the most macabre of ways, using the skin from the dead policeman's face to disguise himself, was almost as much a shock to me as when the head comes through the hole in the boat in "Jaws" which I referred to earlier. I was almost sorry that he had escaped, as that meant that he would no longer be in the film, until his final line, when he tells Clarice that he is "having an old friend for dinner, in the very final scene in the whole film. Without him in it, the film lost its gruesome magnetism to an extent, but was still gripping even without him.

Much of this is due to the overlooked performance of Jodie Foster, who had certainly matured since her days as the child prostitute in "Taxi Driver", and Tallulah in "Bugsy Malone". I'd last seen her being horrifically gang raped in the brutal but brilliant "The Accused", in which she won her first Best Actress Oscar, before winning again as Clarice Starling only three years later. Her award for "The Silence of the Lambs" was totally justified, whereas I'm not sure Anthony Hopkins' Best Actor award was, which again I alluded to earlier.

Hopkins only spends around fifteen minutes of the whole two hour long film on screen, and should really have been nominated for Best Supporting Actor, but such was the power of his portrayal of Hannibal Lecter that the Academy in their wisdom put his performance into the main category. This of course allowed the film to become only the third film in history, and still the last, to win all top five Oscars. It's certainly the only one I've been able to see at the cinema on the big screen, and so I'll forgive the Academy their rather relaxed approach to categorisation.

I'd first seen Anthony Hopkins in a TV movie of "The Hunchback of Notre Dame", one where I had no idea of who any of the actors were as I was only about seven or eight at the time. As with "The African Queen", I'd been flicking through the three TV channels available to me and became engrossed in this classic story, with the lovely Lesley-Anne Down as Esmeralda. Maybe it was her face which hypnotised me, but the sight of Hopkins' Quasimodo was riveting and heart breaking, causing me to cry profusely at the end if I remember rightly.

I must have seen him as Bligh in "The Bounty" as my mum and dad used to watch that film every Bank Holiday Monday it would seem, so I must have sat there with them too. I also remember him in "The Good Father" and another TV movie "The Tenth Man", an adaptation of a Graham Greene novel. And of course I had seen him in "The Elephant Man", as the kindly Dr. Frederick Treves, the man who helps John Merrick overcome his fears and see himself as a man and not just a freak of a man, in another film which had me sobbing profusely.

But it was always "The Silence of the Lambs" in which Hopkins really came to my attention, as John Hurt's performance as John Merrick overshadowed that of Hopkins in "The Elephant Man". This film was the start of Hopkins' golden age, in which he became hands down the greatest screen actor in the world for a few years in the early 1990s.

Obviously his role as Hannibal Lecter gets all the attention, but it is his performances in three later films which I want to focus on now, three films which are as about as English as they come, with the stiffest of upper lips being employed, upper lips which nearly falter in the first two of these, but then finally giving way in the third, causing millions of other lips to give way too, mine certainly included, into sobs and genuine tears. This is of course ironic seeing as these most English of roles are played by one of the fieriest Welshmen ever. Hopkins is in the same vein as Richard Burton, both hard drinkers, both known for their tempers, both born in the same town, Port Talbot, along with another superlative actor in Michael Sheen. Whatever is in the water in Port Talbot, it certainly worked. Maybe it wasn't water at all, just whiskey.

The first of these films was "Howard's End", playing Henry Wilcox, alongside Emma Thompson, who won the first of her two Oscars for her portrayal of Margaret Schlegel, who eventually marries Wilcox. Her other Oscar, for Best Screenplay, was for a film which will definitely get a mention later.

The two would star in another Merchant/Ivory film, perhaps the best film of theirs ever, and one which both Hopkins and Thompson should have won Oscars again. "The Remains of the Day" is the most English of films, which is why these two artists had to be so good. The restraint they both have to show in a world of tradition, manners, morality, class, and even more tradition is pure perfection in terms of acting. The scene in which Miss Kenton is trying to find out what Stevens is reading, teasing him ever so slightly, and ever so slightly flirting with him at the same time, is one of the most beautifully acted scenes in any film of any era. It is touching, heart breaking and so subtly nuanced that whenever I watch it, I know I am watching a true work of art.

Hopkins next work of art, the third of this English trilogy if you will, is "Shadowlands", Dickie Attenborough's beautiful portrayal of C.S. Lewis, author of "The Tales of Narnia", and how his rather passionless existence is broken down by his love for the poet Joy Gresham, played magnificently by Debra Winger. Despite getting married to her in a marriage of pure convenience, he realises that he does love her, and as his love for her grows, so does his emotionless façade slip, which is why it is so gut wrenchingly awful at the end of the film when Joy dies and Lewis breaks down himself.

I challenge anyone with an ounce of emotion or empathy in them not to weep at these scenes, particularly with Joy's son (played by Joseph Mazzello, who had sprung to fame as the little boy in "Jurassic Park"). The bedside scenes are some of, if not the most agonising, the most painful, and the most honest I have ever witnessed on screen. Ever.

These three films of Anthony Hopkins, particularly his roles as Stevens the butler and C.S. Lewis are up there with the greatest pieces of acting of all time. Of course there have been performances by other actors to rival and match these by Hopkins, but I doubt there has been one, certainly not two performances in the same year, that have been better. As I said earlier, Hopkins, at that point, was at the pinnacle of not just his own acting career, but the pinnacle of the craft of acting itself.

But of course, these most human of roles always seem to get overshadowed by his role as a psychotic, almost demonic sociopath who likes to eat his victims with some fava beans and a nice Chianti.

Such is life I suppose.

The Exorcist (1973)   Dir: William Friedkin

From a human with demonic tendencies, to a demon with human tendencies. This film, like "A Clockwork Orange", was still banned in 1992 when I first saw it. It was banned on video at least which is why I'd never been able to see it, which of course intrigued me even more, and made the chance to see it on the big screen even more appealing.

The BBFC in its wisdom had ensured that "The Exorcist" was removed from video shelves after it had been available to rent on video since its release in this format in 1981. Basically the censors bowed to public pressure and agreed that the film was just too darn scary for younger viewers, and so would only be available in cinemas with a strictly upheld 18 certificate.

It had never been shown anywhere near where I lived before I got to university, but the best thing about Reading was that it was close enough to London to go there for the day, or even just go for the evening. "The Exorcist" had gained almost mythical status for me, so when I saw that it was being screened at one of the cinemas around Leicester Square as a midnight showing, my girlfriend and I jumped at the chance. As if this film wasn't going to be scary enough, we thought we'd make a double bill of it and go and see another pretty terrifying film too. Both films, although not pretty, were certainly terrifying.

Martin Scorsese had just released his first mainstream thriller, "Cape Fear" in March 1992, a remake of the 1962 original starring Gregory Peck and Robert Mitchum, both of whom would be given cameo appearances by Scorsese in his version, with Nick Nolte playing the harassed lawyer this time, and who else but Robert De Niro playing the vengeful Max Cady. All these ingredients were enough to make us very keen indeed to see this film, and it even had the added bonus of Jessica Lange, my first ever film crush, as Nolte's wife, who had got sexier if anything. She had been sexy to an extent in "King Kong", but in "Cape Fear", her sultriness and middle aged womanliness was somehow now more appealing than her rather girlish and innocent persona whilst getting carried around by a huge ape.

So, we thought we would go into London and catch both films, not knowing how we were going to get back to Reading in the early hours of the morning. We didn't care; we were going to see a new film by one of my favourite directors, and a film which would become one of my all-time favourites, whether it was banned or not.

"Cape Fear", part one of our fright night extravaganza, was exactly what I had hoped for and expected. De Niro plays the recently released convicted rapist Max Cady with ease, his outward charms masking his simmering anger and vengefulness. Many scenes are memorable, but the one I remember most vividly is the one which involves no violence, no shocks, and no brutality at all, which somehow made it even more disturbing and unsettling.

The scene I refer to is when Cady pretends to be the new drama teacher of Nolte's daughter, played by Juliette Lewis, and they share a deeply unnerving moment of intimacy alone in the drama studio, with Cady kissing her and putting his thumb in her mouth. The feeling that teenage innocence is being corrupted, and that the teenager is a willing partaker in the seduction is the most troubling and unsettling aspect of the scene. Scorsese and De Niro proved yet again that they knew exactly how to get the most uneasiness out of such a low key scene, as they had done when Scorsese himself had been Travis Bickle's passenger in his taxi fifteen years previously.

The rest of the film piled on the suspense, and once it had reached its climax, with Cady speaking in tongues as the boat he is handcuffed to sinks, something else very unsettling to say the least, we came out of the cinema suitably scared and into the bright lights of Leicester Square. We were well in need of something to eat and a couple of drinks by now, which our hour long interval gave us time to do, before commencing with part two of fright night.

The name "fright night" is usually used with horror films which are just lazy, and assume that by just splashing blood everywhere, having lots of screaming, and having lots of gory death scenes, the gorier the better, then that will frighten their audiences. The two films we watched that night had none of those, which is exactly why they are much better horror films, if indeed they can be classed as horror films in the first place. Whatever genre they fit into, they are just plain scary.

Now that "The Exorcist" has been allowed to be released on video again, I remember everyone renting it as soon as they could, with many of the kids I was teaching at the time saying that it wasn't that scary at all, and was nowhere near as scary as some gore fest schlocker like "Saw".

But to me, when I saw it at midnight one dark and chilly Saturday evening in the centre of London, "The Exorcist" was the scariest film I had ever seen. Maybe it was the almost mythical status I'd already given it due to its ban. Maybe it was the strange surroundings, being in a huge city where I had rarely been before, certainly not at midnight. Maybe it was the fact I didn't know how I was going to get back to the safety of little old Reading. Whatever it was, I was petrified by that film.

Right from the start, with the almost dazzling brightness of the opening scene in Iraq, with a sense of foreboding and a real presence of evil being felt, it scared me, and continued to do so once it moved to the streets of Georgetown. The opening scene had unsettled me so much that even the apparent scratching sounds in the attic petrified me. Not knowing what was going to happen, how and when the demon would manifest itself, or what the effects on poor, sweet and innocent Regan would be were what unsettled me the most.

There was never a real and palpable sense of fear in the film; it does not have many moments of pure shock at all, but it was the genuinely psychologically disturbing atmosphere of foreboding and sinister, underlying threat which constantly gnawed away at my nerves, twisting my stomach around, much like the demon itself does to Regan's insides.

The creepiest scenes are the quietest ones. For example when Regan is asleep and the words "Help Me" are discovered on the skin of her stomach, or when Father Karras is talking alone with Regan and the demon conjures up the voice of Karras' recently deceased mother. These scenes for me were the scariest because not that much happened.

All the scenes with furniture flying around, and vile green vomit being spurted out rather violently, or indeed the now infamous crucifix masturbation scene are all too overblown to be genuinely scary. They are shocking, but not particularly frightening. The fear comes from not what is in the bedroom, but from the anticipation of going in there to find out. As the priests walk grimly upstairs before actually entering the bedroom is when the real feeling of horror and genuine fear occurs. True fear lies in the unknown and the unseen, which William Friedkin knew all too well.

So, by the end of the film, and our double header of doom had finished, we found ourselves once again in the heart of London, but this time genuinely paranoid about our mental well-being. This was not due to the fact that we were now stranded in London, with the first train back not leaving for another few hours, but because we had just experienced something so profoundly disturbing that it had actually affected us emotionally. Well, it certainly did to me.

We must have wandered the streets of London, or found an all-night café or bar until we could get the train back to the now even safer streets of Reading, and got back to our rooms to thankfully find that our beds were not being thrown up and down, and that none of our friends' heads were able to turn around 360 degrees. I've always found it more comforting to have friends whose heads don't do that, and so we decided that would be enough scariness for that year thank you very much and decided we would move on in my cinematic journey onto much less freaky, and much less paranoia inducing types of film.

Luckily, we found the perfect video shop to do that. I'll tell you all about it during the intermission. So, get yourself a lolly, top up your popcorn, make as many juvenile noises with your straws as you want, and go to the toilet if you need to. Just make sure you wash your hands please.

Intermission

During our third term of our first year at university, those of us who wanted to leave our hall of residence and fend for ourselves in a shared house were required to actually find a house for the following year, and forego the delights of our tiny little box rooms and shared bathrooms. Myself and four other mates found ourselves an adequate dump of a house, whilst my girlfriend found a much nicer little house with a few of her friends. To get to her house would mean a fifteen minute walk, but in between our two houses we would discover the most awesome collection of films we had ever seen.

The video shop I speak of was owned and run by a lovely old man who had the most encyclopaedic knowledge of films that even surpassed my girlfriend's. His shop was filled with probably what were his own private collection of films, which he had decided to share with the world, and make a living from.

The shop was like our own almost private version of a very rudimentary Netflix. The only difference being that we had to physically go out to choose what films we wanted to watch, and certainly didn't need a broadband connection. That was where the fun lay for us, the browsing, and the actual process of choosing, looking at the video covers and the blurbs, finding out so much about the films themselves, their directors, and their stars.

The films would be either sorted into genres, or by director, or by leading actor, and my girlfriend and I worked our way through most of the shop, with her watching many for the second or third time, and me definitely discovering them for the first time.

To aid with my cinematic education, I invested in a few books about the Hollywood greats of the studio golden age, and got to know as much as I could about these great films, these great directors, and these great stars. From screwball comedy to Film Noir, from Howard Hawks to John Ford, from Claudette Colbert to Marilyn Monroe, from RKO to MGM musicals, I devoured as many films as I could.

During this hugely significant and influential period of my life, my brother and I were writing letters to each other, keeping up to date with each other's lives as I was now so far away from home. He had always been a very good artist, particularly pencil drawings, and he would often include with his letters a drawing he had done for me of these classic film stars which I then framed and hung on my new bedroom wall.

The drawings of the more classic stars are showing signs of age now, as I suppose the stars depicted in them are. They have been on my walls for many years after all, so please excuse the lack of pristine quality. I love the authenticity the ageing gives to them, whereas the more modern stars were drawn much more recently, showing not only a lack of ageing, but also an improvement in my brother's technique. To me, the earlier pictures are so evocative, imperfections and all, making them even more special. The fact that they were hand drawn by my brother makes them extra special.

Anyway, during this intermission, whilst you're enjoying your drink and eating your ice cream from a little tub, have a look at some of the pictures my brother sent to me over the course of that second year at university. Most, if not all of the stars he drew for me are featured in the films which have already been, or will be discussed in the rest of the book.

I hope you enjoy them. They mean a lot to me.

Lauren Bacall 1955

Charlie Chaplin 1918

Joan Crawford 1935

Katherine Hepburn 1937

212

Errol Flynn 1938

Gloria Swanson 1933

Grace Kelly 1955

Barbara Stanwyck 1939

Olivia de Havilland 1936

Claire Trevor 1933

Spencer Tracey 1933

214

 Humphrey Bogart 1945

 Henry Fonda 1935

 Clark Gable 1933

 Cary Grant 1958

215

Rita Hayworth 1952

Veronica Lake 1945

Carole Lombard 1937

216

Ida Lupino 1940

Marilyn Monroe 1958

Gregory Peck 1969

217

Cameron Diaz

Angelina Jolie

Beyoncé Knowles

Al Pacino Marlon Brando   Jessica Alba

Welcome back, and I hope you washed your hands. I also hope you've turned your phones off again, something that the audiences of these next films never had to do.

It would be an actual crime if this first film were to be disturbed in any way whatsoever, especially by a ringtone. I give you my all-time favourite film, by my all-time favourite director.

If you haven't seen it, then you must.

Mr. Deeds Goes to Town (1936)   Dir: Frank Capra

I mentioned earlier about hating Adam Sandler, and this film is the reason for my probably unfair antagonism towards him. I'm a bit like Ken Kesey, who famously refused to watch "One Flew Over the Cuckoo's Nest", as I refuse to watch the remake of the Frank Capra original. If it ain't broke, don't fix it! And this film certainly ain't broke.

After falling in love with "It's a Wonderful Life", "Mr. Deeds Goes to Town", was not the first Capra film I wanted to watch once we discovered our little shop of wonders, with classic films crying out to be watched from every shelf in the video shop. One of the books I had invested in was a year by year account of the films that had made the headlines each year since the Oscars had started in 1929. I obviously picked up quickly that the first film to win all top five Oscars, "It Happened One Night", happened only five years later in 1934, and so that was the priority for me.

I realised just what a great comic performer Clark Gable was, and just how lovely Claudette Colbert's legs were in the famous hitch-hiking scene. I also discovered how Gable had basically been the cause of men no longer wearing vests after he shockingly revealed himself not to be wearing one in the film's

220

final scene, when the Walls of Jericho finally fall, allowing the two stars to finally make union as it were.

Capra had worked with Claudette Colbert years before in his early silent film days, in the 1927 "For the Love of Mike" before working with some of the true greats such as Douglas Fairbanks Jr., Barbara Stanwyck, Fay Wray before she became the object of King Kong's desire, and Jean Harlow in the film which would provide her with her nickname, "Platinum Blonde". But it was the huge success of "It Happened One Night", which would catapult her to true stardom, as it did with anyone connected with the film.

We then watched another of Capra's more screwball of comedies, "Arsenic and Old Lace", with Cary Grant discovering that his new bride's relatives are not quite so friendly after all. We went back to some of Capra's earlier work, with "The Bitter Tea of General Yen" and "Lost Horizon" not making much of an impact on me, until I finally discovered the film which would become so important for me, and consequently cause my dislike for Adam Sandler.

"Mr. Deeds Goes to Town" is perfect. Right from the start, the way that Capra wastes no time in setting the story in motion with a car crashing recklessly off a bridge before a montage of newspaper front pages get us all up to speed. The phrase "up to speed" is very apt here, as within a minute, the film's narrative has been set up perfectly, allowing us to wait anxiously to meet Longfellow Deeds, the man who is about to inherit $20 million, despite being unaware of what this will actually mean for him.

The story of how he is taken to the big city of New York from sleepy little Mandrake Falls, and how the vultures in the big city attempt to use him for their own selfish ends, including at first the rather mercenary Babe Bennett, played by the lovely Jean Arthur, is just wonderful. His bodyguard is played by Lionel Stander, who would go onto play Max in "Hart to Hart", providing the iconic voiceover on the show's opening credits ("It was moyder!"), and even a hard-nosed cynic like his character of Corny Cobb is taken in by the spell of Gary Cooper's innocence and childlike perspective on the world.

Someone else who falls under his spell is Jean Arthur, who has been writing sarcastic and mocking articles for the newspaper, whilst pretending to be a damsel in distress who Deeds saves and falls in love with. She dubs him the "Cinderella Man", but she most definitely becomes enchanted by him in the most beautiful of scenes where Deeds reads the poem he has been working on to her, which is worth quoting in full here:

"I tramped the earth with hopeless beat
Searching in vain for a glimpse of you.
Then heaven thrust you at my very feet--
A lovely angel, too lovely to woo.

My dream has been answered
But my life's just as bleak.
I'm handcuffed and speechless in your presence divine.

For my heart longs to cry out,
If it only could speak,
'I love you, my angel. Be mine. Be mine.'"

At that point he becomes so nervous that he runs off, crashing into some rubbish bins in his innocent devotion to the woman he has no idea has been tricking him.

Longfellow Deeds quickly learns some deep truths about life in New York, which is of course a metaphor for the world of experience compared to the world of innocence where he grew up. He tells his love Mary Dawson, who Jean Arthur is pretending to be, that *"people here are funny. They work so hard at living they forget how to live. Last night, after I left you, I was walking along and - and lookin' at the tall buildings, and I got to thinking about what Thoreau said. 'They created a lot of grand palaces here, but they forgot to create the noblemen to put in them.' I'd rather have Mandrake Falls."*

Once he realises that life in New York is not quite so sweet and innocent as he first hoped it would be, and he decides to give his newly acquired fortune away to help others suffering in The Great Depression of the 1930s, he is obviously considered insane to want to do such a thing. If a man wants to help others, then he must be mad, which makes the film as relevant today as it was then. He is put on trial to prove his insanity, and this is where some of the most powerful and profound lines come in, ones which again we could learn a lot from today.

The trial scene is a brilliant mix of both humour and profound truths, delivered by Gary Cooper in the most innocent yet experienced of ways, along with Jean Arthur, who now defends the man she has fallen in love with too, telling the judge, *"He could never fit in with our distorted viewpoint. Because he's honest, and sincere, and good. If that man's crazy, your honour, the rest of us belong in straitjackets!"*

Cooper's defence of why he wants to give his money away, from his childish, yet extremely sage perspective, should, like George Bailey's outburst in "It's a Wonderful Life", be at the heart of any government's policy:

"From what I can see, no matter what system of government we have, there will always be leaders and always be followers. It's like the road out in front of my house. It's on a steep hill. Every

day I watch the cars climbing up. Some go lickety-split up that hill on high, some have to shift into second, and some sputter and shake and slip back to the bottom again. Same cars, same gasoline, yet some make it, and some don't. And I say the fellas who can make the hill on high should stop once in a while and help those who can't. That's all I'm trying to do with this money. Help the fellas who can't make the hill on high."

He backs this most common sense and kind approach up with another piece of Solomonesque wisdom:

"It's like I'm out in a big boat, and I see one fellow in a rowboat who's tired of rowing and wants a free ride, and another fellow who's drowning. Who would you expect me to rescue? Mr. Cedar - who's just tired of rowing and wants a free ride? Or those men out there who are drowning? Any ten-year-old child will give you the answer to that."

These lines are so simple yet so powerful. Along with the hilarious comic scenes, and the general air of kindness and positivity from Deeds, they are the reason this film is my favourite, and as I said earlier, is why everyone should watch it, and why Adam Sandler should just leave well alone. But I suppose if his remake makes others go and discover the original film, then at least he's achieved that, so maybe I am being overly harsh to Sandler after all. It's just that "Mr. Deeds Goes to Town" is just too important to me for it to be messed with.

The film provided Frank Capra with the film's only Oscar, the second of his three Best Director Oscars, but to me, it should have followed up the success of "It Happened One Night" and taken a clean sweep of all top five awards, particularly Robert Riskin's astonishing screenplay.

Since doing some research for this book, I discovered another reason for me to love this film even more. When the cinema in Lancaster, the one which I saw "Star Wars" and "E.T." in, the one my Gran took me to so many times when I was a small boy, first opened in 1936, the first ever film to be screened there was "Mr. Deeds Goes To Town". I'd like to think that my then thirteen year old Gran queued in anticipation down the street to be a part of the film's first ever audience in Lancaster, and enjoyed its delights and charms, just as I would enjoy them almost sixty years later. I wouldn't be surprised if she had, which makes me love not only her, but the film itself, even more.

The adjective "Capraesque" took on a new meaning for me from that point on, and so this next film needed to be watched as soon as possible, which just so happened to be the next day. It is another film which every politician needs to watch.

Not just every politician, but every member of the human race.

Mr. Smith Goes to Washington (1939)   Dir: Frank Capra

After Longfellow Deeds, and consequently, I, had fallen in love with Jean Arthur, and seeing as I had already fallen in love with James Stewart with just his opening shot in "It's a Wonderful Life", then this film, which starred both of them, looked as though it would challenge the top spot for my new favourite film. It almost did, but not quite.

The story of a wide eyed local boy scout master who gets elected to the Senate, essentially to be the puppet for the Potteresque and corrupt Jim Taylor, who has already blackened the heart of the once innocent Senator Joseph Paine, played brilliantly by Claude Rains, is a metaphor for all political corruption.

Frank Capra would be turning in his grave if he knew that the despicable, narcissistic, corrupt, selfish, heartless, (the list of unsavoury adjectives could go on for a long time) Donald Trump held the highest and most powerful office in not just America, but probably the whole world. Capra would not just be turning in his grave, but spinning at a rate of knots which would make him resemble a lathe. Trump is the antithesis of everything this film stands for, which is just one of the many reasons I despise Trump so much, and love this film so much

Capra's vision, although schmaltzy and rather naïve at times, is needed now more than ever, which is why this film was watched not just by me, but by thousands of people around the world on the day of Trump's election victory in 2016, as a way of holding onto some scrap of hope that things can, and indeed will be better again. I didn't need to watch the film when Barack Obama was elected, as he provided the necessary hope himself. Instead I just enjoyed watching his inauguration with the same sense of wonder as Jefferson Smith has in his eyes when he arrives in Washington and goes on an impromptu sightseeing tour, much to the dismay of those entrusted with looking after him, most notably Jean Arthur's Political Aide to Joseph Paine.

Jean Arthur's portrayal of Saunders is essentially the same as that of Babe Bennett in "Mr. Deeds Goes to Town", a worldly wise urbanite who eventually falls under the spell of our hero, even revealing her first name to Jefferson Smith, with her revelation that she does have a first name too, the very pretty name of Clarissa, being symbolic of her hard exterior breaking down in the face of Smith's callow charms and inexhaustible positivity.

She develops, or rather, rediscovers, her heart throughout the course of the film, and ends up changing her cynical viewpoint, and defending her new hero in the face of the mighty political machine which has so hardened her. The same also happens to

Joseph Paine, when he realises that his corruption is so deep that his protégé's refusal to be corrupted in the same way he was, actually makes him want to kill himself. Truth will always conquer lies, good will overcome evil, and hope will be the victor over despair. And despite those three positives seeming like dirty words right now under Trump's presidency, we have to believe that Capra's message is still possible.

The film has so many memorable scenes, with the filibuster scene being the most obviously powerful one, and one which includes the following lines, lines that are genuinely profound:

"I wouldn't give you two cents for all your fancy rules if, behind them, they didn't have a little bit of plain, ordinary, everyday kindness and a - a little lookin' out for the other fella, too...That's pretty important, all that. It's just the blood and bone and sinew of this democracy that some great men handed down to the human race, that's all."

"That lady that's up on top of this Capitol dome, that lady that stands for liberty. Take a look at this country through her eyes if you really want to see something... And you won't just see scenery; you'll see the whole parade of what Man's carved out for himself, after centuries of fighting. Fighting for something better than just jungle law, fighting so's he can stand on his own two feet, free and decent, like he was created, no matter what his race, colour, or creed. That's what you'd see. There's no place out there for graft, or greed, or lies, or compromise with human liberties. And, uh, if that's what the grownups have done with this world that was given to them, then we'd better get those boys' camps started fast and see what the kids can do. And it's not too late, because this country is bigger than the Taylors, or you, or me, or anything else. Great principles don't get lost once they come to light. They're right here; you just have to see them again!"

"I guess this is just another lost cause, Mr. Paine. All you people don't know about lost causes. Mr. Paine does. He said once they were the only causes worth fighting for, and he fought for them once, for the only reason any man ever fights for them: Because of one plain simple rule: Love thy neighbour. And in this world today, full of hatred, a man who knows that one rule has a great trust."

I told you they were powerful!

But it is the scene when Smith stands in front of Lincoln's statue, watching the old immigrant's grandson recite the Declaration of Independence, with a tear in his eye, which is not only profoundly moving, but profoundly symbolic, and one which is at the very heart of the foundations of America, and one which is insulted by Trump's absurd notion of building a wall to keep these so called aliens out of the country which his own grandfather had emigrated to.

Trump shows how the American Dream can turn not just sour, but bitter and twisted. Jefferson Smith's vision of what the American Dream means is something to hold onto. Yes it is an ideal, possibly an unobtainable ideal, but the principles on which the country was founded still need to be upheld in practice, not just in words. It is these principles which made America great in the first place, and so Trump's rabid desire to "Make America Great Again", would only be achieved if he actually went through with what Claude Rains' Joseph Paine was stopped from doing at the end of the film.

Maybe I am just being too idealistic, but I'd rather be too idealistic than a cynic. I'd rather my politicians were more like Jefferson Smith than Donald Trump, and even if they only exist on screen, they still need to exist to give all us people who care about other people some sort of hope, something that Frank Capra certainly has given to me.

The trilogy of films, starting with "Mr. Deeds Goes to Town", through to "Mr. Smith Goes to Washington", and ending with "It's a Wonderful Life", created the meaning of the adjective "Capraesque". The three heroes of each film, Longfellow Deeds, Jefferson Smith, and George Bailey, are the yard stick which I have tried to measure myself against in my own life. There are elements to these characters in my own life. I was a young, callow and naïve young man who went to the big city and found my own damsel in distress, and have created a family life which hopefully is not just loyal, loving, brave and honest, but also kind. I just hope that Frank Capra himself would approve of what I have achieved with my own family and my own outlook on life. I think he just might.

Capra never bettered these films. James Stewart and Jean Arthur had already teamed up in "You Can't Take it With You", but did not have the same impact as their collaboration a year later would have on me. Similarly, Capra tried to recreate the success of Deeds, with "Meet John Doe" in 1941, with Gary Cooper again playing an innocent and honest Deeds like character, this time with Barbara Stanwyck in the Jean Arthur role. Perhaps it is the absence of Jean Arthur this time which caused this film not to have the same impact on me, or maybe it was the fact that Longfellow Deeds could not be recreated and so viewed the later film with a certain suspicion.

For me, "Deeds", "Smith" and "Life" are the most wonderful of trilogies, even though they are not strictly speaking a trilogy. Each film in itself is a masterpiece, but put them all together, then you have something so wonderful, so pure, so life affirming that if I had to choose only one film to take to my desert island, it would definitely come from these three.

If only there could be some way of combining them into one film, with the hero being called something like Longsmith Bailey. Now he's a man I would like to meet. He'd not only be the best of men, but he'd make a pretty good president too.

If only, if only…

Bringing Up Baby (1938)   **Dir: Howard Hawks**

I'm not sure how to categorise the next set of films, as back in the 1930s and 40s, with the Studio system basically deciding which films should be made, who would direct them, and who would star in them, there are so many different genres, with directors and actors spanning across them all. I suppose I'm having the same difficulty the old man who owned the video shop we rented most of these films from must have had. Do I tackle them by genre, by director, or by starring roles? Let's just see what happens.

One director who seemed to be a master of whatever genre he took on was Howard Hawks. One of his earliest films was the original "Scarface" of 1932, a classic of the gangster genre, with Paul Muni playing Tony Camonte, loosely based on Al Capone. I had this taped from the TV and was one of the many videos I lovingly alphabetised on my shelves. When my housemates were looking for something to watch themselves, they would often raid my stack of films I had taped, and rarely, if ever, chose any of the old black and white classics. But this film would be one that was chosen by them, thinking they were going to be seeing Al Pacino, with his head in a pile of cocaine, demanding that we "Say hello to my little friend". They were not quite as thrilled when they found out it was not that version of the film. Hawks' original, along with William Wellman's "The Public Enemy", starring James Cagney, set the bar very high when it came to gangster movies, films which Scorsese, Coppola and De Palma owe a huge amount to.

The romantic adventure "Only Angels Have Wings", with Cary Grant alongside Jean Arthur would introduce me to another beauty, that of Rita Hayworth in one of the films which would help to break her into the mainstream and become the movie goddess she was.

Hawks' additions to the Western genre are also pretty high on the list of all time greats in this most American of genres, with 1959's "Rio Bravo", starring John Wayne, and most notably 1948's "Red River", again with Wayne, and introducing me to Montgomery Clift, being absolute classics of the genre.

His Film Noirs were also seminal masterpieces of the genre. The two films he made with Humphrey Bogart and Lauren Bacall, namely "To Have and Have Not" and "The Big Sleep" are genre defining, along with John Huston's "The Maltese Falcon" and "Key Largo" in which Huston and Bogart's relationship would be formed before they would go onto make the aforementioned "The African Queen" together. "To Have and Have Not" would introduce us all to Lauren Bacall, who at the age of just nineteen seemed to know not only how to whistle, but also the sexual connotations of putting your lips together and blowing.

"The Big Sleep" would also introduce everyone to the Lolita figure of Martha Vickers and the concept of sitting in Bogart's lap whilst still standing up, a scene which demonstrates the raw sexuality of these classic Film Noirs perfectly, a sexuality which never requires any item of clothing ever being removed, but a sexuality which is bristling with desire and intent.

Hawks was not content at making seminal films in the Gangster, Western and Film Noir genres, but he could also make a pretty good musical too, with "Gentleman Prefer Blondes" with Jane Russell and Marilyn Monroe being the two little girls from Little Rock, who come from the wrong side of the track. It was as though whatever genre he was given, he just came up with a classic of that particular genre almost at the throw of a hat, which of course was not the case. He was a true craftsman of film, and could put his skills to perfect use with whatever screenplay or star he was given to work with.

It is Hawks' comic films which I want to focus on, in particular the genre of comic films which became known as Screwball Comedies. These films were very popular during the Depression of the 1930s, as an antidote to the grim reality of ordinary people's hardships, with Frank Capra's "It Happened One Night" being one of the earliest and most successful films of the subgenre. Along with "My Man Godfrey" of two years later, starring William Powell and possibly the most iconic star of the screwball age, Carole Lombard, the Screwball Comedy satirised traditional love stories, with the female stars dominating the relationships, with slapstick and fast paced witty repartee all adding to the idea of the films being sex comedies without the sex.

Preston Sturges would also add to the genre with three brilliant films: "The Lady Eve", with Henry Fonda and Barbara Stanwyck, "Sullivan's Travels" with Joel McCrea and Veronica Lake, and "The Palm Beach Story", again with Joel McCrea and Claudette Colbert, showing she was still a major star eight years after she won her Oscar for "It Happened One Night".

McCrea would go onto star in one of my favourite comedies ever, Screwball or not, in George Stevens' "The More the Merrier", with my old flame Jean Arthur starring alongside Charles Coburn and his desire to "Damn the torpedoes, full steam ahead." Maybe it was just seeing Jean Arthur again which makes it onto my list of favourites, but the film is another great example of what makes a perfect Screwball Comedy, and the scene in which McCrea and Arthur kiss almost rivals the poem scene in "Mr. Deeds Goes to Town" for romanticism and loveliness.

Howard Hawks' contributions to the genre are, quite frankly, astonishing. His first attempt at the genre became genre defining once more, with Carole Lombard starring in "Twentieth Century", before he would go onto make the film which this chapter gets its title from.

"Bringing Up Baby", with Cary Grant as the rather bumbling palaeontologist David Huxley, is the story of how an unsuspecting man can become smitten with the charms of someone he thought would never be on his radar, especially as she has a pet leopard, the "Baby" of the title, in tow too. Cary Grant becomes involved unwittingly with the scatter-brained Susan, played brilliantly by Katharine Hepburn, in a role she delivered flawlessly, proving she could, like Hawks himself, do any genre of film to perfection.

The story of how Susan's dog steals and buries Huxley's intercostal clavicle, a crucial bone in the brontosaurus skeleton he is working on, leading to much hilarity, is the first Screwball Comedy I first watched, and what an introduction it was to the genre. Grant's line of *"Now it isn't that I don't like you Susan, because, after all, in moments of quiet, I'm strangely drawn toward you, but – well, there haven't been any quiet moments"* not only sums up the madcap pace of the film, but also the charm which Hepburn exudes. It could also be a line I could use toward my youngest daughter too. Even though my daughter does not have a pet leopard, she is certainly a whirlwind who at times has turned my life, not to mention my house, upside down.

Grant and Hepburn would team up again two years later in George Cukor's "The Philadelphia Story", with James Stewart in tow this time, in another perfect example of the Screwball Comedy, and Grant would go onto make some of the finest comedies ever with Howard Hawks, most notably "His Girl Friday" alongside Rosalind Russell, "I Was a Male War Bride", this time with Ann Sheridan, and then "Monkey Business" with Ginger Rogers taking off her dancing shoes, and Marilyn Monroe in one of her most successful earlier films as the female stars.

It's hard to name a Howard Hawks' film which can't be listed as an all-time great, not just in the particular genre he was working in at the time, but films in general. His contribution to cinema is huge. To put it simply and matter-of-factly, many of the greatest films of all time, whether made by him or not, owe him a huge debt, as do the films of the man who directed this next film, another cross genre expert, and one who would also provide career defining moments for many of his leading actors, Marilyn Monroe included.

But this man, unlike Hawks, was born in Austria, and yet made one of the biggest contributions to American cinema ever. Bloody immigrants, coming to America, making life changing films for the whole world to enjoy!

Double Indemnity (1944)   **Dir: Billy Wilder**

Billy Wilder was an Austrian born Jew who, whilst still in his twenties, was already prophetic, realising the dangers Adolf Hitler posed to him, and got the hell out of there, moving to America via Paris in 1933, and went on to have one of the finest careers in film there has ever been. Most, if not all of his films, can safely be called true classics, with many of them becoming entrenched aspects of popular culture and twentieth century iconography. His own personal living of The American Dream is exactly what it was meant to be, so suck on that Trump!

Wilder's first significant success was not as a director, but as a writer, co-writing the screenplay for "Ninotchka", starring the great Greta Garbo, before making an instant impact as a director with "Double Indemnity", one of the noirest of Film Noirs ever. I loved it, and it is definitely my favourite in that genre, mainly because of Barbara Stanwyck being the ultimate in femmes fatales, but also because of Edward G. Robinson and Fred MacMurray's roles, as Barton Keyes and Walter Neff, respectively.

The film is narrated by a man who is literally minutes away from dying, confessing his crimes into a Dictaphone, as he waits for his colleague and nemesis to discover him. Wilder would go one step further with this narrative technique six years later in "Sunset Boulevard", another brilliant Film Noir, but this time the narrator of the film is actually dead, reviewing events from the grave so to speak, as we are introduced to his dead body floating face down in a swimming pool in the opening scene. The technique would also go onto be used much later in Sam Mendes' "American Beauty" with Kevin Spacey narrating the story even though he's had his brains blown out already.

"Double Indemnity", makes even insurance salesmen seem sexy and edgy, or at least Barbara Stanwyck's bored housewife Phyllis Dietrichson seems to think so. The sexiest Phyllis I'd certainly come across wants to dispose of her husband and inherit his wealth, and so ropes her husband's insurance guy into the crime, with a little help from "a honey of an anklet", which Fred MacMurray's Walter Neff can't help but notice. This line is parodied in another film already dealt with, in "The Naked Gun" when Leslie Nielsen's Frank Drebin comments on Jane's similar piece of jewellery, "That's a honey of an ankle bracelet you have

235

there", to which Jane replies, "Did it slip down there again?" You know you've made a good film when it is being parodied over forty years later.

Once Phyllis has hooked her man, she reels him in. In fact she doesn't really have to reel him in as he is the most willing of catches ever. The dialogue between the two in their first meeting is the perfect example of Film Noir slickness, with an undercurrent of sexual tension and humour. The exchange goes like this:

Phyllis: Mr. Neff, why don't you drop by tomorrow evening around 8:30? He'll be in then.
Walter: Who?
Phyllis: My husband. You were anxious to talk to him, weren't you?
Walter: Yes, I was. But I'm sort of getting over the idea, if you know what I mean.
Phyllis: There's a speed limit in this state, Mr. Neff. Forty-five miles an hour.
Walter: How fast was I going, officer?
Phyllis: I'd say around ninety.
Walter: Suppose you get down off your motorcycle and give me a ticket.
Phyllis: Suppose I let you off with a warning this time.
Walter: Suppose it doesn't take.
Phyllis: Suppose I have to whack you over the knuckles.
Walter: Suppose I bust out crying and put my head on your shoulder.
Phyllis: Suppose you try putting it on my husband's shoulder.
Walter: That tears it.

That sort of cracking and crackling dialogue permeates the whole screenplay, also written by Wilder, with a little help from the novel's author James M. Cain, and a certain other renowned author, the Godfather of Film Noir fiction himself, Raymond Chandler.

The only flaw in the film itself, if it even is a flaw, is the worst plan ever to murder Phyllis' husband and try to claim double indemnity on the insurance, as he would need to fall off a very slow moving train in order to do so, a fall of about two feet, something which basically anyone would survive, especially as the train is only moving at fifteen miles an hour. But the murder plan, about as water tight as a sieve, shows just how besotted and crazy Neff has become with the sultry charms of Phyllis.

The plan also means that the two cannot be seen together, and resort to meeting up casually in a supermarket, whispering their desires for each other in amongst the tinned vegetables, a scene which is brilliantly used in "Dead Men Don't Wear Plaid", Steve Martin's Film Noir homage mentioned earlier in this book.

The murderers' plot obviously fails, as Phyllis just gets bored and moves onto a younger sucker, one who does not require secret meetings in the fruit and veg aisle, and the two end up killing each other, using the same gun to finally put an end to the trolley car ride in which there was no getting off until the end of the line where the cemetery was. But before he actually dies, Neff has time to at least confess his crimes and misdemeanours, *"Yes, I killed him. I killed him for money and for a woman. I didn't get the money and I didn't get the woman. Pretty, isn't it?"*

It is the perfect way to end a perfect film, with Neff struggling to light his final cigarette, before Barton Keyes finally lights it for him, striking the match on his thumb, as Neff had always done for Keyes' cigars. There are no winners, no heroes, no consolation; just bleakness and regret, which is how a Film Noir should end as far as I'm concerned.

So, with this instant classic announcing his arrival, Billy Wilder would then go onto make some of the most important films of any era, and of any genre, some of which I am ashamed to say have slipped through my cinematic net and still need to be watched.

The first of these is Wilder's next film, "The Lost Weekend" with Ray Milland playing an alcoholic on a four day drinking binge, who finally finds redemption, and it isn't at the bottom of a bottle. The second film I have yet to see, which is very remiss of me, seeing as it starred Jean Arthur, is "A Foreign Affair", Wilder's last film before a series of films which I definitely have seen, some many times.

"Sunset Boulevard", with a rather deluded Gloria Swanson attempting to recreate her glory days with the help of William Holden, was then followed by a barn storming performance from Kirk Douglas in "Ace in the Hole", with the prisoner of war story "Stalag 17", with Wilder using William Holden again, following on from this.

Holden was then used again in Wilder's next film, alongside Humphrey Bogart in a romantic role, attempting to woo Audrey Hepburn in "Sabrina", a role I was never able to fully accept due to his not exactly romantic roles in his earlier Film Noir hits.

Next came the first film in which Wilder would work with Marilyn Monroe, in "The Seven Year Itch". The film itself is not particularly memorable apart from two scenes, the first being Monroe getting her toe stuck in the tap which leads Tom Ewell to develop his initial itch for her, before one of the most iconic images from any film was created, with Monroe enjoying the breeze from the subway, as it blows her white dress up, much to Tom Ewell's enjoyment, not to mention the enjoyment of most men ever. I think everyone started to get the itch at that point, and many of us are still scratching to this day.

From this light comedy Wilder moved into the genre of biopic, with the story of Charles Lindbergh, as played by James Stewart in "The Spirit of St. Louis", before moving back into romantic comedy, again with Audrey Hepburn as his leading lady, with my old friend Longfellow Deeds, Gary Cooper, being her would be wooer in "Love in the Afternoon"..

Next came the taut courtroom drama, "Witness for the Prosecution", with Charles Laughton attempting to outwit Marlene Dietrich in a classy adaptation of the Agatha Christie novel, before two of the best films of all time, both starring Jack Lemmon, who would go onto star in five more of Wilder's films.

The first of these is possibly the greatest comedy film of all time, "Some Like it Hot", with Lemmon teaming up with Tony Curtis, who, although dressed as ladies, are totally smitten by the sugary charms of Marilyn Monroe, in the second and final film Wilder would use her in. The final line, part of movie folklore now, when Lemmon removes his wig to reveal that he is a man, spoiling Osgood Fielding's plans for that evening with his new beau, only for him to deliver the line "Well, nobody's perfect!" is one of the best final lines ever, in a screenplay again written by Wilder too.

The second film is 1960's "The Apartment", with Jack Lemmon renting out his apartment to his bosses, the biggest of whom is Walter Neff himself, Fred MacMurray, so they can all enjoy a few hours of privacy with their various mistresses, leaving Lemmon's C.C. Baxter literally out in the cold.

MacMurray's personnel director Mr. Sheldrake's latest bit on the side is Shirley MacLaine's Fran Kubelik, who Baxter obviously falls for and rescues, at the expense of his job. After Baxter finally declares his love for her, she delivers yet another great final line from a Wilder script, this time, "Shut up and deal", which stops the film from ever becoming schmaltzy. Although the film is classed as a comedy, and there are certainly great comic moments, but they are all tinged with a certain pathos, with a serious message about infidelity, loneliness and the corporate nature of society underpinning the humour. It is another film I have loved ever since I first saw it, and will gladly watch again whenever possible.

Lemmon and MacLaine would go onto star in "Irma La Douce" three years later, with Lemmon then forming his partnership with Walter Matthau in "The Fortune Cookie", which would then be reprised in Wilder's remake of "The Front Page", with the original film of 1931 being the inspiration for Howard Hawks' "His Girl Friday".

And on that note, with both of these brilliant directors being mentioned in the same sentence, is where I need to move on. They have both given me, and all of us, some truly memorable films, and have contributed so much to the history of cinema. For that I thank them, but must move on to look at a film star too big to not have a chapter devoted to her. But which film of hers should I choose? Actually I won't move on at all, and go back to Howard Hawks. If all else fails, you can always rely on a Howard Hawks film to come up with the goods, and this next one is a diamond of a film.

Lots of diamonds actually.

Gentlemen Prefer Blondes (1953)   Dir: Howard Hawks

As a teenage boy, my bedroom walls had been plastered with posters of Marilyn Monroe. I had a full size poster right in front of my bed of the famous shot of her with her white dress billowing up, so that the first thing I would see every morning would be this blonde goddess. And yet I had never seen any of her films. The nearest I'd got was watching Madonna's video for "Material Girl" in which she famously recreates the "Diamonds are a Girl's Best Friend" sequence from this chapter's title film.

That video was good, but not quite good enough for me at the age of thirteen, and I had no idea just how much better the original version would be. I made it a mission of mine to see the film which it came from, and when it was on TV, I duly taped it and kept it. This was my first ever Marilyn Monroe film, and watched it repeatedly. Well, not the whole film, but the stunningly pink and shiny sequence where Marilyn is surrounded by tailcoat clad men offering her jewels in abundance.

I chose this film to represent the true star she was. She was glamour personified in this sequence, and if you have to pick one shot which sums her up, it would be the shot of her at the centre of a bunch of diamond offering gentlemen, her blonde hair gleaming, along with her lips and eyes. This represents the star quality she exuded a little more than the famous shot from "The Seven Year Itch", due to the almost lurid brightness and shininess of the sequence. Like an actual star, she shone as brightly as anything in the firmament when she was on screen, never more so in "Gentlemen Prefer Blondes". As a teenager, not yet a gentleman, I certainly did prefer blondes, and always have.

My girlfriend and I went through a Marilyn phase, as this was one shelf in the video shop which was absolutely devoted to one particular star. Her films were not put in amongst other genres, or who directed them: she had a shelf all to herself, which in itself is apt, due to her unique star quality, but also her vulnerability and loneliness, which of course led to her eventual early death.

We'd seen her in her earlier smaller parts in "All About Eve" and "The Asphalt Jungle", before moving on in sequence to "Niagara", as we had already seen "Monkey Business". In "Niagara", she had starred opposite Joseph Cotton, who had famously featured in Carol Reed's "The Third Man" alongside Orson Welles as Harry Lime. The tagline for the film is "A raging torrent of emotion that even nature can't control", which of course could be a reference to both the waterfall and Monroe herself. To be honest, the raging torrent of emotion didn't really drown me as I remember very little of the film, or of Monroe's performance in it.

We then watched "Gentlemen Prefer Blondes" again, and my teenage fascination was well and truly reignited, especially after I saw her in her next film, "How to Marry a Millionaire" alongside Lauren Bacall and Betty Grable. Somehow a myopic Marilyn, peering over her glasses, was even sexier than without corrective lenses.

Then came "River of No Return", opposite Robert Mitchum, which again left not much of an impression on me, before "Bus Stop" certainly did, if only for the green saloon showgirl outfit she wears to such wondrous effect. The sight of her in a black pencil skirt, with seamed legs is still a thing of wonder to me now. Yet again though, her vulnerability is shown perfectly in this film, in the way she is bullied by her would be husband, providing another metaphor for the way she was used and abused by the movie industry, whilst always remaining glamourous and the ultimate sex symbol.

In her next film she wanted to try and get away from this blonde bombshell persona, but ironically still plays a symbol of glamour and obsession in "The Prince and the Showgirl", directed by the great Laurence Olivier. In the film "My Week with Marilyn" in which Eddie Redmayne plays the young studio runner entrusted with looking after Monroe, in more ways than one it turns out, we see just how much difficulty she had whilst making this film.

She was the antithesis of everything Olivier stood for. He was famously direct, punctual, and professional, learning his lines effortlessly, whereas Marilyn did not exactly meet the same standards as him. As the film states, she was a star desperate to be seen as an actress, whereas Olivier was an actor desperate to be seen as a star. As a result, the "The Prince and the Showgirl" never really worked for me. Nor did it for many others. Everybody just wanted her to be a star.

Her next film was the one which she arguably gave her best performance in, probably because she was not billed as one of the main stars, playing second fiddle, or rather playing second ukulele, to Jack Lemmon and Tony Curtis, in "Some Like it Hot".

She famously took forty seven takes to say the line "It's me, Sugar", and also took forty takes to say the line "Where's the bourbon?" whilst rummaging through some drawers. After many failed attempts, with Marilyn saying either, "Where's the bottle?", "Where's the whiskey?" or even "Where's the bonbon?", Billy Wilder eventually wrote the correct line, all three words of it, on a piece of paper and stuck it inside the drawer Marilyn was supposed to open. After she then became confused as to which drawer the line was now pasted into it, Wilder stuck it inside every drawer. Fifty nine takes were required for this scene, and in the final cut, she has her back to the camera, causing many to wonder if Billy Wilder just gave up and had her line dubbed in later. Unsurprisingly he did not work with her again.

Marilyn reverted to type in her next film, "Let's Make Love", playing the sex symbol we all craved again, and one who Yves Montand definitely craved, before trying once again to be seen as a serious actress alongside Clark Gable and the post car crash

Montgomery Clift in John Huston's "The Misfits", written by her then husband, Arthur Miller. The couple would finally break up during the filming, and with the drugs she was taking to try and keep her on an even keel doing the exact opposite, she died during the filming of her next film, "Something's Gotta Give" in August 1962.

Her star quality shone brighter than perhaps anyone else's, but ultimately her star was engulfed by a black hole. However, her star still shines on, never more so than in "Gentleman Prefer Blondes". She wasn't the greatest of actors, but she was the greatest of movie stars, in the literal sense of the word. In a way, her contribution to cinema is just as powerful as that of Howard Hawks or Billy Wilder. I'm not sure Billy Wilder would agree though.

On that note, I need a drink. Now, where's the bourbon?

La Dolce Vita (1960)   Dir: Federico Fellini

Glamour didn't just live in Hollywood, or indeed in colour it would seem. I still had my list of must-watch films to get through, which were rapidly being ticked off by now. It was like collecting football stickers when I was a boy, where you either said "Got" or "Need" when I was swapping my stickers in the school playground. I now had more "gots" than "needs", but there was still a significant number of films I needed to see if I was going to complete my sticker album this time. And quite a few required subtitles.

First of all, my girlfriend introduced me to a couple of the French Nouvelle Vague films, namely Jean Luc Goddard's "A Bout de Souffle", or "Breathless" to give it its anglicised name, with Jean-Paul Belmondo and Jean Seberg looking irresistibly cool. We compared it with the 1983 remake, "Breathless", or "Breathless"

244

to give it its anglicised name, starring Richard Gere and Valerie Kaprisky. We decided we liked the original more than the remake, or rather my girlfriend told me I liked it better, seeing as she was the expert, and I must admit, the black and white version is just classier and cooler in a very French kind of way, without the bombast and overt sexuality of the remake.

We moved on to Francois Truffaut's "Jules et Jim", or "Jules and Jim" to give it its anglicised name, and I fell a little bit in love with Jean Moreau, just as both Jules and Jim did in fact. Even though this next film was not on my list, I wanted to prove my dedication to rather poncey arthouse French films, and so I also watched another Truffaut offering, "Tirez sur le Pianiste", or "Shoot the Pianist" with Charles Aznavour showing he could act as well as sing.

I didn't realise that I had already come across Francois Truffaut when I was only four years old, as he had appeared in his good friend, Steven Spielberg's "Close Encounters of the Third Kind." Little did I know then, that sixteen years later, I would be watching Truffaut's films in earnest in a rather desperate attempt to seem as cool as the actors in those Nouvelle Vague films. I just needed to start smoking Gauloises to really prove how cool and hip I was, something I definitely wasn't prepared to do.

There was one other French film which we needed to both see, which was Marcel Carne's "Les Enfants du Paradis", ("The Children of Paradise") starring the great Arletty, which had been called "The Gone With the Wind" of Art films. I preferred the film which starred Vivien Leigh and Clark Gable, and frankly my dear, I didn't give a damn if my girlfriend disagreed with me.

After fulfilling our quota of great French films, we now needed to move into another area of European cinema, and so we crossed

Les Alpes or "The Alps" to give them their anglicised name, and indulged in some of the finest Italian films ever made.

First up was the title film of this chapter, "La Dolce Vita" or "The Sweet Life" to give it its never used anglicised name. Maybe this was because it was a film not restricted to one language, but was a truly pan-European film, with Italian, French, German and English being spoken in it. It simply did not require its title to be translated, it was simply "La Dolce Vita".

This film was one I had wanted to watch whether it was on my list or not, mainly because I wanted to see Anita Ekberg cavorting in the Trevi Fountain. I'd been to the spot of the iconic scene myself as a child when my parents took the family on a day trip to Rome from our hotel on the coast near Rimini. However, by the time the coach had stopped at the iconic fountain, I had fallen fast asleep and my mum didn't want to wake me. Even if I had been awake, I doubt that Anita Ekberg would have been in it though, and anyway I had no idea at the age of eight who Anita Ekberg was, or indeed what the Trevi Fountain was.

By the time I had reached the age of twenty, I knew exactly who Anita Ekberg was after seeing the famous stills from the film enough times in the books I had voraciously been reading. When I finally got to see the film, I realised for sure that, as I said in the first line of this chapter, glamour does not need to be in colour. In fact there was something even more glamourous about the film because it was in monochrome, as if it were trying to prove to Hollywood that European film makers didn't need something so trivial and ostentatious as colour. They were determined to show America, and the rest of the world what true glamour was, and frankly they succeeded.

Glamourous the film may well have been, but in terms of sheer enjoyment, American films were always the winner. With the

European films I was only watching them because I felt I should, as though my film education wouldn't be fully rounded if I hadn't seen them. This was true not only of "La Dolce Vita", but Fellini's other most famous film, "8 ½", or "8 ½" to give it its anglicised name.

We dutifully watched this, and yes I could see the style and the class of the film, but in terms of just all out fun, it lacked a certain something. Probably some musical numbers actually, as when Rob Marshall, the man who had been responsible for the film version of "Chicago" made his own version of "8 ½", simply called "Nine" in 2009, with Daniel Day-Lewis in the Marcello Mastroianni role, I much preferred it to the seminal Italian master work. I'd definitely give "Nine" half a mark higher than "8 ½", if only for the fact that Penelope Cruz, Nicole Kidman, Marian Cotillard all give rather ravishing performances, alongside the Queen of Old School European glamour, Sophia Loren herself. Even Judi Dench did a turn for Day-Lewis, who always seemed miserable in the film, despite a plethora of beauties surrounding him. In comparison, "8 ½" had the gorgeous Claudia Cardinale and Anouk Aimee in it, which almost made up for the lack of Judi Dench. Almost, but not quite.

One Italian film which certainly did not provide much glamour was "Ladri di Biciclette", or "Bicycle Thieves" to give it its anglicised name, the 1948 classic directed by Vittorio De Sica. I know it was on my list, but the story of how a working-class man's bike is stolen in post war Italy, and how he and his son set out to find it, was about as glamourous as that line suggests. There were certainly no scenes of beautiful blondes cavorting in Roman Fountains, and at that point I decided to get back to some good old fashioned American films, and there was no more American a genre than the good old Western.

It was time for me to get off my Lambretta and saddle up.

Unforgiven (1992)   Dir: Clint Eastwood

I was never a huge fan of Westerns as a boy. Maybe this was because my dad had been the exact opposite when he was a boy. He adored films all about Cowboys and Indians, to use the innocent phrase which everyone used before we were enlightened. In the town of Carnforth, where my dad grew up, there is an old cinema, now a Co-op, which my dad used to spend most Saturday afternoons in as a kid. And the films he would usually be watching in the early 1950s would be Westerns. He would saddle up and mosey on down to the cinema to take in at least one cowboy film, sometimes two if there was a double bill being shown, and on his return home he would be galloping along on his pretend horse, slapping his thigh and hollering "yee-hah" all the way to his front door.

As a result of this, my dad was constantly watching Westerns at home when I was a boy. If it wasn't a film, then it would be episodes of "Bonanza" or "The High Chaparral", or "Alias Smith and Jones". If something cowboy and preferably Indian related was on TV, then he'd be watching it. His favourite film I think was "A Man Called Horse", with Richard Harris, as it had loads of Indians, doing not very nice things to our hero, until he became one of them. This was probably the reason why my dad also loved "Dances With Wolves" too. As I said, the more Indians, or Native Americans, the better.

Consequently I'd probably seen most, if not all of the films in this chapter, or at least parts of them, although I wasn't really paying attention to them as a boy, as I was probably building spaceships with my Lego or playing with my Star Wars figures. I was Buzz Lightyear to my dad's Woody, and consequently I just thought that Westerns were a bit old fashioned once I grew up. In fact, the only Western I had truly enjoyed before then was "Blazing Saddles", mostly because it spoofed the genre, and of course had

248

the farting scene which almost made me wet myself giggling when I first saw it, along with Mungo punching a horse.

However, many Westerns were on my list which needed to be watched properly if I was ever going to do the genre justice. So where better to start than the Godfather of the Western, John Ford, and the film which would really make his name, along with a certain John Wayne, in "Stagecoach" from 1939. Wayne starred as The Ringo Kid alongside Claire Trevor, and my eyes were opened properly to the genre.

There have been so many Westerns made that they have become the equivalent of cinema's pulp fiction, which of course many of the films were based on, and no I don't mean the Quentin Tarantino film. I suppose that is why my dad saw so many as a boy as there was always a Western being shown at the cinema, and they were a seemingly bottomless pool of resources for TV schedulers when I was growing up. I thought I would just stick to the ones on my list.

My girlfriend and I worked our way through some great films, some by John Ford, from arguably the greatest Western of them all, "The Searchers", with the iconic final shot of John Wayne turning away as the door closes on him, to "My Darling Clementine" with Henry Fonda, to "Rio Grande" and "She Wore a Yellow Ribbon". We also watched two films which starred the two actors I had fallen in love with in "Mr. Deeds Goes to Town, with Gary Cooper as the ageing town Marshall who was massively batting above his average by marrying Grace Kelly, before having to defend his town against the notorious Miller gang in Fred Zinnemann's "High Noon", to Jean Arthur, as the object of Alan Ladd's affections in "Shane". That film made me realise how much of a hero my own dad was to me as I felt a certain affinity with the young lad who idolises his new found friend in Shane.

Whilst rediscovering John Ford, I also discovered some of his non-Western films, such as "The Quiet Man", "How Green Was My Valley", "The Grapes of Wrath" and "Mister Roberts" but my favourite film of Ford's was one which starred not only John Wayne, but also Mr. Jefferson Smith, James Stewart, and allowed me to fully understand a certain reference in "Reservoir Dogs", when Mr. Blonde says to Mr. White, "I bet you're a big Lee Marvin fan, aren't you?"

"The Man Who Shot Liberty Valance" was shot in black and white as opposed to the colour which John Ford had used in most of his films. Some people say that this was because Paramount Studios wanted to cut costs, others say that it was used to try and hide the fact that James Stewart and John Wayne were not exactly twenty five years younger than they were supposed to be. The film is told in flashback, and the opening scenes with James Stewart, as Senator Ransom Stoddard, returning to bury his old friend Tom Doniphan, played by Wayne, show Stewart as the fifty-three year old man he was at the time to perfection. The only problem was that the majority of the film is set twenty five years previously, with Stewart and Wayne meant to be portraying men in their twenties or thirties, and the black and white shooting would be better at disguising their rather aged looks for much younger men.

The reason I like to think it was shot in monochrome is that it creates a sense of nostalgia, a sense of myth and legend of the old West where outlaws like the truly sadistic Liberty Valance could brutalise the people of one town, before law and order, as symbolised by Stewart's Ransom Stoddard, brought some sort of civility to the West. The brutality of Lee Marvin's Liberty Valance is quite shocking, as he takes real pleasure in whipping, shooting, burning, and generally terrorising the town of Shinbone and its inhabitants. The beating he gives to Stoddard at the beginning of the film allowed me to now get the reference in

"Reservoir Dogs", such was the level of sadism shown by Lee Marvin's character.

The film is all about how the West was founded on myths and legends, with the reputation of the now Senator Stoddard having been formed as a result of his apparent killing of Liberty Valance, only for Tom Doniphan to tell Stoddard, and us, the audience, that he was in fact the man who shot Liberty Valance after all. But as the newspaper editor said, "This is the West, sir. When the legend becomes fact, print the legend." This is one of the most iconic lines from any Western film, and one which would certainly influence the director of this chapter's title film.

I'd already come across many of Clint Eastwood's Westerns, as alongside John Ford's huge contributions to the genre, I'd also been watching many of the so-called Spaghetti Westerns, directed by the great Sergio Leone, especially his "Dollars" trilogy of "A Fistful of Dollars", "For a Few Dollars More", and "The Good, the Bad and the Ugly", which introduced me to the great musical scores of Ennio Morricone, who would score the films of many other great directors later in his career, famously including Quentin Tarantino, who had idolised Morricone as a boy.

My Favourite Sergio Leone film though did not feature Clint Eastwood at all, but "Once Upon a Time in the West" made up for the lack of Clint Eastwood with a few other greats though, namely Henry Fonda, Charles Bronson, Jason Robards, and the even more gorgeous by then Claudia Cardinale, who had travelled from her Italian roots in "8 ½" to Sergio Leone's version of the American West by way of "The Pink Panther", alongside the great Peter Sellers in his first outing as Inspector Clouseau.

Clint Eastwood was perfecting his trade as an actor, but was also preparing for his other great career as a director. His directorial debut would be in 1971 with "Play Misty For Me", in which he directed himself to be the object of one of his radio show's fan's very nearly deadly obsessions, before moving into the genre he had already become synonymous with as an actor.

His first Western was "High Plains Drifter" in 1973, before possibly his greatest film to date, "The Outlaw Josey Wales" in 1976. "Bronco Billy" would follow in 1980, and then "Pale Rider" in 1985, some of which I enjoyed even more than his earlier collaborations with Sergio Leone. But it was not until 1992 that he would make his masterpiece. "Unforgiven", which arrived in UK cinemas just before I started my second year of my degree. It is not just a masterpiece of the Western genre, but a masterpiece of a film. I distinctly remember it as I was still on my summer break, and it was the last film I saw before returning to university to really start my film education when my girlfriend and I discovered our trusty old video shop.

I'm glad I didn't have to see this film on a TV screen, as it is a film which deserves the big screen experience, and if it ever gets shown again at a cinema within an hour's drive of my home, I'll be there to watch it again. I might even manage a couple of hours' drive for this film actually, despite having seen it many times again on the TV since my first viewing. It's that good.

The story of how William Munny, the wizened, gnarled and both physically and emotionally scarred former gunfighter takes on one last job, to find and kill the gang who slashed a prostitute's face, is Eastwood's own eulogy to the Western genre, which uses the same ideas of legend and mythology as John Ford, but this time without any of the romanticism. Munny, along with Morgan Freeman as his old friend Ned Logan, and The Schofield Kid, played by Jaimz Woolvett, go in search of a ransom, but find out many things about themselves along the way.

The Schofield Kid, in a role which harks back to the glamour and infamy the West had for many young men, realises that he is not the killer he thought he was, and decides to pursue a different life after he has finally killed a man. He shoots one of the gang, whilst his victim is enjoying a short toilet break, at point blank range, which shakes him up so much that he realises he does not want his life to become anything like the life William Munny is trying so hard to turn away from. He is not there to see what the brutal Sheriff Little Bill Daggett, played brilliantly by Gene Hackman, does to Ned, putting his body on display outside the town's saloon, and he certainly does not see what Munny does to Little Bill to take his revenge.

The character of Little Bill harks back to the brutality of Liberty Valance, in the way he deals with English Bob, superlatively played by Richard Harris, savagely beating him to within an inch of his life, so that we know he means business when it comes to keeping law and order. Unfortunately for him, so does William Munny when it comes to killing people.

Munny's final encounter with Little Bill, as he is surrounded in the saloon by his cronies, is one of the most deadly, ruthless and brutal endings to a film ever, but never feels gratuitous in any way. He is there to do a job, and if that means killing people, then so be it. He starts by walking into the saloon and asks who owns the establishment. Once the man has identified himself, Munny tells everyone near him to move away before blasting his first victim away.

Little Bill then realises he may have some more work to do, calling Munny a coward for shooting an unarmed man, with Munny simply replying, "He should have armed himself if he's going to decorate his saloon with my friend." He then delivers one of the greatest lines ever, when he huskily and very matter of factly tells Little Bill that "I've killed women and children. I've killed everything that walks or crawls at one time or another. And I'm here to kill you Little Bill."

Even then we have no way of knowing how he will be able to survive this encounter, seeing as Little Bill then tells his men to shoot Munny dead if he is killed, but Munny rediscovers his old panache, and instead shoots them all dead in a glorious blaze of gunfire. Or not quite dead in the case of Little Bill, who is still lying on the saloon floor, cocking his pistol, before Munny steps on his hand. With the dangerous end of a rifle about a foot away from his face, Little Bill tells Munny that he'll see him in hell, with Munny simply replying "Yeah" before making what could only have been a terrible mess on the saloon floor, blowing Little Bill's face clean off.

He then calmly helps himself to a glass of whiskey and rides home, to finally put an end to his former life of brutality. But not before he encounters the journalist Beauchamp, who has now finally witnessed the true facts of the Wild West, and decides to print the legend instead, thus allowing Munny's legendary status to remain.

The film is an elegant, honest, unromanticised, unglamourised and certainly vicious portrayal of the American West, and as I said, is worth driving, or even riding, even though I've never ridden a horse in my life, for many hours to see in a cinema again.

And on that most unglamourous of films, it's time we brought a little glamour back in, with the help of two film stars. I'm going to kill two birds with one stone in the next chapter, a little like William Munny actually, although he was more likely to kill two men with one bullet instead.

Charade (1963)   **Dir: Stanley Donen**

I chose this film not because it is a work of huge gravitas, which changed the face of the cinematic landscape, with the grittiest and most powerful performances from its cast, but because it was exactly the opposite to that type of film. It is a bit of fluff. Stylish, chic, witty fluff, but fluff all the same.

There is nothing wrong with films whose sole purpose is to entertain, without really saying anything to their audience other than asking them to simply sit back, escape, and enjoy watching these two very loveable stars, dressed in very lovely clothes, delivering some mildly amusing lines in a rather silly story which ends with the two stars kissing and planning their wedding. Nothing wrong with that at all. It's what romantic comedies have been doing ever since Shakespeare's day.

"Charade", starring Cary Grant and Audrey Hepburn, could easily have been titled, "Much Ado About Nothing", "All's Well That Ends Well", or even "A Comedy of Errors", as the film is a stylish blend of espionage, tension, intrigue, deception, but ultimately light humour, and Audrey Hepburn looking lovely in dresses that were probably designed by Chanel. There is lots of style to the film, but ultimately not much substance, but again, there is nothing wrong with that at all. It's certainly more entertaining than some of the productions of "A Comedy of Errors" I've sat through.

The story of a recently widowed Audrey Hepburn, who becomes embroiled in a search for the money her late husband had been concealing, with Cary Grant playing a character whose name keeps changing as the web of intrigue and deception widens, is a nice film. It's not great, just nice. It is very much of its time and seems quite quaint now, but it was a huge hit in 1963 on its release.

It didn't win any Oscars, and was only nominated in one category, that of Best Song, which says something about the lightweight nature of the film. It's director was the man who directed some of the greatest musicals ever, including "Singin' in the Rain", and "On the Town", so it was never going to be the weighty piece of work which does in fact win Oscars.

What the film does do is give us two huge stars, and yet one had won a Best Actress Oscar by the time she was twenty four, for her first starring role, and one who made seventy seven films, with only a handful of the very early ones being non-starring roles, and yet had never won an Oscar, only ever being nominated twice for Best Actor in his whole career. The stark contrast here tells us something about the way Cary Grant was viewed as an actor, and how he was constantly overlooked by the powers that be, yet remained one of the most popular stars with audiences there has ever been.

Cary Grant has always certainly been one of my favourite actors, and yet I struggled to think of a film which defines him, which is another reason why the Academy overlooked him on numerous occasions. He never really played meaty roles, the sort of roles which win Oscars, but then again, neither did Audrey Hepburn, and yet she was nominated for Best Actress five times, winning at her first attempt despite only making less than half the amount of films Cary Grant did.

Audrey Hepburn was a fine actress, but she was no nowhere near her namesake Katharine in terms of acting ability. Very few were in fact, seeing as Katharine Hepburn has won the most Oscars ever for Best Actress, with four statues to her name. I'm not criticising Audrey's acting talents, but her looks, her charm, and her general non-threatening loveliness were a major factor in her success. The same could be said for Cary Grant, but he was only given a sympathy honorary Oscar in 1970 after the Academy realised that such a great as he needed some sort of recognition.

Audrey Hepburn's success was immediate with her winning her Oscar for "Roman Holiday" in 1953. It is a wonderful film, and I love it for so many things, principally because of Hepburn's utterly charming performance as Princess Ann, who is shown the sights on a wild twenty four hours of freedom from the restrictions her job entails with Gregory Peck. It is one of my favourite romantic comedies ever, and deservedly holds its place in the category of classic films. It is one of the classiest of classics, and huge fun.

The scene at the Mouth of Truth in which Gregory Peck shocked his co-star by not telling her he was going to pretend to lose his hand was not scripted, but its director William Wyler wisely left the shot in due to its charm. It is a truly lovely scene in a truly lovely film, and set Hepburn on her career in which she would play many other lovely, charming roles, most notably in her next film "Sabrina" opposite Bogart, "Funny Face" opposite Fred Astaire and most famously "Breakfast at Tiffany's" opposite George Peppard, in his days before he became Hannibal, the leader of The A Team. Mickey Rooney also delivers a slightly racist turn as Holly Golightly's Japanese neighbour Mr. Yunioshi, but the film is mostly remembered for the shots of Hepburn wandering around in "that" dress, and for her singing "Moon River". But again, the film is more style than substance. It's not actually that great a film, if indeed it can be called a great film. It has some great iconic moments of course, but as a film, I wouldn't call it a true classic.

Her singing voice is not the best in her rendition of "Moon River" and this was possibly why her songs were sung by the soprano Marni Nixon when she was unfairly chosen to play Eliza Doolittle in "My Fair Lady". Julie Andrews had made the role her own on stage, opposite Rex Harrison, who couldn't sing either, but it was Hepburn who got the part in the film. This was basically because of her looks, not her talents, leaving Julie Andrews to take on the role of Mary Poppins, deservedly winning the Oscar for Best Actress, whereas Hepburn wasn't even nominated for her role as Eliza.

Audrey Hepburn was a great star, but she was not a great actress. She was over rated, whereas her co-star in "Charade" was definitely under rated, which is of course why he received his honorary Oscar. Grant oozed charm, sophistication, and glamour, but he could also play a much wider range of roles than Audrey Hepburn ever could.

His real breakthrough film was when Mae West suggested that he "Come up and see me sometime" in "She Done Him Wrong" in 1932, before he started getting starring roles alongside the other Hepburn, Katharine, in "Sylvia Scarlett" before the great "Bringing Up Baby" truly established him as a star, as well as "Holiday" in the same year, with "The Philadelphia Story the following year.

We forget just how many huge films he made, with some of the greatest actresses in cinema history, from not only Katharine Hepburn, but Jean Arthur in "Only Angels Have Wings" and "The Talk of the Town", Joan Fontaine in "Gunga Din" and "Suspicion", Myrna Loy in "Mr. Blandings Builds His Dream House", Rosalind Russell in "His Girl Friday", Deborah Kerr in "An Affair to Remember" and "The Grass is Greener", Sophia Loren in "Houseboat", Doris Day in "That Touch of Mink", and Leslie Caron in "Father Goose".

The list could go on, as I included all his great roles in Alfred Hitchcock's films in my chapter on "Psycho". However, one name I haven't mentioned is his partnership with Irene Dunne.

He would play opposite her in three of his greatest films ever, the Screwball Comedies "The Awful Truth", of 1937 and "My Favourite Wife" of 1940, before he would gain his first Oscar nomination in 1941 for "Penny Serenade" in an unusually serious and tear jerking film for him.

Maybe that was why he was nominated this time as the Academy simply did not take him seriously enough in his other lighter roles. His only other nomination was for another weightier role, in "None But the Lonely Heart" of 1944, but after that he was completely ignored by the Academy, despite many of his best films ever coming post 1944, until of course his honorary gong was given to him once he had stopped making the films which had given so many people such a huge amount of enjoyment.

He really was up there with the greatest movie stars of all time, and his range was much wider than most actors of not just his generation, but any actor in any generation. However, I don't think he could have pulled Hannibal Lecter off in the same way as Anthony Hopkins, and he certainly wouldn't have been right for the title role in my next film.

There was only one man who could do that, and thankfully for Stanley Kubrick and the rest of us, Peter Sellers was that man, not Cary Grant, although it certainly would have been a sight to behold with Cary Grant in a wheelchair trying to stop his wayward arm from making the Nazi salute and stifling "Heil Hitler".

Dr. Strangelove (1964)   Dir: Stanley Kubrick

I didn't use the full title of this film as it would have taken up too much space, and spoiled my look for each chapter's heading, but this truly great film's full title is "Dr. Strangelove, or: How I Learned to Stop Worrying and Love the Bomb". Even the title is funny, and it remains one of the all-time great comic films, with one of the greatest comic performances ever, or in fact three of the greatest comic performances ever, seeing as Peter Sellers played the roles of Group Captain Lionel Mandrake, President Merkin Muffley, and the eponymous Dr. Strangelove. Sellers showed what a true genius he was, and yet this was not the first time he had performed multiple roles in one film.

I'd seen a few of the great Ealing comedies as a boy, but needed to revisit many of them, and discover some for the first time, so my girlfriend and I embarked on our own little pilgrimage to West London, not literally of course, to watch some of the most truly British of films ever made. One of my favourites was the studio's third ever film to be made, "Passport to Pimlico" from 1949, and then we went onto watch "Whisky Galore!", "The Titfield Thunderbolt", before discovering the Ealing films which had starred none other than OB1 Kenobi himself.

When I first saw Alec Guinness being struck down by Darth Vader when I was only four years old, I had no idea how great a contribution to not just cinema history, but in particular British cinema history he had made. I loved "The Man in the White Suit" and "The Lavender Hill Mob", but was even more impressed with two others, one of which starred Peter Sellers, whereas the other one had obviously inspired him as well.

Sellers appeared alongside Alec Guinness in the brilliant "The Lady killers", which of course would also feature Herbert Lom, who would go onto become Inspector Clouseau's boss Charles Dreyfus in the later "Pink Panther" films, as well as appearing with Sellers in "Mr. Topaze". He would also appear in one of Stanley Kubrick's films, playing Tigranes Levantus in "Spartacus".

As for "Kind Hearts and Coronets", this was a real tour de force, with Guinness playing not just three roles, but nine roles in total, all of them brilliantly, which obviously made Peter Sellers think he could do something similar. When Sellers started getting leading roles in the late 1950s, he starred in two films in which he would play multiple roles, just as Alec Guinness had done, before then going onto making "Dr. Strangelove" five years later.

The first of these was "The Mouse That Roared" where Sellers played three roles, one of which was female, just as Guinness had played both genders in "Kind Hearts and Coronets". He then played two roles in one of my favourites of Sellers' early work, "I'm All Right Jack", alongside Terry Thomas, Ian Carmichael and Dickie Attenborough. With his apprenticeship in multiple roles having been successfully negotiated, it was now time to meet with Stanley Kubrick.

My girlfriend and I still had a few of Kubrick's films to watch, seeing as most of his films were on my must-watch list. I'd already ticked off "The Shining", "Full Metal Jacket", and "A Clockwork Orange", and I'd seen "Spartacus" as a boy as my dad loved it and we'd always watch it whenever it was on the TV, usually on a Bank Holiday Monday afternoon. However, this was not strictly speaking a true Kubrick film, as he had been brought into direct the film a week into shooting, after its original director Anthony Mann was sacked by its star and producer, Kirk Douglas. This was the only film in Kubrick's canon which he did not have full control over, but Kirk Douglas obviously thought he'd do a decent job. Millions of people have since agreed with him.

Kubrick had first worked with Douglas in the film I watched next, "Paths of Glory", which is arguably the greatest film about the First World War ever made, even after Sam Mendes released "1917" recently. I loved it, and so wanted to see the other earlier

Kubrick films too. "The Killing" with Sterling Hayden, who would go onto become the mad and wonderfully named General Jack D. Ripper in "Dr. Strangelove", was enjoyed, before I then saw Kubrick's first film with Peter Sellers, and one which I had definitely wanted to watch, as I had read Vladimir Nabokov's book from which it came.

Peter Sellers would play two roles in this film, those of Claire Quilty and Dr. Zempf, before being cast in Kubrick's next film, and still to my mind his best ever. I love "Dr. Strangelove", not just because of Peter Sellers. George C Scott's performance is brilliant too, along with Sterling Hayden and Slim Pickens as Major "King" Kong, a role which had also been meant for Sellers before Kubrick and maybe even Sellers himself decided that three roles were enough.

There are so many favourite lines and scenes in the film that the list would just go on, but some just have to be mentioned. The telephone call between the two presidents; the first appearance of Strangelove himself, with him trying desperately to control his Nazi gloved hand, even biting it to stop it from being raised in the Nazi salute; and the line "You can't fight in here! This is the War Room!" are just three of the countless list of gems in a remarkable script written mostly by Kubrick, although Sellers was allowed to ad-lib many of his lines.

My favourite line though is when Mandrake is telling General Ripper about when he was tortured by the Japanese, and he delivers this line in the most beautifully understated way, with the stiffest of upper lips ever: "I don't think they wanted me to talk, really. I don't think they wanted me to say anything. It was just their way of having…a bit of fun, the swines. Strange thing is they make such bloody good cameras." Absolute classic.

The whole film is basically perfect. There is nothing that could be improved on, and it makes me wonder why Kubrick never did another comedy film, seeing as he did such an astonishing job with this film.

Sellers of course would go onto make some hilarious films, ones which I remember watching with my brother and dad. The later "Pink Panther" films, along with the original, would always cause my dad to almost wet himself, and I particularly liked Clouseau's encounters with Cato. I think my dad did actually emit something in his underwear when Clouseau is swinging on the parallel bars and jumps off, only to fall straight down the stairs in "The Pink Panther Strikes Again".

Sellers would also make some absolutely awful films, which seemed to sum up his mental state. He could be both brilliant and bemusing in equal measure, something which his final three films highlight. "The Prisoner of Zenda" and "The Fiendish Plot of Dr. Fu Manchu" are awful, but sandwiched in between is a piece of brilliance, with Sellers' performance as Chance the gardener in "Being There" being possibly his best ever performance as a serious actor, earning him an Oscar nomination for Best Actor, as did his perfect comic performance in "Dr. Strangelove".

As for Stanley Kubrick, the next film of his I would watch would be the rarely mentioned "Barry Lyndon" of 1975, but maybe a reason it is rarely mentioned is because it gets so overshadowed by his other more famous, and frankly better films, one of which was still on my list, but one which I didn't want to watch on a TV screen, as if any film needs to be seen in the cinema, then it is "2001: A Space Odyssey".

Luckily, it was the film's twenty fifth anniversary in my final year of my degree, and the film was re-released in selected cinemas, so that I could experience it properly. Another trip into

London was required, but unlike with "The Exorcist" I did not come away feeling emotionally exhausted and petrified. I was a bit bored and bemused by it actually.

Yes, the film is stunningly beautiful, particularly the iconic scenes of the spaceships waltzing to Strauss' "The Blue Danube", and because of these I felt privileged to have seen it on the big screen, but ultimately the film left me cold. Like space itself, it left me in a vacuum, emotionally at least, and as for the film's final sequence, life is just too short to try and work out its full meaning.

I tried again on the film's next re-release, this time taking my then nineteen-year-old son to see it on its 50th anniversary to The Dukes Theatre in Lancaster, where I had been to watch so many arthouse films as a teenager. I still couldn't figure out the ending, and found myself being just as bored, and just as bemused as the first time I saw it.

Maybe I'm a bit of a plebeian, but I'd much prefer to watch a film about the world being blown up accidentally in a nuclear holocaust than a rogue computer in space, even if it did have dancing spaceships. The future depicted in "Dr. Strangelove" was certainly a funnier future than the one Kubrick depicted in "2001", and one I'd take any day.

I'd rather watch people dance than spaceships, and who better to watch than the greatest dancer of them all? Ladies and gentleman, I give you Mr. Frederick Austerlitz, better known as the one and only Fred Astaire

The Band Wagon (1953)   Dir: Vincente Minnelli

Before I got to university and met my film loving girlfriend, I'd only been aware of Fred Astaire from his appearances on

"Parkinson", or from the odd clip I'd seen on the TV. I had certainly never seen any of his films, as my parents, my dad in particular, had an aversion to films with any sort of ballroom dancing in them. He loved his Westerns, and Fred Astaire's films were hardly Westerns, although like that more rugged of genres, film musicals are one of the few true American creations.

My dad's aversion to anything dance related was mainly due to the rain. At school, if it was raining, instead of him being allowed to play football outside, the whole school would have to cram into the hall, pair up with a similarly reluctant girl and practise his ballroom dancing. This would probably have put me off for life too. To this day I have never seen my dad dance in any way, shape or form, and just the mention of my enthusiasm for "Strictly Come Dancing" brings him out in palpitations.

So it was no wonder that I'd never seen any Fred Astaire film. Thankfully, my girlfriend introduced me to a whole new world of grace, elegance and beauty, just as my dad had done with football, which could also occasionally provide grace, elegance and beauty, though maybe not in the early eighties when I started watching it.

The first Fred Astaire film I watched was probably "Top Hat" as the BBC were showing a selection of his most famous films over the Christmas period in what was probably my second year at university. This film featured the absolutely iconic routine to "Cheek to Cheek" with Ginger Rogers' feathery dress floating around, getting up Astaire's nose, although you would never notice his irritations due to his utter professionalism and perfectionism.

The storylines of these films were all basically the same, but like me, nobody cared. They were just a way to link together the dance sequences, the money shots so to speak. Just like porn films, nobody is interested in the storylines, and everyone who cares to watch them watches them for one thing. And as with the films of Astaire and Rogers, Fred and Ginger certainly provided lots of hardcore dance porn.

From "Top Hat", I watched "Follow the Fleet" with the great songs "We Saw the Sea", and "Let's Face the Music and Dance", then moved onto my favourite of all, "Swing Time". In this film, particularly in the routines for "The Way You Look Tonight", and "Never Gonna Dance", I don't think Astaire and Rogers ever danced more beautifully together. Ginger Rogers looked gorgeous, and of course she had to do the same moves as her male partner, but backwards, whilst wearing high heels, as she famously said.

They might have outdone themselves in their next film, "Shall We Dance" with "Let's Call the Whole Thing Off" being performed whilst they both wore roller skates. They could make any routine look elegant, graceful and beautiful, which is of course the point, and which is why they were so successful in the 1930s when the reality of most people's lives contained no grace, elegance or beauty, and certainly no glamour. Fred and Ginger provided that for millions of people.

I tiptoed my way through the other Astaire/Rogers films, from their first ever together, "Flying Down to Rio", through to their last, "The Story of Vernon and Irene Castle", a biopic about a couple who revitalised ballroom dancing in the years before the First World War. This was perfectly suited to a couple who did the same for dancing in the years preceding the Second World War, and just as the war was breaking out in Europe, so the relationship between Fred and Ginger would break up.

Astaire had already danced with one of the greatest stars of all, Joan Crawford, in "Dancing Lady" in 1933, and he would then move onto working with many more of the greatest stars of all time after he and Ginger had split up. First would be Eleanor Powell in "Broadway Melody of 1940" from, surprisingly enough, 1940, before dancing with Paulette Goddard, who had starred alongside Charlie Chaplin in his great "Modern Times".

Then came a couple of under rated films with one of, if not the most beautiful film star of all, although she became ultimately famous not for her dancing, but for removing a single glove in "Gilda", much to the delight of movie goers for evermore. The prisoners in "The Shawshank Redemption" certainly enjoyed it, leading to Andy Dufresne covering his huge hole in his cell with the iconic poster of Rita Heyworth. That film was based on the Stephen King novella which was actually called "Rita Hayworth and the Shawshank Redemption", but before she took off that glove, had starred alongside Fred Astaire in "You'll Never Get Rich" and "You Were Never Lovelier". Some of the dance routines rival those Astaire did with Ginger Rogers, and Rita Hayworth really was never lovelier, until she became Gilda of course, a film famous for only one thing, a song and a glove.

Astaire would then work with Judy Garland for the first time in "Ziegfeld Follies" in 1945, before they both headlined in "Easter Parade" three years later. I loved this film, even though Astaire's role was intended for the other great dancer, Gene Kelly, and especially the numbers "Stepping Out With My Baby" in which Astaire performed solo, "Shakin' the Blues Away" which introduced me to another great, Ann Miller, as well as the numbers performed by both Astaire and Garland, namely "A Couple of Swells", "It Only Happens When I Dance With You" and the title song "Easter Parade". This was one of the first films Astaire would make for a studio renowned for the greatest film musicals, MGM, a studio who would reunite him with Ginger Rogers in 1949 with "The Barkleys of Broadway", before dancing on the ceiling in "Royal Wedding" although thankfully his co-star was Jane Powell and not Lionel Ritchie.

He made a couple with Vera Ellen, who had made Gene Kelly's night in "On the Town", before teaming up with a dancer who had possibly the most iconic pair of legs ever. Cyd Charisse, whose pins were famously insured for $5 million, had hypnotised everyone the year before in "Singin' in the Rain". She had certainly hypnotised Gene Kelly with just one leg, and it was the success of this scene which made MGM realise that she needed to be paired with Fred Astaire for the title film of this chapter.

I chose "The Band Wagon", as it contained the coolest, the most thrilling and one of the most difficult dance routines I had ever seen. It was also the sexiest routine I had ever seen, despite Fred Astaire being the grand old age of fifty-three by then. The "Girl Hunt Ballet", with Cyd Charisse wearing the sexiest of red dresses, along with her black gloves and black wig, is a show stopping routine harking back to the gangster and Noir films of the early 1930s. Even one of the dancers was employed simply because he looked like Jimmy Cagney.

The routine is so good that I can happily watch it over and over again, and has inspired many other routines in not just films, but in "Strictly Come Dancing" too. Jake Wood's routine with Janette Manrara at Blackpool was basically a rip off of this routine with Astaire and Charisse, one which the "Eastenders" star did justice to thankfully.

Astaire and Charisse would go onto star alongside each other in "Silk Stockings", a musical remake of "Ninotchka", but despite the title, Charisse would not be as sexy as she was in "The Band Wagon". Their second film had many moments of real beauty, but without the red dress, they were no comparison for me. In between these two films, Astaire would make "Daddy Long

Legs", opposite Leslie Caron, and "Funny Face", with Audrey Hepburn, but "Silk Stockings" would be his last great dancing role, as even he had to hang up his dancing shoes. He was fifty-seven by then after all.

Fred Astaire was for me the greatest dancer of them all. He could dance just about any routine he was given However, although he created the "Girl Hunt Ballet", even he would admit my next film needed Moira Shearer, rather than him, to perform real ballet. I'm not sure the shoes would have fit him either.

The Red Shoes (1948)   **Dirs: Michael Powell,
                                             Emeric Pressburger**

I had already seen Moira Shearer in "Peeping Tom" in those first few weeks at university when my girlfriend had been studying Hitchcock films, and watched this as a comparison to "Psycho" which had been released in the same year, but without the same sort of reception by critics and audiences alike.

"Peeping Tom" had caused all sorts of revulsion, and tarnished the reputation of its director, Michael Powell, such was its force and its ability to shock, fascinate, challenge, and twist the minds of anyone who watched it. It was all about voyeurism and about the power of the gaze, with the central character torturing his victims, capturing their final moments on camera at the point of death.

It sounds hugely shocking now, so just imagine the response this brave and challenging film got on its release, in the days when even "Lady Chatterley's Lover" was still banned from being sold in bookshops. Powell's reputation was only really restored to its rightful place due to Martin Scorsese's championing of him. To be blunt, if it wasn't for Michael Powell, along with his collaborator, Emeric Pressburger, then Martin Scorsese would not have become a film maker. If he valued Michael Powell so highly, then I thought it was about time I did too.

The films I would then discover could have a whole book devoted to them, rather than the chapter I'm giving them. There have in fact been many books written about them, but this is not that type of book, and so I apologise for this rather desultory recap. Each of their films deserves so much more than this chapter, as each one is a masterpiece. Every single one of the great modern film makers, from Scorsese to Spielberg, from Lynch to Loach, from Coppola to Cronenberg, all pay a huge debt to the remarkable films made by Powell and Pressburger.

My girlfriend had told me about one of her favourite films, "I Know Where I'm Going" and so I gladly was introduced further into these wonderful films. I watched Roger Livesey in this lovely little film for the first time ever, but it would certainly not be my last. I saw him again in "The Life and Death of Colonel Blimp", and once more in one of the most dazzling films ever to be made, the jewel in the crown of Powell and Pressburger's output, "A Matter of Life and Death".

This work of true art had David Niven talking to Kim Hunter from the cockpit of his doomed aircraft, before entering a world of fantasy which deals with some really quite profound subjects. If Aristotle, Plato and Jesus are mentioned by Niven in his ponderings about what the next life will bring, you know this is not going to be the simplest of films. Romance, fantasy, comedy and spirituality, along with the nature of morality are all dealt with in a film which had to have its title changed in America to "Stairway to Heaven", as any film with the word "Death" in it was simply too off-putting for American audiences.

Thankfully, us Brits were made of sterner stuff and we got to see the film exactly as its directors wanted us to, in both black and white for its scenes set in Heaven, and bright technicolour for the scenes set on Earth. It really is a masterpiece of cinema, and one which has been influential and inspirational for so many directors, not just the ones listed above.

I followed this with another true work of art, "Black Narcissus" starring Deborah Kerr who is trying to set up a convent in the foothills of the Himalayas. The premise sounds about as exciting as watching paint dry, but the film is another astonishing piece of cinema, the whole film being shot in England, with the directors and their genius crew creating one of the most beautiful, atmospheric, yet dark and disturbing films ever.

The next film by Powell and Pressburger, who would come to be known as "The Archers", the name of their production company, and nothing to do with a Radio 4 long running soap opera, was also the next one on my list, the one which would reintroduce me to Moira Shearer, and the film she is most famous for. She only made six films, three of them with her muses, Powell and Pressburger, but if she had only made this one film, she still would have gone down in cinematic history and folklore.

The story of a ballerina torn between her lover, the ballet company's composer, and the company's powerful Director, is echoed in later films, notably "Black Swan" with Natalie Portman, but more obviously in Baz Luhrmann's "Moulin Rouge", with all three films ending not very happily for the female protagonists. "The Red Shoes" is again a stunning piece of not just cinema, but theatre and ballet wrapped into one.

It is the film which Martin Scorsese, the man who gave us some of the most brutal films ever made, says "plays in my heart". Indeed, Scorsese literally could not have made his films if it hadn't been for Thelma Schoonmaker, his long-time editor, winner of the Oscar for Best Editing three times, all of which for films made by Scorsese, and who would go onto marry Michael Powell after Scorsese had introduced them. The two film makers are inextricably linked, so anyone who likes Scorsese films had better go and watch "The Red Shoes" and "Black Narcissus" too. They may be a bit different to "Raging Bull" and "Taxi Driver" but one thing is for sure, these last two films would not exist if it were not for the first two.

Another very British film which must be mentioned here, is one which was certainly not directed by Michael Powell. It was directed by another truly great British film maker, and another whose influence has been crucial to many film makers since, thanks to such epic films as "Lawrence of Arabia", "The Bridge on the River Kwai", Doctor Zhivago", and "A Passage to India". And the film I'm talking about, although not quite so epic, was filmed, or at least parts of it were, only a few hundred yards from the house where I would spend the first six years of my life, and would feature my dad's uncle in it too.

David Lean's "Brief Encounter", one of the most romantic but ultimately heart breaking films ever, was filmed at Carnforth station, the town where I grew up and the town which shaped me. Little did I know that when I was waiting for the train to take me to Lancaster to go to the cinema, that I was standing on the same platform that filmed some of the most memorable scenes in British film ever. The scene where Trevor Howard and Celia Johnson meet for the first time, where she famously gets a piece of grit in her eye, was filmed in the tea room of Carnforth station. The two fall in love, but as she is married already, their romance is doomed and can never continue. I remember watching it and surreptitiously wiping tears away from my eyes when the two finally part.

In my over romanticised mind, when my girlfriend and I had to part from each other to go and visit our families, I imagined that some of the pain Alec and Laura were feeling was similar to mine. Little did I know what real love would feel like at that point, and thankfully never have felt that way, seeing as my wife is still with me now after almost twenty-two years. I certainly never understood what real heart ache could feel like when I was just a twenty-year-old boy, pretending to be in love with my then girlfriend. It would take a lot more than a film to make me realise what true love was, although that film gave me an idea, that's for sure.

It is a film which I will always have real affection for, especially as my dad's uncle, a train driver back in the 1940s, was the driver of the train which takes Alec away from Laura on that train platform where I have stood so many times, underneath the huge station clock, waiting for a train which would take me to the cinema, and take me to a world where an old black and white film can make me weep.

Such is the power of the cinema, or maybe it was because when I was growing up, that lovely old tea room had long since gone. There was no chance of a brief encounter for me on that station platform. Thankfully, the tea room has been restored and my old home town has realised the commercial potential of the film, creating a "Brief Encounter" museum, where anyone can now get a piece of grit in their eye if they want, for a small charge of course. They just won't be able to disappear from view with smoke billowing out of the train, nor with my dad's Uncle Alf driving it away.

Now where's that handkerchief?

Singin' in the Rain (1952)   Dir: Stanley Donen

MGM Studios really were the studio to beat when it came to musicals, and this film was the best of the lot as far as I'm concerned. However, if it wasn't for a man whose greatest work was for one of MGM's rivals, then maybe they would not have become the force they would be.

Busby Berkley, the man who directed and choreographed some of the most dazzling musical numbers ever, had worked for Warner Bros when he made his most stunning dance sequences. "42nd Street", "Footlight Parade", "Gold Diggers of 1933" and "Dames" were all huge smash hits in the early 1930s, mainly because the dance sequences were completely new. There had literally never been anything like them, with Berkley's camera often being used above the dancers to create mesmeric and almost hypnotic kaleidoscopic effects with his dancers. The dancing itself was not particularly beautiful, but the way it was shot definitely was.

Berkley's films paved the way for musicals to realise they could do whatever they wanted with their camera work, and led to MGM using the same techniques not with dancers, but with swimmers, led by Esther Williams, who would have represented the USA in the Olympics of 1940 had the Second World War not cancelled them. Instead she was picked up by MGM and thrust into a series of films which became known as "Aquamusicals", with Williams being the focal point of basically some extremely fancy synchronised swimming routines, many filmed using the style which Busby Berkley had created.

MGM were already a huge studio by the time Esther Williams dived into her first main role in "Bathing Beauty" in 1944, and had some huge musical hits to their name. Their use of Esther Williams showed how they could innovate, as well as look to the past, something that the studio's next major star, and possibly their greatest ever, could do too.

Gene Kelly, after having a few bit parts in films such as "Cover Girl" with Rita Hayworth and "Christmas Holiday" with Deanna Durbin, was given his first major role in "Anchors Aweigh" in 1945, alongside its primary star, Frank Sinatra. In this film, Kelly famously danced with another character who was arguably bigger than either himself or Sinatra; not Mickey Mouse, but Jerry Mouse, he of "Tom and Jerry" fame. This made Kelly's name, and he was then paired with Judy Garland in "The Pirate", and with Esther Williams in "Take Me Out to the Ball Game", which was in fact directed by Busby Berkeley too.

But Kelly's big break came in 1949 with "On the Town", one of the most joyous musicals ever, and one in which many scenes would be shot on location in New York, at the insistence of its director, who just happened to be Gene Kelly too, in his debut behind the camera, as well as being its major star, surpassing his co-star Frank Sinatra now in terms of box office appeal. Kelly's brand of muscular, high energy and yet graceful dancing was able to personify the joy and excitement the three sailors felt as they embarked on a night of shore leave in New York, with Ann Miller and Vera Ellen providing ample support for Kelly's abilities.

From there he appeared in "Summer Stock", another with Judy Garland, before he teamed up with her husband, Vincente Minnelli, although the couple were going through a divorce at the time, in "An American in Paris". This film would introduce the world to Leslie Caron, and would include possibly the most ambitious piece of musical dance sequence ever filmed. The climax to the film is "The American in Paris ballet", a seventeen minute, dialogue free dance featuring Kelly and Caron set to George Gershwin's "An American in Paris". The ballet sequence cost almost half a million dollars to shoot, and involved using forty-four sets on MGM's back lot. Gene Kelly certainly had big ideas, which he invariably pulled off.

His next film would top even the extravagance of "An American in Paris", maybe not in sheer size, but in terms of charm, dance routines, songs, and most crucially, storyline. "Singin' in the Rain" helped to develop the genre of film musicals from a series of set piece song and dance routines where the narrative was secondary to the singing and dancing, to films where the song and dance routines would be integral to the actual story. Basically, "Singin' in the Rain" would still be a great film if it didn't have any singing or dancing in it at all because the storyline is so strong.

Thankfully, it did have singing and dancing, which is of course part of the storyline about the problems studios faced with the arrival of sound in films. Kelly, as Don Lockwood, an old time star of silent films, has to move with the times, and so decides to turn his next picture into a musical, with the storylines of the actual film, and the film within a film all tying together beautifully, just as every single aspect of the whole film did.

Kelly's performance is obviously outstanding, with his iconic routine to the title song, with him swinging round a lamp post, becoming part of twentieth century iconography. But his co-stars Donald O'Connor and Debbie Reynold also gave career defining performances. Even Kelly's pretend on screen partner, the squeaky voiced Jean Hagen is brilliant in her role, adding to the perfect ensemble.

The title routine is obviously a huge moment in the film, but every routine is truly memorable, from "Fit as a Fiddle", "Good Morning", "Make 'Em Laugh", and of course "The Broadway Melody", which features the aforementioned Cyd Charisse's perfect pins. It is a perfect film, and even though I prefer to watch Fred Astaire dance, it is this film of Gene Kelly's which beats any of Astaire's hands down in terms of being an all round masterpiece. Kelly would never better this film, and frankly neither would anyone else.

After this masterpiece of musical film, many others I watched simply did not have the same appeal. I watched a few others such as "Show Boat", "Meet Me in St. Louis", "High Society", a remake of "The Philadelphia Story" with Grace Kelly playing the Katharine Hepburn role, and "Gigi" with the lovely Leslie Caron. In this last film however, I could not stand Maurice Chevalier and the way he didn't really sing, but spoke his songs, something else which has always put me off another of Lerner and Loewe's great musicals, "My Fair Lady". Rex Harrison just annoys me in that film, and I still think it would have been better had Julie Andrews just been given the role, instead of opting for the out of her depth Audrey Hepburn.

I'd obviously seen Julie Andrews in "The Sound of Music" or "The Sound of Mucus" as Christopher Plummer always called it, and of course in "Mary Poppins", but had never really enjoyed them as a kid. They were always on the TV on wet Bank Holidays, and back then I'd rather have been building Lego or kicking my football around rather than watching Julie Andrews sing and dance, but it was another of Andrews' films which I discovered which would give me more enjoyment.

"Thoroughly Modern Millie" is an under rated musical in my opinion, and has some cracking songs in it, performed brilliantly by Dame Julie. The film was set in the 1920s, the time of the flappers, and that whole era fascinated me so much more than little kids riding around Salzburg on their bikes, or chimney sweeps pretending to be cockneys.

I also discovered the work of someone who must be included in any chapter about great musicals. Bob Fosse, whose choreography has always fascinated me, directed one of my favourite musicals, "Sweet Charity" with Shirley MacLaine putting in a show stopping performance in "If They Could See Me Now", which also won Tom Chambers the "Strictly Come Dancing" title in 2008 as he used the track for his unforgettable Show Dance routine with Camilla Dallerup. "Sweet Charity" also included one of the sexiest dance routines ever, with "Big Spender" blowing my mind.

This led me onto watching another of Fosse's films, the brilliant "Cabaret", which is more than a musical. Yes it has some amazing musical numbers in it, particularly Liza Minnelli's Sally Bowles singing "Mein Herr" whilst dressed in her iconic black stockinged outfit topped off with her bowler hat, but it certainly is not a jolly piece of fluff which many other musicals are. A musical about Nazi Germany does not sound that light and fluffy, unless of course Mel Brooks made it, with "The Producers" becoming another of my favourites once I had seen "Springtime For Hitler" being performed.

The choreography of Bob Fosse would play a major role in another hugely significant show and consequently film for me, but I'll come to that later. I need to move onto another actor who has already featured in this book, one who was not known for musicals, and yet had given a great performance in "Guys and Dolls" as Sky Masterson, singing "Luck Be a Lady". In fact, any lady would be in luck if they were to star with Marlon Brando, especially in his earlier films when he was simply not only a formidable actor, but one of the most handsome men ever to have walked the earth.

I think even I had a bit of a crush on him, as did just about every female who ever saw him in those early roles in the 1950s. He was the most masculine of "The Men", which was incidentally the name of his first film, but it wouldn't be until his second film where he would wear a ripped T-shirt and scream "Stella" that the whole world would come walking down the stairs and embrace him.

A Streetcar Named Desire (1951)   Dir: Elia Kazan

I obviously saw Marlon Brando for the first time when I was just five years old when my Gran took me to see "Superman", and if she'd have told me then that the man on screen in 1978 was once the most handsome, the most desirable, the most godlike of men, then I would not have believed her. If she'd also told me that he was the most intense, the most powerful, and the most formidable of actors, then I doubt whether I would have believed her about that either. I was more bothered at that point that his son was just about to be sent to Earth from Krypton to save our planet from Lex Luthor.

The first proper film I'd seen of his, apart from "Apocalypse Now", was one of his much later ones, which still didn't make me realise just how handsome and intense he had been in the early 1950s. After being slaughtered by Martin Sheen, he took a break for around ten years and then returned to the big screen with two films I saw during my sixth form days. The first of these was, "A Dry White Season", an apartheid courtroom drama in which Brando played a liberal white lawyer who challenges the white establishment.

The other was "The Freshman", opposite Matthew Broderick, who probably couldn't believe his luck to be appearing with Marlon Brando in another film where Brando played a mobster Godfather. The role required a certain amount of self-parody, with Brando almost lampooning his most famous screen role. After this he appeared in some half decent films, such as "Don Juan DeMarco" with Jonny Depp and Faye Dunaway, but some truly awful films, such as "The Island of Dr. Moreau". The less

279

said about that the better. It was a strange and rather sad way to end a career which had started in the most phenomenal of ways.

Brando burst onto the scene and the screen in Fred Zinnemann's "The Men" in 1950, before he blew the whole world away with his smouldering, angry, vulnerable, and downright dirty portrayal of Stanley Kowalski in the film adaptation of Tennessee Williams' play "A Streetcar Named Desire". When I first saw this, I had already read the play and was keen to see some sort of version of it either on stage or on screen. As the film was readily available in our magic video shop, my girlfriend and I both drooled over Brando, although she drooled slightly more than me, the same way my wife now still drools over this film or any stills of Brando in it.

Marlon Brando, in a dirty white vest, with his hair almost being covered by his cap, drinking a bottle of beer, is a sight to behold, and whether it got my girlfriend then, and my wife now all hot and bothered, it certainly did the same for Vivien Leigh as Blanche DuBois. Leigh had gone from the prissy and spoilt Scarlett O'Hara to this older, insecure and sexually frustrated southern belle. Her performance was wonderful, but Brando's overshadowed it.

He was nominated for the Best Actor Oscar but lost out to Humphrey Bogart in "The African Queen" as the academy probably thought Bogart might never get another chance to win, whereas Brando certainly would, as would another young firebrand who was nominated that year, Montgomery Clift, for his performance opposite Elizabeth Taylor in "A Place in the Sun", a film which had nothing to do with couples looking to buy a holiday home on a daytime Channel 4 TV show.

Brando would also lose out in the following two years, with his role as Emiliano Zapata in "Viva Zapata!", also directed by Elia

Kazan, and Mark Anthony in "Julius Caesar" being overlooked by the Academy. His next film was overlooked completely, and he wasn't even nominated for his role as Johnny Strabler, the leader of a leather clad biker gang in "The Wild One", which also featured a younger Lee Marvin on his way to becoming the sadistic bastard Liberty Valance.

The film was perhaps deemed too wild for the Academy, and definitely too wild for us very proper Brits as it was banned in the UK until 1968, not allowing the British boys and girls to hear him deliver one of his most famous lines ever. When he is asked what he is rebelling against, he famously replies, "Whadda you got?"

After seeing that film, and because I thought I was such a cool rebel, I bought the famous poster of him from that film and stuck it on my university bedroom wall, next to my other faux cool posters of "Easy Rider" and "Apocalypse Now". But who was I kidding? I had never worn a leather jacket in my life and had certainly never ridden a motorbike. My most rebellious act up until then was to take two sausages for my breakfast, when I was only allowed one.

However, Brando's next film, another directed by Elia Kazan, could certainly not be ignored by anyone, including the Academy, and he won his first Oscar for Best Actor playing the role of Terry Malloy, opposite the almost ethereal Eva Marie Saint, who I had already fallen in love with in "North by Northwest", even though she was five years older in that film. In "On the Waterfront" though, she was the most gorgeous blonde ever, and I often tell my wife she reminds me of a young Eva Marie Saint, or even an older Eva Marie Saint, depending on how big a hole it is I'm trying to dig myself out of. This huge compliment usually ends up winning her over, as she herself knows just how gorgeous Eva was.

Brando's performance as Terry Malloy is almost on a par with that of Stanley in "A Streetcar Named Desire". Almost, but not quite, although his brilliant "I coulda been a contender" speech with Rod Steiger, showed everything his earlier performance had shown, this time with just a little more restraint, something he would keep learning until his next Oscar for "The Godfather" almost twenty years later.

In between he played some strange roles. I've already mentioned his Skye Masterson in "Guys and Dolls", and there was his famous portrayal of Fletcher Christian in the second of the three film versions of "Mutiny on the Bounty", but apart from these two films, most of Brando's output was rather forgettable. It was as though he knew he wouldn't be able to top what he had achieved in the three films he made with Elia Kazan, and so couldn't be bothered any more, until Francis Ford Coppola gave him the role of Vito Corleone of course. Even after this he then went onto make the rather bizarre "Last Tango in Paris", which I only watched to see what other use there was for a knob of butter other than greasing a cake tin.

Kazan, on the other hand, would go onto make "East of Eden" which starred another famous rebel, James Dean. This was Dean's breakthrough film, and then of course went onto star in "Rebel Without a Cause", opposite Natalie Wood. This film allowed me to finally understand the reference in "The Exorcist" to Sal Mineo, as I finally realised who he was and how Father Karras did indeed look more like John Garfield than Sal Mineo, according to Lee J. Cobb's detective.

Dean's third and tragically final film was "Giant", in which he played another rebel, the cowhand Jett Rink. The shooting of the film was coming to an end when Dean crashed his car and broke his neck, killing him instantly. So much for being a rebel. At least Brando didn't break his own neck through his own stupidity. I often wonder just how good James Dean would have been, whether he would have ever rivalled Brando, or whether he would have fizzled away.

Another cocksure young actor with fire in his belly was Montgomery Clift, who I already mentioned for his great performance in "A Place in the Sun". He'd already made his name by then of course in Howard Hawks' "Red River", and would go onto star with Burt Lancaster and George Bailey's wife from "It's a Wonderful Life", Donna Reed in "From Here to Eternity", a film which features the beach kissing scene, wonderfully spoofed in "Airplane" of course.

Whilst shooting his next film "Raintree County", Clift would almost do a James Dean, crashing his car, but not killing himself. Nearly but not quite, and he would be left with severe facial injuries, which would be noticeable once he recovered and started reshooting the film. He was never the same actor again, despite appearing, as Brando had done, in a Tennessee Williams' play which had been turned into a film, this time in "Suddenly Last Summer", alongside Elizabeth Taylor again, and also with the great Katharine Hepburn. He then was also in "The Misfits" with Clark Gable and Marilyn Monroe, but his earlier successes would not be matched even here. That'll teach him not to fall asleep at the wheel of his car after leaving a Beverly hills dinner party. Just take a cab!

I can't leave this chapter on the bad boys of Hollywood without mentioning someone who definitely looked like James Dean, and is probably just as good an actor, if not better. The two men even get a mention in the lyrics of R.E.M.'s song "Electrolite", along with another bad boy, Steve McQueen, who I had loved not only in "The Great Escape" but also in "Bullitt", basically because of the coolest car chase ever, and his ability to make even a polo neck look cool.

The other name mentioned in that song was Martin Sheen, who had of course slaughtered Marlon Brando like a sacrificed ox in "Apocalypse Now". I don't know why he hadn't gone on from there to star in some really huge films as the leading star. He was certainly talented enough. Maybe again, like Brando and Dean, he peaked too early, this time in his debut film "Badlands", in which he is famously known for resembling James Dean, directed by Terence Malick, where he and Sissy Spacek go on a killing spree in South Dakota. I loved that film, especially Sheen's boyish charm, and how sweet and innocent he looked when he was blowing people away.

And speaking of sweet and innocent, it was time for me to relive my own days of sweetness and innocence. Steven Spielberg had another blockbuster out in the summer of 1993, and I would be at home to watch it, in the same cinema that I first saw another of his films which featured a creature with very sharp teeth.

This time, however, the creatures would not swim in the sea, but live in a park, and be billions of years old. It was time to be blown away by Mr. Spielberg once more.

Jurassic Park (1993)   Dir: Steven Spielberg

As well as all these classic older films I'd been watching, there were quite a few memorable trips to the cinema still going on. The first of these took place in May 1993 when my girlfriend and I had been on a day trip to the south coast. My housemate had allowed me to borrow his old knackered car, so I swept my girlfriend down to the south coast so she could see where she had grown up, in the Hampshire countryside. We had a lovely day if I remember rightly, walking along the prom at Southsea, before stopping for a drink in a couple of beautiful little pubs in the South Downs on our way back up to Reading.

We fancied taking in a film too, so on our way back we stopped at the most nondescript of retail parks to get something to eat and go to the cinema which was also in the retail park. You know the type of place; huge outlet stores, huge multiplex, huge choice, huge everything. Just very little charm, as it was just outside the most nondescript of towns ever. Bracknell is not known for its beauty or charm, but the film we would watch that evening was definitely charming, and beautiful in its own way.

"Groundhog Day", directed by Harold Ramis, who had starred with the film's main star, Bill Murray in "Ghostbusters", was, and remains, an absolute little gem of a film. We had not heard that much about it, but there wasn't much choice that evening, so we opted for this film, and were more than pleasantly surprised. We were exceptionally delighted with it in fact.

The film's story, if anyone doesn't know it, is of grumpy weatherman Phil Connors being stuck in not only the isolated little town of Punxsatawny, where he has been sent to cover the annual groundhog festival, where a rodent can apparently forecast the weather too, but also stuck in time, as he has to relive the same day until he learns how to change himself and thus change his future. If you didn't know the story then surely you must have heard the phrase "groundhog moment" or something similar being used. This film created a new phrase for us all to use when the same thing seems to keep happening to us. Not many films introduce a new idiom into our language, but this one did.

It is one of the sweetest, funniest, and actually one of the most romantic films we had both seen in ages. It made a change from my girlfriend having already seen the films we were watching on video, as this time it was a truly shared experience, with both of us not knowing what to expect, and both of us feeling exactly the same emotions for the first time. It really was a lovely and romantic way to end what had been a lovely and romantic day.

Bill Murray's object of desire is Andie MacDowell, who I had first seen in "Sex, Lies and Videotape", before she moved into more mainstream films, starring opposite Gerard Depardieu, who had done the same, in "Green Card", another of the films I had seen during my sixth form years. She then made a bit of a stinker with "Hudson Hawk", opposite Bruce Willis, before coming back to form in "The Player". "Groundhog Day" was the next film of hers which I saw, and still remains my favourite, more so even than "Four Weddings and a Funeral", which I will come onto in a later chapter.

The biggest compliment I can give to the film is that if Frank Capra had been making films in the 1990s, then this is the sort of film he would have made. It is very Capraesque in its tone although it deals with similar issues, but reversed. Instead of a man coming to the big city to realise that his values should be adopted by the city dwellers, as in "Deeds" and "Smith", this time it is a man coming from a big city into the smaller town and taking on a much simpler, a much kinder, and ultimately a less cynical and more hopeful outlook on life. As I said, it really is a little gem of a film. As I said, it really is a little gem of a film. As I said, it really is a little gem of a film. Sorry I went all a bit groundhog there.

My second year of university finished, and me and my girlfriend returned for the summer to our parents' houses, which we now did not really consider home anymore. We would see each other every weekend, and one of the alternate weekends she would be staying with me would coincide with one of the biggest movie releases ever. The anticipation surrounding Steven Spielberg's next blockbuster was huge. The press had built it up until the public were almost in a bit of a frenzy, waiting for the film to be released, as Spielberg had not had a massive hit since his third Indiana Jones film, four years previously.

Apart from this third instalment in that series, since the second film of the series had come out in 1984, Spielberg had veered away into more adult orientated films, with "The Colour Purple" in 1985, which introduced the world to Whoopi Goldberg, who would go onto star in some of the biggest films ever made, and "Empire of the Sun", which would introduce the world to Christian Bale, who would go onto become Batman, and a psycho from America who liked to chop women up with a chainsaw, and no he wasn't playing Leatherface in a remake of "A Texas Chainsaw Massacre".

Both "The Colour Purple" and "Empire of the Sun" were very good films, very worthy films, and very adult films, and so had passed me by somewhat as a teenager. I had gone to see Spielberg's rather dreary film of 1989 called "Always" which had reunited him with Richard Dreyfuss, and of course the damp squib "Hook" on my nineteenth birthday. And so I, along with millions of other kids, both young and old, were very excited about "Jurassic Park" as it was bound to provide the same sort of blockbuster entertainment Spielberg had made his name for.

It seemed that everyone else was as excited as me when my girlfriend and I arrived at the cinema in Lancaster one warm Monday evening in late July. I'd never seen a queue that long before, not even for "Star Wars" on my first ever visit to that cinema. It stretched right round the corner of the street, and then turned two more corners, almost meeting itself again, forming a kind of human barrier for the block in which the cinema was situated.

Luckily, we had got there fairly early, anticipating a queue, and we were around the first corner, in a queue which must have resembled the queue my own Gran had been in as she waited to get into to see "Gone With the Wind" over fifty years previously. I spent the whole time shuffling forward, wondering whether we would in fact get in to the cinema, or whether we would be two of the unlucky ones who would get all the way up the stairs, only to be told that it was full.

Thankfully, we did get in, but I don't know how many people were left disappointed that evening, as the auditorium was already almost full when we squeezed into our squeaky seats. Despite the squeakiness of the seats, they made me feel more comfortable than ever. These were the seats I had grown up sitting in, before I had become a big ponce and gone down south to study literature and watch a load of arty films. I was back where I had started my cinematic journey, in a packed theatre, with the buzz of anticipation being palpable in the air, waiting for a true blockbuster of a movie to escape into.

To be honest, "Jurassic Park" is not one of Spielberg's best films actually. It had nothing like the impact "E.T." "Jaws" or "Raiders of the Lost Ark" had on me. Maybe that was because I was that much older now, not even being a teenager anymore by this point. But the film itself, if you take away the dinosaurs, is not that great. But of course nobody cared, me included, as we all had the same expressions on our faces as Laura Dern and Sam Neill, when they first saw the huge Brachiosaurus standing on its hind legs to reach the very highest leaves. Our jaws dropped even more when we saw the T-Rex, and as for the scene when the "bloodsucking lawyer" as Dickie Attenborough's character John Hammond, the park's owner, calls him, gets eaten whilst sitting on the toilet, well, I was agog and aghast.

It was huge fun, and also referenced the first ever film I had "almost" seen, when Jeff Goldblum's character mentions the gates of Jurassic Park looking like the gates that kept King Kong out. The film itself would be referenced by other films, most notably in "Toy Story 2" when Rex the dinosaur is chasing the toys around the toy store as they drive Barbie's car, with the shot of him in the rear view mirror replicating almost exactly the shot of the other, much bigger CGI T-Rex in Spielberg's film.

I'm sure that Spielberg was also referencing one of the early Screwball classics which has already had a chapter devoted to it in this book. In almost the final scene in the film. When the dinosaur skeleton collapses whilst Sam Neill, who has developed his parenting skills somewhat over the course of the film, is ushering the two kids away from the velociraptors, is very reminiscent of the scene in "Bringing Up Baby" when Katharine Hepburn accidentally demolishes Cary Grant's pride and joy of a dinosaur skeleton. I am in no doubt that Spielberg was a huge fan of Howard Hawks, and wanted to pay his respects to him, although of course in "Bringing Up Baby" the scene wasn't ended with one vicious and very much alive dinosaur being eaten by a much bigger, and equally vicious and alive dinosaur.

Looking back now, the CGI dinosaurs in "Jurassic Park" seem quite crude now, but back then they were nothing short of a phenomenon. Nobody had ever seen such sights before, in such realistic and life like detail. Yes, we'd all seen monsters, but never like this, where the digital magic seemed to fit seamlessly in with the actual live action. The film opened up the gates for CGI films to out do each other, to the point where CGI is now almost expected in a blockbuster, and we almost yearn for a film without its use.

Spielberg cleverly left the possibility of a sequel open with the stolen dinosaur embryos being buried in the mud after the fat guy's failed attempt to escape with them, and also with the warning from Jeff Goldblum coming true that the dinosaurs had bred in the wild, and that life had indeed found a way. And sure enough, there have now been five sequels to the original film, but none of them for me captured that same moment of awe I experienced in the original film. As I said, CGI has become part of our cinema experience now, whereas in 1993 it almost bit you in two with its scale and wonder, a bit like the T-Rex did to the lawyer actually.

From this CGI fest of a blockbuster, Spielberg's next film would be the complete opposite. He would not need computers to show the horrors on screen as the Nazis would do that for him in "Schindler's List", which provided a cinema experience just as powerful as his last film, although for completely different reasons.

In complete contrast to "Jurassic Park", "Schindler's List" was shot almost entirely in black and white, with only the image of the little girl in her red coat being seen in colour, which became a motif for the film. I'd heard people sobbing before in one of Spielberg's films, in "E.T." but for wholly different reasons than the sobs I heard and indeed experienced myself whilst watching the extraordinary story of one man's attempt to save as many Jews as he could from Nazi extermination.

It really is an extraordinary film as well, particularly when you think it was released only seven months after "Jurassic Park". Spielberg must have been planning it and visualising it in his head as he was actually filming the scenes where dinosaurs rip each other to bits. It really showed how huge Spielberg's range was and also how huge his talents are.

As a Jew himself it was obviously a very personal film to him, and I believe it has done so much for the world's general understanding of what went on in those Nazi death camps, and deservedly won him his first Best Director Oscar, as well as the film winning Best Picture, Best Adapted Screenplay, Best Cinematography, Best Art Direction, Best Editing, and Best Music for John Williams' score. From the worst period in humanity, came one of the best films ever.

Changing the tone completely, my year at the cinema in 1993 ended with a film which definitely wasn't black and white, and certainly was meant for a different demographic than "Schindler's List", although me and my three best mates, all either twenty or twenty-one years old by this point, joined in this much younger demographic for one afternoon just before Christmas.

Disney's "Aladdin" also won an Oscar for its original score, although Alan Menken's music would be very different to that of John Williams, and Menken also won the Oscar for Best Song for the awful "A Whole New World". Me and my mates much preferred "Friend Like Me" or "Prince Ali", as that was more in tune with our very childish, and very drunk minds that particular afternoon.

It was either Christmas Eve, or the day before, and we were all at home, having returned from our various places of "study" to be with our families. We'd all spent enough time with our families by then so decided to meet up, get the train into Lancaster, and get drunk, just as we used to do during our sixth form days, or rather our sixth form evenings. But this day we would start in the early afternoon, so that by around 4pm we were completely hammered, and rather than just carrying on in the pub, we were now in the mood to go and relive another of our sixth form pastimes; going to the cinema together.

"Aladdin" was the next showing when we arrived at the cinema, so into the queue we went, along with the many small, giggly children and their parents. We actually fitted in quite well in the queue, as although we were taller, much taller in the case of my six and a half foot tall mate, we were of the same mindset, equally giggly, equally giddy, and equally as excitable.

The other children's parents gave us some disapproving looks, and could probably smell the beer on us, but apart from swaying slightly, and almost falling down the stairs up to the auditorium, we behaved even better I would say than some of the five and six year old kids. And we certainly enjoyed the film as much, if not more than our younger audience members.

Disney's star had not been shining so brightly as it did in the 1930s, 40s and 50s, and had not had a huge animated film since probably "The Rescuers" in 1977, another film my Gran had taken me to in the cinema I now sat in. In fact, Disney had been trundling along with its live action films, and had only recently had a resurgence of its hand drawn animated films since "The Little Mermaid" of 1989. This would be the first of "The Big Four" films, which also included "Beauty and the Beast" from 1991, and "The Lion King" of 1994. "Aladdin" proved to be the third film in this quartet, reigniting the public's enthusiasm for what Disney had become famous for in the first place.

Since then Disney would release a new hand drawn animated film every year, with "Pocahontas", "The Hunchback of Notre Dame", "Hercules", "Mulan" and "Tarzan" all being very worthy additions to their hand drawn canon, before John Lasseter came along and made "Toy Story" which frankly changed everything in the world of studio animation. More on that later, but at the time when me and my mates were giggling like small children to Robin Williams' brilliant voicing for the Genie, this was the first truly great Disney film we had ever watched at the cinema, unless of course I was counting the re-released films I had seen as a small boy.

I loved "Aladdin". It was perfect drunk viewing, and to this day, I very much enjoy a Disney film after I've had a few. The visuals become brighter, the humour becomes more puerile, the storyline remains nice and simple, and there is always a happy ending to

292

keep the drunk from becoming an angry or depressed drunk. The magic carpet ride Aladdin takes in the cave, the first appearance of the Genie, with the song "Friend Like Me" being an absolutely hilarious show stopper, and the talking parrot on Jafar's shoulder all made us giggle or gasp quite possibly disproportionately to the other kids, although I'll always remember one little lad who forgot he was supposed to be whispering when he shouted out to his mum "If I see that parrot one more time, I'm gonna wee my pants," which of course almost made me and my mates nearly wee ours. And I, as an English Literature undergraduate even got the joke about the parrot's name being Iago. I bet the five year old kid didn't, not that I'm being childish.

That afternoon with my mates, watching a kids' film, was one of the most joyous experiences I have ever had in a cinema, and reminded me why we go to the cinema in the first place: the shared experience. I've seen it plenty of times on video or TV since, indeed my girlfriend's mum bought it for me on its video release, but watching it at home on a small screen has never been able to capture the sheer sense of joy, excitement and fun that I felt that afternoon. It made me not just feel like a kid again, but to think like one, and experience like one. And for that, the film will always have a special place in my heart, as will the next film, a film whose central song also makes me feel childish, sweet and innocent every time I hear it.

Are those raindrops I hear outside?

Butch Cassidy and the Sundance Kid (1969)
Dir: George Roy Hill

I didn't include this film in my chapter on Westerns before as I wanted it to have its own chapter, as it is very special to me. I don't really consider it a Western really anyway. Yes it is set in the West, with gunslingers, bank robberies, cowboys, and whorehouses above saloons, but it is more of a modern day buddy movie, which just happens to be set in the West.

It is more about the death of the West as symbolised by the famous scene which the song I referred to, "Raindrops are Falling on my Head" is set to, in which Paul Newman as Butch takes Katharine Ross, as Etta, for a spin on his new bicycle, which would of course eventually replace the horse as a means of transport. The scene where Butch and Sundance are watching the Marshall try to drum up a posse to catch them, before the bicycle salesman opportunistically diverts his audience's attention is comedy gold, and sums up the sense of humour, fun and irreverence the film brings.

Whatever it is, it is a huge great romp of a film, with moments of real comedy, real drama, and real beauty. The beauty is provided by Katharine Ross as Sundance's girlfriend Etta, particularly in the scene in which she is forced to undress at gunpoint by Sundance, shaking her hair and unbuttoning her underwear, whilst we the audience do not yet know who she is. It is one of the sexiest, yet also tenderest strip scenes in a film I have ever seen, not that I'm a specialist in these scenes I might add.

I'd already seen Katharine Ross in "The Graduate", riding the bus away from her sexually warped and frustrated mother, with Benjamin Braddock by her side, the graduate of the film's title, who her mother had tried to famously seduce. As I was now well into my third and final year as an undergraduate and would soon become what Dustin Hoffman was playing (not the object of an older woman's desire I might add), but a graduate, then I thought it was about time I ticked this film off my list. I already knew all the songs, as I'd listened to so much Simon and Garfunkel during my university years, and was frankly quite embarrassed that I had not yet seen the film which arguably their most famous song had been written for.

I very much enjoyed "The Graduate" but did not fall in love with Mrs Robinson's daughter at that point. I probably fancied Anne Bancroft, her mum, more in a weird kind of MILF way. Katharine Ross became another sort of MILF when I watched the 1975 version of "The Stepford Wives", and always remember that film for Ross and Paula Prentice overhearing one of the robot wives screaming in ecstasy to her husband Frank that not only was he the best in bed, but also the king, the champion and the master! But it will always be "Butch Cassidy and the Sundance Kid" which I will remember her most fondly in.

I love the shot of her face as she has just locked the bank manager in his own safe room, after he had invited her and Sundance down there, not realising they were then going to rob him. I love how she repeatedly says, "show me the money", trying to get Butch to repeat it in Spanish, which suggests a certain prostitute relationship between her and the two loves of her life. She is, after all, their kept woman, but is obviously deeply in love with both men as she is not prepared to watch them die at the end, in what is one of the most iconic final shots of any film.

The film is split into two halves really, the first half being set in America, with the second half in Bolivia, cut in two by the most lovely montage ever on screen, with George Roy Hill's use of music beautifully transitioning the two halves of the story, telling of the threesome's journey from North to South America. There is not a single part of that film which I would change. It has so many memorable scenes, memorable lines, and memorable laughs.

One of my favourite shots does not involve any character at all. Just as the three depart their old lives in America, Butch rolls the bicycle he had wooed Etta with away, shouting "The future's all yours ya lousy bicycles!" The next shot is of the fallen bicycle, its wheels still spinning in a stream, slowly coming to a stop, symbolising how time and nature will continue, but progress will always necessitate change.

With the ending of one type of West, then another will come along, which is also symbolic of Hollywood itself. The Wild West transformed into Hollywood, which of course was where this film originated. Progress is necessary, however painful it may be. This of course is what Butch and Sundance cannot cope with, moving to Bolivia to try and continue the only lives they've ever known, but even there the law catches up with them, putting a very permanent end to their lives in a volley of gunfire.

So, yes the film is a Western, and was certainly one of my dad's favourites, but it is more than a Western. It is simply a wonderful film, and probably in my top five of all time. I could watch it at least three or four times a year, and even though I know the script almost word for word, I never get tired of saying the lines out loud as I watch, much to my wife's eternal annoyance.

She loves the film too, but not for the same reason as me. Well Paul Newman is just one of the many reasons I love it, but for her, he is the most obvious reason why she does not mind me watching it over and over. Simply put, Paul Newman is my wife's kinda guy. I often catch her gazing at pictures of him on her phone, and to be honest I don't blame her. There are certain shots of Newman, just like Brando, which make me go all a bit of a flutter too.

Another film of his made me go more than just a bit of a flutter, as I watched the most suggestive and seductive of car washes ever in "Cool Hand Luke", another scene my wife strangely doesn't mind me watching, seeing as it features Paul Newman all sweaty and bare chested. My favourite scene from that film though is when Newman is challenged to eat fifty hard boiled eggs in one hour. I have always loved eggs, in any form, with hard boiled being one of my favourites. I've often thought whether or not I could, or indeed, should take on the same challenge too. I'd like to think I could do it, although I doubt my wife would be that enamoured of that particular scene once my digestive system started breaking all those eggs down.

One of my favourite films of Paul Newman is his debut, "Somebody Up There Likes Me" from 1956, in which he played the real life Rocky, Rocky Graziano, before Newman really made a name for himself, just as Brando did, in a not just one film version of a Tennessee Williams play, but two, with "Cat on a Hot Tin Roof" opposite Elizabeth Taylor, and "Sweet Bird of Youth".

In between these two films was possibly Newman's best ever performance, in "The Hustler" in 1961, playing "Fast" Eddie Felson, a role he should have won the Oscar for Best Actor in 1962, losing out to Maximilian Schell in "Judgement at Nuremberg". Maybe that was why he won his Best Actor Oscar for that film's sequel, Martin Scorsese's "The Colour of Money" in 1987. Strangely though he'd already been given an Honorary Oscar, in the same way that Cary Grant had been given one, with the Academy obviously thinking that Newman would not get another chance. He proved there was life in the old dog yet, and won a proper Oscar anyway, just to confirm his status as one of the greats. He had plenty of life in him in fact, as he would appear in two more very significant films in my life, which will definitely be mentioned later.

As for The Sundance Kid, Robert Redford had already made his name in "Barefoot in the Park", as one half of a newlywed couple, with the gorgeous Jane Fonda as his new bride, in the film version of Neil Simon's play. This is such a lovely film, and Fonda is ravishing in it. Redford certainly was lucky to get married to her, but many women would probably not say that he was punching above his weight as he went onto become one of the throbbiest of heart throbs ever, particularly in the huge hit "The Way We Were" opposite Barbra Streisand, a film which also featured one of my earliest heart throbs if you remember, Lois Chiles, who had played Holly Goodhead in "Moonraker".

Chiles would also feature with Redford in "The Great Gatsby", a film I too have already mentioned, before Redford would make one of his most important films of his career, "All the President's Men" alongside Dustin Hoffman, another film I duly ticked off my must watch list.

One of his biggest hits, "A Bridge Too Far" was more like "A Bridge Too Young" for me, as I was only four when it came out and then passed me by ever since, as did "Out of Africa" with Meryl Streep" as I was twelve by then, and soppy films set in colonial Kenya were not really my bag then.

One of my favourite films of Redford's was Barry Levinson's "The Natural" from 1984, a film about an almost divinely talented baseball player, which I watched on video during that spate of Baseball films around the late eighties and early nineties, which included "Bull Durham", and "Field of Dreams", both starring Kevin Costner, and "A League of their Own". Redford's film was better than Kevin Costner's, and way better than the other one even though it starred Tom Hanks and Geena Davis, with even Madonna giving a good performance in a film. I also saw Redford in the rather forgettable, "Legal Eagles", "Havana", and "Indecent Proposal", but "Sneakers" from 1992 was lots of fun.

Unlike Paul Newman, who had dabbled with directing his own films, but without much success, Redford's directorial debut in 1980, "Ordinary People" not only won him the Best Director Oscar at his first attempt, but also won Best Picture. It was as though whatever he did turned to gold, which could also be said for his film festival, The Sundance Festival, which from quite humble beginnings in 1978, in which independent films were showcased, has now become a huge event on the cinema calendar.

The media extravaganza which encircles it now seems to go against Redford's original intentions, and there have been several measures put in place to stop the festival becoming another media circus. But then again, just like the bicycle in the film the festival takes its name from, progress, be it bad or good, is inevitable, and sometimes it can change the very nature of its original meaning, again just like the American West.

Redford would not direct another film for another eight years, and sticking to his indie principles, made a couple of very independent films, with "The Milagro Beanfield War" in 1988 and the one which I most fondly remember, as it quickly became one of my fly-fishing loving father's favourite films, "A River Runs Through It".

He then went slightly more mainstream in 1994 with "Quiz Show", a film my then girlfriend was desperate to see as she had the hots for Ralph Fiennes, who would play Charles Van Doren in the story of the scandal over the cheating which went on in 1958 on the TV quiz show "Twenty-One".

The only other of Redford's films I have seen which he directed was "The Legend of Bagger Vance" starring Will Smith, Matt Damon and Charlize Theron, which still remained less than mainstream, and almost quite mystical, in the same vein as "A River Runs Through It" had also been.

There is one glaring omission in this chapter about Paul Newman and Robert Redford, a chapter whose title film was directed by

George Roy Hill, and that is because it is the only other film in which that director directed those two stars. George Roy Hill had already directed "Thoroughly Modern Millie" before he really hit the big time with Butch and Sundance, and after the success of this last film, the obvious thing to do was team up again, but this time they would not be making a Western, but a 1930s crime caper, with Newman and Redford as con men trying to pull one over their nemesis, Doyle Lonnegan, played by Robert Shaw..

"The Sting" was one film I had seen many times when I was young, as my brother and dad loved it, my brother loving the use of Scott Joplin's ragtime music in particular. He especially loved the film's theme tune, "The Entertainer" and he learned to play it on the piano quite adroitly, another of my brother's many talents which he never really followed through on.

The film itself was another wise-cracking buddy movie, but just did not have quite the same appeal as the director and stars' first collaboration. Maybe it was the script, which although very good, did not quite hit the target in the same way as William Goldman's astonishing screenplay had for "Butch Cassidy and the Sundance Kid". But then again, few films do hit the bullseye quite like that script.

When I watched "The Sting" as a kid, I had no idea who Robert Shaw was back then. It was only after he'd been bitten in half by a shark that I realised who he was the next time I watched "The Sting". Even that didn't make me love the film more than "Butch Cassidy and the Sundance Kid".

That really was a film which showed real vision, whilst the rest of the world wore bifocals.

Four Weddings and a Funeral (1994)   Dir: Mike Newell

This film is included not because it is one of my favourites, or because it's such an artistically impressive one. It is neither of these things. It is a sweet, gentle, very English comedy which made a huge star of Hugh Grant, and gave Andie MacDowell's career another boost. It also made its writer Richard Curtis very rich.

Curtis had written some of the funniest comedy of the 1980s, creating one of the best sitcoms ever in "Blackadder", before trying his hand at a film script for "The Tall Guy", which Mel Smith, who Curtis had written much material for in "Not The Nine O'Clock News" directed, starring Jeff Goldblum and Emma Thompson in her debut on the big screen. This was yet another film I saw during my sixth form years, and featured a memorably comic sex scene, with Goldblum and Thompson getting very messy amongst the breakfast things, in which toast gets stuck to Thompson's rear end.

The film did ok but would be nowhere near as successful as Curtis' next screenplay, which arrived on our cinema screens in the middle of May 1994, right in the middle of my final exams. My girlfriend and I had allowed ourselves a night off from our revision and preparation, and went along for what would turn out to be our last film together as undergraduates.

Maybe it was the fact that I just couldn't properly switch off my mind from the exams I had coming up that I did not enjoy the film that much when I first saw it, or maybe it was the fact that the film is very British. I do not mean that in a derogatory way, but the British Film Industry in the years before "Four Weddings" came out had not exactly experienced a boom or heyday in its long and distinguished life.

The 1980s had been a rather lean period for British films, with the odd hit occurring, mainly by the team of Merchant/Ivory or an independent sleeper of a film such as Stephen Frears' "My Beautiful Launderette", or Lewis Gilbert's "Shirley Valentine", or even Bruce Robinson's "Withnail and I". The trend continued into the early nineties with Merchant/Ivory films keeping the British end up, and so watching a huge success of a film such as "Four Weddings" was a bit of a novelty for me.

For the past few years I had engulfed myself in mostly American films, some of them great, some not so great, and had become accustomed to American accents. To then be presented with accents which were not just British accents, but really quite posh English accents, was all too much of a contrast for me, even with Andie MacDowell's broad South Carolina accent included too.

And maybe the other reason I did not really enjoy the film was because it was very romantic, and my girlfriend and I had been drifting apart over the previous few months. Maybe it was because we had basically watched just about every film in that video shop we had discovered two years previously, or maybe our studies were finally becoming more important, or maybe even we were getting a bit bored of each other. Whatever the reason, the sight of Hugh Grant delivering charming and romantic lines, in the words of David Cassidy in fact, while he was still with The Partridge Family, such as "I think I love you", was again something which did not really appeal that much at the time. I've obviously seen it many times since then, and have grown to love it more with every viewing, but it still does not get onto my list of all-time favourites.

Possibly the reason I have included "Four Weddings and a Funeral" at all is because the film came at a real crossroads moment in my life, a moment that has become known as a "Sliding Doors" moment, the phrase being created by another

British film, which will also be dealt with later. At that point in my life, with me taking my Finals, bringing to an end my formal education, something that had been my life for the past seventeen years, I now had a choice to make: what the hell was I going to do with the rest of my life?

I had considered journalism quite seriously and also teaching, but I suppose my real dream at that point was to become a part of the film industry myself, writing screenplays, or maybe even directing a film myself. That would have been the answer I would have given had a Fairy Godfather or a genie in a lamp come along and granted me one wish, but I had neither the confidence, the contacts, or indeed the bravery to make that wish come true by myself.

I had fancied myself as someone with stories to tell, but had no idea of how to go about becoming a film writer or film director. Maybe I just didn't have the common sense either, or deep down, the burning desire to make it happen. I've had loads of what I think are good ideas for film scripts, one of which is based on "Four Weddings and a Funeral", or at least the basic premise. For the second part of his working life, my dad was a funeral director, and had told me many stories of his funeral days. Some were downright ghastly, some were tragic, some were bland and very ordinary, and some were just absolutely hilarious.

As such, I have often thought of writing a script for a film based on these stories, but this time I would invert the original idea and call mine "Five Funerals and a Wedding", with one extra funeral added into the mix to really put the fun into funeral. Maybe I will still write it, and maybe I will see my own idea turned into a film and shown on the big screen. Maybe, maybe not. Maybe I could have been a contender myself, just like Brando, but instead I didn't have the guts, and so became an English teacher instead.

I've rarely regretted choosing this as a career. It has given me some wonderful moments, along with some not so wonderful ones, but I wonder what might have been if I had gone through a different sliding door, and travelled on a different train. One thing is for certain, I wouldn't have met the woman who became my wife and provided me with my wonderful family.

Maybe I have had a wonderful life after all, despite not conquering Hollywood. But the first step on my journey to teacher stardom was to train to become one in the first place. And to graduate of course, or at least to become a post graduate, something that Benjamin Braddock never was I bet.

Part Five

The Postgraduate

The Hudsucker Proxy (1994)   Dirs: Joel and Ethan Coen

And so I graduated with a Second Class Honours Degree in English Literature, a 2:1, which would be the equivalent of a Grade B in terms of school grades. My brainbox of a girlfriend got a First, keeping up her A Grade status. I'd like to think I would have got a similar sort of grade had my Final exams been on the history of cinema and the key films of a range of film stars and directors. I think I may have much rather enjoyed taking exams on those topics rather than Romantic Poetry, The Theatre of the Absurd, Geoffrey Chaucer, Charles Dickens, and Shakespeare, to name a few of the topics I actually was examined on.

After my decision to become a teacher, I had to take an extra postgraduate teacher training course, which would mean another year in Reading. Despite me and my girlfriend drifting apart, we still kept what was becoming a bit of a dead shark of a relationship going by getting a small flat together, where I would be able to do my teaching course, and she would get a temporary job, on the proviso that we then move to London the following year to start my career, and whatever career she decided on. We got a nice little one bedroom flat just round the corner from where her first student house had been, and still just up the road from our wonderful video shop.

However, we seemed to watch very few films from there anymore. Admittedly, we had watched probably the vast majority of films in the shop, and were now on first name terms with the old man who owned it, but I was so busy with my course, and my girlfriend was usually so tired from work, that we tended to just slump in front of the TV and watch any old rubbish that was on. We'd become almost like a married couple who were just becoming bored with each other, with our lives now taking different directions now that our shared degree had ended.

We did however still treat ourselves to a night at the cinema, more to alleviate the awkward sense of boredom we felt with each other's company. A night at the pictures would at least mean we didn't have to share our increasingly separate lives, despite ironically sharing a flat together for the first time.

The first film we saw would be one of the films I mentioned which Paul Newman would prove he still had some life in him, and it would also highlight the change in my girlfriend and I's relationship quite starkly. The film in question is an affectionate homage to the director that my girlfriend had introduced me to almost three years before, one who I had fallen in love with, but this time, the film would be a less charming, and quite harsh depiction of an innocent young man arriving in a big city. It was as though the innocence and charm had gone from our own relationship too, but that didn't stop me from thinking it was still a great film.

"The Hudsucker Proxy", is the Coen brothers' affectionate homage and tribute to Frank Capra, and some of the Screwball Comedies of the 1930s and 40s. It is the story of a wide eyed and naïve young man, Norville Barnes, played by Tim Robbins, who I had very much enjoyed in "The Player", but maybe not enjoyed so much in "Jacob's Ladder", who arrives in New York City full of ideas and hope, a bit like Longfellow Deeds did, and Jefferson Smith did in Washington D.C. He soon finds that life is not quite so carefree and innocent, becoming Newman's Sidney J. Mussburger's stooge in the jungle of the business world, being eaten up by the lions, despite inventing the Hula Hoop, "You know, for kids!" which was meant to have been a flop, but unwittingly became a huge success.

In a direct parallel with "Mr. Deeds Goes to Town", Jennifer Jason Leigh plays a newspaper reporter, Amy Archer, who even has an alliterative name, just like Jean Arthur's Babe Bennett had done in the earlier film. The scene in which her newspaper editor berates his team of reporters for not getting any scoops on "The Ideas Man", is an almost shot for shot recreation of the same scene in Frank Capra's predecessor, with Deeds being referred to as "The Cinderella Man" for the first time by Babe Bennett, a nickname which she would make stick once she gets the exclusive story she promised her editor.

In order to get this exclusive, she has to pretend to be a damsel in distress, just as Amy Archer does in the Coen Brothers' film. Archer becomes Norville's personal secretary, and pretends to be helping her new boss, even pretending to be from the same small town of Muncie, Indiana, in another direct reference to Mandrake Falls from "Deeds".

Once Mussburger's plan doesn't quite go to plan, his solution is to prove Norville to be insane and a fraud, in a further parallel to "Deeds", and there is even a Germanic sounding professor brought in, with diagrams and graphs, to prove Norville's mental derangement, just as Longfellow Deeds was subjected to in the court scene of Capra's film.

Inevitably Amy's hard exterior is broken down by Norville's naivety and innocence, and she realises she has played a huge role in corrupting her callow young boss, with the two falling in love and kissing to the swirling crescendo of "Adagio of Spartacus and Phrygia", the best use of that music since it became the theme tune to "The Onedin Line". But safe to say that all ends well, with Mussburger being taken away in a straitjacket instead of Norville, leaving our hero to live happily ever after, presumably with Amy by his side. Mr. Norville Barnes esq. even has the time to launch his new product onto the market, another toy, "You know, for kids!" which is similarly circular, similarly simple, and similarly successful: the Frisbee.

308

Jennifer Jason Leigh's portrayal of Amy Archer harks back to the quick fire banter of the Screwball Comedies, with her playing the role in the style of Rosalind Russell in "His Girl Friday" but combining it with Katharine Hepburn's voice. Her performance was a bit of a mish-mash of styles, and the whole film was a bit of a mish-mash, being part satire, part homage, part fantasy. It also lacked something which the films it was paying homage to had in abundance: humanity and warmth.

There are elements of these two traits present in "The Hudsucker Proxy", but I don't blame the Coen brothers for not wanting to make the sort of schmaltzy homage which would have just been overbearingly simplistic. The cinema, and indeed the world, have progressed since Frank Capra's films had been huge successes, and similarly so had mine and my girlfriend's relationship. The innocence we felt at the beginning was now waning, being taken over by the realities of everyday life, just as Norville Barnes had been.

I still love the film though, especially the New Year's Eve climax, with Barnes falling from the top floor of the Hudsucker building, only for the clock to stop his deadly descent about a foot away from the ground, enabling him to joyously run off to safety once he finds out that he in fact has now inherited the whole company after being told to finally open and read the blue letter which he tried to deliver to Mussburger in the first place. Waring Hudsucker, the man Norville Barnes had replaced as President, becomes his guardian angel, in yet another direct reference to a Capra classic, with Clarence the angel being responsible for George Bailey's redemption in "It's a Wonderful Life".

Whatever "The Hudsucker Proxy" is, despite its flaws, it is an innovative piece of film making, one which fondly and affectionately looks back to the past, just as I was doing in my relationship with my girlfriend.

Other notable cinema trips that year were few and far between. We had enjoyed Richard Donner's take on the Western genre, "Maverick", with Mel Gibson, Jodie Foster, and James Garner in a really enjoyable romp of a film. Donner had moved from scaring the living daylights out of everybody in "The Omen" in 1976, another film I love and will gladly watch again and again, despite Billie Whitelaw's petrifying portrayal of Mrs Baylock, to making everyone believe a man could fly in "Superman", well sort of anyway, before making some of the most successful films of the 1980s, including "The Goonies", "Lethal Weapon" and "Scrooged", all of which I have much affection for too.

One blockbuster we both definitely escaped into was Jan de Bont's "Speed", with Dennis Hopper now playing a bit of a psycho, surprise, surprise, toying with the lives of innocent people on a bus, which made Sandra Bullock into a household name, and pushed Keanu Reeves into the stratosphere.

If it wasn't for "Speed", I doubt whether Reeves would go onto star in another truly awesome film, another of my all-time favourites, along with millions of other blokes of a certain age, particularly Simon Pegg who homaged it frequently in "Spaced", the best sit-com ever made as far as I'm concerned. Keanu Reeves of course would become, "The One", playing Neo in "The Matrix" and its subsequent sequels, and the rest is history, or rather the rest is a virtual world into which people are plugged, with reality being a computer generated cyberspace construction of course.

The other notable cinema trip we took was just before I started my ten week teaching block in February 1995, which definitely made me escape from lesson planning and creating resources for my classes, and ironically it is the story about someone else attempting to escape. There's not much to say about "The Shawshank Redemption", as it has been on TV so frequently that everyone seems to have watched it and fallen in love with it too. Everyone knows it almost word for word, and everyone knows the scenes where Tim Robbins' Andy Dufresne locks the warden's door and plays the opera music to the other inmates, or the scene when he finally emerges from the sewage pipe and lifts his arms up to the sky in the rain.

Everyone knows it too well for me to say anything new about it. It's so well known that it was even hilariously parodied in an episode of "Family Guy" along with another couple of Stephen King penned films, "Stand By Me" and "Misery", two more films I love, and will never get bored of, just like "Shawshank", despite it being on TV almost constantly. I love that the final word in the whole film is "hope", something we all need at this point in life, with a President of America who is much more corrupt and nasty than even the warden of Shawshank prison. If only Donald Trump's treachery would be legally found out, causing him to blow his brains out too!

And speaking of brains being blown out, my next film certainly had quite a bit of that in it, some on purpose, and some by complete accident. It was time for Quentin Tarantino to blow all our minds again.

Pulp Fiction (1994)   Dir: Quentin Tarantino

I'd been training to be a teacher for just under a month when this most Tarantino of Tarantino films was released on October 21st, 1994, and I saw it twice in two days. I'd become friendly with two of the other male student teachers on my course, and discovered they both enjoyed the cinema too, as did a few of the female student teachers. So, what better way to bond than to all go and be blown away by a film which still manages to blow me away to this day, despite me knowing it almost word for word and scene by scene, even shot by shot for most of it.

I'm sure there are so many others out there of a similar age to me who can say the same. The film has become so engraved on our collective memories and become such a part of popular culture that many of the lines of dialogue, many of the shots or stills from the film, and much of the soundtrack has simply become iconic. It became iconic for me after just one viewing, with my girlfriend joining me and my new colleagues at the cinema the day it came out. As soon as we emerged from the cinema that night, we both agreed that we not just wanted, but needed to see it again the following evening, but this time it would just be our treat.

The first viewing blew our minds so much that another viewing was absolutely crucial to be able to take in its vast array of highlights properly. In fact the whole film is just one long highlight, and is still the best film Quentin Tarantino has made.

After "Reservoir Dogs" had introduced the world to Tarantino, then this film turned his films into a genre of their own, using many similar techniques as his first film, but adding to them, refining them, and improving them. Many music artists talk about "that difficult second album", but this was obviously not the case for Tarantino. This film showed a man at the peak of his creative powers, and as I said, he has not improved on it since. It's hard to improve on such a thing of wonder as "Pulp Fiction".

When teaching my students about genre, I have always asked them to list the ingredients for certain genres, be it in literature or film, such as Sci-Fi, or Westerns, or Horror, or Rom Com, but you could easily argue that Tarantino's films belong in a genre all to themselves. Part gangster thriller, part romance, part comedy, part buddy movie; there are so many parts to this film which make it into its whole, and the ingredients have become standard fare for Tarantino films ever since. It even contains an animated sequence, something else which would be used again by Tarantino, just before the young Butch is quite hilariously told of the significance of his father's watch by Christopher Walken.

First there is the violence, which is never gratuitous, but always strangely enjoyable and satisfying; then there is the non-linear narrative, with the storyline not being told chronologically; then there is the dialogue, an almost ultra-real style of dialogue, very often included not to progress the narrative, but just for the sheer hell of it, such as the opening scene in "Reservoir Dogs" and the many examples of it in "Pulp Fiction", from Vincent and Jules opening chat in the car on the way to sample a Big Kahuna burger, to their chat in the diner in the final sequence, along with Mia and Vincent's seemingly innocuous and sometimes awkward exchange in Jack Rabbit Slim's diner, the awkward silences even being a part of their dialogue. And of course there is the soundtrack, which has provided so many songs which have become a part of not just my life, but those of my children's too.

I have danced around my living room so many times to "Hooked on a Feeling" from "Reservoir Dogs", with one of my children in my arms, particularly with my youngest daughter, whose lips were definitely as sweet as candy, bouncing her up in the air just before the title lyric is sung. Thankfully for them I have not recreated the scene in which "Stuck in the Middle" features though.

My children and I have all danced around to "Jungle Boogie", and Dusty Springfield's "Son of a Preacher Man" became very special to me and my wife seeing as I actually am the son of a preacher man, and I'd like to think that I've been the only one who could ever please and teach her properly. And "You Never Can Tell" and "Misirlou" provided us with our favourite "Strictly

Come Dancing" moment ever when Jay McGuiness and Aliona jived to a medley of both songs in Movie Week, in week three of his journey to the glitterball in 2015, over twenty years after I'd first watched John Travolta and Uma Thurman do their own most idiosyncratic of jives.

The scene in which that iconic sequence takes place is also Tarantino's homage to the 1950s and its great film stars, with screen idols such as Jayne Mansfield, James Dean and Marilyn Monroe all featuring as waiters or waitresses in Jack Rabbit Slim's diner. That one scene has provided so many iconic shots, in particular Mrs Mia Wallace's coolest of looks, with the Louise Brooks style bob, the classic white shirt, the cigarette, and the red lips.

The film is littered with so many iconic shots and sequences that it would be pointless just listing them. We all have our own favourite shots, our own favourite bits of dialogue, our own favourite moments. The film has become so well known and such a part of popular culture that Harvey Keitel has even rather disappointingly made a series of insurance commercials using the same iconography. There is no need for the advertisements to explain themselves as anyone who knows the film knows exactly what they refer to.

One of the things I enjoyed doing most on my second viewing was piecing together the narrative, and working out the actual chronological order of the three discrete stories, and it is apt that the film would end with another classic ingredient of cinema, with our hero, or one of them, if indeed any of the characters are heroes, riding off into the distance on his motorcycle, with his girl behind him. It would be the perfect way to end the film, but of course with Tarantino this perfect ending occurs two thirds of the way through the film, leaving the final image to be of two ruthless gangsters leaving a diner dressed in beach wear.

Tarantino would never end this film with such a cliché as the hero driving away to a new future on his motorcycle.

But of course it wasn't even Butch's motorcycle, it was Zed's, and "Zed's dead baby, Zed's dead," and it wasn't even a motorcycle, it was "a chopper baby", bringing to an end "without doubt the single weirdest fuckin' day of my life" according to Butch. It was certainly the single weirdest and most brilliant fuckin' film of my life so far, and still remains so.

Now where's my watch?

Seven (1995)   Dir: David Fincher

Apart from the films just mentioned in the previous two chapters, I don't remember any others from my teacher training year. I was so busy, not just with teaching, but then with trying to get a job, which I succeeded in doing by securing my first ever teaching post at a school in North London. My girlfriend and I would then have to find a flat in London, move all our stuff, and start our careers.

By this point, one of my best mates from my sixth form days had moved in with us into our little one bedroom flat. He was unsure of what to do with his life and thought moving to London would be a good idea too, so for the last few weeks of our lives in Reading, we shared them with my mate, who needed somewhere to stay. He was kipping on our sofa and as flats in London were proving to be much more expensive than we expected, the obvious solution was to get him to share a flat with us, so we could split the rent three ways.

My girlfriend and I both knew that our own relationship was coming to an end. Our dying shark was on its last legs, so to speak, and I think we both knew that we would probably split up once we got to London. With me having a mate living with us, I wouldn't be left on my own if she decided to move out into a much nicer flat, which wasn't difficult as the only flat we were able to afford was a complete dive. But still, it was a flat, which gave all three of us access to London, me to go out towards the suburbs, whereas my girlfriend and best mate would go into central London every day.

Once we'd settled in and I'd started my teaching career, and the other two found themselves work in London, we would occasionally go into central London together, and sometimes even go to the cinema together. We were a little like the threesome in "Jules et Jim", although it was certainly no love triangle. My girlfriend and I were drifting apart week by week, now that we no longer had university to bind us together.

The first film we would go into London to watch was "The Usual Suspects", Bryan Singer's brilliant thriller starring Kevin Spacey, who may or may not have been Keyser Soze. We saw it in the Odeon Leicester Square, and I was constantly reminded of happier times, when me and my girlfriend had been to watch "Cape Fear" and "The Exorcist" that evening a few years before. Despite the content of the films that night, it was a much more loving and romantic evening than the night we went to watch Kevin Spacey bamboozle everyone in the later film, including most of the audience too. I should have enjoyed it much more than I did, but the dead shark kept rearing its head out of the water, like a decomposing Jaws, reminding me that my four years with my girlfriend were coming rapidly to an end.

We tried one more film to try and rekindle something between us, leaving my mate at the flat one Sunday afternoon the following month, so that we could go back into Leicester Square together to watch "To Die For", with Nicole Kidman as an ambitious news reporter who is willing to do anything to pursue her career, even if it means getting rid of her husband. The plot seemed almost ironic as my girlfriend was now pursuing her own career, and if that meant getting rid of me, then so be it.

The afternoon we saw the film was gloomy and depressing, with overcast cold, grey skies seeming to threaten rain at any point. Even the weather that day was a metaphor for our relationship, and a few weeks later, on New Year's Eve 1995, the inevitable happened, and we decided that the dead shark was well and truly deceased and really wasn't worth trying to resuscitate. We parted amicably, although I was still a little bit heart broken. I had spent my whole university life with her, and she had helped me to discover a whole new world of cinematic treats, and widened my film experience so much. For that I will always be grateful to her, and it was for the best really that we split up. I did not realise on that last evening of 1995 that 1996 would be the year which would really change my life.

The New Year started with another film which has since become one of my favourites, despite it being one of the darkest, the gloomiest, the sickest, the most depraved, and most sinful of films I have ever seen. The darkness of the film still seemed to sum up my mood only a couple of days after my now ex-girlfriend had moved out.

Me and my mate went to see "Seven", the day after it was released, on the Saturday before I would start my second term as a teacher, the first one without my girlfriend. I will always remember it as the first film I ever saw without her, after almost every cinema experience I had enjoyed over the past four and a bit years had been with her. As I said, it really is a bleak film, and one which perfectly suited my mood. When the final line of a film is "The world is a fine place and worth fighting for. I agree with the second part", you know that you've just watched a film which does not really offer the same sort of optimism of "The

Shawshank Redemption", the other film I had seen that year with Morgan Freeman voicing the final line. "Seven" offers little hope, just a brutal insight into how dark humanity can be.

The film is shot in gloom and the whole atmosphere is foreboding. When it rains, it absolutely sheets it down; when it is creepy, it is one of the creepiest films ever; and when the man who has been kept alive by Kevin Spacey's John Doe character suddenly starts coughing, despite already looking like a skeleton, I don't think I've ever jumped out of my seat in shock and horror as much since the decapitated head rolled into view in "Jaws", when I was only about seven myself.

To piece together the effort, the patience, the dedication, and the determination which John Doe has to have in order to preach his sermon on the sins of humanity really did blow my mind, in a completely different way than Quentin Tarantino had done. Unlike "Pulp Fiction", there wasn't really much to enjoy about this film, although "Seven" is still a hugely satisfying experience all the same. After the darkness of the majority of the film, the final horrifying sequence takes place in bright sunlight, which disorientates the audience, and certainly leaves Brad Pitt disorientated. At least he was only disorientated, whereas his lovely wife, played by Gwyneth Paltrow, was decapitated by the whole experience.

I thought the most appropriate way to end a chapter about this film would be with a sick joke, which is of course what Brad Pitt had had played on him after all. His character's life would certainly be different at the end of the film, now that he'd lost his wife. Despite my girlfriend's head not being posted to me in a box, I too had lost my partner, and so my life would change too.

I doubt Detective David Mills found the same sort of happiness I would find though.

Heat (1995)   Dir: Michael Mann

Part of being young, free, and single meant that I could now watch whatever film I wanted, whether my girlfriend wanted to or not. Samuel L. Jackson's character Jules in "Pulp Fiction", had said that his girlfriend was a vegetarian, which pretty much made him a vegetarian too, which was why he so enjoyed that very tasty burger before he blew its owner away, quoting Ezekiel Chapter 25, verse 17 as he did so. Like Jules, my ex-girlfriend had been a lover of classic films, which pretty much made me a lover of classic films too, and I was longing to watch some silly, stupid, and downright puerile films too. As long as they were hilarious that was all that mattered. I needed an antidote to the gravity of some of the films I had been watching recently.

The first of these was one which I had seen a long time before, but needed revisiting, seeing as my work colleagues had now given me a nickname based on one of its characters. Seeing as my surname is Small, and my initial is D. one of my new colleagues decided to start calling me Derek, as a weird sort of tribute to Derek Smalls, the bass player in the band Spinal Tap.

I had seen the mockumentary "This is Spinal Tap", directed by Rob Reiner, whose own father had made the spoof "Dead Men Don't Wear Plaid", during my sixth form days, after I had discovered the younger Reiner's films with "Stand By Me" and then "When Harry Met Sally". I'd gone onto watch "The Princess Bride" which everyone seems to love, but I preferred Rob Reiner's second film, "The Sure Thing" with a young John Cusack attempting to bed Nicolette Sheridan, but being diverted by the less obvious charms of Daphne Zuniga. I would also watch "Misery" and then "A Few Good Men", before enjoying "The American President" very much, which would actually be the last film I would see of Rob Reiner's.

In amongst all these somewhere, I caught up with his debut as a director, and possibly his best of all, the hilarious and ground breaking "This is Spinal Tap", which wasn't as ground breaking as everyone thought. Before Spinal Tap and the whole Heavy Metal music scene had been so brilliantly lampooned by Reiner, the British comedy group "The Comic Strip", which included three quarters of "The Young Ones", Rik Mayall, Nigel Planer and Ade Edmondson, along with Peter Richardson, had already created a spoof band, "Bad News" and had already released their own pre-cursor to "This is Spinal Tap".

Both satires were so good that audiences did not realise at first that they were spoofs at all, assuming them to be actual documentaries, which of course kills the joke somewhat. This was a little like Ricky Gervais' sit-com "The Office", which didn't really get going until everybody realised it was all a joke, as the performances were so subtle and realistic.

The performances in "This is Spinal Tap" are also subtle yet marvellously accurate depictions of rock stars, with many rock stars themselves not actually liking the film as it was too close to the bone, with Aerosmith's Steve Tyler apparently not finding much to laugh about, particularly the scene where the band get hopelessly lost backstage. Perhaps the film hit too much of a nerve with Steve Tyler, one of the heaviest of Heavy Metal stars, although not in terms of weight.

The film has provided so many great moments, with the man I had been nicknamed after getting stopped at airport security and being asked to remove all metal items, before finally having to empty his underwear of the cucumber wrapped in tinfoil which he had been using to enhance himself with. He is also the man who gets trapped inside his alien pod onstage, as well as the man responsible for writing the band's seminal move into a different musical direction with "Jazz Odyssey". The whole film is mercilessly accurate and thus cringingly hilarious. It certainly turns the humour, as well as the volume, all the way up to eleven.

Another film which would turn the humour control up to eleven, if you like dumb, puerile comedy that is, was "Dumb and Dumber", which me and my mate watched on video one drunken evening in our flat. Some people can't stand the film. Some people love it. I just happen to be one of those who loves it. When a film has the line "We got no food, we got no jobs, our pets' heads are falling off!" you know what sort of humour I am talking about. Yes it is childish, yes it is dumb, but that's kind of the point. It is certainly no "Dr. Strangelove", but that doesn't make it not funny.

I still sometimes pretend to be running really fast if I'm in the passenger seat of a car travelling down the motorway. Whenever I see someone wearing big boots, I have been known to shout "Killer boots man" at them, and if I have to give some sort of tablet to my dogs, I will always cajole them into swallowing them with the line "Pills are good!"

If you don't like the film yourself, then fair enough, but I still giggle like a kid whenever I see it again, and giggle to myself whenever anybody uses a mouth freshener spray, whether they use it properly or not, as in the case of Lloyd Christmas. My son and I can communicate very easily by just quoting lines from that film, and the fact that he loves the film too is one of my proudest achievements as a father.

Apart from comedies, my flatmate and I would also watch one of the best heist movies ever made, arguably the greatest heist movie of all time. I'd already seen and loved Al Pacino in a very different sort of heist movie, in the fact that the heist in "Dog Day Afternoon" did not quite go as planned. He would do a much better job of catching the robbers rather than being one himself in

Michael Mann's "Heat", which opened on the first weekend of February 1996.

The film is a tour de force from everyone involved, and despite it being almost three hours long, never fails to get me watching it again if it is on the TV, despite me owning the DVD or it being available on many different streaming services. It is a masterpiece of crime cinema, and is notable for the fact that it brought two of cinema's greatest actors together for the first time.

Al Pacino and Robert De Niro had both played key roles of course in "The Godfather Part 2", but had never been on screen together, seeing as De Niro was playing Pacino's father before Michael Corleone was even born. Two of the greatest actors ever, who had starred in some of the greatest films ever, had never acted together, until one scene in "Heat", which is placed right at the heart of the whole film's narrative. The two actors are only on screen together for just under ten minutes, with the central coffee shop scene taking up three quarters of that time, but is literally pivotal in not just the plot, but also the actual structure in the film. Like the fulcrum of a seesaw, it is no accident that this scene is placed in the centre of the film.

The film has so many great scenes, but the one sequence which really stood out is probably the best shootout scene there has ever been on screen. The bank heist which goes wrong, with Pacino's men arriving on the scene just as De Niro's men are leaving the bank with huge bags full of cash, is breathless and breath taking. The amount of bullets fired is ridiculous, with around a thousand blank rounds being fired in each take, so I have no idea how many were fired to shoot the whole sequence. The scene is so realistic that it has been used to train US Marine recruits as an example of the proper way to retreat while under fire, and Val Kilmer was very proud when he was told that the moment in the gun battle when he runs out of ammo, and rapidly changes his magazine, is regularly shown to Marine recruits as an example of how to perform the action properly.

The scene also became the basis of one of the best missions in another computer game I would become slightly obsessed with. I have already mentioned how "Boyz N The Hood" was referenced in "Grand Theft Auto: San Andreas", but that was not the only time this franchise would use the cinema as a reference. In "GTA 3", many of the songs on the radio stations are on the soundtrack to another of Pacino's films, the 1982 version of "Scarface", which in itself would be the whole inspiration for the next game in the franchise, with "GTA: Vice City", being basically a rip off of the same film, set in a city based on Miami, complete with chainsaw wielding coke fiends.

"GTA 4" would feature a very similar bank robbery shootout as the one in "Heat" as its most explosive mission, causing me to play that particular mission over and over, immersing myself in the chaos and carnage which the film depicts brilliantly. But the film is not just guns and carnage. It works on so many levels, in particular the domestic scenes between Pacino's Lt. Hanna and his wife and daughter, showing that it was basically impossible for a detective to have any sort of successful home life, whereas the much happier, almost familial scenes between the gang members and their families show the complete opposite. It's much easier to be a baddie than a goodie it would seem, although of course the baddies eventually get their comeuppance, with Pacino's character at least having some sort of hope for a future with his wife and daughter by the end.

"Heat", would also be notable as the first time anyone had seen Jon Voight looking anything other than fresh faced and almost angelic looking, at least not in any sort of decent film. I'd first seen him probably around the age of nine or ten in "The Champ", the 1979 remake of the 1931 original, which had won Wallace Beery a Best Actor Oscar.

The original also starred Jackie Cooper as Beery's son, who would go onto become Clark Kent's editor on The Daily Planet in the Superman films almost fifty years later. In the remake of "The Champ", Voight played the boxer who was trying to be the best dad he could be to his young son TJ, played by Ricky Schroeder, fighting for his affection against his wife, played by Faye Dunaway, who he had separated from seven years previously.

I must have been the same age as TJ when I saw the film, and like TJ, wept profusely when his dad, his hero, dies at the end. I suppose this was the first realisation that my own dad could indeed die, which is probably why I sobbed so much as my dad was, and still is now to an extent, my hero.

The next time I would see Voight was in my first year of university, in Voight's memorable debut, "Midnight Cowboy", which won its director, John Schlesinger a Best Director Oscar, as well as picking up the award for Best Film. Voight played Joe Buck, a naïve young Texan who heads to New York, hoping to become a male prostitute, helped by Dustin Hoffman as Ratso Rizzo. From that point on, Voight would become known for his youthful looks which emanated naivety and innocence.

This fresh faced image would be compounded in "Catch-22" the following year, Mike Nichols' adaptation of Joseph Heller's classic novel, in which Voight played Milo Minderbinder, before then being tied to a tree with his own belt and being forced to watch his friend squeal like a pig, in "Deliverance", a film I would not see until a few years after I had seen "Heat".

Voight would then become a father to Angelina Jolie, who was born in 1975, and after winning a Best Actor Oscar for "Coming

Home" in 1979, Voight would then become The Champ, before his fresh faced looks began to desert him. Not only would his looks desert him, but as a consequence so would his roles.

Throughout the 1980s and early 1990s he would appear in a few very forgettable films, and even had to make a few TV movies to keep working, before he realised that his once youthful looks, which had brought him so much success had become gnarled and quite sinister. He embraced his new found gnarliness and went onto restart his career playing sometimes seedy and disreputable characters, as in "Heat", as well as some not so seedy characters like Tom Cruise's boss in "Mission Impossible", and even played the father of his own daughter when Angelina Jolie became Lara Croft. Let's just say I didn't watch that film because of Voight's appearance in it, considering the charms of Lara Croft and the actress who played her.

Three weeks after the release of "Heat" would see another film featuring Robert De Niro, and another which I was hugely eager to see, as it was basically "Goodfellas" in Las Vegas. Martin Scorsese's "Casino" would reunite De Niro with Scorsese for the first time since "Cape Fear" had terrified me, and would also reunite both of them with Joe Pesci, the first time all three had worked together since "Goodfellas".

In between these films, Pesci had taken lots of fairly forgettable roles, with many of them such as "My Cousin Vinny" playing on the image he had so violently created for himself in the first of these films. He was even directed by De Niro in "A Bronx Tale", acting alongside him too in De Niro's first effort as a director, but it would not be until Scorsese directed him again that the old brutality would be so viciously released once more.

Pesci moves on from causing vast amounts of maiming and suffering with guns and kitchen knives in "Goodfellas", to doing

325

much the same with other household implements in "Casino". A hammer, a vice, and even a pen are all used with extremely painful and quite imaginative consequences this time, with Pesci increasing his unique brand of psychotic mania, in an attempt to reach even greater heights than the former film. And this is part of the reason I do not like the latter film as much.

"Casino" was too obvious an attempt to be "Goodfellas" but this time in a different city, and also in different decades. For some reason I just preferred the authenticity of 50s and 60s New York to the Las Vegas of the 70s and 80s. It just seemed grittier and more real, which is not surprising seeing as Las Vegas is the epitome of artificiality. Though both films had killer soundtracks, I also preferred the melodies of "Goodfellas" to the sounds of the seventies in "Casino", although of course there is some overlap between the two films and their soundtracks.

Maybe the main reason I just did not like "Casino" as much was because of Sharon Stone. I've never really liked her as an actress, and never really thought she was that great, almost not worthy to be in a Scorsese film. But he obviously thought she was good enough himself, and she does give the best performance of her career, providing her with her only Oscar nomination in her whole career. I just didn't like the fact that she had made her name in such a trashy film as "Basic Instinct", whereas Scorsese's films were anything but trashy.

Whatever it was, the film has just not stayed with me in the same way "Goodfellas" has, although the scene with Joe Pesci using a vice to burst his victim's head open like a water melon has certainly remained with me. It may well have inspired another character in my next film due to his own rather intense levels of intimidation and fear.

This character did not come from New York, or Las Vegas. He came from Edinburgh, and his name was Francis Begbie.

Trainspotting (1996)   **Dir: Danny Boyle**

In between "Heat" and "Casino" came a film both me and my flatmate had been looking forward to even more than either of these two great films. We had both devoured Irvine Welsh's novel about Renton, Sick Boy, Spud and Begbie, and so were desperate to see how it had been translated onto the screen.

It opened on Friday 23rd February 1996, and I met my flatmate in central London as soon as he finished work, so we could have a couple of pints before the 6pm screening. We wanted to see it as soon as we possibly could, and had even considered pulling sickies so we could watch the afternoon screening, but had chickened out. The film was definitely worth the extra four hours' wait and it instantly became a film we knew we would have to watch again as quickly as possible, which we did the following afternoon.

The film, although very different in some respects to the book, remains true to the author's intentions, and even improves on the book in some regards. Its director, Danny Boyle, was able to condense the essence of the book into just over an hour and a half of brilliant film making. Like the book, it was gritty, funny, sickening, scary and euphoric, sometimes all at once, almost imitating the drug induced rush that the book quite harrowingly depicts and almost gives to its readers. What the book did, the film magnified even more, making the rush more heart pounding, more exciting, but also more harrowing.

The opening sequence, with Ewan McGregor as Renton, being chased by the police as his now iconic "Choose life" monologue is voiced over the thumping opening bars of Iggy Pop's "Lust for

Life", instantly takes us into a world where heroin controls and rules its users. What the film then does is not judge these characters; it simply portrays their lives, and their habits, and the sometimes hilarious, sometimes horrendous consequences of these habits.

The scenes with Spud having verbal diarrhoea as he speeds his way through his job interview, and actual diarrhoea when he passes out in the bed of the girl he has managed to pull, or Begbie's realisation that the girl he has pulled is not in fact what he first thought she was, or the dog being shot by Renton using Sick Boy's air rifle, whilst they both imitate Sean Connery, causing the dog to then attack its sleeping owner, are all some of the hilarious scenes.

On the flip side, Renton's overdose to Lou Reed's "Perfect Day", his subsequent cold turkey nightmare, Tommy's death, and funeral, and Begbie's casual and quite savage violence are just a few of the more horrendous situations the characters find themselves in.

Both sides of this deceptively shiny and alluring coin are mixed together to make the film a modern classic. It instantly became one for me and my flatmate anyway. It wasn't just the film, but the soundtrack was a heady mix of classic songs, and drug fuelled electronica, and the soundtrack quickly became an album we would constantly be listening to back at our flat. We both knew certain songs by certain artists like Lou Reed, Iggy Pop, Blondie, Pulp, Blur and Elastica, combining old classics with the energy of Britpop, which was sweeping the nation, but it also introduced us to a new type of music, one which we would want to explore more.

Tracks such as Bedrock's "For What You Dream Of" played during Renton's first ecstasy experience in a London club, and especially Underworld's "Born Slippy", which ends the film as Renton finally decides to choose life after walking away from his mates, would become very important tracks over the next few months for me, and remain so to this day.

The film gave me a much needed shot in the arm, and made me realise that instead of moping about after splitting up from my girlfriend, I too should choose life, and get on with enjoying the experience of being young and living in one of the most thrilling and vibrant cities in the world at that time.

I read Irvine Welsh's other books, and decided I wanted to experience something along the lines of Renton's clubbing experience. A few months later, on the evening after England had beaten Scotland during Euro 96, which made the whole of London, if not the whole of England throb with excitement, me, my flatmate, and a few other mates who'd come to stay with us, would have our eyes opened to proper clubbing, after mostly going to clubs where we would have to drunkenly make our way home. My decision to choose life was starting to pay out, and it was the start of a glorious summer, which would end with a new beginning for me.

Our Saturday evenings began to consist of going to watch a film at the cinema, before then going onto a club, knowing that the clubs we were now frequenting stayed open until much later than the ones we had previously been going to. We watched a few really good films, some really bad ones, and some really quite ugly ones over the summer of 96.

The good included "Fargo" another excellent film from the Coen brothers, which starred Frances McDormand in her first leading role, and the first film I had seen her in since "Mississippi Burning", just after I had finished my GCSE exams in what seemed an age ago for me by now.

Another film in the good category was "Mission Impossible" with Tom Cruise. I had seen most of Cruise's films since his early career, and definitely all of them since he had burst ono the world's consciousness in "Top Gun". But the real reason I wanted to watch his latest film was because one of his co-stars had already taken my breath away when I was still a sweet and innocent sixth former.

If you remember, one of the biggest screen crushes I had was for the French actress Emmanuelle Beart, who I had fallen in love with after I had seen "Manon des Sources". She had now been given her first major role in a Hollywood blockbuster, and so I was very keen to see how she had matured, even if I hadn't particularly done so. She did not disappoint, and she'd got even more beautiful if anything, even though she was now no longer blonde.

The film was also memorable for the iconic scene in which Tom Cruise is lowered into the room on a wire, with Brian De Palma showing us that his skills at building tension, which he'd already displayed so brilliantly in "Carrie", were still in fine working order.

As far as the bad category, we saw Arnold Schwarzenegger continue in the same vein as I remembered him from my teenage years in "Eraser". It wasn't so much bad, as just more of the same really. Since I saw him in "Terminator 2", I'd also seen him in "Last Action Hero", directed by John McTiernan, who had given us "Die Hard" and "Predator", and James Cameron's "True Lies", films which had at least tried to do something different with Arnie's action persona, but "Eraser" just seemed to revert back to type.

It wasn't that it was bad or indeed boring, it was a really enjoyable Arnie type film, with James Caan as the baddie, and

Vanessa Williams as the love interest, who had previously been the first African-American Miss America. But that was all it was, a standard Arnie action movie, full of muscles, guns, and one-liners.

As for the ugly category, we went to watch that summer's blockbuster "Independence Day", which was quite laughable in its plot and its jingoistic tub-thumping. It was as though Donald Trump had already become President of America in that film, and the only thing I did enjoy about it was the huge alien spaceship destroying The White House. If only Trump had been President back then in real life, then maybe he too would have been blasted into smithereens by a massive flying saucer. I doubt Will Smith would have saved him, if he even wanted to in the first place.

And so with the summer holidays coming to an end, I was about to start my second year as a teacher. Little did I know that I was about to have the biggest sliding doors moment ever.

Sliding Doors (1998)   **Dir: Peter Howitt**

Even though this film was not released until May 1ˢᵗ 1998, three months before my wedding day, I include it now to show how I went from a raving young singleton, to a man who by the time the film came out had met the one true love of his life and become a dad to a ready made family too. And like Gwyneth Paltrow's character Helen in the film, it all resulted from a chance encounter on a train. There are so many sliding doors moments in everyone's life, but the biggest for me occurred on a train too, a train that I had been getting to work every morning.

There are so many what ifs which had to be negotiated before I would actually meet my future wife, and mother to my children: what if I had got a job at the first school I had been interviewed for? What if me and my ex-girlfriend had found a different flat in a different area of London? What if the woman I would meet was happily married? What if she already had a daughter from that marriage? What if that daughter hadn't accepted me as her dad? What if I'd never met her mother in the first place because I was on a different train, leaving from a different station, at a different time? So many what ifs, but thankfully they were all answered for me. My wife has been answering questions for me for almost twenty-four years now, and will hopefully do so for at least another twenty-four, preferably many more than that.

During my first year of teaching, I'd noticed a very pretty girl who would get on the same train as me two stops further up the line. Some mornings she would be there, some mornings she was nowhere to be seen. I assumed that she was a temp or something, and only got on my train occasionally. I lived with the constant apprehension that I may never see her again. Her getting off the train and walking to her little flat after work may well be the last time I ever see her. I would wake every morning in the hope that she would be on my train in the morning, and I would catch even the slightest of glimpses of her.

The fact that I became almost her stalker is a constant source of amusement in our marriage. I started noticing which carriage she would get on, if indeed she was standing at the platform, and so I started to sit in that carriage too. Some mornings she would get on the train and sit at the other end of the carriage, whilst I tried to watch her from behind my newspaper. Just getting a glimpse of her fascinated me. Some mornings she would sit really quite close to me, still blissfully oblivious that there was some strange northern bloke gazing wistfully over his paper at her.

One particular morning she actually sat opposite me in the nest of four seats, causing me to have mild heart palpitations. I was desperate to talk to her, to discover who she was, where she worked, and crucially whether she would perhaps like to go for a drink after work sometime. But I was almost paralysed with nerves. For all she knew I may have been some weirdo who thought about her at night, which of course is what I was.

That one particular morning, the morning she had sat opposite me, gave me the opportunity to do some serious stalking, and after she had got up to exit the train, I hung back to see in which direction she would go on her way to work. I didn't exactly follow her strictly speaking, as it turned out that she took almost exactly the same route as I did to get to school.

I walked to school that morning watching her every move, the sway of her hips, the way her blonde hair fell to her shoulders from underneath her hat, the way she would change her bag into her other hand, and the way she would walk into the office building which was directly opposite my school. Joy of joys!

I then started to notice which train she would return home in. Some afternoons after work I would stay behind to mark books and prepare lessons, other days I would get out as soon as possible and do that teacher stuff at home. I noticed that she would be on the later train, and so I made a point of doing my teacher stuff at school every day, so that I could get the later train home too. Even when I didn't really have much to do, I would still wait for that later train, hoping that one day I would finally gain the courage to start a conversation with her.

When I finally did, sometime soon after my second year of teaching had begun, she definitely must have thought that I was a weirdo, as I casually mentioned to her once I had slyly sat down close enough to chat, that she had not been at work the previous day, as I hadn't seen her on the morning train. Alarm bells should have started ringing wildly in her ears, and maybe they were, but obviously my charms won her over. I had wondered so much about her, whether she was with anyone, whether she would like me. For all I knew she may have been married with a child.

This in fact turned out to be the truth, as during our chat she told me how she didn't always get the same train in the morning as it depended on her childcare arriving on time. That childcare happened to be for her then two year old daughter, who would spend the day with her husband's mother. My heart fell into a slump, but then was revived when she told me that she had left her husband a few months before, and was now a single mum.

From then on we would chat on the train every time we were on it together, and eventually, she agreed to meet me for a drink one lunchtime, but little did I know that two of her best friends, one of whom would be her chief bridesmaid on our wedding day, were sitting in the corner of the pub we met up in, to keep an eye on me, to see whether or not I was indeed a weirdo who should be avoided at all costs. I passed the weirdo test and she eventually invited me round to her flat for dinner, which I quite incredulously accepted.

I was falling in love, head over heels in fact, and I would then do the same with her daughter, who I gradually gained the confidence of with every dinner I would gladly eat at my new girlfriend's house. I started arriving for dinner at 7.30 on the dot, which gave Emma, my new girlfriend, the time to get Lottie, her daughter settled into bed, allowing Emma and I to get to know each other properly. However, I knew that if this relationship was going to last, I would need to take on the role of father to Lottie too. I then started getting to Emma's flat at 7pm, which would then give me a chance to spend a bit of time with Lottie, and even read her a bedtime story.

The rest, as they say, is history. I have already mentioned in the second chapter of this book about mine and Emma's first ever trip to the cinema was to see the re-release of "Star Wars" and how even that didn't put her off me, and soon enough I proposed to her and we got married in the summer of 1998, three months after the release of "Sliding Doors" a film which we did not see on its initial release, but have watched many times since. As you can see, the film holds special significance for both of us.

The film itself was written and directed by Peter Howitt, who had starred in the 1980s Carla Lane sitcom "Bread". I had also seen him in the TV adaptation for Robert Swindells' novel "Stone Cold", a book I had read with many of my classes in those first three years of my teaching career, a book which I still love teaching whenever I can. He had played a psychopathic serial killer of homeless people in this role and so I was very surprised when I next became aware of him, as what he came up with was one of the loveliest and most romantic of films.

He had obviously gone away and written a screenplay, got funding, and acquired a couple of huge Hollywood stars to play the female leads, in Gwyneth Paltrow, with her head still attached this time, and Jeanne Tripplehorn, who I had first seen getting almost raped by Michael Douglas in "Basic Instinct" before starring in "The Firm" with Tom Cruise, and "Waterworld" with Kevin Costner, both of which I had seen with my previous girlfriend.

The film would also star John Hannah, the man who had read out Auden's poem so movingly in "Four Weddings and a Funeral", and John Lynch, as the philandering Jerry, who I had only ever seen once before, appearing alongside Daniel Day-Lewis in "In the Name of the Father", yet another film I had seen with my girlfriend whilst at university.

By the summer of 1998, on the release of "Sliding Doors", my own prayers had been answered, and my new girlfriend was now

335

my fiancée. I had chosen the best sliding door to enter a train ever. But before we would begin our matrimonial bliss, I would have my own little girl to tutor in the way of classic cinema. But which film should I begin this tutelage with?

I would need to go and ask a certain wizard for help, which would mean a trip down the yellow brick road of course.

Part Six

Second Childhood

The Wizard of Oz (1939)   **Dir: Victor Fleming**

As I started spending more time at Emma's flat with not only her but also Lottie, I thought it would be nice if we got to know each other a little more by watching some films together. I raided my video collection for anything remotely suitable, and after deciding that my now three year old little girl was probably not ready yet for "Citizen Kane", or even "Carrie", I decided on something more suitable. I doubt whether her mum was ready for "Carrie" either after her traumatic experience with her own mum and the pig's blood.

I had a few films which were not only suitable, but ideal for her. The most obvious place to start was in Kansas, before she would meet a wicked old witch, a scarecrow, a tin man, and her favourite, the cowardly lion. There is absolutely no point in describing the film, as if you haven't seen it then stop reading immediately and go and watch it. We all know it so well. It has become part of everyone's consciousness, part of our culture, especially for those of us of a certain vintage where we remember the film being shown every Christmas morning in our own childhoods, or so it seemed anyway.

I was now starting to spend most of the weekend with my two new girls, and on Sunday afternoons we would very often snuggle up on the sofa and watch Dorothy travel down the yellow brick road. I had forgotten not only how magical it was, and how brilliant the songs were, but also just how scary it was at times. The Wicked Witch of the West scared me as a kid, and still affected me as a young man, and as for the flying monkeys, they had the same effect on Lottie as they had on me when I was three or four; absolutely petrifying. Of course that only meant that she would snuggle up to me even more.

I would also often make her giggle her head off with my own impression of the Cowardly Lion, imitating his "Put 'em up. Put 'em up. I'll fight you with one paw" line, which had always been one of my favourite bits in the film as a small boy.

We then progressed onto a few Disney films which I also had. Her mum had already got her a couple of singalong videos featuring a range of famous songs from Disney films, one of which was the classic "King of the Swingers" routine in "The Jungle Book" with King Louis and Baloo performing some of the funkiest moves ever. Lottie and I would often perform our very own duets to this song, dancing around Emma's front room, again making Lottie giggle her head off. Lottie was convinced that my fingers were an actual trumpet and was very disappointed to find that her own fingers did not play the same sounds as mine. It is not unusual for my wife even now to find me having a bit of a boogie to that song whilst doing the washing up, still playing my very own magical trumpet with my fingers.

We watched "Aladdin" together, and maybe "Snow White", and I also started to buy her videos occasionally, to start her own collection, one of which was "Hercules". When it was hot enough for me to wear my sandals, Lottie would always refer to them as my Hercules sandals, which was nice, although that was about my only similarity to the Greek demi-god. Even without my sandals on, I was aware that I was becoming a bit of a hero figure to Lottie, and was rapidly taking the place of her own father, who she begrudgingly saw every other weekend. Whilst he was her father, I was becoming her dad, and quite frankly, I loved it.

More Disney films were bought and watched, and she kept all these films when she took then to university with her, many years later once she had become all grown up, although she in many ways has never properly grown up, a bit like me really. In her first student house her and her housemates only had a tiny little

TV, one with a built in video player, and as they had no aerial, or indeed TV licence, she would spend her evenings with her housemates watching these old Disney films, most of which I had bought for her when she was three or four years old.

Her degree was, just like her, unique. She didn't just go to any old place of education as I had done. She chose to do fine hand embroidery as a degree, once she realised that it was an option, which would be offered by the Royal School of Needlework, which tutored its participants at Hampton Court Palace.

Very often her, and her handful of almost as equally talented and idiosyncratic girls who had got onto this most idiosyncratic of courses, would wile away the hours, perfecting their stitches whilst singing songs from these Disney films. Her favourites would always be from "Hercules", particularly "A Star is Born" and "The Gospel Truth", both sung by the great Jocelyn Brown, who my then fiancée had introduced me to after playing me "Somebody Else's Guy", which we would then see her perform in a club in north London, with Todd Terry on the decks beside her. What a night that was.

On her first ever morning on her new course, she cycled from her flat along the banks of the River Thames, singing "I Can Go the Distance", through the gates of Henry the Eighth's palace. She certainly did go the distance, and graduated with flying colours, with a little help from "Hercules" and "Mulan".

Although she loved these Disney animated films, she preferred live action films. Maybe this was due to "The Wizard of Oz", and so I bought her some very girly and very lovely films, although they were the sort of film I would have hated as a small boy at the age of four when Lottie watched them. She devoured the 1993 version of "The Secret Garden", and 1995's "A Little Princess" directed by Alfonso Cuaron, who would go onto direct the third of the Harry Potter films, as well as "Gravity" with Sandra Bullock getting lost in space, before winning a Best Director Oscar for "Roma" in 2019.

Probably her favourite back then was 1997's "Fairy Tale: A True Story", which featured an array of acting talent, from Paul McGann, to Lord Percy from "Blackadder", Tim McInnery, Lawrence of Arabia himself, Peter O'Toole as Sir Arthur Conan Doyle, Anna Chancellor, Bob Peck, who I had last seen being ripped to shreds by velociraptors in "Jurassic Park", Bill Nighy, Peter Mullan, and Winston Wolf, or even Mr. White himself, Harvey Keitel as Harry Houdini. Mel Gibson even turned up at the end of the film to make the girls in the film believe not only that fairies did indeed exist, but that their dad will not let them down, something I was determined not to do for Lottie.

Whenever we went for a walk in the woods once Emma and I got married and moved up north, Lottie would always go looking for the fairies in one particular little dell, and would always be playing in our own garden whilst wearing her fairy costume, complete with wings which her mum had fashioned for her. Lottie's needlework skills had certainly been inherited from her own mum, although as ever, Lottie would take them to another level.

The other film she would watch almost on repeat was "Matilda", Danny DeVito's adaptation of the Roald Dahl classic. Pam Ferris' Miss Trunchbull became a figure of fear for not just Lottie, but thousands, if not millions of other small kids, although she didn't much scare me. I too never got bored of watching that film with her, mainly due to the loveliness of Matilda's inspirational and caring teacher, Miss Honey, played by Embeth Davidtz, who would go onto feature in "Bridget Jones' Diary", before becoming Spiderman's mum in the rebooted version of still my favourite hero's film franchise in "The Amazing Spider-Man" of 2012, along with its sequel a couple of years later.

"Matilda" was also memorable for Bruce Bogtrotter eating that huge chocolate cake, and whenever I bake a chocolate cake myself, I always think of that scene where Miss Trunchbull makes Bruce eat the whole cake, whilst his classmates are cheering him on. I've never needed that much encouragement to eat chocolate cake, although I doubt even I could have finished off the one which Bruce did. I'm more likely to complete the hard-boiled egg challenge from "Cool Hand Luke", though strangely enough Lottie has always hated eggs, and so would not have a chance on that one.

Lottie became obsessed by owning her own version of Miss Honey's Lissy Doll, and when Emma and I eventually did tie the knot, Lottie stayed with my parents for a week whilst we went exploring a couple of Greek Islands for our honeymoon. We brought her the perfect gift back, which was a china doll which instantly became her very own Lissy Doll, a doll which we have kept to this day, which miraculously managed to survive Lottie's childhood.

One doll which didn't survive, at least not in the way it originally looked, was her very own Ariel doll from "The Little Mermaid". My parents took her to see a re-release of this film whilst we were in Greece, the first film they would take their new granddaughter to see in a cinema. In a strange parallel to my first ever trip to the cinema with them, she too had to leave the auditorium as she was so scared, although not because of a huge ape which was about to bite a woman in half, which of course had been the reason for my distress. The cause of Lottie's anguish was not even a mammal, but an octopus, as the sight of Ursula, the film's baddie, freaked her out so much that she could not cope any more.

My parents then bought her an Ariel doll to make up for the fact she had not withstood the trauma of being under the sea with a scary octopus. The film had obviously left a deep scar on her as only a few weeks after receiving the doll, Lottie decided to kind of mutilate it, cutting off Ariel's mane of hair, fully expecting it to grow back in time so that she could restyle it. She came to us crying a few days later, when she realised Ariel's hair had not in fact grown back at all, despite us having promised her that it would do.

"The Little Mermaid" was the second of the "Big Four" Disney films of that era which she had not been able to watch. She had managed "Aladdin" with no problems, and loved "Beauty and the Beast", so much so that Emma and I treated her to a trip into the West End to see the stage version at the Dominion Theatre one lovely Saturday afternoon. However, when it came to the other film which had also been turned into a massive musical hit on the stage, "The Lion King", she could not get past the point in that film where Simba has to watch his father die.

We were snuggled up on the sofa, watching one of the greatest animated films ever, and she just could not deal with the concept of Simba losing his dad. I had obviously become such a father figure now to her that she simply would not watch the film anymore as even the suggestion that I might not be with her forever was too much for her to take, which of course made me fall in love with her even more, and make me even more determined not to let any such thing happen.

After all these hand drawn animated films, or live action films, there would be one other film in particular which would become very special to both of us, as it has done for millions of others around the world, of any age and of any generation. It was neither hand drawn nor live action, and consequently it was a film which I was suspicious of at first, but within a few seconds it engrossed

343

me completely, just as it did with Lottie about six o'clock in the morning on Boxing Day 1997. Even though I was a bit grumpy at her for waking up so early, my fuzzy head was cleared almost instantly by a cowboy and a spaceman. I had no idea that I was about to go to infinity and beyond, and the memories the film brought will certainly last for me into infinity.

Toy Story (1995)   Dir: John Lasseter

I am now slightly embarrassed by my admission that I was rather suspicious about this film at first, seeing as it has become a film which truly will last into infinity. I had been used to traditional hand-drawn animation being used in films, although CGI had also begun to creep into these too, particularly in the magic carpet ride sequence in "Aladdin". The announcement that Pixar Studios would be releasing the first ever full length CGI animated film was pushing the boundaries for me a little too much, and passed it off as a fad or novelty which would be short-lived and fleeting. How wrong I would be.

The film was released in 1995, before I even knew Lottie existed, and I only bought her it on video because Woolworths were having a three for ten pounds deal on. I had chosen two films for Lottie and picked up "Toy Story" simply because I could pick a third film to make up the numbers. It became a film which would make up some astonishing numbers of its own, along with the subsequent films from the phenomenon that Pixar Studios was in the late 1990s and early 2000s. Pixar had made a deal with the giant corporation of Disney worth $26 million to make three fully CGI films, the first one being "Toy Story". This film then went on to make $373 million worldwide. This was just the start of the Studio's meteoric rise into the stratosphere.

Inevitably the two companies started to fall out over the money being made, but after this initial seemingly tiny deal had got Pixar up and running, Disney eventually bought the company in 2006 for the ever so slightly larger figure of $7.4 billion. Pixar had smashed box office records with every single one of their films, each film making many more millions than its predecessor, until in 2010, "Toy Story 3" managed to not just make millions, but grossed over a billion dollars. As I said, they really were a phenomenon. The studio have become the Disney of our time, with each new release being as eagerly anticipated as the early films by Disney themselves back in the 30s, 40s and 50s. Which is why they were prepared to spend $7.4 billion on them I suppose.

So, when Lottie woke me and Emma up that Boxing Day morning, I really had no idea of the phenomenon that I was about to watch. Seeing as she had got up unusually early for her, I told Emma that I would do the first shift, allowing her to stay in bed, before she could take over at about 8am, so I could then go back to bed and have another hour's snooze. Little did I know that those two hours would give me one of the most joyous experiences of my life.

Lottie suggested we watch a film, and seeing as she had watched the other two of the three the previous day on Christmas, there was only one choice left to us. We were both hooked instantly by the charm and the warmth of the story. Whatever medium a story is told in, as long as the story is engaging, then the characters, the dialogue, the tensions, the climax, will always be invested in. The special effects and the computer wizardry were just a means of telling that particular story. But the story itself was much more important than the fact that it had all been created by what I thought would be a soulless and inhuman computer.

The film is one of the most human, the most soulful, the most life affirming ever, and again I really don't need to describe the story. As with "The Wizard of Oz", if you haven't seen it, then go and do it now. It changed the course of film history, as of course the "The Wizard of Oz" did too, fifty-six years previously, with its use of special effects and technicolour, along with another film of that era, Walt Disney's first ever feature film "Snow White and the Seven Dwarfs", which had been released in 1937, two years earlier than "The Wizard of Oz.".

"Toy Story" is the Snow White of CGI films. It is the daddy of them all so to speak, which is what I felt like as Lottie snuggled up to me, and we both fell in love with Woody, Buzz and all the other timeless characters of Andy's toy box. It is a film which everybody should watch at least ten times before the age of ten, a number I reached before the age of twenty five, despite being only a few months off that age when I first saw it that wonderful December morning in 1997. It became another repeat viewing film, with Lottie literally rewinding it once it had ended, with Woody and Buzz being reunited with Andy after their experience in Sid's house next door, and starting it all over again.

Once Emma and I were married and moved back to where I had grown up, I was able to take Lottie to the same cinema my own parents, and my Gran of course, had taken me to when I was her age. The first film I would take her to see would be Pixar's second film, "A Bug's Life" and although it was not as enjoyable as "Toy Story" (very few films are) it was still a brilliant and hugely captivating film. It was nowhere near as captivating as the sequel we had both been waiting for, and when "Toy Story 2" was released in 1999, I think I was looking forward to it more than Lottie.

The sequel is another perfect film, possibly even better than the first, with the introduction of Jessie, and the most moving of sequences when she recounts how she had been abandoned by her own kid, with the beautiful "When She Loved Me" as its theme. I can't stop myself from weeping every time I see that sequence,

346

even now, so you can imagine what sort of state I was in when I first saw it in the cinema. I almost resembled my eight year old self when I first saw "E.T." such were the sobs.

By this point other studios realised they had to adapt their own films, with traditional hand drawn films becoming almost obsolete. Dreamworks Studios had released their own CGI insect based film with "Antz" in 1999, but their next one would be another game changer, and would nearly rival "Toy Story" in my affections.

"Shrek" was released in 2001, and for some reason I had not been able to take Lottie to see it in the cinema in Lancaster. There was no way I was going to let us both miss out on this film, so we drove down to Preston to go to the same cinema I watched "Dances with Wolves" and "Taxi Driver" in. To be honest, I would have driven much, much further to see this film.

It is the story of an ugly green ogre who has his world disrupted by a short arsed little man, before falling in love with a princess, who instead of remaining a beautiful princess when the spell is broken, turns into an ugly, yet also very beautiful ogre too. From the very first scene, the film literally wipes its arse with the conventions of the fairy tale genre, with Shrek tearing out and using as toilet paper the first page of the traditional fairy tale book he is reading. From that point I knew I was going to love this film. I loved it right from the first scene, and then once Eddie Murphy's Donkey came along, the enjoyment went to another level.

Once Princess Fiona showed off her Matrix style moves whilst beating up Robin Hood and his Merry Men, who looked strangely similar to Errol Flynn, then my love for the film went off the scale. I had only recently watched "The Matrix" myself, and so for it to be referenced in a supposed kids' film, then I really knew that these films were no longer just for kids. I've probably watched it more times than most children actually, and have used it many times in my classroom when teaching about generic conventions and how these ingredients can be played around with, which "Shrek" did hilariously.

Shrek's voice was played by Mike Myers, who would be responsible for another film franchise which all my kids would love. Lottie was the first to be introduced to Austin Powers, when I rather inappropriately let her watch the first of those films with me. Whilst I was hypnotised by Elizabeth Hurley, in what is her best role of her career seeing as it did not require much acting ability, Lottie kept asking me the meanings of some of the jokes, and didn't seem to understand why I was laughing so much at the name Alotta Fagina. Thankfully, she was too young to come with me to see the sequels, as even she might have understood by then why Fat Bastard, Ivana Humpalot, and Felicity Shagwell made me crack up. She would have to wait until that one came out on video.

My son and younger daughter have both been introduced to Austin Powers and his rudely named associates, although my youngest was only interested in watching the third film because Beyoncé Knowles, one of her favourite pop stars ever, was Austin's foxy sidekick Foxxy Cleopatra, another name which thankfully she was too young to understand why it had me sniggering.

By 2003, with the release of Pixar's fifth film, "Finding Nemo", Lottie had been joined in the cinema by her little brother, who was almost four by the time this most lovely of films swam onto our screens. I'd had Lottie all to myself for "Toy Story", "A Bug's Life", "Toy Story 2" and "Monsters Inc,", but from that point on, she would have to share me with her little brother too, my only son, Tom. The fact that this wonderful story of a father desperately searching to find his own son was my own son's first Pixar experience makes it another very special film for me.

The vast ocean in which Nemo becomes lost is inhabited by a wonderful array of characters, including two sharks, one of which resembles Jaws, who is trying desperately to stop eating fish, with quite scary yet hilarious consequences. Marlin's sidekick on his quest to locate his son is a fish who never seems to be able to remember anything, and from that point on my daughter became known in our family as Dory, as she too was rather forgetful from time to time, forgetting how to open her own bedroom door at one point, forgetting that her door knob turned anti clockwise, despite having turned it that way all her life.

Dreamworks Studio, in another strange consequence in their attempt to cash in on the Pixar phenomenon, had set their next film in an underwater world too. "Shark Tale", which was released the following year, would feature some huge Hollywood names providing the voices, including Robert De Niro, Will Smith, Renee Zellweger, and Angelina Jolie. Even Martin Scorsese had a part, but despite all these stars, the film was not a patch on "Finding Nemo", just like "Antz" was not as good as Pixar's "A Bug's Life" a few years before.

It seemed that Dreamworks' attempt to muscle in on Pixar's patch was based on just using celebrity voices. They had used Woody Allen, Sharon Stone, Gene Hackman, Sylvester Stallone, Dan Ackroyd, and even Mrs Robinson herself, Anne Bancroft to try and beat Pixar in their first CGI film, and would fail again with "Shark Tale". Pixar proved that the strength and warmth of their stories would always win out over star voices. I know that some huge names have voiced many of the Pixar characters, including Kevin Spacey in "A Bug's Life", Ellen DeGeneres and Willem Dafoe in "Finding Nemo", and obviously Tom Hanks as Woody, but these were not the films' selling points. I'm sure some of you could tell me who provided the voices of Marlin and his son Nemo, but they certainly were not household names, and still aren't, despite the massive success of the film (Albert Brooks and Alexander Gould by the way). Pixar's films had more heart than those of Dreamworks, and although I have enjoyed many of their films, they will never hold the same place in my heart as the classics of early Pixar.

Another studio which would become significant, more for Lottie than for me, would be Studio Ghibli. After all these CGI films, I wanted her to see an example of hand drawn animation which was not Disneyfied. Hayao Miyazaki's "Spirited Away" certainly was not Disneyfied in any way. Studio Ghibli films seemed to go in the complete opposite direction to Disney's schmaltz. We watched "Spirited Away" with fascination, more for her than me actually. The weirdness and strange imagery of the film captivated her much more than it did for me. It was all just a bit too strange for me. I wasn't able to completely let go of my reality and get inside the mind of a child like Lottie was at the age of seven.

Lottie loved it though, and so I thought I would encourage her to watch a few more films from this most inventive and ground breaking of animation studios. I bought her DVDs now, not videos any more, and some of the first discs I would get her were "Princess Mononoke", "The Cat Returns", and "Grave of the Fireflies". Little did I know that this last film is the least Disneyfied of animated films ever. It is absolutely harrowing in fact, and another film which I maybe should have waited until she was a bit older to watch.

When a film starts with a Japanese boy dying of starvation in a train station shortly after the atomic bomb has obliterated much of his country, you know it's not going to be that happy and schmaltzy. Even Disney would struggle to get a happy ending out of that scenario. Studio Ghibli went the other way, and had the two main characters, Seita and Setsuko die of starvation in an abandoned bomb shelter, after finding out that their father, a captain in the Japanese navy, is most likely dead too after Japan's navy has been sunk. As you can see, it was certainly no "The Little Mermaid" although strangely, Lottie managed to watch the whole of the dark and foreboding post-apocalyptic "Grave of the Fireflies", whereas she had been too scared of the cheery and upbeat Disney offering.

Despite having a fascination with fairies, Lottie has always been a bit of a conundrum to me, and has always been slightly fascinated with the darker aspects of life, just like her mum. When she used to draw pictures on the Etch-A-Sketch type thing Father Christmas brought for her one year, she would alternate between pictures of rainbows, and creations which were nothing like rainbows. She would often present the screen to me which had just been filled with black, with the title of her new masterpiece being simply, "Darkness", adding to my own fascination for her.

She's always liked her films to take her into a world which is not all sweetness and light, which is why she would become obsessed with the next film and its subsequent parts in the trilogy, as they would feature some of the darkest forces ever created, either in a book, or on the screen.

We were about to go to Middle-Earth together, somewhere she quite possibly has never completely returned from actually.

The Fellowship of the Ring (2001)   Dir: Peter Jackson

Now that my son Tom had started to accompany his big sister to the cinema, it was rare that Lottie and I would share that experience just on our own any more. However, Tom was still far

351

too young to watch the trilogy of films which this chapter gets its title film from. So, for three consecutive years, years which would also include the birth of her younger sister, I had Lottie all to myself for a couple of hours every Christmas.

Each trip was much longer than a couple of hours, more like four hours actually, as the first two films in this trilogy would be almost three hours long themselves, and with an interval included, the only films I'd taken Lottie to see which had needed an interval, the whole trip would be around double the length of our usual cinema trips. Neither of us minded though. It just meant we had double the time together without being interrupted by nappy changing duties.

I'd never got into "The Lord of the Rings" when I was a boy. Two of my best mates who I would go to the cinema with during sixth form, one who would eventually become my flatmate in London, both loved the books, and would have really nerdy chats about the books, leaving me and my other mate excluded. I'd read "The Hobbit", but it just never really captured my imagination, and ever since, I've never been enthused about the fantasy genre. If I wasn't prepared to read the books, at least I would now be able to join in the conversations about the films. However, if it hadn't been for Lottie's excitement, I doubt very much whether or not I would have gone to see them at all, as my wife certainly wasn't interested.

I must admit though that I was hugely impressed by the first film, and the brilliant opening sequence recounting the mythology of the One Ring definitely hooked me in. The next few scenes in The Shire, where we meet Gandalf, played by Sir Ian McKellen, dragged on a bit, but as soon as the Orcs come into play, I perked up again.

By the end of the film I was very satisfied indeed and couldn't wait for the next one, but of course I would have to wait a whole year for that. I understood why my mates had loved the books now, although it still didn't make me want to read them. I bet the film blew my mates' minds actually. It certainly did that for my Lottie, who demanded to go again a few days later, which I really didn't mind doing. It filled another afternoon of my Christmas holidays up, and got me off more nappy changing duty.

I refused to do the same the following year for "The Two Towers", the second film in the trilogy though, which frankly bored me in certain parts. By now I had a very energetic and very mobile-for-her-age eight month old baby girl, as well as a son who was now almost three, plus of course Lottie, who was nearly nine by now. Maybe I was just so tired, now that me and my wife had become outnumbered, that all I remember about the second film was the introduction of Gollum, who had been played by Andy Serkis, a graduate of Lancaster University I might add, who would also go on to play King Kong in Peter Jackson's next venture after this trilogy.

The second film was maybe just one trip too many into Middle-Earth, and I discovered another wonderful experience which the cinema can provide; the pleasures of a nap. I probably dozed off for an hour or so, seeing as my two younger children, especially my baby girl, had probably been up in the night, so it was the obvious time to catch up with a little shut eye.

I've taken a little nap in plenty of other films I've taken my kids to see, as many of them have been fairly rubbish, quite frankly. I definitely fell asleep thankfully during "The Magic Roundabout", which my son was very keen to see when he was five. It was nothing like the TV programme I fondly remembered, and even whatever Zebedee was taking would probably not have kept me awake during that film, despite Robbie Williams, Sir Ian

McKellen, Bill Nighy, Jim Broadbent and even another of my boyhood crushes which had carried on into manhood, Kylie Minogue, as Florence all providing their voices. I think films such as "Barnyard", "Over the Hedge" and "Kung Fu Panda" may well all have sent me into the Land of Nod too amongst many others.

Back in the Land of Middle-Earth, the third film, "The Return of the King" at least kept me awake the following year, and I remember this one in a little more detail, with some truly breath taking battle scenes certainly keeping me awake. Whatever my feelings about the films, the most important thing was that Lottie saw them and enjoyed them so much more than I did. She became a little obsessed with them actually, and she and her three best friends developed a game in the school playground where they were all hobbits, with Lottie as Frodo, trying to evade the evil gaze of their evil teacher, the evil Mrs Jenkins, who they imagined to be Sauron.

On World Book Day that year, my wife created an awesome costume for Lottie so that she could become Frodo properly, and she even went to school with hair stuck to her feet with glue, although I don't recall her walking to school barefoot, but I wouldn't have put it past her.

Lottie still loves the films to this day, and her boyfriend is also a self-confessed Rings geek. Even Lottie's name on our family's WhatsApp group is Gollum, and she keeps nagging me to watch the films again. I think I may have only seen them once more since Lottie and I watched them in the cinema, and I may well have to have a Lordathon, and see if I can stay awake for all three films in one day. Just writing about them now has piqued my interest again, so I may well just do that.

See you in about twelve hours then my precious.

Chitty Chitty Bang Bang (1968)   Dir: Ken Hughes

I've just realised after writing the title film for this chapter that this is the first film since the first few chapters of this book where I was not sure of the film's director. I had to look up the names of the directors of both "King Kong" and "Herbie Goes Bananas", in chapters one and three respectively, and it is only now, on film number sixty-six that I have had to do the same for this most famous of films. The film itself, its main star, the car, many of the songs, and certainly the Child Catcher are all quite rightly famous, and have become integral to so many childhoods, but as for the director, even when I'd looked his name up, I'd still never heard of him.

Apparently, the rather blandly named Ken Hughes started his film directing career with the much more interestingly named "The Brain Machine" in 1955, before moving onto other "classics" such as the equally intriguingly named "Jazz Boat" five years later. Neither of these films featured anyone I had heard of before, although Patrick Barr, the lead in "The Brain Machine" also appeared in "Octopussy" almost thirty years later, so I had actually seen him before.

Ken Hughes' next film after "Jazz Boat" would be a bit bigger, starring Peter Finch, he of the famous line "I'm as mad as hell, and I'm not gonna take it anymore", from 1976's "Network", which I loved. It was a great insight into the inner workings of TV networks, and how they can send one of their own assets crazy once they are no longer popular, ironically becoming more popular because of the craziness which they create in the first place. In Hughes' film, Finch played Oscar Wilde in "The Trials of Oscar Wilde" alongside James Mason, who of course had tried to kill Cary Grant in "North by Northwest" amongst many other great films.

So, as you can see, Ken Hughes was moving up in the world, and his next hit would be an adaptation of Somerset Maugham's "Of Human Bondage", with Kim Novak. His now semi-meteoric rise continued, with his next "hit", which would star Tony Curtis and Zsa Zsa Gabor in "Drop Dead Darling" in 1966, before really hitting the big time with the title film of this chapter, and the reason why I have just given you this little summary in the first place.

After making a car fly with "Chitty Chitty Bang Bang", he made "Cromwell" with Richard Harris and Alec Guinness as Cromwell and Charles I respectively. This would seem to have been the peak of Ken's powers, as after that he would make some rather tawdry looking 1970s sex romps, the first of which being "Alfie Darling", in which the Michael Caine character from nine years previously was back to behave in a very 1970s manner towards women, one of whom happened to be Joan Collins.

The second of these films was possibly his most intriguingly named film to date, one which he would not beat, seeing as he only had one more film in him, with 1977's "Sextette" which bizarrely starred Timothy Dalton alongside Tony Curtis, Ringo Starr, George Hamilton, Alice Cooper, and possibly the most bizarre of them all, Mae West, who was almost eighty years old by then, in a film which definitely would be her last appearance on screen. She played, appropriately enough, an ageing glamourous sex symbol of the silver screen. I wonder how many of those male stars would actually want to come up and see her sometime by that point in her career.

One name who had appeared in some of Ken Hughes' early films would be Lionel Jeffries, who would then become Dick Van Dyke's father in "Chitty Chitty Bang Bang", a film which my three year old son became obsessed with. He didn't care who starred in it, or even who directed it, and certainly didn't care about its director's back catalogue. All he cared about was the fact that it had a car which could fly in it.

Ever since I could remember, my son had always been intrigued by cars. Not just cars, but most modes of powered traction actually. The film he loved most when he was really young was a film starring Peter Fonda. I would love it if the next film title I wrote was "Easy Rider" as that would mean I had the hippest, coolest one year old son ever, but sadly the film in question was "Thomas and the Magic Railroad".

I think it's fair to say that out of the three male stars of "Easy Rider", Peter Fonda had fared the least well. Whereas Dennis Hopper had gone onto feature in many of the films already mentioned in this book, with Jack Nicholson winning Oscars and featuring in even more, this film is the second and only other time Peter Fonda will be mentioned. Henry Fonda's son, and Jane's brother, had not quite had the same success as his other co-stars it would seem.

This film, Thomas the Tank Engine's feature film debut no less, was bizarre, but my son seemed to love it. However many times I had to sit in the same room as him whilst the film was on the TV, I still never understood the plot. It also featured Alec Baldwin, and Matilda herself, Mara Wilson, in a plot which literally made no sense, but then again, neither does the plot of "Chitty Chitty Bang Bang", when you think about it.

Whether I understood the plot or not, it featured a big blue train, which was good enough to keep my son amused, as would a big red car whenever "The Wonderful Wonderful Car" was driven onto the set of Vic Reeves and Bob Mortimer's reboot of "Shooting Stars" in 2002. This red Ferrari type car, which inexplicably had a human posterior as its rear end, was used as a replacement for "The Dove From Above", which had featured in the original series of the show, and my son definitely thought it was wonderful. Like most things on the show, the car's human rear end was inexplicable, but my son didn't seem to mind that instead of two exhaust pipes, it had two buttocks in their place.

Whatever he was doing whenever we watched the show, he would stop and just gaze at the car in an almost worshipful manner, becoming transfixed by its wondrous wonders. As soon as it was no longer on screen he would go back to playing with his own cars, which he rather worryingly used to just line up in rows very carefully, rather than actually driving them along the carpet, making jumps for them, causing crashes etc, the usual sort of toy car play. For some reason, and no he is not on the autistic spectrum, he just loved to arrange his cars in nice neat rows, and would only stop doing this when "The Wonderful Wonderful Car" appeared.

However, once he discovered "Chitty Chitty Bang Bang", a film which his older sister had introduced him to actually, the cars would be abandoned, and he would become transfixed on this very special car, a car that could actually fly. This truly was the most wonderful of wonderful cars, although its rear end was not shaped like an arse sadly.

I've never really been a fan of the film, as the Child Catcher probably petrified me as a kid, and it was all a bit too old fashioned for my liking when I had first seen it. I did very much enjoy Dick Van Dyke's "Me Ol' Bam-Boo" routine, my favourite of all his song and dance routines, and you can't help but sing along to the film's theme song. One song which my wife would definitely sing along to was "Truly Scrumptious", so much so that it became the song she would sing our baby girl to sleep with.

My wife would often be caring for our baby girl Becky, or more than likely stopping her from destroying things, whilst Tom was watching the film, and whenever the "Truly Scrumptious" song was sung by the children and Truly Scrumptious herself, played by Sally Ann Howes, my wife would notice that Becky would calm down and become much less energetic.

My wife, usually in desperation by that point, would sing the song over and over again to try and restore some peace and quiet to our front room, and even I tried it once when I was struggling to get her to settle in her cot for the night. Consequently our youngest's first ever nickname would be Truly Scrumptious.

The nickname would be replaced once she discovered her own favourite Pixar film, but before that, Tom would discover his first Pixar film which he would truly love, a film which didn't just feature one car, but loads of them, despite none of them being able to fly at all. But they could all talk, and some could even drive backwards in a really cool way too. And one of them had a much cooler name than Chitty Chitty Bang Bang.

This car was called Lightning McQueen.

Cars (2006)   Dir: John Lasseter

Before my son would watch Lightning McQueen dash around the track, he would first get to know, and even pretend to be someone else who dashed everywhere. After having his first Pixar experience with "Finding Nemo", which he was a bit too young to remember, his first proper Pixar fix, or PixFix as I have now christened them, was just before he would turn five years old with "The Incredibles". Even though this is supposedly a kids' film, it is still one of the greatest superhero movies ever. My son certainly thought so, as did I. And still do.

359

It was directed by Brad Bird, who had already directed the excellent "The Iron Giant", in 1999, before being recruited by John Lasseter to work for him at Pixar. He has since made two other Pixar classics, in "Ratatouille" in 2007, and the long awaited sequel to "The Incredibles" in 2018. The sequel is not as good as the original though, with the first film becoming very special to not just me and Tom, but to our whole family. It made such an impact on me, Lottie and Tom, that obviously we got the DVD as soon as it came out, so that the whole family could enjoy it, including our then three year old daughter Becky too.

It became apparent that the five members of my family shared certain characteristics with that of Bob Parr and his wife Helen, although my wife was not able to stretch her legs and arms quite as far as Elastigirl could, and I was not able to lift anywhere near the weight of a train as part of my "fitness" regime. Like Mr. Incredible though, I had the fiercest desire to protect my family, and would probably have become superhuman had anyone threatened any of us, as no doubt most dads would.

Lottie by then was almost a teenager, and like Violet Parr, would feel rather awkward as she was starting to enter her adolescence. Boys were starting to notice her by now too, which probably just enhanced her sense of otherness. She never felt different within our family, but at school she was realising who she should stay away from and who to stick close to.

Tom, like Dash Parr, sped around everywhere. Why walk around the park when he could run? Why just amble along next to me whilst out with the dog, when he could sprint up and down the canal towpath instead? And our own version of Baby Jack-Jack, or Baby Beck-Beck as we called her then, certainly had the same sort of fiery temper that the youngest member of the Parr family had started to display. When she threw a temper tantrum, the whole street knew about it, although she at least did not have laser eyes, at least not yet. She was able to cause destruction almost at will, something she has been perfecting ever since she worked out how to unlock baby gates and also climb out of her cot at much too young an age.

For Tom's sixth birthday, we decided to have an Incredibles party. We got a little party pack which included a mask for each of us, a sticker with the Incredibles logo to be stuck on our chest, and we sat there in our "costumes" around our family table in our dining room, eating steak and cake, not on the same plate I might add. Tom, again like Dash, liked his meat, and we would also refer to him as "the carnivore" just as Helen Parr did to her son.

There is a scene towards the end of the film in which the family have to protect each other from Syndrome, with Mr. Incredible and his wife clutching their three children close to them, whilst Violet creates a force field around the whole family. Sitting around our big, strong family table, a symbol of our family's own strength, it felt like there was a force field around us that day, or at least that is how I felt.

Since meeting my wife back on the train all those years ago, I had created something very special, something very super, something very incredible actually, and at that moment, sitting with my sticker on my chest, and my eye mask around my face, I did feel almost as though I had superpowers. My strength came from my wife and children, and together we could get through anything if we worked together. Hence my huge affection for the film, apart from it being just completely awesome, it has always made me feel "totally wicked" to use the phrase the Parrs' little neighbour shouts to them after the force field scene I just mentioned.

By now my son was just like me when it came to Pixar films, and was chomping at the bit for the next one. When "Cars" was released in the summer of 2006, Lottie's awkward stage meant that she didn't really want to accompany me to the cinema anymore. She was a proper teenager by now and being seen with her dad in the cinema, watching a kids' film all about cars was probably not the coolest of activities, and so she passed the baton over to her little brother as dad's cinema buddy. Me and Tom had a wonderful time watching Lightning McQueen almost win the Piston Cup, which of course he denies himself the victory by finally realising that winning is not the most important thing in life, and that helping others is also quite important.

The film would be the second of the two films I mentioned which allowed Paul Newman to carry on showing off his talents, although only his voice would be used this time, playing the ageing Doc Hudson, who relives his past through Lightning McQueen. I'm not sure Lottie would have liked the film anyway. It is very much a boys' film, although I am in no way stereotyping gender roles there. I certainly felt like a little boy again as me and my son sat there in the new multiplex cinema which had finally replaced the old cinema I used to go to.

I would have loved that cinema to still be there to allow me to take all my kids to watch films with me in it, but alas, only Lottie would have that same squeaky chaired experience. Tom got to see his first three Pixar films, or PixFlix as I have now christened them, in a state of the art auditorium, with a Dolby surround speaker system. I'm not sure it made "Cars" any better. It would have been just as good in whatever cinema we had watched it in.

This new Vue Experience would become the norm for me and Tom over the next few years. We would see many of the seminal films of his young life there, including "Robots", which was entertaining enough, and another CGI film which I remember little of apart from one moment which for some reason made my son giggle so much that I'm sure he leaked a little. The film was "Hoodwinked", a fairly ordinary reimagining of the Little Red

Riding Hood story, with rather crude CGI animation being used. By now many other studios had jumped on the CGI band wagon and there was a plethora of usually inferior kids' films being released, at least one, quite often two being screened every school holiday. I've already mentioned a few of them, but Disney's first attempt in this area, "Chicken Little" was particularly bad. It was then that the once great Disney Corporation realised that if you can't beat 'em, then buy 'em, leading to the $7.4 billion takeover I mentioned earlier. Anyway, at least this one scene from "Hoodwinked" which involved a singing goat, if I remember rightly, was a hit with my son.

We both very much enjoyed the Pixar spin off "Bolt", one of Disney's own CGI films which had much more of a Pixar feel to it, mainly due to the fact that John Lasseter was its executive producer. Lasseter was the man who could do no wrong as far as me and Tom were concerned. He also produced another masterpiece in "Ratatouille", and the truly astonishing "WALL-E", the final true PixFlix, before the Disney takeover.

I'd taken Tom to see "WALL-E" with my brother and his two sons, the youngest of whom was a year younger than my own youngest Becky, who was six when the film came out in 2008. Lottie had even agreed to join me, Tom, Becky, my brother and my two nephews for this one, and the film was memorable for me for one incident in particular.

Actually it was memorable for many things: from the beautiful opening scenes with the little robot existing on his huge pile of trash in which he watches Barbra Streisand in "Hello Dolly", to the most stunningly mesmeric sequence in which WALL-E and EVE dance in space. The incident in particular I referred to earlier was when WALL-E thinks that his new robot girlfriend is going to be hurt, and he cries out to her in genuine anguish. At this point, my youngest nephew genuinely started to cry because of the emotional investment he had in the film. The film had taken him on such an emotional ride, at the very young age of just five, that it had overwhelmed him.

My brother, who was never quite so comfortable as me when it came to sobbing at films, could not understand why his son Luke was crying genuine tears. I knew exactly why he was crying, and I was extremely proud of him for doing so. He had become so wrapped up in the film that his suspension of disbelief had also been suspended, and he really and truly empathised with the characters on screen, feeling the same amount of panic and distress that this little robot was feeling. In that one instance, the power of film was displayed, and it is again another moment in my cinematic life I will never ever forget.

I think the same thing happened for me and my wife when we both watched "Up" together with our two youngest. As most adults who watch the opening ten minutes or so of that film, we both had tears streaming down our faces as we watched Carl Fredricksen watch his wife, and his dreams die. It is one of the most heart-breaking opening sequences to any film, and the film was a welcome addition to the now Disney/Pixar catalogue.

But, after coming up with the goods with "Cars", the first film Lasseter had directed himself since "Toy Story 2", the sequel was underwhelming and was a complete let down, for Tom as well as me. It felt as though from 2011 onwards Pixar's magic had been dissolved to an extent by Disney, and I don't think they have ever reached the same heights since, apart from the third and what should have been final piece in the "Toy Story" trilogy. More on that later.

"Brave" was good, but not great, but at least it made my wife cry with the mother/daughter thing going on, just like me and Tom had had the father/son thing going on in "Cars". And as for "Cars

3", which was the first of the series not to be directed by John Lasseter himself, well, it is simply not worthy of being called a Pixar film in my humble opinion.

Pixar's films, or rather Disney/Pixar's films from then on were always good, but never really great, something which every single one of the first eleven of their films was. The sequels to "Monsters Inc.", "Finding Nemo" and "The Incredibles", along with "The Good Dinosaur" and "Inside Out" are all perfectly good films and very enjoyable, but not great films. It would not be until "Coco" in 2017 that Pixar would reach the same sort of heights as their earlier masterpieces. Again, more on that later too.

One other CGI film needs to be mentioned in this chapter, the wonderful Robert Zemeckis film "The Polar Express". Zemeckis had given me some of my favourite ever film experiences with his "Back to the Future" trilogy, and would then give my own kids a similarly awesome ride when the film arrived exactly on time for Christmas in 2004. Tom was almost five by then and so believed completely in Father Christmas, whereas Lottie was almost eleven, and had reached the age where she was having serious doubts about the whole thing. She probably knew the big secret already by that point, but at no point did she ever let onto her younger brother what her new found wisdom and experience meant.

It was a significant moment in her childhood when she finally realised the truth which us deceptive adults had kept from her for as long as possible, but was determined that her brother would also believe for as long as he could. The final sequence of that film was so magical that it even made me believe again in the true magic of Christmas.

That magic would return in another film which was released just before Christmas, but five years after "The Polar Express". It was a film which my son became obsessed with, and it was given to us by the same man who had made such an impact on me as a kid when Arnold Schwarzenegger had blasted countless police officers dead after promising that he would be back, in "The Terminator".

James Cameron was certainly back for me, but this time he'd become rather blue now he had reached his fifties.

Avatar (2009)   **Dir: James Cameron**

A very good friend of mine described this film as "Dances with Wolves meets The Smurfs" which I thought was a bit harsh. His description didn't exactly fill me with confidence as me and Tom walked down to the cinema. Tom was filled with anticipation though as one of his friends had already seen it, and had told him how great it was.

Tom was almost ten now, and had entered that period where he wanted to be as grown up as it was possible for a nine year old to be. I think that he too by now had realised his parents' evil deception about Christmas. This film would more than make up for his disappointment though.

We spent a brilliant afternoon together, nearly as long as one of those afternoons I had spent with Lottie watching "The Lord of the Rings" films, as this too was a film which was almost three hours long. However, it never felt like it, and like the film my friend had compared it to, "Dances With Wolves", the film sped by and instantly became a film I could quite happily watch again and again. I think we may have even seen it again over that Christmas break, and my son loved it so much that bizarrely he started to teach himself the Na'vi language, the language the blue

366

inhabitants of Pandora speak. He would often greet me using words, and even sounds that I had never heard before, and encouraged me to respond to him accordingly, which I bemusedly did, once he taught me how to. However, apparently one of the phrases he had taught himself was "shut up you moron", and so I have no idea what the reply was that he taught me. I had enjoyed the film very much, but maybe not to the extent my son had.

He loved it because of the breath taking action sequences, the massive artillery used in the battle scenes, and the way his blue hero Jake bonds with his direhorse, which reminded me of how Perseus had tamed the winged horse Pegasus, in another great film from my childhood, "Clash of the Titans".

I refer to the original version of "Clash of the Titans", and not the remake which also starred Sam Worthington, who had made his name in "Avatar" to start with. The original was a film from my childhood which I loved, another one which my Gran took me and brother to see at the cinema, with Harry Hamlin as our hero attempting to kill Medusa so he could save Andromeda, played by Judi Bowker, who had made her name in the TV series, "The Adventures of Black Beauty", which always seemed to be on during the school holidays, causing me to hate it with a vengeance, as it was so girly and insipid, which then made me not really care too much whether Perseus actually saved her from the Kraken or not.

The film had starred a huge host of stars, from Laurence Olivier, Ursula Andress, Maggie Smith, Claire Bloom, and of course, Rocky's trainer Mickey, Burgess Meredith, although at that point, when I was only eight, I had no idea who any of them were. All I was bothered about was whether Harry Hamlin would be able to cut Medusa's head off and save the day, even if that did mean saving that annoying girl from "Black Beauty".

My son Tom also loved "Avatar", because of the story, and the eco-message it subtly yet powerfully portrayed to him. For the first time he realised that this was not a film meant for kids which adults could enjoy too. This was a film which both adults and kids could learn something from, and it made him feel even more grown up because he was now starting to get the allegorical meanings of films. He had now progressed from being a kid to being a young man, even though he was still only ten by now, and very much a kid in my eyes, and still is to this day, even though he is now into his third decade rather than his second.

His entry into more adult orientated films had begun when he joined me for what was ultimately a fairly satisfying end to the series of three "Star Wars" prequels, which had let me down so badly with "The Phantom Menace" in 1999. The highlight of that film was just seeing those famous words "A long time ago, in a galaxy far, far away…" back on the big screen, before the music burst into our ears again, something I hadn't seen for over sixteen years. Since my last experience of it, in "The Return of the Jedi", I had gone from boy, to not just a man, but a husband and dad too. "The Phantom Menace" made every one of my age who saw it feel like they were about five years old again, yet even though the film featured a quite cool double ended light sabre, and a quite spectacular pod race, the rest of it was a massive let down, particularly the annoying and very punchable Jar Jar Binks.

Thankfully Jar Jar didn't feature that much in the next film, the much better "Attack of the Clones", which began to restore my faith in George Lucas, so when Tom joined me to watch Anakin Skywalker finally become Darth Vader in "Revenge of the Sith", my anger from the first film had been sufficiently quelled. At least I introduced him to the Star Wars world on the big screen in a fairly worthwhile addition to the saga, although it was still not as good as any of the first three films.

Tom's introduction to "Star Wars" was at least worthy of the series, and he would go onto watch all the other films at home on DVD, before we would both go and experience the latest trilogy together over alternate Christmases between 2015 and 2019. The first and third of this trilogy would be directed by J.J. Abrams, a director who had already given me and Tom a great cinematic ride in 2008, in his homage to Steven Spielberg, the awesome "Super 8".

The title of this film refers to the type of camera used by the kids in the film who were making their own home movie, before extra-terrestrial forces disrupt their plans. It was the same camera that Spielberg had started making his own home movies with, and no doubt the same sort which Abrams used too. "Super-8" the film is a brilliant film in itself, but when you realise how many homages to Spielberg it contains, it gets better, which is why I loved it probably even more than Tom and one of his best friends, who were both transfixed by it. They especially loved the train crash scene, which blew their minds so much that they both just looked at each other after the train and ensuing carnage had come to rest, both mouthed the word "wow" to each other, and promptly burst out laughing with sheer joy at the physically palpable experience they had just had.

That moment was a sign to me that Tom didn't just watch films, but like me, he felt them. We would both feel the same experience eight years later when the Star Wars spin-off "Rogue One" was released. This, as far as I'm concerned, is the best Star Wars film outside of the original trilogy, and may even be better than "Return of the Jedi". It allowed me and Tom the same chance to experience the old and the new of the Star Wars saga together. We both felt the excitement and the sense of doom as Vader's ship approached at the very end of the film, just as I had done in the cinema, and Tom had done on TV, at the beginning of the very first film of the saga, the one I had watched with my

369

parents at the age of four, which certainly felt like "a long time ago, in a galaxy far, far away" by now for me.

I also introduced Tom to another series of films which had featured heavily in my youth, when we went to see a new type of James Bond when Daniel Craig became 007. "Casino Royale" was a great way to introduce him to Bond, and like me when I had first seen "The Spy Who Loved Me" and "Moonraker" when I was about the same age as him, I'm sure he had a huge crush on Eva Green as Vesper Lynd. Can't really blame him. She was absolutely stunning in that purple evening gown.

"Quantum of Solace" was a bit of a disappointment though, but "Skyfall" was a welcome return to form, with Tom definitely feeling that film again, or at least feeling something in his soon-to-be teenage loins for Berenice Marlohe, as the sumptuously glamourous and enigmatic Severine. I think we both felt the same feeling during that film.

With Tom becoming all grown up, it was time for him to pass the baton, just as his big sister had done. It was now time for me to unleash the force of my youngest child into the cinemas. The force certainly awakened anyone who was trying to have a nap when she was in the cinema.

Nativity! (2009)   **Dir: Debbie Isitt**

My youngest child, Becky, or Baby Beck Beck as we had called her by now, has always provided my wife and I with more challenges than our other two children shall we say. She was a different kettle of fish than our first two, and has had us pulling our hair out with anger and frustration at certain times, almost literally actually. Like Tom with what we thought might be autism as he lined his toy cars up in a very regimented fashion, so we thought Becky may have ADHD or something similar.

It turns out that she hasn't got it, but is just really annoying, and can't concentrate on anything for too long unless whatever is vying for her attention is really interesting or captivating. As such, she has always been the harshest of critics when it comes to films, and if a film in the cinema is not doing it for her, then she'd be off trying to find something which would hold her attention, even if that meant flushing all the toilets in the loos, turning on all the taps, and pressing all the buttons on the hand dryers just to see which was the most powerful.

She was certainly not as relaxing a child to take to the cinema. Maybe I had just been lucky with my first two, as they would happily become engrossed in most films I took them to see, but for Becky, she required something extra special.

Apart from Truly Scrumptious and Baby Beck Beck, she had also acquired the nickname of Becky Boo, after she had seen "Monsters Inc." with the rest of the family when she was probably around the same age as the little girl in the film, who is also called Boo. I must add that this was in our own front room on DVD. I hadn't yet discovered her penchant for cinema toilets and hand dryers by then.

Sully's blue hairiness seemed to catch her attention, and she would even laugh at appropriate times to Mike Wazowski's jokes or pithy comments which always went down a treat with the rest of the family. As such, our Becky became a version of Boo. I was supposed to be the big, hairy, and protective Sully in this scenario, but I was very proud of my own Boo when she got all soppy at the end of the film, just as I do every time I watch it, and when she saw that Sully was getting all tearful when he finally gets to say hello to his Boo again, after thinking he would never see her once her door had been shredded, my Boo came up to me and gave me a cuddle too. She has always had a knack of being the most annoying child ever, but then being the sweetest little thing ever too.

So the name Becky Boo stuck, and soon enough she decided that she was old enough to join me and Tom at the cinema, even though she was nowhere near ready to sit still for a couple of hours. And so it proved for the first three years or so of her cinema going life. She'd probably started coming with me and Tom when she was around four, and Tom was six, and because she wasn't prepared to sit still for a prolonged period of time, or maybe because the films she was taken to see just weren't interesting enough for her, she developed a habit of needing to go to the toilet quite frequently.

I was starting to worry that she was having bladder problems as she needed the toilet so often, before I realised this was just her way of getting out of her seat and doing a bit of exploring. A trip to the toilet did not necessarily mean a trip to sit on the toilet. It invariably meant an opportunity for her to test every single flushing mechanism on each loo, turn every tap in the sinks just to make sure they were working ok, and then finish off by pressing the button on each of the hand dryers, making them all go off simultaneously.

The first few of these trips to the loos meant that I would end up missing quite a lot of the film, as I would be standing outside the ladies' toilets, wondering what the hell she was doing in there. It was only once I heard all three hand dryers being turned on, one after the other, that I knew I would soon be able to take my seat again, disturbing all those people again who we had already disturbed on the way out.

After a few of these experiences I just let her go by herself. She knew exactly where the toilets were, and where I was if she needed me, and if she wasn't back after ten minutes I would go and find her. It always seemed that she had a sixth sense to know exactly when ten minutes would be up, almost waiting for me to disturb the other families in our aisle, before reappearing at the bottom of the stairs, causing all manner of tutting from the equally as frustrated and annoyed audience who would then have to move aside again.

After three or four attempts with various films to give her the chance to show me that she could in fact be a good girl, and sit nicely, and just watch the bloody film will you, but after each failure, after each time the toilets had their regular Becky check-up, I gave up and refused to take her with me anymore, not until she was a bit older at least. I think she'd failed on "Cloudy with a Chance of Meatballs", "Monsters v Aliens" and even on Disney's "The Princess and the Frog", their first traditional hand drawn animated film since "Brother Bear" had flopped six years previously.

This film was Disney's attempt to go back to basics, with a story based on a fairy tale, with high quality traditional animation, and a few catchy little songs thrown in. Although this worked to an extent with Becky, she didn't last the whole film. A good mate of mine had come along to see it too with his daughter, so at least I didn't have to sit on my own watching Princess Tiana attempt to turn herself back into a human, whilst Becky yet again flushed every toilet, turned every tap on, and pressed every hand dryer.

This film would pave the way for the phenomenon that was "Frozen", Disney's highest grossing film ever at the time of its release in 2013, even beating "Toy Story 3" despite it not having any Pixar influence at all. So far it has made almost $1.3 billion and proved that when Disney do what they do best, which is traditional hand drawn, fairy tale based stories, using great songs which would be sung the world over, then they are the best.

"The Princess and the Frog" had been released in February 2009, and I had given up on Becky by then, at least on animated films, whether CGI or hand drawn. Maybe she would be ok with a live action film, and so, undeterred, I suggested the whole family should go and see a Christmas film that year. Becky was coming up for eight years of age by then, and the whole family would be able to go to the pictures, watch a nice little Christmas film, and then go for a pizza afterwards. It all sounded wonderful. The question now was whether Becky would embarrass me again, this time with her mum, brother, and older sister there too.

A threat of no pizza for Becky was administered if she messed about. I was desperate for her to succeed this time, partly because I didn't want to have to take her home and miss out on pizza too, but mostly because I'd been recommended the film we were going to watch. "Nativity!" was a lovely little British film, starring Martin Freeman and Ashley Jensen, both of whom had come to my attention in Ricky Gervais' sitcoms "The Office" and "Extras", respectively. As well as these two, there would also be a host of British talent on display, including Jason Watkins, Miss Trunchbull herself, Pam Ferris, Alan Carr, Ricky Tomlinson, and Marc Wooton, as the infuriating but very loveable Mr. Poppy.

Joy of joys, and like Mr. Poppy, Becky was more loveable than infuriating that day, and managed to sit in her chair throughout the whole film. She proved that if the film had the ability to captivate her, then the toilets no longer seemed particularly intriguing. She absolutely loved it, and still does to this day. No doubt she will have the same sort of joyous day with her own kids, once she has some, and maybe she might even invite me round to watch it again too with her and my future grandchildren.

Whether it was the threat of no pizza, or just the fact that the film happened to be one of the most wonderful of cinema experiences I had ever had, with every other member of my family feeling the same way too, which stopped Becky from going to the toilet during the film. She may well have had to have her toilet fix straight after the film, but by then I no longer cared how many hair dryers she would turn on simultaneously.

"Nativity!", exclamation mark included, hit all the right spots in all the right places for all of us that day. Not just Becky, but every one of us had the loveliest of afternoons. We all laughed out loud, we all sniggered, we all felt nervous with the children who were performing their sweetest of nativity plays, and we all cried at some of the soppier bits. We all thoroughly enjoyed ourselves. It was the first family day at the cinema we had all attended, and Becky passed her test with flying colours. The pizza tasted even better, and she was even allowed extra sprinkles on her ice cream afterwards. Not just sprinkles, but marshmallows, Smarties, various sauces, and a range of other brightly coloured things which entirely covered the ice cream underneath.

The miracle of Christmas, which the film portrayed so sweetly and hilariously, had become our own little miracle too. Even the creator of the film's name seemed miraculous, as Debbie Isitt's surname is pronounced "I sit", which Becky proved she could finally do. It really was the best day of the Christmas period, much better than Christmas Day itself. Becky had given me an early present by proving that I could now take her to the cinema without having to listen for the hand dryers being turned on to realise she was on her way back.

I now had to test her with Pixar films. This was going to be tricky and emotional, seeing as the next family day at the cinema would be very emotional for everyone involved, especially a young boy called Andy, who was now not so young, and would be going to college very soon.

Toy Story 3 (2010)   **Dir: Lee Unkrich**

Now that Becky had proved herself, this was the real test. If she
disturbed the whole family's viewing of this film, I would not
have been happy at all. It was too important a film for not just
me, but my wife and two other kids, especially Lottie, who had
now reached sweet sixteen, and so was starting to think of what
she would like to do after she left school. She had grown up with
Andy and his toys, and I had watched her do it. My wife and I
were preparing ourselves for the same moment that Jessie had
experienced in the second film of the trilogy, when she would be
abandoned, except this time it would be us who were being
abandoned by Lottie.

Of course I'm being a tad melodramatic here, as Lottie would
never abandon us. But she would be flying the nest in the next
few years and this film brought that truth home to me and my
wife, very tearfully so for not just us two, but for most people in
the cinema that day actually. I defy anyone not to well up at the
end of "Toy Story 3", when Andy passes his beloved toys onto
Bonnie.

It wasn't just parents who were sniffling and quietly sobbing all
around us, but when I looked over to Lottie, she had tears
streaming down her face. She was a complete mess to be fair, and
thankfully the film had also held Becky's attention, particularly
with the inclusion of Barbie in this film. She had behaved
impeccably, allowing the whole film to be one of the most
perfect, the most endearing, and also the most emotional I have
ever seen.

Pizza and ice cream were thoroughly enjoyed again, making our
whole day a brilliant one, and I think I may even have suggested
to Lottie that just us two go again the following week. We had
seen the first of the trilogy together, early that Boxing Day when

she was still only three years old, before I would take her to see the second film at the old cinema in Lancaster. I needed to watch this one just with her too, and we both sobbed profusely, possibly even more in the second viewing. Woody, Buzz and all the other toys had become part of our lives together, just as they had done for millions of other parents and their children. We cried not only because of how the film ended the whole trilogy so perfectly, but I think we also cried as we knew there would be no more of these films for us to watch together.

But of course we would be proved wrong, because inexplicably, as far as I'm concerned, Disney/Pixar decided to make a fourth "Toy Story" film in 2019, to further continue what was starting to become not just a story, but a saga. Frankly, I am not including this film in the saga, as I do not think it should have been made in the first place.

"Toy Story 4" is still quite a sweet film, and is much better than most of the guff that is churned out these days, but for me it somehow detracts from the perfection of the original trilogy. It doesn't quite fit, and is unnecessary. It adds nothing significant to the characters, and just seems to be a money making exercise, which of course the original film was certainly not when John Lasseter started working on it. He made that film back in 1994/95 because it was a labour of love for him. He had no idea back then whether it would even be commercially viable, let alone a financial success. And to see his creation turn into the phenomenon that it did must have been beyond his wildest dreams. The fourth film was not made for the same reasons I believe.

This is exactly like another unnecessary fourth film which was made much later than the original trilogy. I don't like to criticise Steven Spielberg, but I share the same feelings I have for "Toy Story 4" as I do for "Indiana Jones and the Kingdom of the

Crystal Skull", which came out in 2008, almost twenty years after the original trilogy had ended. Again, it is a decent addition to the series, but was not needed, and detracts from what would have been an almost perfect trilogy.

I say, "almost perfect" trilogy, and would also put the three "Godfather" films in the same "almost perfect" category. The third film of each of these trilogies slightly lets the whole down for me, as does the second film in the "Back to the Future" trilogy. But I will argue with anyone who cares to do so that the three "Toy Story" films are the best trilogy of films that have ever been made. Each one is a perfect film in its own right, but when they are added together, the three little pieces of perfection make up one even bigger slice of pure perfection. There has not been a better set of three films made before, and it will take something very special indeed to knock John Lasseter and Lee Unkrich's creations from their highest of perches.

And there endeth the lesson according to Woody and Buzz. I promise I won't mention them again and just let them drift off into infinity. The films will continue to provide the ultimate in cinematic family delight for many generations, and will be written and talked about for many, many years to come, which is exactly what I'm doing now I suppose. And I've just broken the promise I made only a few lines ago.

There would be one more PixFlix which would become very special to me, as this one would become Becky's PixFlix. It had been "Toy Story" with Lottie, "Cars" with Tom, but the film I would watch just with Becky would require a journey into another land. It was time to go with her into The Land of the Dead.

Coco (2017)   **Dir: Lee Unkrich**

Before we would enter The Land of the Dead though, Becky and I would go to university together first, well, a university for monsters anyway. As Becky had acquired one of her nicknames from "Monsters Inc.", we were able to then graduate together in 2013 when we went to watch the sequel "Monsters University". She was now eleven years old and had definitely got over her phase of pressing things in the cinema toilets. She had proved this the year before when she had managed to watch the great little film, "Wreck-it Ralph" with me.

This had been the first time she had lasted a whole film without going to explore the toilets without any other members of the family being with us. We both enjoyed this film very much, especially as it took me back into my arcade playing days of my own childhood, and she loved it because she knew just how proud I was of her to just sit and watch it with me.

That same year, in 2012, she proved that she could not only last a whole film which was a couple of hours long, including the adverts and trailers, but she would also prove to be able to go the distance with a much longer film. That year was the centenary of the sailing and the subsequent sinking of Titanic, and James Cameron's film of the same name, the one everyone seems to hate, was re-released on the big screen to mark the centenary. Becky suddenly decided that she would like to go and see it too.

The film has always been a bit of a guilty pleasure of mine. I know it's a bit cheesy, and the love story set on that fateful maiden voyage is a little contrived, but I have always really enjoyed the film, especially the scenes after the ship has hit the iceberg. Whatever people say about the plot, they can't fail to be impressed with the actual demise of the ship, and the destruction of the once proudest and grandest of ships.

So, when the opportunity to watch the very impressive ship sink in a very impressive, if rather tragic way, then I was well up for another viewing of the film, especially as I had never seen it on the big screen. Becky lasted the whole film again, and we both had a lovely afternoon's entertainment watching hundreds of people drown or freeze to death in the North Atlantic. I'm not even going to refer to it as a guilty pleasure any more. It is just a pleasure watching that film for me, I have no guilt about saying that whatsoever. There, it's out now, I really like the film "Titanic", and I don't care who knows it.

Becky didn't care who knew that she had been to see the film, especially her guitar teacher. She had just started learning the guitar at school, and once her teacher knew she had seen the film, he found her the bloody awful theme song by Celine Dion to learn over the next week. She dutifully brought her homework home and started to practise playing a rather rudimentary version of the instrumental version. I was just grateful she didn't try and sing along to it as well, as although she was a quick learner, her musical ability has never been that great.

Forget about Celine Dion's heart going on and on, Becky's practising would do exactly that too. Wherever we were in the house we could hear her plucking and strumming away to a song I couldn't really stand in the first place. Even when my wife or I would escape for a bath, if we hadn't locked the door she would join us in the bathroom, sitting on the toilet seat and practise for us. This was actually worse, as once in the bath, there was no escape at all. Even with the door locked, she would sit on the step outside, serenading us whilst we were supposed to be de-stressing in the tub. Becky has always had a knack of making situations which are meant to be calm and relaxed the complete opposite.

Becky's enjoyment of "Titanic", theme tune and all, obviously made her feel a little more grown up. Having now watched a

380

supposedly grown up film, she wanted to do the same with her mum, as well as me, so when we told her that we were going to watch Idris Elba as Nelson Mandela in "Mandela: Long Walk to Freedom", she was now ready to join us on our date night. I told you she had a knack of making relaxed evenings into stressful ones.

We were going to see the film at The Dukes Theatre, the independent theatre and cinema which I had frequented so much in my life, but this would be Becky's first visit, and there would be a whole new ladies' loos for her to try out, with different flushing mechanisms, different taps, and possibly different hand dryers. I wouldn't actually know as I've never been in there, but the blokes' loo only had hand towels. This could be very interesting indeed for Becky. But she was as good as gold, and actually made our evening really lovely. We were watching her grow up and learn about one of the most important figures of not just black culture, but human culture, and she thoroughly enjoyed herself too. And she still managed to resist the temptations of the toilets and their possible lack of hand dryers.

She had enjoyed it so much that she then asked to accompany us again the following week to see another important film about black, and indeed human culture, but even our independent cinema would not let an eleven year old in to see a 15 certificate film, and so she would watch that one a few months later, as soon as it was released on DVD, as I knew she was ready to watch such a film, despite her still only being eleven. And because she watched it, she grew up a little more.

With all this growing up she was doing, I thought it was best to balance it out a bit by taking her to see another Pixar film, this time "Finding Dory", the nowhere near as good sequel to "Finding Nemo". We still enjoyed the film, but it proved that Pixar had lost their Midas touch. The following summer, Pixar's mantel would slip still lower with "Cars 3, the first film of theirs I would not see at the cinema, and only caught up with it eventually on TV at some point just to see if it was as bad as everyone had said. Sadly, it was.

However, a few months later, after their worst film, came one of their best, and one which would also help Becky to grow up and realise just how important family is, as it did for me. "Coco" is a film which is special to Becky and I for a few reasons, but mainly because it is simply a great original story, and not some rehashing of older triumphs, as in the case of "Monsters University" and "Finding Dory". The film is worthy of the studio's name, and can rightly sit alongside their best films. Not quite up there with the very best, but certainly on the podium somewhere.

The other reasons are much more profound. The film is about passing on memories to the next generation, and with John Lasseter having passed on the directing duties in "Toy story 3" to the next generation in Lee Unkrich, who had cut his teeth on the early films as co-director, he would put his trust in Unkrich again with this film. He did not let his father-figure down. And neither would my daughter let her grandmother down.

Becky's grandma, my mother-in-law had been diagnosed with cancer almost ten years before the film was released, and had endured many surgeries and various chemotherapy treatments, but in February 2018, a few weeks before we would see the film, had lost her fight against the disease. This was the first time that my daughter had experienced the loss of a member of her family since my own grandmother, her great grandma had died when she was only four. She remembers very little of the grief she felt, but with her grandma dying, it affected her much more profoundly. She experienced grief, not just loss, and realised that they are not the same thing.

"Coco" is the story of a young boy called Miguel who attempts to reconnect with his ancestors by travelling to the Land of the Dead, and meeting his great, great grandparents. This then allows their daughter, Miguel's great grandmother, the eponymous Coco, to remember who her real father was. It is all about being guided by your family and making your ancestors proud of you by creating and sharing memories which can be passed down through the generations.

Well Becky certainly did that for not just me, but for her grandma who had died only a couple of weeks before we went to see the film. Just to go and see the film under the circumstances required a certain degree of bravery from my daughter, knowing what the film was about, especially as her own mum was not ready to see something so raw yet.

We saw the film in between her grandma's death and the funeral, and the final sequence, in which Miguel sings the same song to Coco as her own father used to sing to her as a tiny little girl, was emotional to say the least, especially as the song is called "Remember Me". It was tough for me to watch, but for a teenage girl, who was experiencing real grief for the first time ever, then it must have been even tougher.

But that's the thing with great films. They do not always bring joy and laughter, of which there is plenty in "Coco" by the way, but they can sometimes be tough to watch. This is what makes them ultimately so much more rewarding, and Becky rewarded me that day for putting up with her many foibles over the years. She reminded me of the same thing that Miguel learns, that "nothing is more important than family", something which I have lived by all my life, and am trying to do even now by writing this book.

I hope this book will be read by future generations of my own family, helping to keep not just my own memory alive, but those of all my other family members, my Gran and my brother especially, who, like my mother-in-law, are still alive in spirit, and with us in the Land of the Living.

"Coco" was a film which I believe helped my daughter become the young woman she is now. She turned eighteen earlier this year, and at some point soon will be flying the nest, along with her older brother and sister. Me and my wife will be left on our own, until of course we become grandparents too. That will mean I'll be able to have a third childhood, as I definitely intend to take my grandchildren to the cinema too, as often as possible, just as my own Gran did with me.

But that stage of my life will have to wait. I'm happy to watch a few more adult films before my third childhood begins. My second childhood was the most wonderful of experiences, but it's kind of finished now. My kids are all grown up, but it doesn't mean that I have to be too.

Part Seven

Finally Reaching Adulthood

Well, almost

Saving Private Ryan (1998)   Dir: Steven Spielberg

Whilst having children has been the best thing to happen to me, they did have the knack of preventing me and my wife from going to the cinema. After going to watch a film on the big screen at least once, and sometimes two or three times a week at university, I then entered a period of my life in which I rarely, if ever, went to the cinema with anyone else. If I did go, my wife would stay at home looking after our children, and so most films would be watched at home, either on TV or on DVD. I was still able to watch films which I didn't want my children to watch, or at least not with me. Not until they were much older anyway, which is about now in fact. I would gladly watch the following films with any of my children now. Some of them I know they have watched too, just not with me. Maybe I still will.

I chose the title film of this chapter as its main star, Tom Hanks, is just too huge a star not to dedicate a chapter to. He has proved himself to be arguably the most versatile actor there has ever been, and remains the only actor ever to win consecutive Best Actor Oscars, which he did in 1994 and 1995 for "Philadelphia" and "Forrest Gump" respectively. He has become the nearest thing to a National Treasure in America. He is their equivalent of Dame Judi Dench, although I'm not quite sure how he would take that compliment, which it very much is.

He'd first been nominated for an Oscar in "Big" where he played a teenage boy who suddenly finds himself in the body of an adult. His ability to portray youthfulness and innocence made the film memorable, in particular the scene in which he and his boss of the toy company he gets a job at play "Chopsticks" on the huge piano on the floor of the famous toy store, FAO Schwarz.

This was the film in which he really became "big", after appearing in mostly light comedies, some romantic, some not, ranging from "Splash" in 1984 where he fell in love with a mermaid, played by Darryl Hannah. I next saw him in the not quite as rude as I was hoping it to be "Bachelor Party", starring with Tawny Kitaen, who I would salivate over in the videos for the band Whitesnake's songs "Here I Go Again" and "Is This Love?", as she was then married to the band's creator and vocalist, David Coverdale. Many a Thursday evening would be spent with me drooling over her on "Top of the Pops" when I was at that particularly drooly age of fourteen.

Hanks would then appear in a few relatively big films such as "The Money pit", "Dragnet", "Punchline", "The 'Burbs" and "Turner and Hooch" as well as the aforementioned "Big", before he would become the huge star we know today in the 1990s.

This decade would start with another film I would see on one of those Wednesday afternoons in which I would bunk off school, going to the cinema instead of doing PE. "Joe Versus the Volcano" was the first film he would appear in with Meg Ryan, before he would then appear in the film version of Tom Wolfe's novel "The Bonfire of the Vanities" alongside Bruce Willis and Melanie Griffith. The film would also feature someone else I had drooled over around the age of fourteen when I first saw "Porky's" and watched Kim Cattrall get very turned on by the smell of the boys' changing rooms, consequently making some very remarkable noises, much to the amusement of the rest of the school.

"A League of Their Own" came next, which I have already mentioned previously, before he would meet up again with Meg Ryan, this time on top of the Empire State Building in "Sleepless in Seattle", Nora Ephron's attempt to replicate the success of her screenplay for "When Harry Met Sally", but this time as director.

After all these quite light comedies, Hanks would play his first serious role, as the lawyer dying from AIDS in "Philadelphia", before then opening up a box of chocolates in "Forrest Gump", a film which I've never really liked for some reason. I can understand why he won his first Oscar for "Philadelphia" but I'm not too sure about his second. I would have much preferred John Travolta or Morgan Freeman to have won that year for their roles in "Pulp Fiction" and "The Shawshank Redemption" respectively.

Then came "Apollo 13", Ron Howard's not quite out of this world account of the very nearly fatal failed mission to the moon, before Hanks would become the voice of Woody in the "Toy Story" films. I've just broken my promise again not to mention that film any more, but I don't really care seeing as the role would make Hanks into a favourite of not just adult film fans, but millions and millions of kids too.

Hanks would then have a go at directing, with "That Thing You Do", directing himself too in a decent first time effort, before then starting what would become a hugely successful relationship with Steven Spielberg, in "Saving Private Ryan", which I'll come back to later. One more film with Meg Ryan, in "You've Got Mail" came next, again directed by Nora Ephron, before he would end the twentieth century in Frank Darabont's attempt to replicate his first prison drama "The Shawshank Redemption" with another prison drama, the good, but not quite so good "The Green Mile".

As for the twenty first century, Hanks films would be even huger than the previous century. Some were great films like Robert Zemeckis' "Castaway", Sam Mendes' "Road to Perdition" the Coen brothers' remake of "The Ladykillers", Paul Greengrass' "Captain Phillips" and Clint Eastwood's "Sully: Miracle on the Hudson". Some were charming films like "Saving Mr. Banks", as

Walt Disney himself trying to persuade P.L. Travers, played brilliantly by Emma Thompson, to allow him to make her story "Mary Poppins" into a film, and playing another National Treasure, Fred Rogers in his latest film at the time of writing, "A Beautiful Day in the Neighbourhood".

Some of his films though would not be particularly great, or even particularly good, namely the two films he teamed up again with Ron Howard, who directed the film versions of the phenomenal best-selling books by Dan Brown. "The Da Vinci Code" and particularly its sequel "Angels and Demons", were not Hanks' finest moments, and I didn't really like him in "Charlie Wilson's War", although many other people did.

But it was his films directed by Steven Spielberg which would become some of his greatest ever, starting with the film with the most astonishing opening sequence to a film ever filmed. It is a film which showed the true range of Tom Hanks, and also reminded us all what an bewilderingly brilliant film maker Steven Spielberg is.

The opening twenty minutes or so of "Saving Private Ryan" are truly remarkable. They are the most visceral of sequences ever seen on screen as far as I'm concerned. Not just seen, but also heard, as the brilliant use of sound, with bullets fizzing into the English Channel, and also fizzing through the soldiers as they emerge from the landing vehicles on the beaches of Normandy on D-Day, add to arguably the most intense sensory experience ever on film.

The use of slow motion, first person perspective, long shots, close ups, sound effects and many other techniques I'm not an expert on, create a completely enthralling yet truly harrowing piece of cinema. The scenes of men dragging their mutilated comrades across the beach, some looking for their own limbs, others screaming for their mums as they lay dying, is an absolute tour de force in terms of film making, and one which I loved playing in the computer game "Medal of Honour: Allied Assault", although if I got shot, wounded or killed on that beach, at least I could just start the assault on the beach again, which those men who actually were shot, wounded and killed on those beaches on June 6th, 1944 definitely could not do.

Despite the game being a first person shooter, with all the computer wizardry available to its creators, it still came nowhere near the visceral force of Spielberg's film, and deservedly won him his second Oscar for Best Director. The rest of the film is not particularly brilliant, but those opening sequences make up for anything the rest of the film may lack.

Hanks' other films with Spielberg have all been exceptional, following on from "Saving Private Ryan" with "Catch Me If You Can", four years later, and "The Terminal", two years on from that. Hanks and Spielberg would not work together again for another ten years, but then made the brilliantly taut "Bridge of Spies", with Mark Rylance finally making his breakthrough onto the big screen after Spielberg had recognised him as possibly the finest stage actor around, and then "The Post" which gained Meryl Streep her twentieth Oscar nomination of her remarkable career, having already won three statues already, for "Kramer vs Kramer", in a supporting role, and Best Actress for "Sophie's Choice", and "The Iron Lady".

Tom Hanks has proved throughout his whole career that he can provide the best entertainment to any type of audience, in almost any type of film. He really will go down in cinema history as one of the true greats.

However, I'm not so sure he would have provided the same sort of entertainment as that provided in my next film. I really don't think Tom Hanks would have had the same impact if he'd been the one shouting to the audience in the most blood thirsty of arenas, "Are you not entertained?" It's time to unleash hell.

Gladiator (2000)   Dir: Ridley Scott

Ridley Scott has made some cracking films in his time, as well as some fairly awful ones. Russell Crowe appeared in examples of both. From making the iconic Hovis advertisement, where the little lad pushes his delivery bike up the hill, before zooming back down, Scott went onto make his debut feature film in 1977 with "The Duellists", before making possibly his most seminal film ever in "Alien". I just about remember this being on the TV for the first time when I must have been nine or ten, and being allowed to stay up with my brother to watch it, and predictably freaked out when the creepy little monster bursts out of John Hurt's belly.

Then came "Blade Runner", which I didn't see until I was much older, although I did see one of its stars, Rutger Hauer when he basically put anyone off hitchhiking ever again in "The Hitcher" in 1986, another one of the videos my brother was able to rent out when I was only thirteen.

I then saw one of Scott's lesser known, but actually one of his best films, in "Someone to Watch Over Me" starring Tom Berenger, before "Black Rain" in 1989 and "Thelma and Louise" in 1991 were a big part of my sixth form days. At university I distinctly remember watching one of the two films which came out celebrating Christopher Columbus' 500th anniversary of his "discovery" of America, with Scott's "1492: Conquest of Paradise", but then did not see another film of his until the most epic of epics ever was released just after the turn of the century.

Although Scott's much later "The Martian", is a not particularly close second, which I can watch happily again and again, "Gladiator" is by far my favourite of his films, and one which I simply cannot help myself from watching whenever I flick onto it when it's on TV. It's one of my go to films if I ever just want a barnstormingly brilliant film to chill out to. But before I come onto this film properly, I need to go down a bit of a worm hole which films and the way they link together tend to take you down quite often. I promise I'll come back up into the dazzling light of the Colosseum in due course, but I just want to mention a couple of other stars which are linked to "Gladiator".

I'd first seen Maximus Decimus Meridius in another brilliant film, although in "LA Confidential", Russell Crowe is not the lead, but one of a very impressive ensemble cast. First of all there is Guy Pearce, who I'd first seen as Mike in "Neighbours" when I was a teenager. Little did I know that when I was watching him with Kylie Minogue and Jason Donovan, that he would go onto become a huge film star, and star in one of my favourite films of all time.

Then there was James Cromwell, who I'd only seen dancing with a pig in "Babe", another film Lottie and I would watch together very often. From being a sweet farmer who trains his pig to herd sheep, he became a ruthless, corrupt, and really very nasty chief of police in the order I watched the films in. It was all a bit of a shock when the man who had said "That'll do pig. That'll do", started murdering the police detectives he was supposed to be in charge of. Maybe if I'd watched the films in chronological order then the shock would have been much more pleasant.

One of the detectives Cromwell kills in "LA Confidential", is Jack Vincennes, played by Kevin Spacey, who in a nice parallel to one of his other great films, brings about the downfall of Cromwell's chief of police by mentioning the name Rollo

Tomasi. This rather cryptic clue is similar to another mysterious name Spacey had uttered to a policeman, that of Keyser Soze in "The Usual Suspects", for which Spacey won his first Oscar, as Best Supporting Actor.

Spacey would then go onto voice one of the insects in Pixar's "A Bug's Life" before winning his second Oscar, but his first as Best Actor, as Lester Burnham, in "American Beauty" who discovers he is no longer in love with Annette Bening, who played his wife. Her performance made me realise I was still very much in love with her, and again the film has become another one of my go to films.

The most recent film I saw Annette Bening in deserves a mention too. In "Film Stars Don't Die in Liverpool", she plays the ageing and fading star of films such as "The Bad and the Beautiful", for which she won the Oscar for Best supporting Actress, "In a Lonely Place, "The Big Heat", and of course has a small but significant part in Frank Capra's "It's a Wonderful Life".

The star in question is Gloria Grahame, and in 1981 she was appearing in a production of Tennessee Williams' "The Glass Menagerie" in none other than Lancaster, my home town. Little did I know that when I was only eight years old, a true Oscar winning star of old Hollywood would be performing only a few miles from my house, that is until she became ill and had to give up the part.

She rings an old boyfriend of hers in Liverpool, the much younger Peter Turner, played by Jamie Bell, and tells him that her cancer has returned. He then helps her get through the final years of her life, before she returns to America to die. The film is beautifully played by both leads, and the romance between the two is really quite touching, with Bening giving yet another wonderful performance to add to the many films I love her in.

"American Beauty" became one of the films I could very happily watch over and over mainly because of the brilliant script, which won Alan Ball (no, not the World Cup winning England midfielder) an Oscar for Best Original Screenplay. Ball would then go onto create one of my all-time favourite TV programmes, "Six Feet Under", also featuring James Cromwell in the later seasons, which had special significance for me seeing as it is all about the lives of a family of funeral directors, something which I knew the reality of. However, my own dad was about as far removed from Michael C. Hall's David Fisher as was possible. My dad is neither young, gay, nor has ever taken Ecstasy in an LA nightclub. Now that would have been a sight to behold.

The other leading star in "LA Confidential" is someone I fell in love with fifteen years previously, but this film made me realise I still loved her too, especially as she was dressed as one of the most beautiful stars of the golden age of Hollywood, Veronica Lake. I had first seen Kim Basinger, and fallen head over heels in love with her, as most thirteen year old boys did when they first saw "9 ½ Weeks", and realised that the contents of a fridge did not simply have to be used as food. I very much wanted to be Mickey Rourke at that point. The film was also significant as being the only time I have ever liked a song by "Roxy Music", with the use of "Slave to Love", as the backing song to a very steamy episode in the film, where Rourke and Basinger become very friendly in a clock tower if I remember rightly.

Basinger would then go onto appear in "No Mercy" with Richard Gere, "Blind Date" with Bruce Willis, where there was no sign of Cilla Black at all, "Nadine" with Jeff Bridges, before becoming the sexiest alien ever opposite Dan Ackroyd in "My Stepmother is an Alien", all of which were fairly forgettable. She would then play Vicki Vale in Tim Burton's "Batman", before appearing again with Richard Gere in "Final Analysis", another film I saw on those Friday cinema nights with my girlfriend at university.

We would also see her in Robert Altman's "Pret-a-Porter", but then again, we would see most Hollywood stars in that film due to the amount of cameo appearances it featured.

And then of course came "LA Confidential", where she fell in love with, and even tamed the brutality of Russell Crowe's Officer Bud White. I love the film not just because of the stars in it, the script, the storyline, and the brilliant 1950s Hollywood atmosphere, but also because it harks back to the Golden Age of Hollywood and its legacy. Basinger appears as a high class escort working for the "Fleur de Lis" agency who specialise in delivering movie star looks to their clients. Not only does Basinger's Veronica Lake make an appearance, but also Rita Hayworth and the "real" Lana Turner, with the film paying homage to the great Film Noirs of the 1940s and 50s, becoming in itself one of the greatest of Noir films ever, despite being filmed in colour, with the dazzling California sunshine highlighting the darkness of Hollywood's underbelly.

It was Russell Crowe's performance which was the most arresting of all though in "LA Confidential", and then when I saw "Gladiator", he became one of my favourite actors, despite me having only seen a few of his films. I saw him next in "A Beautiful Mind", as the tormented Maths genius John Nash opposite the now even more lovely Jennifer Connelly, who I had last seen in "The Hot Spot" over ten years before, and then in Ron Howard's "Cinderella Man", the biopic of a real life Rocky, Jim Braddock, in a true story of glory in the boxing ring.

For some reason I haven't seen any of Crowe's other films, apart from ironically a film which many people thought he was severely miscast in, "Les Misérables". I have yet to see Crowe's "Robin Hood", "American Gangster", "Body of Lies" and "A Good Year", all directed by Ridley Scott, although from what I have read this last one is not worth watching at all. I haven't even seen Peter Weir's "Master and Commander", or "Noah", two other epics in a series of epics which Crowe has become famous for. Maybe I haven't seen any of these because his first epic was just too epic for me. I could not, and maybe even did not want to see him in anything other than gladiatorial armour.

For me, Russell Crowe as Maximus, is one of the best roles ever, in one of the best films ever. It is not just about the astonishing fight sequences in the arena, but the storyline is perfect too. I had just become a father when I first saw the film, with Tom being born only a few months before its release. The scene when Maximus finally arrives home after his ride through various landscapes, only to find his son and wife crucified and burnt, had a huge impact on me, which of course made Maximus' revenge on Joaquin Phoenix's Commodus even more satisfying in the final fight sequence.

My son's birth prevented me from actually seeing the film on the big screen, which is something I have to rectify at some point. If ever a film deserved to be watched on the big screen, then "Gladiator" is it, and I vow that I will watch it one day in a cinema, even if I have to unleash my own sort of hell to get there. I think I'd even ride cross country for many days and nights to see it on the big screen.

My name is David John Small, husband to a gorgeous wife, father to three wonderful children, and loyal servant to the true cinematic greats.

And I will see "Gladiator" in a cinema, in this life or the next.

Sense and Sensibility (1995)   **Dir: Ang Lee**

My wife has always loved a good period drama, and I'm not talking about the sort she and our daughter seem to have every month now that their cycles have synchronised.

Seeing as I have devoted a few chapters in this book to films I've very much enjoyed with each of my three kids, it seems only fair to do the same for my better half. She is never as willing to watch a film with me as I would like, and often just isn't prepared to commit herself properly to a film, usually falling asleep half way through if we're watching it in bed. Some of the films though in this section keep her awake very happily, whilst some just keep her awake, at whatever volume I turn them down to. More on those later, but for now, let's concentrate on the ones she actually is happy to stay awake to.

Ironically, I'm going to start with a film which she's never really loved. She likes it, and enjoys it, but unlike me, she does not love it. That's because this period drama is all about a dramatist she has never really got on with, whereas I've been teaching him for the last twenty five years.

"Shakespeare in Love", has become a film I've watched many, many times, or at least one particular scene. I've watched the whole film a few times but there is one scene which I know shot by shot, word for word, as I have used it in my lessons on many occasions. The story of how William Shakespeare falls in love with Lady Viola, which inspires his writing of "Romeo and Juliet", is wonderful. It is romantic, funny, sometimes heart wrenching, witty, and above all, tremendously satisfying, all thanks to the brilliantly inventive Oscar wining screenplay by Tom Stoppard, who enjoys playing around with the Bard, as he also created "Rosencrantz and Guildenstern are Dead", for both stage and screen.

Joseph Fiennes and Gwyneth Paltrow, who won her only Oscar for this film, are just lovely together, and the ensemble cast, including Geoffrey Rush, Tom Wilkinson, Anthony Sher, Martin Clunes, Simon Callow, Colin Firth, Imelda Staunton, Jim Carter, Ben Affleck, and not forgetting Rupert Everett as Shakespeare's friend and sometimes rival Christopher Marlowe, and Judi Dench, giving an Oscar winning performance as Queen Elizabeth I, are all equally good. Two stars of "The Fast Show", one of my favourite comedy sketch shows ever, also feature, with Simon Day as the gregarious river taxi driver, who can't stop telling his passengers "You'll never guess who I had in here last week", and Mark Williams as one of Shakespeare's troupe of actors, who has the unfortunate problem of a stutter to deal with, before he hit the big time as Arthur Weasley in the Harry Potter films.

The story, which mixes elements of the comedy "Twelfth Night", with the tragic elements of "Romeo and Juliet", is very clever indeed, with some knowing winks to our own age as well as lovingly using Shakespeare's language. The scene I have watched so many times is the actual performance at The Rose Theatre of the play within a film, which shows exactly what it must have been like to experience Shakespeare's theatre back then. When I have taught the context to Shakespeare, looking at the actual theatres and what their design meant for the performances of the plays, I have always used the scene from "Shakespeare in Love" as the perfect way to try and get my classes to empathise with the theatre goers of the 1590s.

The scene starts with the crowds of people all pushing into the theatre, jostling for position in "The Pit", before having their minds blown by the power of Shakespeare's drama, to the point where they are not sure whether to clap or cry, and end up doing both once they realise that what they have just witnessed was all just make believe. It is a brilliant scene which shows not just the power of stage drama, but also that of screen drama to create emotions so contradictory, yet so powerful, that they completely overwhelm us, something the cinema has been doing to me since that first film when I was just four years old.

As I said earlier, I have always loved this particular period drama, but it was a little too early a period for my wife to truly love it. She's always preferred a bit of Georgian, in particular a bit of Austen power to completely lose herself in the past. The Georgians did things much more genteelly, with much prettier dresses, with much more handsome men, especially when they walk out of lakes wearing white shirts, and much, much nicer architecture, which has always been one of my wife's ultimate passions, apart from me obviously.

"Sense and Sensibility", ticks almost every single one of those boxes, with the possible exception of the dresses. Another film would provide those in abundance a few years after Emma Thompson adapted Jane Austen's novel and wrote the script for the film which would bring her a second Oscar, to put next to her Best Actress Oscar in her downstairs loo.

I'd never really enjoyed Jane Austen, and even though I am an English teacher, have never had to read a single one of her novels. As a football mad young boy, the thought of reading a story about prissy girls looking for a husband was about the worst sort of story I could possibly imagine reading, and so I have always tried to avoid her novels and their film adaptations. But this one won me over, and has joined the not particularly exclusive club of films that I could watch happily again and again.

I was swept away with the film's wonderful script and subtle direction by Ang Lee, and was completely floored, a little like Kate Winslet, when Mr. Willoughby turns out to be a complete arse to Marianne Dashwood, and was completely uplifted, again a little like Kate Winslet when the dependable Colonel Brandon, played by Alan Rickman in possibly my favourite of his roles, helps to bring her back from the brink of life. The scene at Marianne's bedside, where her sister Eleanor begs her not to leave her, showed the same sort of emotional intensity Emma Thompson had displayed with Anthony Hopkins in "The Remains of the Day" and "Howard's End", and could quite easily have won her another acting Oscar as well as the one she did win for her screenwriting.

Hugh Grant is his charming self as Edward Ferrars, who eventually makes Eleanor very happy when he proposes to her, with Eleanor's sisters trying desperately to see into the window from their magical garden. The scene is so lovely, and the house is one my wife would pay an obscene amount of money, if she had that sort of money of course. She has even been known to say that she would happily lose a limb to own that dreamy little cottage, although I think I'd rather have all her four limbs in perfect working order.

The ironic thing is that the Dashwoods considered the simply stunning cottage in the heart of the Devonshire countryside as a step down from their previous grandeur, and had only moved there as a way of cutting back on their dwindling reserves, having to slum it in this most beautiful of houses, which would be worth millions today. If only we could afford to "slum it" in a house like that.

One house we definitely could never afford is Chatsworth House in Derbyshire, a place my wife and I visited on a rare weekend away from our children for our fifth anniversary many years ago. Even though it is almost seventeen years ago at the time of writing, I still remember which dress my wife wore that day and how beautiful she looked as we wandered through the magnificent gardens, stopping to shelter in a small pagoda when the sky threw a sudden shower. It was one of the most romantic afternoons we have ever spent together, and one which one of the previous occupants of the house would dearly have loved to experience with her husband.

Georgiana, Duchess of Devonshire, was married to the man who actually owned the house in 1744, and became the subject of another of my wife and I's favourite films. "The Duchess" provided the most stunning of dresses and costumes for not just my wife to admire, but also for me to ogle the wearer of them, as the outfits which Keira Knightley wears are works of art in themselves. The film is Georgian outfit porn, as well as Georgian architecture porn, with many scenes filmed in Bath, another city my wife and I have spent a couple of weekends away in, mainly to see some of the film's locations and generally pretend that we are Georgian aristocrats, "pretend" being the most apposite of words here.

Speaking of outfits worn by Keira Knightley, the green dress she wears in "Atonement" is another absolutely stunning creation, showing Miss Knightley's exquisite charms off to perfection, as did the corset she had to wear in "Pirates of the Caribbean", the only thing which kept me awake I think when I took my son Tom to see this overblown and frankly quite dull film, despite Jonny Depp's attempts to salvage some sort of humour from it.

We would next see her in "Love Actually" in a rather simpering role, unlike Emma Thompson's character in the same film, who yet again shows just how wonderful an actor she is, when she has to hold back the tears after opening a Joni Mitchell CD from her husband, and realising that he has been a philandering git.

Knightley would then go onto star in her own Jane Austen adaptation in "Pride and Prejudice" in 2005, playing Elizabeth Bennet, but this film lacked the power of Emma Thompson's version of Austen. The next period film we would see her in was one we went to The Dukes Theatre to watch on a date night. "Anna Karenina", the adaptation of Tolstoy's classic novel, was very sumptuous, but so dull that we were both glad when the eponymous leading lady decided to throw herself in front of a train. The only thing I remember about that film, apart from the unfortunate train incident, was the amount of impressive facial hair going on with the male actors. Jude Law's beard was particularly notable, and was possibly a factor in me deciding to grow one of my own, although maybe not quite as impressively.

Although not a period drama, Knightley was much more likeable in "The Imitation Game" alongside Benedict Cumberbatch as Alan Turing, another film we enjoyed at The Dukes. This was followed a few weeks later with another film about a remarkably brainy yet troubled genius, Professor Stephen Hawking in "The Theory of Everything", but the female lead this time would not be played by Keira Knightley, but by the equally lovely Felicity Jones, who would then go onto play the lead in "Rogue One" the aforementioned Star Wars spin-off, in quite a departure from the film set in Cambridge with Eddie Redmayne. The scene where the two fall in love with the lights sparkling in the grounds of Trinity Hall is gorgeous, and Cambridge became another city my wife and I have spent many hours wandering around, although never on our own. We always had our kids with us, something which will be rectified as soon as we are able to.

Finally, one of our favourite period dramas is "The Favourite", with Olivia Colman as a sickly Queen Anne, who has to try and choose between the affections of either Rachel Weisz or Emma Stone. The film showed just how good us Brits are at portraying strong women throughout history, winning Colman an Oscar for Best Actress, carrying on the traditions started by the best of them all, Dame Judi Dench in "Shakespeare in Love" and Dame Emma

Thompson in "Howard's End" but particularly for "Sense and Sensibility".

Colman is well on the way to National Treasure status, a status Dame Judi has definitely achieved, and for my money, Dame Emma has too, although she will never be able to compete with my own Dame Emma, my wife, who has watched all these films with me. I have fallen a little more in love with her with every viewing and so I think I may just watch one of these period dramas again later tonight.

That makes complete sense and sensibility to me.

Kill Bill: Vol. 1 (2003)   Dir: Quentin Tarantino

From the most sedate of films and genres, I come back to possibly the least sedate of directors and films. After "Jackie Brown" had underwhelmed me, Tarantino was almost back to his best with this "roaring rampage of revenge", which I went to the cinema to see one Sunday afternoon all by myself, seeing as my kids were only nine, three and one years old, and definitely were not ready to see this film yet. I wasn't exactly on my own though, as the cinema was packed, as was to be expected with a new release by Tarantino, especially as this was his first film for six years.

The reason he took so long in between films was that he was making not just one film, but two, which for me is the film's weak point. The fact that it comes in two volumes detracts from the overall film it could and should have been. The first part is brilliant, but the second part, released the following year, lets the whole film down.

The two part nature of the film means that the first film ends unfinished. Tarantino was starting to become rather too self-indulgent, and lacked discipline to an extent. Instead of making two films which take over four hours to watch together, nobody would have complained if he'd condensed the whole thing into one film of two and a half or even three hours. The whole thing would have been tighter, and presumably would not have included so much rambling as the final sequence of the second part contains. Instead of listening to Bill drone on, just kill him and complete the revenge. The second film is hardly a rampage, nor is it roaring, unlike the first film, which was definitely both.

As with many of Tarantino's films, there are links between this one and "Pulp Fiction". In the earlier film, when Mia and Vincent are on their evening out, which definitely wasn't a date of course, she tells him of a failed TV show she made a pilot for called "Fox Force Five", where the five female characters, all foxy chicks, each had their own speciality in terms of killing. Well each one of these characters would become part of the rampaging revenge in "Kill Bill" nine years later.

Uma Thurman's The Bride kills, or at least severely maims four other foxy chicks over the course of the two films, which of course should have been one complete film. The first girl she mentions from "Fox Force Five" is the leader, the blonde, who obviously becomes Darryl Hannah's Elle Driver in "Kill Bill", who makes her appearance in Volume 1, but is not actually dispatched until Volume 2, along with Michael Madsen's character Budd.

Then comes the Japanese fox, who was a kung fu master, who becomes Lucy Liu's O-Ren Ishii, along with the black girl, the demolition expert, or Vivica Fox's character Vernita Green, who The Bride dispenses with first in front of her victim's daughter. Finally comes the French fox, whose speciality was sex apparently, who becomes Julie Dreyfus' Sofie Fatale, although I'm not sure how good she'd be at this speciality anymore after having both her arms chopped off and left alive to tell Bill of what happened in The House of Blue Leaves.

That particularly bloody scene, with Uma Thurman dressed in her now iconic yellow outfit with black piping, stolen directly from Bruce Lee's "Game of Death" proved that she was the fifth and final fox, whose speciality was knives, or in this case, swords, particularly samurai swords created by the legendary Hattori Hanzo. The exaggerated violence, with blood literally gushing out of her victims like hellish geysers, creates an almost cartoon like quality to the violence, and relates to one of my favourite parts of the film, the anime section which shows the roots of O-Ren Ishii, and how she eventually became the Head of the Council of Yakuza bosses, which also features a blood geyser gushing out of O-Ren's first ever victim, the paedophile Matsumoto.

The penultimate scene in the film, where The Bride and O-Ren fight on the rooftop with snow all around them, with O-Ren finally being scalped, is astonishingly shot. The use of colour and black and white, along with sound and slow motion shows just what an innovative and expert film maker Tarantino had become, and his use of the soundtrack had also got better, particularly with Santa Esmeralda's version of "Don't let me be Misunderstood" playing over the fight scene. The song has become a favourite of mine and my kids now, seeing as I have played it so often in the car that they know all the words too. I'm also proud that they have all seen the film now too, and has become one of my son's favourites as well.

"Kill Bill" has so many iconic shots and scenes, that it too has become part of popular culture. If anyone was stupid enough to actually call their vehicle "Pussy Wagon" then we all know what that would refer to, just as most film lovers know who "The

Crazy 88" are, and have probably, like me, counted each one of their demises in that iconic scene.

The second film has some great sequences too, particularly the scene where The Bride gets buried alive, and consequently punches her way out of the coffin after the flashback sequence of her "Cruel Tutelage of Pai Mei" shows us how she was able to get herself out of such a horrifying position as being stuck inside a coffin, buried six feet under the ground.

If only these sections had somehow been incorporated into the first film, making a whole and complete experience, then maybe "Kill Bill" would even have knocked "Pulp Fiction" off its perch as my favourite Tarantino film. Instead it languishes in probably fourth place, with "Reservoir Dogs" still retaining a podium spot in third place.

As for my second favourite of his films, it would probably be "Inglorious Basterds" of 2009. In between he had made the two exploitation homages, "Grindhouse" and "Death Proof", which were fun and interesting, but his next film, which would be his first with Brad Pitt and Christoph Waltz, gets my nod for second place because it is a fully rounded film, where the director's self-indulgence had been reeled in a little. The opening scene with Waltz's Colonel Hans Landa ever so stealthily, but oh so ominously interrogating Monsieur LaPadite, is one of the most tense scenes I have ever seen, and sets the film up to become one of Tarantino's best ever.

I quite enjoyed his next film, "Django Unchained", but my love for Tarantino was starting to wane by now, to the point that I have never even got around to seeing his next film, "The Hateful Eight". Even his latest film, "Once Upon a Time in Hollywood", although having elements of his best work in it, in particular the use of naturalistic dialogue, was still a bit of a disappointment to me and my son, who came to watch it with me at the cinema, the first Tarantino we had ever watched together on the big screen. Maybe Tarantino will astonish us all once again, but even if he doesn't, then the legacy he has left with "Pulp Fiction", "Inglorious Basterds", "Reservoir Dogs" and "Kill Bill: Vol. 1" is certainly enough to put him amongst the great directors and innovators of cinema history.

One other film which Tarantino played a major role in needs to be mentioned in this chapter. I saw "Sin City", again in the cinema on my own, and thoroughly enjoyed the graphic violence on display. It certainly was the most graphic of graphic violence, as the film was an adaptation of Frank Miller's series of graphic comic books, directed by Robert Rodriguez, with a guest slot as director reserved for Tarantino, who had worked closely with Rodriguez before.

In "Four Rooms" in 1995, both directors had shared duties along with a couple of others, before Rodriguez would direct the vampire horror thriller "From Dusk Till Dawn" which Tarantino had written. Rodriguez would then go onto make three films which my eldest daughter Lottie would love, the "Spy Kids" trilogy, and so when I heard that he would then be making "Sin City", I was intrigued. This one would definitely not be suitable for Lottie though, despite now being a big girl having started secondary school by the time it was released.

The quite gruesome and brutal story of the characters of Basin City featured another one of Lottie's childhood film heroes, with Elijah Wood playing a completely removed character from that of Frodo Baggins. This time he would play a full sized person at least, but one who was a mute cannibalistic serial killer of prostitutes. I told you it was a bit of a departure from a hairy footed Hobbit.

This character is not even the weirdest or the sickest in a film filled with weird sick bastards, but they all add up to some great, if gruesome, graphic gore, which of course is what Tarantino had introduced me to all those years ago as a sweet and innocent young undergraduate reading the poetry of William Blake.

Tarantino has certainly helped to change my Song of Innocence into one of Experience, and I am eternally grateful to him for that.

Moulin Rouge! (2001)   Dir: Baz Luhrmann

This is now the second film I've chosen which ends with an exclamation mark, both of which are musicals. Well "Nativity!" is sort of a musical film, but there is no doubt that this film by Baz Luhrmann is not only a musical film, but one of the greatest ever, and no doubt will replicate its success on stage once the stage version is released in the near future.

You will know from previous chapters that I do love a good musical film, but it is fair to say that the genre wasn't experiencing its hey day from 1973 onwards, the year I was born. MGM studios had stopped making them, and were releasing compilations of their greatest hits in "That's Entertainment" in 1974. In that year, there were only six films released which could be classed as musical. One was a compilation of past glories, one was animated, and one was Russian. The previous year had seen only nine musical films released, the same as 1972. However one of those was "Cabaret" which kind of made up for the lack of other musicals.

Ever since talking movies began, musicals became a staple part of Hollywood, with "The Jazz Singer" being the first smash hit musical ever in 1927. By 1929, and throughout the 1930s, there were usually at least fifty musical films released every year, with over sixty in some years. This continued right through the 1940s, with even the Second World war not being able to stem the flow of musical films pouring onto cinema screens.

The trend continued for most of the 1950s too, but by the end of that decade, cinema seemed to change, as did popular culture in so many ways with the baby boomers of the war years becoming teenagers and young adults by now. They wanted something less old fashioned, and although musicals still thrived in the 60s, there were much fewer of them, tending to be huge releases like "West Side Story", "The Sound of Music" and "Oliver!" to name just a few.

The genre was changing, and unless a musical film was new and fresh, then audiences just didn't want to know. The glory days of MGM studios and their classic musical films were becoming nostalgia for the new generation's parents to reminisce over. Along with "Grease", which ironically harked back to the 1950s, Bob Fosse injected some new life into the genre during the 60s and 70s, but by the 1980s, the musical film genre was becoming almost obsolete, being taken over by the might of the super-musicals on the stages of the West End and Broadway.

There were obviously a few exceptions throughout the 1980s, but films like "Fame", "Annie", and "Footloose" were few and far between. The second half of the 1980s, the time when I had really started my cinematic journey in earnest, saw hardly any musical films at all. I'm not even sure you could call "Dirty Dancing" a proper musical. The only "proper" musical would be "Little Shop of Horrors" in 1986, which again harked back to an age when the musical genre shone brightly.

The only musicals which were being produced in the 1990s would be Disney or other animated films, again with a few notable exceptions, such as John Waters' "Cry-Baby" which has already had an honourable mention in this book. But there had been one film in 1992 which would have a huge impact on the future of not just musical films, but also musical TV programmes, as this particular film would help to spawn "Strictly Come Dancing" and its various offshoots around the world.

Baz Luhrmann's "Strictly Ballroom", although again not strictly a musical, showed that there was life in the genre yet, and awakened people's appetites for something a little more old-school, which brought a bit of glamour and pizazz back onto the screen, and also had some good old fashioned musical numbers in them. Luhrmann realised he was onto something, and then came back nine years later, after developing his own visual style in his version of "Romeo and Juliet", the one most GCSE students have seen rather than reading the actual play, with one of the most visually stunning films ever created, with music, dancing, glamour, and sparkling diamonds bombarding the senses into a state of near overload.

"Moulin Rouge!" is a visual and aural feast. Nicole Kidman really was a modern day Marilyn Monroe as she sung the updated version of "Diamonds are a Girl's Best Friend", whilst swinging above her adoring audience on a trapeze, making everyone's eyes pop with excitement, especially Ewan McGregor's as the naïve young idealistic playwright who has just arrived in Paris to live the bohemian life. He got more than he bargained for, as did everyone who saw the film. It blew most people away when they first saw it, and it certainly blew my mind and my senses, placing a huge stick of dynamite into the musical genre and giving it the shock therapy it deserved. It didn't just bring the genre back to life; it supercharged it, paving the way for other musicals to do the same to my mind and my senses.

It also did the same for one of my favourite novels to be adapted for the screen. Luhrmann's version of "The Great Gatsby" with Leonardo DiCaprio as the title character was perfect for

Luhrmann's style. I know many people couldn't stand his version of the story set in the bright lights of the Jazz Age in the Roaring Twenties, but I thought Luhrmann's eye for visual glitz and glamour perfectly suited the themes of superficiality and frivolity.

"Moulin Rouge!" also led to another of my favourite ever "Strictly Come Dancing" moments, when Simon Webbe danced the same version of The Police's "Roxanne" which was used to such brilliant effect in the film. The film's routine is the most sensual of Argentine Tangos ever, and Simon Webbe and Kristina Rihanoff did an awesome job of recreating the same sexiness and sensuousness in their own Argentine Tango at Blackpool in 2014.

However, whereas "Moulin Rouge!" is an original work for the screen, the other musical films I would see would mostly be adaptations of the stage hits they already were. I loved Rob Marshall's Best Picture Oscar Winner "Chicago" so much that I yearned to see the original stage version, finally fulfilling my new found desire for all that jazz, choreographed of course by the great Bob Fosse, by taking my wife to see it in the West End for our tenth wedding anniversary, whilst her relatives still down in London looked after the kids. I enjoyed it even more than the film, seeing as it was so warm that summer of 2008, and as we were sitting on the second row, the sweat from the dancers as they performed "Cell Block Tango" splashed onto my already hot and sweaty face, making the whole experience truly moist for me.

The same night, my eldest daughter Lottie, who was fourteen by then, was being taken by her granny and grandad to watch "Hairspray" on stage, and the excitement on her face when we caught up with her later, instantly made me realise that this was another musical I had to see. Until then I would have to put up with the awesome film version of the stage hit, which had in turn been based on the original John Waters film of 1988. I would eventually see it on stage ten years later when it came on tour to Manchester, but this time I would see it with my youngest daughter Becky, providing us both with a wonderful day out, and a wonderful soundtrack to sing along to in the car ever since.

Another musical film inspired by its original stage play I would love watching with Becky was "Mamma Mia!" yet another one requiring an exclamation mark! I'd taken Becky into London one evening when we were staying with Emma's parents and we suddenly decided to get a couple of tickets for a show, as it was the only show which both appealed and was within our price range.

We had a lovely evening on the Greek Islands watching Sophie try to figure out who her actual father was. We didn't get the best seats, and by the end of the show I had a bit of a crick in my neck as I had to peer over the balcony at a very uncomfortable angle. I enjoyed the film version more, and thought this was a rare case of a film adaptation actually improving on its source material, especially the routine for "Dancing Queen" where Meryl Streep leads her long line of dancing queens all through the streets of the village before all jumping into the Aegean Sea. They couldn't do that on stage.

The same could not be said for its sequel, the rather pointless "Mamma Mia! Here We Go Again", which was ok and had some nice songs and routines in it, and of course the lovely Lily James to hold my attention. Whatever Lily James has been in has been worth watching, if only to see her career progress, but it was one of her co-stars, someone who has already had a hugely successful career, who spoiled the film for me. The appearance of Cher seemed to change the whole atmosphere of the film, as though the whole film had to be altered to suit the decision by Cher to deign to appear in it. The film became just rather bizarre towards the end, and took some of my enjoyment of the first film away too, such was the disappointment I felt due to Cher's rather Norma Desmondesque and desperate performance.

I actually preferred Cher alongside Christina Aguilera in "Burlesque", which my wife and I went to see one evening. It was as cheesy as an old piece of stilton, and as camp as Christmas, but it was at least a lot of fun. It wasn't trying to be anything other than it purported to be, which was an old fashioned rags to riches story with some good song and dance routines, topped off with some very sexy outfits which we both could enjoy. It did exactly what it said on the tin, and that was fine by me.

In complete contrast to this glamourous world of LA showbiz came the very glum, the very grim, the very miserable, but the absolutely stunning film version of "Les Misérables", directed by Tom Hooper in 2012. I had never seen the stage version and didn't know very much about the story, as it had never really appealed to me. I did not realise that all the fuss the stage version had caused on its release in 1985 was completely and entirely justified.

I went into the cinema with a slight amount of trepidation, not just as to whether I would enjoy it, but also whether I would still have my wife sitting next to me by the end. She has been known to get up and leave certain performances if she is not enjoying them, whereas I'd rather give something the benefit of the doubt, and will stick with something to the bitter end.

She was definitely there with me at the end of this one though. We both fell in love with not only the film, but the songs and the sheer epic scale of its storyline. The songs, particularly "I Dreamed a Dream", sung by Anne Hathaway as Fantine, and "Stars", with Russell Crowe doing a surprisingly epic job as Javert, were able to focus on the intimacy of their lyrics and the characters' faces. Other numbers such as "One Day More", were able to showcase the ensemble nature of the song, being brilliantly cut together by Tom Hooper to make me fall in love with the song and to make me want to wave my tricolore with all my might.

As soon as we had watched the film version, I made it a mission of mine to watch the original stage version, which we eventually did, this time for our twentieth wedding anniversary. It was brilliant, and we gave it a standing ovation, but it lacked something which the film was able to bring to it.

The static nature of a stage musical, despite the most ingenious of props and stage design, still cannot match the scale which the cinema can bring. The film had the ability to make the moments of intimacy much more intimate, and the moments of epic soaring majesty become even more epic on screen. I've seen both versions again since my first viewing and love them both for their different qualities, but at least I don't have to pay almost a hundred pounds a ticket to watch the film version every time I want to enjoy it.

Hugh Jackman was brilliant as Jean Valjean, but in another original musical film, one which had not been based on a stage version, he was awful. I know a huge number of people loved "The Greatest Showman", my daughter being one of them, but whilst me and my wife were watching it in the cinema, even I almost walked out after half an hour. I can't quite believe how I managed to stay until the end, as it was just showy, overblown, narcissistic nonsense. The songs weren't particularly good, and the routines lacked any sort of subtlety or charm. Sorry, but for me, "The Greatest Showman", was simply all show, and certainly not great.

A much nicer film, another original musical film, was "La La Land", which we both very much enjoyed right up until a few minutes before the end, when we then find out that the lovely Emma Stone and Ryan Gosling do not in fact end up happily ever after. Instead we are shown what might have been between the two. I know in this post modern era we are supposed to accept less predictable endings, but as far as I'm concerned, films about two people falling in love whilst singing and dancing together, especially when they do it in such cheery and magical surroundings, then they definitely need to end up together.

I don't want a realistic version of what would probably have happened. Since when have musicals been about what might have happened? They should always be about what should happen, and in the case of "La La Land", then the couple should most definitely have lived happily ever after.

The opening number, "Another day of Sun" is meant to be a satirical comment on the superficiality of Los Angeles, but I'd rather the film ended with our couple continuing their endless days of sunshine. Forget post-modern, I'm old school when it comes to musicals. Give me one day more of schmaltz and cheesiness every time. I want to come out of the theatre or cinema feeling uplifted and full of sunshine, which is of course why musicals were invented in the first place all those years ago, as soon as films realised they could sing and dance in the first place back in 1927.

So, I'm going to start a campaign to change the ending of "La La Land". Will you join in my crusade? Who will be strong and stand with me?

Well at least I can dream a dream of it happening.

The Artist (2011)   Dir: Michel Hazanavicius

Someone else who dreamed a dream was Peppy Miller, a dream about becoming a movie star just like her hero, in another film about the transition from the days of silent films to talkies. My wife and I went to see "The Artist" without knowing too much about it, and had the most lovely evening at the cinema we had had for a long time, despite never having heard of its director, its male lead, and definitely not the actress who played Peppy Miller, Berenice Bejo. It was truly adorable, and Berenice Bejo was possibly the most adorable part of the whole adorable film. She reminded me of why I fell in love with another French actress, Emmanuelle Beart, many years ago, although Bejo had in fact been born in Argentina, which gave her her dark and smouldering looks.

The story is of an amiable if egotistical silent film star, George Valentin, played by Jean Dujardin, who is literally run into at his latest premiere by a hopeful young actress, full of dreams for the big screen. Our hero gives her a break into the movies, and she becomes a huge success, taking the limelight away from the man who gave her the opportunity in the first place.

The advent of talking pictures brings about a reversal in their fortunes, as the young actress Peppy Miller embraces the new technology and her fresh face seems perfect for this new era of the cinema. However, Valentin resists the entire notion of "talkies" and has to watch his star fade whilst Peppy's star shines ever brighter. He watches his money dwindle away and then loses it all in the stock market crash of 1929, forcing him to even make his loyal butler, played by James Cromwell in one of his sympathetic roles, redundant. This leads to his depression and near suicide, before being saved by the woman he had helped years before, the same woman who had fallen in love with him too.

The scene where Peppy puts her arm through George's coat arm, and pretends that she is being embraced by him is so touching and romantic that it made my wife and I go all soppy, in a film packed full of lovely moments, but none of them with any dialogue at all. Seeing as the film is about the silent movies era, the film itself is shot in black and white, and is silent, with only a musical score and speech boards to aid the narrative, just as the silent films of the 1920s had.

Yet the film never feels as though it is trying to replicate the glory days of the silent era. It is such a modern film despite not using even the most basic of technology now available. It proves that great storytelling does not need fancy special effects, or colour, or even dialogue to be a great film. It was deservedly awarded five Oscars, including Best Picture, Best Director and Best Actor, although I suppose it's fair that it was beaten in the Best Screenplay category by Woody Allen's "Midnight in Paris", a film with a lot more speech than "The Artist" ever had.

I mentioned much earlier in this book how I had managed to see a couple of great films from the silent era, namely "Metropolis" and "Battleship Potemkin" during my sixth form days, and having rediscovered the joys of silent films I watched as many as I could at home, as well as watching a few documentaries about the great silent comedians of the era. I watched a few programmes about Charlie Chaplin, and discovered just how brilliant "Modern Times" was, and still is, as well as a Buster Keaton documentary, along with his great film "The General". I realised just how innovative, just how ground breaking, and most of all, just how funny these two geniuses of early cinema were.

There have been many books written about these two stars, and if you want a detailed insight into their achievements, then you'd better go and read those books instead, but all I will say is that anybody who came after these two, along with Harold Lloyd, stood on the shoulders of giants.

Just after I had seen documentaries on all three of these great stars, Harold Lloyd's seminal "Safety Last", was being screened at The Dukes Theatre in Lancaster, accompanied by a live piano score, just as would have accompanied the film in 1923, when it was first released. This was such a fantastic opportunity to see one of the greatest film stars of not just the silent era of cinema, but cinema as a whole, in one of his greatest ever films, the one with the iconic scene of Lloyd hanging from a clock face hundreds of feet above the street below.

The camera trickery used by Lloyd was flawless, even back then in 1923, and watching it almost a hundred years after its first release on the big screen, was not only a privilege, but a real insight into how such films were made. It was a brilliant experience because I completely forgot that I was watching a silent film; I was just watching a great film, speech, or no speech, similar to when I watched "The Artist", despite both films being divided by almost ninety years of film history and new technologies.

Soon after watching a real silent film, I saw a film all about another couple of greats from the silent era, one of whom happened to be born only a few miles from where I was born and bred. Stan Laurel hailed from the town of Ulverston, just the other side of Morecambe Bay from where I lived and grew up, but whereas I'd gone to London and come back home to the area, Stan had gone to Hollywood, met a bloke called Oliver Hardy, and became one half of arguably the greatest double act in cinema history.

The film "Stan and Ollie" came out in January 2019, and I just had to see it. Not only was it about two greats of cinema, one of whom was fairly local, but it also starred possibly the greatest comedian from my own era, at least in terms of TV. Steve Coogan, who played Stan Laurel to perfection, was someone whose output for TV I had watched over and over again, to the point that whenever I saw him act in other films, I just couldn't get past the fact that he was Alan Partridge. This is in no way a criticism of his acting, but more a compliment to the brilliance of his Norwich based DJ and failed talk show host persona.

Coogan's only other film which I have truly enjoyed was "Alpha Papa", but this was only because this was Alan Partridge's first foray onto the big screen. That's why I loved it so much as it was my favourite comedy character on the big screen, in a proper film, with a proper story, and not in half hourly episodes as I was so used to.

Coogan's portrayal of Stan Laurel was the first time I could get over the fact that the man up there on the screen wasn't Alan Partridge, and wasn't even Steve Coogan pretending to be someone who wasn't Alan Partridge. In this film, the man up there on the screen was Stan Laurel, just as John C Reilly's performance made me think that it was Oliver Hardy on the screen too.

The film itself was a little lightweight in terms of story, but some films are worth watching just for the performances of its stars, and John C. Reilly's and especially Steve Coogan's performances are definitely worth watching. His brilliant ability to not just mimic, but inhabit and become a character, almost in the same way Peter Sellers could do, was the perfect vehicle for Steve Coogan. It certainly wasn't another fine mess he'd got himself into this time, although his performance was not even nominated for an Oscar, which is a crying shame.

If only he'd have won an Oscar, I wonder whether he'd have shouted "A-Ha!" to the world in his acceptance speech. I doubt it somehow.

Apocalypto (2006)   Dir: Mel Gibson

I said before that there were certain films which keep my wife awake whether she likes them or not. This is definitely one of them. I'd flicked onto the film quite by accident after only about five minutes or so into it, and was instantly hooked. It was just so different from anything I'd ever seen before, especially as the dialogue is all in the original Mayan language which its characters speak.

The whole look, feel, plot, characterisation, and bravery of the film transfixed me. The story is that of a Mayan tribe who are captured so they can be used as human sacrifices, and the subsequent escape of the protagonist. His journey home to his pregnant wife and child, all the while being pursued by his captors, is completely gripping and displays bravery in abundance, as did the film's director just for having the courage to make the film in the first place.

Mel Gibson had been a major part of my childhood, with his breakthrough coming in 1979 with "Mad Max". This was one of the first films my big brother rented out on video as soon as he looked anywhere near eighteen, and so obviously I watched it too. I may well have seen him in the four episodes of the Australian soap opera, "The Sullivans", which he appeared in during the late 1970s. I remember the programme as it was always on once I'd just arrived home from school before the kids' programmes started., and so I wouldn't be surprised if I'd already met the man who would then go onto star in "Peter Weir's "Gallipoli", and "The Year of Living Dangerously" which I discovered after I'd become very closely acquainted with his

Martin Riggs character in the "Lethal Weapon" series, films which were part of most teenage boys' staple diets in the late 1980s.

I also saw him in "Tequila Sunrise" opposite Michelle Pfeiffer at her most ravishing best, and with Goldie Hawn in "Bird on a Wire" which passed the time of day one Wednesday afternoon whilst I should have been doing some cycling whilst at sixth form.

He even did a great job as Hamlet in Franco Zeffirelli's 1990 version of the Shakespearean tragedy, trying to stay sane whilst also trying to kill his uncle Claudius, the biggest of uncle Knobheads ever, played by Alan Bates, and also trying not to harm his mother, Gertrude, played by Glenn Close, and his girlfriend Ophelia, played by Helena Bonham-Carter. He manages to mess it up ever so slightly, with not just his uncle Knobhead dying, but everyone he ever cared for, including himself.

I would then see Mel Gibson in his debut as a director, "The Man Without a Face" in 1993, before the whole world saw his face painted blue in "Braveheart", which he of course also directed, bagging himself a couple of Oscars for Best Picture and Best Director. The next time I would hear him, but not see him was as Rocky the chicken in "Chicken Run", Aardman Animation's first ever feature film after their successes with Wallace and Gromit on the small screen. I'd taken Lottie to the cinema to watch it, and had a very enjoyable time, which is probably why I was so surprised and even shocked when the next film of his I would watch would be his next as a director, and one which is one of the most brutal watches ever.

"The Passion of the Christ", depicts the final twelve hours in the life of Jesus, and Gibson certainly did not hold back in the treatment Jesus received at the hands of the Romans. The flogging scene and the eventual crucifixion are not just tortuous for the Son of God, played brilliantly by Jim Caviezel, but also for Mary Magdalene, played by Monica Bellucci in certainly one of her less glamourous roles, and Mary Mother of God, played by Maia Morgenstern. It is also tortuous for us the viewers, as bits of flesh are literally ripped from Jesus' body with the cat o' nine tails being shown as the truly brutal instrument of torture it was.

The almost visceral pain is relentless, which of course is what Gibson intended, although I'm not sure he intended for his star to be left with a fourteen inch scar on his back from the whipping scene, or a dislocated shoulder from the weight of the cross. He even contracted hypothermia and pneumonia from filming the crucifixion scenes in sub-zero temperatures. If ever a man felt the pain of his character, then Jim Caviezel is that man. He truly must have felt like the son of God, if ever that was possible.

It was meant to be a tough watch, and certainly didn't end with John Wayne telling us all that "Truly this man was the Son of God", as he had done in George Stevens' "The Greatest Story Ever Told" back in 1965. Mel Gibson did not need any star cameos to impress us all in his telling of the story, and he did an astonishing job. Whether you believe the actual story of Jesus' crucifixion was the greatest ever told or not, Gibson's film was certainly the greatest telling of the story, particularly as the languages spoken in it are Latin and Aramaic. It really is a remarkable film and proved that films do not need to be in English or even a language which is spoken at all anymore, at least not widely, for them to be eminently watchable.

So his decision to use the Mayan language for "Apocalypto", two years later, was not particularly surprising but it was definitely another brave one, but he succeeded once again in making a beautiful, yet brutal film, but one which, although showing scenes of quite savage intensity, never shows the people he is depicting to be savages themselves. The Mayan people are depicted as a proud culture, whose traditions, which are massively different to our own cultures and traditions, still care for their loved ones in a simpler, but somehow much more meaningful way.

Despite seeing babies being ripped from their mothers' arms and slaughtered in front of them, or fathers having their throats slit whilst their sons are made to watch, or watching decapitated heads literally bounce down the sides of a great stone pyramid, or the headless bodies of these victims being thrown in a horrific mass grave, there is never a sense that these people are mere savages.

The second part of the film in which Jaguar Paw, played astonishingly by Rudy Youngblood, almost becomes a black jaguar himself as he emerges from the quicksand, to then be his captors' nemesis, is enthralling. It is one of the most gripping and heart thumpingly tense pieces of film making I have ever seen, which is why whenever it is on TV, or whenever I fancy streaming it late at night in bed, my wife can never get to sleep. Not only is it a brutal watch, but it is also brutal listen.

No wonder she ends up watching it with me again as she simply cannot ignore the screams of anguish, and the sounds of flesh being punctured by the most deadly of wooden traps, and the blood thirsty chewing of a jaguar as it pulls the face off its human prey, amongst other brutal ways of dying. Most people would struggle to drift off peacefully to sleep with those kind of background noises going on.

Gibson would then not direct another film for ten years, but when he did get round to it, my wife gladly stayed up to watch the brilliant "Hacksaw Ridge" with me, despite it being filmed in English and not having any babies being slaughtered in front of their screaming mothers. The story of a soldier who refused to fire a shot, as he was a conscientious objector, instead becoming a medic, saving many of his comrades' lives in The Battle of Okinawa, shows a different type of brutality and slaughter. But as with "Apocalypto" and "The Passion of the Christ", it always has a message of hope and redemption underlying the brutality and viciousness on display. I look forward to Gibson's next film with huge anticipation, whatever language it is filmed in.

Other films my wife has not been able to sleep through are a rather eclectic mix. We first saw "The Texas Chainsaw Massacre", Tobe Hopper's original I might add, and not the pointless 2003 remake, one night as we were lying in bed. I had never seen it before but had only heard about it in almost mythological terms. The almost legendary brutality of the film which I had only been told about proved to be absolutely true.

My wife and I just lay there in bed, open mouthed in disbelief at what we were seeing on screen. The relentless gnashing roar of the chainsaw itself was enough to cause severe nightmares, but when you add the scene where the most fucked up family ever sit around the table watching their desiccated Grandpa attempt to kill one of their victims by hitting her over the head with a hammer, along with many other of the most fucked up scenes in film history, then it was no wonder that neither of us could get to sleep that night. It really is the most remarkable film in terms of just how dark, twisted, sordid and sadistic it is, with no hope of redemption or even explanation coming from the film. The final scene of Leatherface just swinging his chainsaw in rage and frustration is one of the most bleak but brilliant final shots ever.

Another film which rather randomly kept us awake one night, open mouthed again, but not in horror this time, but in bewilderment, was "Vampire Circus", an old Hammer film from

1972. It is one of the most bizarre films I have ever seen, and we just could not stop watching it.

The story is of a mysterious travelling circus who arrive in a plague quarantined village. Soon after their arrival, young children begin to disappear, and the locals suspect the circus people are hiding a horrifying secret. I won't spoil the plot any more for you, but when a film's tagline is "Human fangs ripping throats – no sawdust can soak up the torrent of blood!" then you know it's not going to be the sort of film to fall asleep to.

The last film which my wife is usually more than happy to watch with me is another one which displays lots of blood, so much so that it's hero's costume had to be changed from white to red because he couldn't get the stains out in the wash, even on a hot whites wash. "Deadpool", kept my wife awake partly because she really fancied Ryan Reynolds, but mainly because it is so hilarious.

The opening slow motion scene from within the car as the titles roll, with Julie Newton's "Angel of the Morning" playing on the stereo, instantly made me a huge fan, and the combination of awesome violence, the coolest death scenes ever, and some side splittingly hilarious jokes in the amazing script, meant that Deadpool the character almost overtook Spiderman as my new favourite super hero. It is the funnest superhero film ever, and redefined what it actually meant to be a super hero.

I'm certainly not going to get into an existential argument about the nature of superheroes and their role in society; Deadpool himself would think that was so dull, and would probably kill me if I did. But at least he would kill me in the most entertaining way possible. I would expect nothing less from him to be frank. He may even speak Latin, Aramaic, or even Mayan whilst killing me. Again, I wouldn't put it past him.

Marvellous (2014)   **Dir: Julian Farino**

I've covered some huge Hollywood blockbuster films in this book, as well as some European Arthouse classics. Some of the films have been extremely violent, some extremely distressing, some extremely serious. I thought it would be appropriate to end with a couple of films which could never be described in such terms. They are certainly not Hollywood blockbusters, nor are they Arthouse, and frankly it would be an insult to them both if they ever were described in such a way. What they are is genuinely touching, heart-warming, and life affirming, as well as being laugh out loud funny at times, qualities which, at my age, are much more important than serious and violent.

If you've read my first book, "Just Me and My Football", you will know that football has played a huge part in my life, and so I need to include another film based around this subject. I've already included "Escape to Victory", which had a football match as its finale, played by a star studded cast from both the football and film worlds, but I wanted to also include a film which features none of these types of stars; but it does feature a football match.

"Marvellous", is the sweetest little film which definitely lives up to its title. It is the almost true story of Neil Baldwin, a man who has his own very unique way of dealing with life's ups and downs. This is quite necessary seeing as he is a supporter of Stoke City Football Club. As a lifelong supporter of another smaller club who rarely wins anything, I fully understand Neil's passion for his club and his own idiosyncrasies which supporting such a team brings about.

Neil Baldwin, or Nello, as he has become known, was diagnosed with a learning disability as a child and required speech therapy. He left school at the age of sixteen to run away and join the circus, becoming a registered clown, which he still is to this day. He lived with his mother until a few years before she died, and in that time she would see her son become an honorary life member of Keele University Students' Union, despite never having studied there, and also become the kit-man for his beloved Stoke City after the then manager, Lou Macari, who I had watched so many times on TV playing for Manchester United in the late 1970s and early 80s, appointed him, and went on to call him "the best signing I ever made" as Nello's sense of humour and fun were so good for team morale.

He was even brought on as a substitute by Macari for the last five minutes of a testimonial game, and later devoted seven pages of his autobiography to him, describing him with real warmth and affection as "a man without an angle, and there aren't many of them in football". Nello certainly didn't have an angle; he was as straight as they come, because he didn't know how to be anything else. He was, and still is, a genuinely lovely, simple man, and someone who deserved to have a Bafta winning film made about them.

Nello is played by Toby Jones in the film, and his mother by Gemma Jones, who was of course the Dashwood girls' mother in "Sense and Sensibility". The two give beautifully subtle performances, showing the deep bond between the two. When Neil loses his mother, the scene where he breaks down is truly heart wrenching, but thankfully this kind of scene is far outweighed by those of genuine affection for the film's subject, often laced with some absolutely hilarious lines of dialogue.

I spat my tea all over my bed when Nello goes to the job centre and says he wants to become a football manager, and if he can't be Stoke's manager then he doesn't mind which team will have him really, "but I draw the line at Port Vale". To get the joke you need to understand the deep rivalries within the world of football

427

and its local teams, in particular the fact that the city of Stoke has two football teams, and they don't really like each other very much.

The whole film is just the most lovely and charming of films, with the narrative being cut in with scenes of Nello's local church choir singing songs about him, from hymns to football chants, as well as the real Neil Baldwin popping up from time to time to confirm or otherwise whether the film is telling the exact truth.

I don't care if the film is not exactly how it may or may not have happened. As with "The Man Who Shot Liberty Valance": when the legend becomes fact, print the legend. Neil Baldwin is certainly a legend in not just the footballing world, but also to thousands of undergraduates who have benefitted from his unique skills as a student counsellor.

The film has made him a legend for thousands more people, whether they like Stoke City or even football at all. It is a story not about football, but about the most remarkable of football people, and I hope this chapter may go a small way to make him a legend to thousands more.

After all, "There's only one Neil Baldwin, one Neil Baldwin, there's only one Neil Baldwin!"

Paddington 2 (2017)   Dir: Paul King

And so we come full circle. I started this book with a film about a wild animal travelling thousands of miles across the ocean, only to find himself in captivity, and so I finish this book in the same way. But I'm guessing King Kong didn't carry a marmalade sandwich under his hat.

"Paddington", and its sequel "Paddington 2", are quite simply for me, life affirming, in really quite a literal sense actually. Apart from being the most charming, lovely, kind, polite, sweet, and friendly of films, they have played a part in changing my life, making this book possible in the first place.

Maybe I am regressing slightly, but in the past few years, my wife and I have watched a few films whose main target audience is somewhat younger than us. I write this on the morning of my wife's fiftieth birthday, as I wait for her to get up and see the lovely spread of presents and flowers me and the kids have got for her. But as we have both got that bit older, then so have we felt the need sometimes to watch what could be classed as films for kids.

This book has been split into seven parts, and as in Shakespeare's "seven ages of man" speech from "As You Like It", the seventh stage involves a "second childishness", where we regress back into our childlike state. I'm not quite there yet, as I am not "sans teeth, sans eyes, sans taste, sans everything" just yet, although I am certainly sans as much hair on my head as I was as a child. But I have felt the need to watch simpler, more childish films from time to time, but learning from them in a very adult way.

We watched the live action version of Disney's "Cinderella", directed by Kenneth Branagh, or Kenny B as I like to call him, starring Lily James as our heroine, and found that we very much enjoyed it. We then found ourselves compelled to watch another of Disney's live action remakes when it was released in March 2017, this time "Beauty and the Beast", with Emma Watson as Belle. We enjoyed this one even more, and even found ourselves both quietly weeping at the end. This was a sign that our second childishness was progressing, so when "Paddington 2" was released later that year, I certainly felt the need for something which would help to take away some of the weight of adulthood from my shoulders.

I don't mind admitting, and maybe it's good for me that I do, that the few years before the release of "Paddington 2", I had been struggling with stress, anxiety, and ultimately depression from my job. I was no longer enjoying teaching in the way I had done for the majority of my career, and my mental health was suffering as a result. My mind had been taking me to some dark places, and I am not ashamed to say that I had thoughts which I never want to have again. "Paddington 2" helped me to not only find solace, but helped me find a way out of my struggle. It helped to put me on a new path, one which I am still travelling on now, but one which is a much brighter path, and also one which has produced not only this book, but my first one too.

After a particularly stressful Friday at work, I got into my car to drive home to the safety of my wife and home. As usual on a Friday, I turned the radio on to listen to Simon Mayo and Mark Kermode on Radio 5 Live, to listen to their film review show. That particular weekend saw the release of "Paddington 2", and the way they both talked about the film, along with countless emails and messages from the listeners, made me realise that I needed to see it too. I had not seen the first film yet, so as soon as I got home I suggested to my wife that we both go to the cinema the following afternoon and watch the sequel, after having watched the first film at home on the Friday evening.

My wife had been listening to the show at home too, and as soon as I suggested my plan, she instantly agreed. She knew that I had been struggling at work, and could tell that I needed to watch these films not simply to pass the time of day. So we downloaded the first film and instantly fell in love with a little bear who we had both grown up watching.

Michael Bond's books about a bear from darkest Peru had been a staple part of any child's television viewing in the late 1970s, and had been very charming then. The film version upped the charm offensive hugely, and gave us one of the loveliest Friday evenings in front of our television ever. We both fell instantly in love with the little bear once more, and both wept tears of joy when he finally becomes adopted into the Browns' home. We couldn't wait for the next afternoon to arrive so we could continue our double bill of charm and warmth and loveliness.

The cinema was packed that dreary Saturday afternoon in November 2017, with parents and their young children, all looking forward to the film they had probably been waiting for the last three years since they too had fallen in love with the first film. And there we were, right in the middle of all these children, full of just as much anticipation, despite having only had to wait about sixteen hours since we'd fallen in love with the first film.

We fell in love even more, not just with Paddington himself, but with the whole Brown family, and even the dastardly Phoenix Buchanan, played memorably by Hugh Grant, in what is one of his finest ever performances, kids' film or not. And of course, we wept even more when Paddington's Aunt Lucy turns up on the Browns' doorstep after he had been released from prison. He had been incarcerated for the theft of a pop up book he wanted to buy for his Aunt which would allow her to see the sights of London, and of course at the end, Paddington is not only able to give the book to her, but also to show her the sights in person, or more appropriately, in bear.

Both films certainly relieved my depression that weekend, and made me realise that I needed to change something if I was to get away from the dark thoughts I had been having. The films caused me to take a long, hard stare at myself and realise that I needed to get some help, which I did later that week.

To cut a long story short, those films led me to leaving my job, taking a break to do some supply teaching, a period I entered into with the promise to myself of finally writing a book, which had always been an ambition of mine. Well, as you can see, not only did I write my first book during that year, but also this one after I had resumed my full time career the next year, but this time with my head clearer, wiser, in perspective, and also a little more childish.

The two "Paddington" films made me realise that having a more childish outlook, one which did not include the same adult stresses and strains which I had been suffering from, was in fact a much healthier way of living my life. I became more childish, and yet wiser in my older age, and am now enjoying life again almost as much as I did as a boy, when I'd get home from school and watch a television programme all about a little bear, who had a penchant for marmalade sandwiches, who found a home with his new family.

My own family and my home have always been my sources of sanctuary, but after watching the two films about that same bear, I also felt safer in my own mind, although I've yet to develop the same love for marmalade sandwiches as Paddington. As I said earlier, the films were not just life affirming, but they were life changing. They may well have even been life saving for me. And for that I will forever be grateful to that little bear.

My wife had always been fascinated by pop-up books as a young girl, and "Paddington 2" was special to her because it brought this fascination back for her. So when I was wondering what to get for her as a Christmas present that year, there was one obvious choice. The film's merchandising included its own version of the pop-up book in the film, with London scenes being brought vividly to life. She had been taken into London quite frequently as a small girl, and the book which Santa delivered to her, by way of not darkest Peru, but another part of South America, namely via deepest, darkest Amazon, and its delivery service, brought her own childish happy memories back to her. My own second childishness helped my wife to rediscover hers too, and the pop-up book has been cherished by her ever since.

***

And so, just as Paddington's journey ended with him being safe and secure at home, surrounded by a loving family, so does my own cinematic journey. These films throughout this book have given me so much happiness, well most of them anyway, and I hope you have enjoyed being a part of my journey too.

But of course, the journey will continue. My second childishness, when maybe I will also be sans teeth by then, will continue once I become a grandad, and I can start the whole process again. I can't wait for the rest of my life to happen, which is proof enough that me and my films have been good for each other.

To use one of the most famous and iconic final lines ever from a film, my films have provided me with not just the start of a beautiful friendship, but one which will continue into infinity and beyond. Thank you for being a part of this friendship too.

The End

Fin

Printed in Great Britain
by Amazon